The Eye for Innovation

The Eye for Innovation

Recognizing Possibilities and

Managing the Creative Enterprise

Robert Price

Yale University Press

New Haven and London

Published with assistance from the Louis Stern Memorial Fund.

Printed in the United States of America.

The Library of Congress has cataloged the hardcover edition as follows:

Price, Robert M., 1930–
    The eye for innovation : recognizing possibilities and managing the
creative enterprise / Robert Price.
      p.   cm.
    Includes bibliographical references and index.
    ISBN-13: 978-0-300-10877-4 (hardcover : alk. paper)
    ISBN-10: 0-300-10877-X (hardcover : alk. paper)
    1. Control Data Corporation—History.   2. Technological innovations—
Management.   3. Information technology.   4. Creative ability in business.
I. Title.
HD9696.2.U64C66 2005
338.7′61004′09–dc22

              2005013218

A catalogue record for this book is available from the British Library.

The paper in this book meets the guidelines for permanence and durability
of the Committee on Production Guidelines for Book Longevity of the
Council on Library Resources.

ISBN 978-0-300-12370-8 (pbk. : alk. paper)

10 9 8 7 6 5 4 3 2 1

Contents

Foreword by William C. Norris, vii
Preface, xi
Acknowledgments, xv

Introduction, 1

Part One Habitats for Innovation and Their Inhabitants

1 The Once and Future Company, 13

2 On the Edge of the Possible, 36

3 Meeting Vital Needs, 53

4 Fostering the Courage to Innovate, 65

5 Building a Framework for Innovation, 82

Part Two **Technology, Innovation, and Strategy**

6 Journeys in Strategic Space, 99

7 The Care and Feeding of Strategy—The Technology
Food Chain, 120

Part Three **Forging a Strategic Journey: The Decision Trichotomy**

8 Collaborate to Compete, 131

9 The Art of Acquisition, 155

10 "Make": Relying on Internal Resources, 176

11 Accepting Daring and Unusual Challenges, 190

Part Four **Strategies for the Unexpected and the Unusual**

12 When It Hits the Fan: Perilous Journeys—Innovation
in Times of Crisis, 209

13 Innovating Beyond the Walls, 224

14 Extraordinary Innovation, Extraordinary Collaboration, 236

Epilogue, 251

Appendix 1 Control Data Timeline, 261

Appendix 2 Organization Charts (1957–1986), 265

Appendix 3 Robert Price Presentation to the Control Data
Corporation Board of Directors (March 14, 1985), 277

Appendix 4 Seymour Cray Letters, 283

Appendix 5 Robert Price Speech to CBEMA Panel—"Microelectronics: 'The Crude Oil of the '80s'" (April 7, 1981), 289

Appendix 6 *New York Times* article: "Computer Accord Signed
by Soviets," 295

Appendix 7 Memoirs of Carolyn Firouztash, 299

Appendix 8 Spin-offs and Start-ups by Former Control Data
Employees (partial list), 303

Notes, 305
Index, 311

Foreword

William C. Norris

We opened the doors of Control Data in 1957 in the face of what some might have seen as insurmountable odds. We were up against entrenched competitors with vastly superior resources. Yet there was in Control Data both optimism and fierce determination. That optimism was based on a core group of professionals with a proven track record of technological innovation. That determination was based on a desire, stemming from earlier disillusionment, to forge a different kind of company, a company in which innovative ability could flourish. We succeeded to a remarkable degree. Control Data's people created a company that was at the leading edge of electronic digital technology, management practices, employee relations, community relations, and the innovative application of business techniques, products, and services.

Control Data was all about innovation—harnessing the imagination, ingenuity, and energy of its people to meet the technology needs of customers and ultimately, on a larger scale, the urgent needs of society. Control Data was at the forefront of using technology to make the world a better place—from education to health care, from urban renewal to rural revitalization, from full employment to enabling small business to achieve its full potential.

All of this didn't just happen. It was the result of creative business strategies and strong leaders like Bob Price.

Bob's leadership skills are grounded in technological innovation. After graduating magna cum laude from Duke University, he was hired as a mathematician at the Lawrence Livermore Laboratory, where he worked with a veritable Who's Who of brilliant scientists, including Edward Teller and John von Neumann. Bob's first project leader was Harold Brown, then a newly minted UC Berkeley Ph.D., who went on to become president of the California Institute of Technology and Secretary of Defense under President Jimmy Carter.

At Lawrence Livermore and later at Convair (General Dynamics) and Georgia Institute of Technology, Bob worked on the largest and most powerful early computers. In developing numerical modeling applications in high-energy physics, aircraft design, and other engineering problems for the ERA 1101, ERA 1103, and the UNIVAC I, Bob developed a user's perspective of the innovative digital electronic design that would be a hallmark of Control Data systems.

When Bob joined Control Data in 1961 as a programmer in Palo Alto, California, the company was beginning a major push to develop its own software. By 1963, Control Data was expanding rapidly outside the United States. There were a thousand loose ends. I needed someone to pull everything together and provide guidance and leadership. Frank Mullaney, a cofounder, suggested I talk to Bob. So I flew to Palo Alto to offer Bob the position of Director of International Operations.

I was never a master of small talk. I told Bob what needed to be done. Was he interested or not? He was. I was fortunate because in Bob I found a kindred spirit. We were on the same wavelength from the very beginning. He was intelligent and had all the necessary technical knowledge, his integrity was the highest, and I could count on him to give me the facts no matter how painful they might be. You can't ask for more than that.

One of my lifelong passions has been technological collaboration. Companies don't think in terms of collaboration; they think in terms of competition—beating the hell out of each other. Control Data was a maverick in that we viewed collaboration as a vehicle to get us where we needed to go. And we were good at it. We conceived and initiated the Microelectronics and Computer Technology Corporation (MCC) and numerous other successful collaborations.

Another of my passions is education. Control Data's PLATO system was a major pioneering effort in computer-based education and computer-managed learning. On my departure from Control Data, the William C. Norris Institute was established to foster both technological collaboration and new initiatives to improve education using computer technology.

Bob shared my passion for education. Since he retired from Control Data in 1990, Bob has continued to pursue the basic concepts that were the foundation of Control Data's strategies: assisting numerous innovators and small business entrepreneurs; serving as a member of the Governor's Business Executives for Education in New Mexico, where he helped set up the advisory committee for improving technology utilization in education; sponsoring the practice of Total Quality Management in the public school system; founding the National Center for Social Entrepreneurs and serving as chairman of its Board of Directors. As executive-in-residence at Duke University's Fuqua School of Business, Bob has taught management of technology and innovation, corporate strategy, entrepreneurship, and human resource management. For his outstanding contributions to education, business, and society, Bob was honored as the 1998 Distinguished Alumnus of Duke University.

Bob Price deserves much of the credit for the greatness Control Data achieved. He served as its president, and later as my successor as chairman. He was the right man to lead the company through the turbulence of the late 1980s when the still immature computer industry was beset by an unprecedented degree of change. The strategies he put in place as chief executive officer allowed Control Data to emerge in the '90s as a services company. His leadership provided the environment for innovators and inventors to flourish and excel. He made hard decisions when they had to be made.

Bob Price is the best person I know to tell the story of Control Data and the incredibly talented individuals who, beginning in 1957, built a dynamic enterprise that accomplished what most people can only dream about, and, in the telling of that story, to be able to capture its valuable lessons for posterity.

Preface

In *Present at the Creation,* Dean Acheson concludes his Author's Note with this quote: "'History,' writes C. V. Wedgewood in her biography of *William the Silent,* 'is lived forward but it is written in retrospect. We know the end before we consider the beginning and we can never wholly recapture what it was to know the beginning only.'" Acheson then adds: "In a way this volume is an attempt to do that: for those who acted this drama did not know, nor do any of us yet know, the end."

Thoughts very much along those lines have strongly reinforced my taking pen in hand, or keyboard to fingertips, to recount the drama and capture the legacy of Control Data. Moreover, while we certainly do not "yet know the end," we do know that the Control Data story has much to offer to future generations of managers. While my friends and colleagues have urged me to "tell the Control Data story," it has been the Executive MBA students at the Fuqua School of Business, Duke University, who have inspired me to attempt to extract from that story insights regarding management for the future.

To be privileged to take part in the early growth of a company and of an entirely new industry is a great good fortune that few people are privileged to experience. I am truly grateful to have had the opportunity and grateful to the people who helped me learn along the way.

My involvement with computers began at the Lawrence Livermore Laboratory, where pushing the envelope of physics, math, and numerical analysis generated excitement and great energy in all who worked there. My first project leader was Dr. Harold Brown, later President of Cal Tech and Secretary of Defense in the Carter administration. We had as consultants to that project John von Neumann and the director of the laboratory, Edward Teller. That was heady company for a twenty-one-year-old mathematician.

Control Data was the major part of my forty-year adventure in the birth and growth of the computer industry. In 1961 my colleague and friend Dick Zemlin convinced me to join his little band of software mavericks at Control Data. It is with great admiration for Dick as a person, and with humility in light of the opportunity he gave me, that I include Dick, now deceased, in these notes.

As I trust I have captured in the stories in this book, Control Data was a great adventure and a wonderful learning experience. The company was founded by men of rare quality, with Bill Norris and Frank Mullaney in the lead. In the early years I was blessed in working with executives such as Bob Kisch, Clair Miller, Ed Strickland and Trevor Robinson. Many years later, when a full-blown crisis engulfed Control Data, I had the opportunity to chart a successful course through that crisis. The true reward of executive leadership is to solve complex problems and achieve difficult goals through the success of others. That may seem a hopelessly Pollyannaish assertion today, when the public is rocked by the blatant greed and egregious grasping at monetary gain by a few prominent corporate leaders. It is nonetheless true, and it is more enduring than temporary aberrations. Certainly it has been true for me, and in particular in the challenges Control Data faced in the second half of the 1980s.

In recent years Bill Norris has received more fitting accolades than was the case twenty years ago, and Seymour Cray has achieved near mythological status, but Control Data's other leaders have received scant credit for the company's awesome range of innovation, its strategic wisdom in the pursuit of its computer and information services strategy, its use of collaboration as a principal means of executing that strategy, and its visionary human resource policies and practices. While it is not possible to recognize every individual contribution appropriately in these pages, I hope in some small way to correct that lack of recognition.

The people of Control Data were a dedicated and industrious lot who

Mario Fernandez, *Spirit of the Entrepreneur*

worked mostly in anonymity. But we profoundly affected one another in immeasurable and enduring ways, including inspiring the title for this book. A young Cuban refugee named Mario Fernandez, who started an engineering firm in which Control Data invested and with which we closely worked, painted the icon of our company for our twenty-fifth corporate anniversary—a soaring eagle. It aptly portrayed how far we had climbed since the company's inception, but it also depicted the *freedom* of thought and action we prized as well as the *observational ability* to spy opportunity from afar. Regardless of rising revenues and stock value, new problems inevitably presented themselves, and the bold search for fresh solutions never ended. From the start, we well understood that it would be impossible to thrive if we weren't creative, and that we would remain creative only if we tried. That is, we considered innovation to be an active process, a way of thinking, and, in turn, held the well-founded beliefs that the principles of innovation could be taught and its spirit instilled. And that, really, is what this book is about.

As a participant in shaping Control Data's achievements—particularly in shaping and leading the strategic move from hardware to services—it is not possible for me to write with total objectivity. I do, however, write with a true love for the adventure we call business, especially for my fellow adventurers who founded and grew the computer and information services business over the first half century of its existence, and most especially for those who have done so, and continue to do so, with creativity and innovation.

Acknowledgments

This book simply would never have come into being had not three very special people given me the encouragement and support that made it possible. Don Lamm, retired President of W. W. Norton Company, was a wonderful sounding board for my ideas and helped strengthen my belief in them. He also provided, in his words, "drive-by editing" that kept me from crashing as I undertook a task new and different for me. Jan Schwettman, a friend and colleague, was simultaneously an inspiration and unrelenting in pushing me to express my thoughts more vividly and readably. She has been unwavering in her support and unstinting in her gift of time. Sandy Holt, my assistant of many years, provided both the skills and perseverance without which the many file searches, electronic and paper, would have been a hopeless task. She suffered through revision upon revision. Without her my thoughts would never have become a manuscript.

In gathering the information and data necessary to illustrate the history of Control Data and facts regarding its remarkable innovators, I was particularly dependent on the marvelous memories and extensive files of Frank Dawe and Norb Berg. Sue O'Donnell was invaluable both in delving into the files of the Charles Babbage Institute and in assisting me in many of the early interviews. Mike Moore, Director of The William C. Norris Institute of the College of Business, University of St. Thomas, has been helpful in plugging gaps and sorting through conflicting historical data. The Ford Library of the Fuqua School of Business, Duke University, has been a valuable source of management literature and historical data. Any unattributed quotations are from my personal files.

One of the more pleasant aspects of gathering the material for the book has been the interviews it involved and information provided by old colleagues. The following people were particularly helpful: Roxie Aho, Ray Allard, Judy Alnes, David Anderson, Eugene Baker, George Bardos, Steve Beach, Gerard Beaugonin, Donald Bitzer, Dick Broeker, Ellen Brown, Peter Brown, Pat Conway, Nate Dickinson, Willis Drake, Homa Firouztash, Bill Fitzgerald, Wilbur French, James Harris, Larry Jodsaas, Nasser Kazeminy, Robert Kisch, George Latimer, Robert Lillestrand Family, Neil Lincoln, Joseph Minutilli, the Mormon Church (Dr. Monson and Richard Scott), James O'Connell, Daniel Pennie, Brian Roth, Robert Schmidt Family, Derrel (Sam) Slais, Edward Strickland, Duane Thoms, Lloyd Thorndyke, James Thornton Family, Herbert Trader, Tony Vacca, David White, Gaylon White, and Henry White.

The ideas contained in the book grew out of decades-long association with Control Data colleagues and business executives in many other companies. Their distillation is a result of many classroom hours of interchange with the gifted students, particularly the Weekend Executive MBA students, at the Fuqua School of Business, Duke University. I thank each and every one of them. Along the way I had great help and much pleasure in working with outstanding academic colleagues: Janet Bercovitz, Rich Burton, Wes Cohen, Gerry DeSanctis, Heather Haveman, Joel Huber, Arie Lewin, John McCann, Will Mitchell and Wanda Wallace. Most importantly, it was Dean Thomas Keller at the Fuqua School who believed I had something valuable to bring to the students. The support of the Fuqua School and of the College of Business at the University of St. Thomas has been important in making the book a reality.

Review of the book and considerable early editing has been provided by Norb Berg, Frank Dawe, Mike Moore, Sue O'Donnell, Jan Schwettman and Gerry Souter. I am deeply appreciative of the assistance they have provided.

I have been most fortunate in having Michael O'Malley at Yale Press as my editor. Working with Mike has given rise to excellent ideas and challenging questions, all of which have made this a better book and a great learning experience for me.

My family has indulged me through the many years of my devotion to business and academic endeavors. I am grateful to my wife and three wonderful daughters for their patience and love. In turn, I am sure they are grateful that this book is completed.

The Eye for Innovation

Introduction

He who seeth the abyss but with eagle's eyes,—he who with eagle's talons graspeth the abyss: he hath courage.
—Friedrich Nietzsche, *Zarathustra*

This is the story of a company, Control Data, and the lessons learned from its incubation, operation, trials, and successes, as it grew to become one of the premier corporations in the information technology world. We'll take the lessons apart and see what fueled the innovative engine that gave employees and managers alike the excitement of participation in this decades-long event. We'll find out how one company's evolutionary path can be applied to any business, large or small, domestic or international. This is a story of people and the tools they used: tools that are available to everyone who has the vision and the will to use them.

As we enter this third millennium the entities we call "businesses," and, more specifically, companies and corporations, are taken for granted as part of the world in which we live. Yet considered in the total sweep of humanity's history, the large or even modest-sized company is a very recent development in economic organization.

At the beginning of the second millennium, a mere blink of the eye ago in time, there was no such entity. At that point, the focus of economic endeavor centered on the individual craftsman or agrarian laborer. Organized, collaborative labor for the most part found its locus in monasteries or feudal fiefdoms. That is hard for us to imagine in today's world in which business enterprises are integral aspects of societal structure, for better or worse touching every aspect of human activity.

What has been the driving force behind the rise of the corporation? The answer is technology. The increasing complexity of technology over the past thousand years—especially the past two hundred—is the powerful driving force that has stimulated the birth and growth of the complex organizations necessary to use technology effectively. That means technology deserves intense study, not for its scientific intricacies, but for its influence on and shaping of enterprises of all kinds.

At this point you, the reader, no doubt are saying to yourself: "Oh, dear, another book for computer technology geeks." Not so. As you will see, Control Data provides stories and lessons that will help all of us become more valuable to our businesses as well as to our communities. We will learn, for example, about Hilda Pridgeon, who used company policy and resources to start the National Alzheimer's Association. We will learn about Bob Lillestrand, a brilliant scientist and innovative computer designer who devised a backup navigational process for astronauts that didn't depend on computers at all. He personally tested his celestial navigation ideas by assisting expeditions to the North Pole. Control Data provides us with an exciting spectrum of such stories: of individuals who are intent on devising and implementing technological innovations; of individuals whose needs are better met by those innovations; and of common sense management practices that nurture innovation.

Since "technology" is so integral to the stories of this book, it is necessary to strip the word of its mystical aura. In today's vernacular, the word is not only overused, it is *misused*. Many people, including prominent business executives, tend to think of technology as the esoteric fringe of science and engineering. This leads us to fall into the trap of relegating technology to the concern of specialists. A common belief is that only those executives in electronics and other such "high tech" arenas need concern themselves with technology. In academia, "technology" is for the most part left to engineering schools. Wall Street is even more confused in its use of the term. The demise of ill-conceived startup, Internet-based businesses was recently referred to as the "bursting of the technology bubble." Their failure had nothing to do with technology and everything to do with extraordinarily poor judgment.

A dictionary's definition of technology is straightforward: "know-how." Technology is the know-how we apply to basic science or to already existing products, tools, processes, and services to fashion a solution to some problem, some need. This idea of the equivalence of know-how and technology is easily understood and accepted in developing and producing products and services. However, it is also true for all the other processes of an enterprise: marketing, administration, human resources, and financing. The know-how—technology—used to devise these processes is essential to competitiveness. It may even be the source of superior competitiveness. Dell's direct sales process for personal computers is a vivid example.

In this light, technology becomes much more encompassing. Understanding its dynamics is essential to understanding the task of management. In this book, therefore, the terms *know-how* and *technology* will be used interchangeably. The reader who thinks in terms of know-how will be wiser and far more perceptive.

If the word *technology* has led us astray in understanding the primary task of management, the word *innovation* is even more formidable. To make matters worse, more often than not, strategists inform us that we must produce "technological innovation." By now most of us feel like the child in the *New Yorker* cartoon who says to his mother, "I don't care what you call it, I say it's spinach and to hell with it!"

Innovation, like technology, has a straightforward meaning: problem solving. Problem solving is something we do every day. On most occasions, we rely on well-established old skills, or know-how, to solve our problems. And, curious and inquiring by nature, we constantly are acquiring new know-how that not only makes us better problem solvers but allows us to look at problems in a new light. And so it is with innovation.

Unfortunately, often our first exposure to problem solving comes in the form of the notorious bane of beginning algebra students—"the word problem." The motivation to tackle such a problem is fear—fear of parents or teachers. That's hardly an auspicious beginning for a life of innovation.

By the time we are employed as adults, this barrier of disinterest in problem solving has been erected and with us for many years. The key to overcoming that barrier is to become reengaged with the world around us: to reawaken caring for those things that matter most to us. The key to innovation is not a set of rules, company policies, or slogans on a wall. The drive to solve problems, to innovate, derives from personal concerns and perceived needs. Without fascination and excitement, without the conviction that a need is worth satisfying, innovation will be stifled. In the stories of Control Data, the reader will see how we invigorated people through immersion in a wide array of needs, and how the passion for innovation, for solving problems, can be engendered in any organization.

Immersing people in, and making them cognizant of need, formed the prehistory of Control Data, which began in the dark days of World War II when a group of young engineers and scientists were working desperately to devise computing devices and algorithms for breaking enemy secret codes that would give the U.S. Navy a competitive advantage over the Japanese. Later, immersion in need gave rise to the rocket launch of Control Data with the design of its Model 1604, the world's most powerful computer at the time. It continued to evolve with ever more advanced computers for the next twenty years. Early on, however, this immersion in need branched out into education, healthcare, and employees' personal and work-related problems, underemployment of minorities, and urban and rural revitalization. The resulting outpouring of innovation was truly remarkable.

This concept of problem solving—innovation—is far more interesting, however, than just its role in the formation of Control Data and its strategic evolution. For there is another curious fact about publicly held companies: on average their existence is relatively brief. The life expectancy of a Fortune 500 company has averaged less than fifty years. Those companies that claim to be centenarians are a source of wonder and admiration, and Methuselahs of business—either public or private—are truly a phenomenon. (There are nine members of Britain's Tercentenarians Club—companies more than three hundred years old). Why should this be? Is the purpose they serve, the need they meet, so fleeting, or do they blindly embrace Darwinian evolution?

People going full throttle in the day-to-day leadership of businesses have scant time to reflect on such questions. Rather, business people tend to rely on instinct and on belief in the pontifications from on high. In today's world, divine guidance comes from Wall Street financial analysts who solemnly state the purpose of business to be stockholder value and from academic prophets who state it to be profits. In addition, we receive shallow advice from practitioner-oriented gurus who advocate that we "be number one or two in our markets," or "stick to our knitting."

To be sure, stockholder value, profit, and market strength are truly desirable and crucial outcomes of business, but like many lofty nostrums for success they can oversimplify and mislead. Indeed, in the longer term, they actually can undermine the very outcomes they purport to produce. Witness Enron. In any event, they provide little in the way of basic principles to guide the business leader's task of developing and maintaining a winning strategy. The sooner you free yourself from their grasp, the better.

It is important to ask at this point the most elementary of questions: "Why do companies exist?" and "What purpose do they serve?" Surely we can find a more helpful answer than: "So people can compare the stock price from one quarter to the next." In this book, I offer a straightforward and rigorous answer, one that has served me well over the years: Businesses exist because they meet some economic need of society. To the degree that they meet that need more effectively than any other enterprise, they not only have a right to exist, they will grow and prosper. And the key to doing so is innovation.

This task of "meeting economic need" inevitably leads to the subject of people—both the people whose needs are being served and the people who fashion new and better ways to meet those needs. Of course, there are other people involved: people who provide necessary financial wherewithal and the people of the community at large. But at its most basic level business strategy is about people.

Here, however, guidance for management leaps from the frying pan into the fire, from the blistering simplicity of outcomes to the inferno of recipes for management behavior at the micro level of day-to-day action. The torrent of such recipes in publications, books, articles, case studies, magazines, lectures, and consultancies is ample proof of the continuing and frustrating search for answers.

Through the fog of conflicting advice, is it possible to discern a more enduring characterization of corporate functioning than that based on the conventional wisdom of the moment? Such a characterization must proceed directly from the basic underlying fact that in the end what counts is the success of a company's customers and the success of the people who effect customer success, that is, employees of the company. I strongly believe there is a way to think about companies that makes them more enterprising and adaptive.

I have pared what I understand of corporate innovation to seven overlapping principles. I use the term *principles* because they are really ways of conceiving fundamentals rather than recipes to be followed by rote. I wish I had discovered them long ago without the labors of trial and error. But as with so many other things in life, revelation comes only after a great deal of experience, introspection, and honesty. So, then, with those definitional caveats in mind, the creation of an innovative company demands a belief system that embraces the following principles:

1. *Innovators are made, not born.*
2. *Strategy is a journey of sequential steps toward an objective. Each step involves innovation in some combination of process, product, and targeted market.*
3. *Strategy must coevolve with technological change and the changing nature of the world it addresses.*
4. *Technology is the strategic manager's best friend.*
5. *Collaboration, especially technological collaboration, is a powerful strategic tool.*
6. *Crisis is inevitable. Crisis can result in chaos, but innovative leaders can use crises to galvanize people for positive change.*
7. *Public–private partnerships present important but frequently overlooked strategic possibilities.*

These seven principles form the basis for the narrative of this book. They are the recurring themes that underlie much of what I have to say. None of these alone seems remarkable. Indeed the greatest tribute I could wish for, is for the reader to say: "Well, that's obvious, it's just common sense!" Organizational and strategic insights, like the most powerful insights in physics are not to be measured by their complexity. Taken together these seven principles may not rival $E = mc^2$, but they do form a straightforward and cohesive framework for enlightened and powerful management.

Innovators are made, not born.

It is useful to illustrate technological innovation ranging from the design and development of the most powerful computers of their time to the promulgation of innovative human resources policies and practices. Many remarkable individuals contributed to this. These examples show there was something about the nature, the culture of the company that not only made these individual contributions possible, it also enhanced and nurtured them in a way impossible to any of these individuals working alone. Many of their abilities undoubtedly were genetically encoded, but Control Data enabled their expression. Even more interesting than the stories of these people themselves is the impact their innovations had on others. By looking at this "results" side of the innovation equation in terms of the individual, we gain a more meaningful perspective on technological innovation.

The company culture of nurturing technological innovation reached be-

yond the people in the company. It was Control Data's foresight and support
that made possible the PLATO computer-based learning and management system developed by Dr. Donald Bitzer at the University of Illinois. PLATO was
in every sense a seminal technology that exists today in everything from the category of software known as "groupware," or facilitated group distance discussion and learning, to enhanced individualized learning programs.

Despite the self-evident need for creativity in organizations, it is truly amazing
how few in management know how to produce the conditions that engender it.
Understanding the characteristics that nurture innovation is helpful, but it leads
naturally to answering the question of the strategic purpose of innovation. This,
then, focuses our attention on yet another much used yet elusive concept: *strategy.*
As with technology and innovation the key to understanding is to strip the word of
its mystical aura. Strategy is a commonsense process of solving the problem of how
to reach an objective with a defined set of resources. Then the second principle is:

***Strategy is a journey of sequential steps toward an objective. Each step
involves innovation in some combination of process, product, or targeted
market.***

This process is by its very nature dynamic because strategy must deal with:
changing technology, competition, changing economic conditions, and demographic and cultural change; it must also accommodate often capricious actions by governments both globally and locally. So strategy, the strategic thinking process, is dynamic, a matter of trial and error, and thus evolutionary.

***Strategy must coevolve with technological change and the changing na-
ture of the world it addresses.***

This in turn leads to the fourth principle:

Technology is the strategic manager's best friend.

The individual business has little power to change the evolution of demo-
graphics and culture, nor is it capable of significant influence on economic
change. Affecting government policy and actions is desirable but very difficult
for a single company. But technology know-how resides in the minds and skills
of employees, as well as in the world at large. Thus technology is the resource
most readily available to the successful business strategist.

Strategies for business growth all involve a basic decision trichotomy: do we
make, buy, or collaborate? Since the acquisition of desirable and necessary technology—know-how—can be expensive in terms of both time and money, we
come to the fifth principle:

Technological collaboration is a powerful strategic option.

The other two branches of the strategic trichotomy, make and buy, present their own particular challenges. And the buy branch, acquisition, is more noted for failure than success. Control Data's success at growing its know-how, new markets, new services as well as financial and other critical supporting capabilities by means of acquisition was unrivaled in its industry until the considerable success of Cisco a quarter of a century later. By examining a few of these acquisitions in more detail, valuable lessons can be learned in better understanding the art of successful passage through the treacherous terrain of the strategic "buy."

The "make" branch of the trichotomy is vividly portrayed in Control Data's early expansion into global markets. These days the global nature of business is generally understood and taken for granted. Both business people and the general public are aware of global interdependency in everything from the economy's dependence on fossil fuels to meeting the somber threat of terrorism. That wasn't so common a half century ago, especially in the United States. Control Data, however, was acutely aware, even as a start-up, of the opportunities offered by global expansion. It was also attuned to the problems and threats involved. In no small part this awareness grew out of the involvement of its founder Bill Norris in the American–British World War II collaboration in breaking the Axis's cryptographic codes. Not long after Control Data's formation, as a result of these wartime connections, one of the company's earliest high-speed computers was shipped to England for the British intelligence service. These wartime experiences also provided valuable lessons regarding the realization of the benefits and overcoming the difficulties of international collaboration.

Global market access is a major problem for small business in particular. For advanced technology companies faced with the high cost of the research and development, such as supercomputers in the case of Control Data, the additional difficulty of national security issues introduces another whole level of challenge. Not only is creative and innovative thinking required, but so are patience and persistence.

Control Data's trials demonstrate that no strategy, no matter how well conceived, can avoid the crises that derive from the competitive, economic, policy, regulatory, social, and technological forces that beset business. They likewise show that determination, devotion, and action are the hallmark of survivors.

Crisis is inevitable.

Outstanding leaders can use crisis to galvanize people for positive and dynamic change. In his epic biography *John Adams,* author David McCullough relates the story of Adams's voyage to France as a commissioner appointed by the fledgling U.S. government. During the voyage his ship encountered a violent storm and was struck by lightning. Years later, McCullough tells us, Adams wrote to Thomas Jefferson about the voyage as being "symbolic of his whole life." McCullough then makes this observation: "The raging seas he had passed through, he seemed to be saying, were like the times they lived in, and he was at the mercy of the times no less than the seas." Beyond that, Adams also had to face the possibility that his young son, John Quincy, who was accompanying him on the voyage, shared his very real prospect of imminent death. "Possibly," McCullough writes, "he saw, too, in the presence of John Quincy, how directly his determination to dare such seas affected his family and how much, with his devotion to the cause of America, he had put at risk beyond his own life." McCullough concludes,

"He may also have seen, the voyage had demonstrated how much better suited he was for action than for smooth sailing."

One of the most common aphorisms of today's world is "The only constant is change." Like many such sayings, although it is a clever juxtaposition of words, it masks the most compelling challenge of change: it is the unevenness, sporadic nature and unknown implications of change that really matter. Trying to cope with this uncertainty is the challenge of strategy—and for that matter, of life. Success lies in discerning the *discontinuity* in continuous *change*.

Public-private collaborations present important but frequently overlooked strategic possibilities.

Control Data had such undertakings at the local, state, and national levels in the United States. These governmental partnerships took on several different forms, but the results were the same: better opportunity for people who had been bypassed by the mainstream economy, better communities in which to live, and profit to the company itself. It was in these endeavors that Control Data demonstrated both leadership and its particular strength in devising innovative approaches to the pressing problems of minority unemployment and underemployment, economic development in blighted urban and rural areas, and in remedial education.

Control Data swept into being on the technological wave that resulted from the wellspring of scientific achievements of the first half of the twentieth century. Technological change brought opportunity. Control Data was also born because management practices in its predecessor company stifled innovation.

The result was an exciting business that helped achieve success for its customers, from government scientific laboratories, space agencies, and intelligence services to disadvantaged inner-city youth and rural farmers, and also brought an extraordinary sense of success and fulfillment to its employees. As Judy Alnes, a former executive, told me in an interview: "Control Data was the best place in the world to work." This is a simple and apt summary of the feelings of many of us who worked there.

The principles and lessons to be learned from this extraordinary enterprise are not just once-upon-a-time curiosities. They are keys to the future; they are seven principles for effective business and management practice in the twenty-first century.

Part One Habitats for Innovation and Their Inhabitants:

Innovators Are Made, Not Born

Understanding this first principle of the strategic management of innovation is essential to understanding and applying the other six. Perspective can be gained by looking at numerous examples of people engaged in innovative endeavors. With that perspective, and with examples of environments and infrastructure that nurtured those people, it is possible to provide practical guidelines for managing in accordance with this first principle.

Chapter 1 The Once and Future Company

The Corporation was organized to engage in the design, development, manufacture and sale of systems, equipment and components used in electronic data processing and automatic control for industrial, scientific and military uses.
—Initial prospectus for Control Data Corporation common stock at $1.00/share, July 8, 1957.

On October 4, 1957, the Soviet Union launched Sputnik, the first space satellite. Physically it was a rather insignificant, 183-pound orbiting sphere the size of a basketball, but its impact on global politics and economics was destined to assume colossal proportions.

Three months earlier, on July 8, there was another launch. In the dry language of legal business documents, the "Nature of Business" statement noted above was at first glance unimpressive. But that business launch also proved to be historic and, indeed, would soon cross paths with that of U.S. space programs and the historical path of the Soviet Union. Control Data built its influence through an awesome array of products and services, corporate and industry initiatives, and national and international policy initiatives within a new but aspiring industry. That journey offers many lessons in innovation that are applicable to any business at any time. Companies change, but the inherent nature of innovation does not.

The wellspring of Control Data's successes was a reservoir of creative energy supplied by an extraordinary group of people and beginning with its 1957 launch and lasting more than thirty years. In the initial 1957 prospectus, the official beginning of Control Data listed the founding stockholders as: W. C. Norris, 70,000 shares; A. J. Ryden, 20,000 shares; Fremont Fletcher, 5,000 shares. The balance sheet showed total assets of $25,000 and no liabilities.

During World War II, W. C. (Bill) Norris and Howard Engstrom were key members of the U.S. Navy's Communications Supplementary Activity–Washington (CSAW, pronounced "seesaw"), a group that focused on code-breaking. At the end of the war, when the group's members returned to civilian life, the navy wanted to continue its research and development of electronic tools and techniques for cryptanalysis. In 1945, with the navy's encouragement, Norris founded Engineering Research Associates (ERA), along with John E. Parker, the principal stockholder of ERA, Engstrom, and Ralph Meader. ERA's story is a fascinating one and is most interestingly documented in David L. Boslaugh's book *When Computers Went to Sea.*

Engineers founded ERA. Its innovation was nurtured and encouraged by one of the most technologically forward-looking units of the mighty World War II U.S. military. The navy insisted on reliability as well as performance, and kept an on-site presence to monitor developments at ERA. The results were impressive. ERA finished the construction and delivery of its first large-scale digital computer, the Atlas, by the end of 1950. After a remarkably short installation time for that period of eight days, CSAW's cryptologists began using the computer as soon as it was "powered up." The machine immediately demonstrated remarkable reliability, requiring only sixteen hours of unscheduled maintenance in its first five hundred hours of operation.[1]

As the company grew, ERA had the typical startup's need for capital, and in 1951 it was acquired for $1.7 million by Remington Rand. The previous year Remington Rand had bought another computer startup—the Eckert-Mauchly Computer Corporation—for $538,000 plus 50 percent of the net profit from its patents for eight years. With those two acquisitions, Remington Rand had both a formidable technological lead and ready access to the most accomplished computer minds in the young industry. But over the next few years it proceeded to fritter away that lead to IBM and its hard-as-diamonds marketing machine. ERA was rightly referred to as an "engineer's paradise."

That paradise, however, became "paradise lost" after the acquisition by Remington Rand.[2]

The struggles of ERA's innovative and energetic young engineers against a highly bureaucratic and unimaginative culture shaped by decades of selling typewriters, was like watching a powerful young horse caught in quicksand. To make matters worse there were technical rivalry and management conflict between ERA and Eckert-Mauchly. The top management of Remington Rand and, later, Sperry-Rand had little skill and less stomach for managing such intensity. Far less equipped were they to devise successful strategies to compete with IBM.

By 1957, Bill Norris, Frank Mullaney, and Willis K. (Bill) Drake had had enough. Finding common ground with Arnold Ryden, they decided to start anew. They began with a novel financing idea that became an oft-told story in Minnesota lore: this upstart startup with no products and no revenues—not even a contract—sold stock to the public at a dollar a share. This unconventional beginning included selling stock at coffee parties in kitchens and living rooms. As a consequence, a wave of entrepreneurial startups in Minnesota was launched.

The company was incorporated on July 8, 1957, and opened its doors for business in September of that year with $600,000 in proceeds from its public stock sales. The assets consisted of hard cash and the determination to build computers at the leading edge of technology. Control Data's saga is first and foremost a collection of stories about innovation and, especially, the courageous individuals who recognized need and took the risks.

To better appreciate the stories of the protagonists, it will be useful to summarize a few facts and figures of the company's history. A detailed history of the company and the leading figures would require volumes; the abbreviated history that follows is intended only to provide a frame of reference for the events and strategies described in the rest of this book.

THE FORMATIVE YEARS—1957–1966

For the first decade of the company's existence, the computer systems business was the focus and driving force of its success. Its accomplishments in that regard were astounding. Before the company was a year old, the U.S. Navy had ordered the first model of Control Data's computers. This wasn't blind luck, but rather the result of the proven track record of the company's people, especially premier computer designers Seymour Cray and Jim Thornton. Its first computer, the Model 1604, was the first fully transistorized electronic digital computer to be a commercial success. It was delivered to the U.S. Naval Postgraduate School in Monterey, California, in 1960. By 1964 some fifty systems worth more than $75 million had been delivered, and the total revenues exceeded $100 million that year—a spectacular start for a company whose founder, Bill Norris, had remarked shortly after it began operations, "We're aiming at sales of $25 million a year within five years."[3]

The rapid growth put a strain on financial resources. The young company also faced serious competitive threats, particularly from IBM, which aggressively sought to squash challengers. Tough as these problems were, they all the more stimulated the excitement felt by employees. There was a palpable feeling of predestined greatness instilled by the leaders who were giving shape to the company. The desire to excel, to be best, was an intrinsic trait of employees throughout the organization—a quality that was relentlessly reinforced.

One particularly defining characteristic of this young company was manifest in the lifeblood of all who worked there. Control Data's people had a history of working closely with customers, going back to the early days of ERA. The company's major customer, the U.S. Navy, continuously challenged the leading edge of technology. The Naval Computing Machine Laboratory (NCML), CSAW, and customers that followed over the next decade were faced with increasingly complex, intransigent tasks. The digital electronic tools needed to help solve their problems were essentially undefined and, consequently, undeveloped. As a result, mutual problem solving between supplier and customer became a way of life. Success requires more than a lifeless statement of specifications. It requires an intuitive, deep-rooted understanding of the daily operational challenges faced by customers. This kind of partnership between Control Data and customers became an ingrained part of the company culture.[4]

That relationship with customers said, in effect: "We're in this together. Technology has answers. Together *we* can discover the best answer if we are asking the right questions in order to find it." Contrast that with the more traditional mode of a company doing its R&D under wraps—often in operational isolation—then unveiling the resulting product with fanfare, promoting its features, advantages, and benefits to a public who does not fully understand its usefulness.

Seymour Cray was, without doubt, a brilliant conceptual designer and architect of powerful digital electronic circuits. But the unheralded key to the success of his computer designs was his fundamental understanding of what his customers faced in trying to solve their complex mathematical and physical problems. This was not the pandering we all too often find today under the banner of "being close to your customer." Instead, his was a deep and passionate concern for, and understanding of, the problems customers faced every day.

During the early years, Bill Norris assembled executive leaders to guide this fledgling company: Frank Mullaney, who headed the Computer Division; Bob Kisch, who directed engineering operations in that division; Bill Keye, in charge of Research and Engineering; Jim Harris, who had the responsibility for bringing some administrative order to this ferment of design engineers; and Seymour Cray, already a shining star in the design of digital electronic circuitry. They were bright and energetic and had had a taste of heady success at ERA. The company likewise was fortunate in having a wise and gifted corporate counsel—Bob Leach of the law firm Oppenheimer, Brown, Wolff and Leach.

A host of talented people worked under their leadership, and I will have more to tell about them later. For now it is enough to say that the innovative designs of those individuals provided a spectacular beginning for this upstart computer company. By 1961 the original $1 stock had reached $29 a share and split three for one. Still it continued its meteoric rise. It began trading on the New York Stock Exchange (NYSE) on March 6, 1963. It split three for two in 1964, and by August 1968 had reached $140 per share. An initial investment of $10,000 was now worth $6.3 million. Not bad.

The equity created was quickly reinvested. Acquisitions, beginning with Cedar Engineering in 1957, were an integral part of the company's actions to augment its computer technology and its people skills. Control Data's notable success with its computer designs obscured the fact that in these earliest years the company started two new lines of business that would play major roles in its future: the original equipment manufacturing (OEM) peripherals business and the data services business.

Although the Model 1604 computer was a performance whiz, there was a problem in the total system. Getting external data into the machine was difficult because of the limitations of input–output devices. In addition, the available products poorly met the need for large, reliable, external auxiliary storage. Data input and storage devices that were available at the time were punched paper tape and punched cards—both unacceptably slow—and magnetic tape.

Magnetic tape had been around for some years when the first 1604 was delivered in 1960. It was used extensively in analog recording for audio and in the young TV business. Tape was adopted as both a digital input–output medium and an auxiliary data storage medium for digital computers. Except for IBM's magnetic tape transports, however, the input–output devices were unreliable and slow. But IBM would sell to other computer manufacturers only at the full end-user retail prices. They offered no OEM price breaks. Because magnetic tape transports and other data handling and printing devices represented as much as 30 percent of the total price of a computer installation, this was a major competitive disadvantage in terms of total profitability of the system.

There was considerable imperative, then, for a company such as Control Data to design and build its own magnetic tape transports. The barrier, of course, was cost—both research and development cost and manufacturing cost. These costs dictated the need for high volume. In Bill Norris's mind there was an obvious answer to this dilemma, and that was to make Control Data magnetic tape transports and sell them to competitors—in other words, to any computer company that wished to buy them. Almost fifty years ago Bill Norris well understood the dynamics of this burgeoning industry and the basic sources of competitive advantage. He practiced "co-opetition" long before it became a catchword in business. Fortunately, the company had the technical talent and sales skills for such a business. Veterans Bob Perkins, Paul Bulver, and Lloyd Thorndyke eagerly undertook the task. Tom Kamp, plant manager of that first acquisition, Cedar Engineering, became the chief cheerleader of Control Data's OEM peripherals business and its chief executive as well.

Thus it was in 1960 that Control Data's OEM peripherals business was born. The model 606 magnetic tape transport was developed and with it the start of this new enterprise. The OEM peripherals business provided Control Data the economies of scale required to build cost-effective, high-performance peripherals for its powerful computers. The lineup of peripheral products began with magnetic tape transports. Soon printers, magnetic disk drives, computer terminals, and other devices followed.

While OEM peripherals were getting their start in 1960, the Data Centers business was launched that same year. Data Centers sprang from a basic cultural premise in Control Data: "If you have to have it for yourself, you might as well sell it to everyone else, because it'll be cheaper (economies of scale), and it'll be better because you'll learn a lot from why and how other people use computers."

Control Data used its computers in its internal design and development processes. That cost money. Why not turn that internal cost center into an external revenue producer? To make that happen, Bill Norris didn't turn to one of the company's many gifted design engineers, or even to the marketing and sales organization. No, he chose Jim Harris, the company's vice president of administration who had proved his tenacity and organizing abilities. There was plenty of technical talent around with whom Jim Harris could confer. Bill Norris understood the task at hand and the personal traits that would be required to pull it off. Jim Harris was the man for the job.

The Data Centers Division was the cornerstone of what ultimately became the major strategic thrust of Control Data's business: computing, education, consulting, and information services. For example, in 1967, the acquisition of C-E-I-R added commercially oriented data centers and an initial entry into so-called time-shared computing. C-E-I-R also brought with it Control Data's first true database information services business, American Research Bureau, the leading provider of audience measurement services for radio and local TV broadcasting. That business changed its name to its initials, ARB, and later to Arbitron. It competed with the Nielsen Company, which dominated network TV audience measurement, but Arbitron was the leader in measuring local market TV advertising. By the 1980s, Arbitron had become the company's most profitable business unit. ARB's transformation from a struggling, purely research-oriented backwater of the information industry into a dynamic marketing and service-oriented company was the work of Theodore F. Shaker, a former group vice president at ABC-TV.[5]

While the services business gained a strong foothold in the company's first decade, its potential was hardly visible in the glare of publicity and excitement surrounding the company's powerful computers. But there was no question about Bill Norris's support. In a 1981 interview, Jim Harris referred to services as one of Norris's sacred cows in that first decade: "[Norris] is a very persistent man and when he decides something is going to get a damn good trial, it gets a trial and he backs it up with actions, not just words."

That said, it was an exciting time for the computer hardware business. By the end of 1962, there were forty-one installations of 1604s. In addition, two hundred of the smaller 160 and 160-A computer models had been installed. That same year, the Model 3600 was announced and Michigan State University ordered the first one. As has been true from the beginning of computer development, the 3600 had several times the power of the 1604 at only about twice the price. A typical 3600 system sold for $2.5 million in 1962.

The 1604 achieved great market acceptance from the beginning. The much-anticipated successor machines, first the 3600 and then the even more ambitious and powerful 6600, entered a market eager for the new models. In 1964, the first 6600 was shipped to the Lawrence Livermore Laboratory. The 6600 was the first computer to be dubbed a supercomputer. IBM's marketing tactics became ever more aggressive; they included selling computers still in the design stage. Such computers were derisively termed "paper machines" since they existed only on paper: design specifications, drawings, and marketing literature. However, by 1967 the 6600 was well on its way to ultimate success. By 1974 the 6000 series, led by the flagship 6600, had amassed profits of $43 million on sales of $889 million.

Control Data's growing reputation in large-scale computing naturally gained global attention. The company's first sale outside the United States went to British intelligence. In collaboration with the U.S. National Security Agency (NSA), the British intelligence facility at Cheltenham received a Model 1604 in 1961. The project was kept secret. Even inside Control Data the customer was known only as "Webster" and was generally represented as being NSA. Also by 1961 there were already discussions with the Weizmann Institute in Israel. These were but harbingers of what the global scientific community would mean to Control Data's rising prosperity.

The market potential outside the United States was large, and it provided scope and scale to help amortize the large R&D expenditures involved in designing large-scale computers. At that time Philips, the large Dutch electrical and electronics firm, greatly desired to get into the burgeoning young computer industry. Philips and Control Data began seriously seeking an agreement, but ultimately the discussions broke down.

The company's treasurer, Ed Strickland, was then dispatched to Europe to set up a European headquarters. In the second half of 1962, Ed had established his office in Lucerne, Switzerland. Late that year the newly formed operation made its first computer sale in continental Europe—a 1604 was sold to the Danish research and data center organization, Regnecentralen. By June 1963, Control Data subsidiaries had been established in Switzerland, France, West Germany, Sweden, and the Netherlands. After the 1604's success in Europe, the first international installation of the 3600 was in November 1963 at the Societé d'Economie et de Mathématique Appliqués in Paris. A year later, a 6600 was ordered by the European Center for Nuclear Research (CERN), an organization with thirteen member nations. In 1963, Europe accounted for 4 percent of the company's total revenues. In 1965, that figure was 12 percent and growing. By the end of its first decade, Control Data had operations in twenty countries and had delivered $100 million worth of computers outside the United States.

In 1962, in another part of the world, the company established a manufacturers' representation agreement in Australia with the E. L. Heymanson Company and would soon extend its reach into other international markets. Control Data acquired Bendix Corporation's Computer Division in 1963. Although the primary purpose of the acquisition was to obtain people with maintenance services know-how, Bendix also had operations in Canada (Computing Devices of Canada) and manufacturers' representatives in Japan and Mexico. The Japanese representative was C. Itoh and Co.

By Fiscal Year 1967, International had operations in twenty countries and was contributing 20 percent of Control Data's $245 million in total revenues. The principal thrust in International's early years was the sales and service of large-scale computers and the expansion of the OEM business. Prestigious customers in the computer business, such as CERN, Electricité de France (EDF), French AEC, German Weather Service, Regnecentralen, and multiple universities around Europe reinforced the company's position in engineering and scientific computing.

The OEM peripherals business expanded its capabilities in a number of ways, including a joint venture with Holley Carburetor Company to form Holley Computer Products; acquisition of Digigraphic Systems from Itek; acquisition of Bridge Inc., makers of card punch and card reader systems; and acquisition of Rabinow Engineering and its state-of-the-art expertise in optical character recognition technology. Foreign manufacturing capabilities were added with the purchase of a majority share in Electrofact, N.V., of Amersfoort in The Netherlands, and the acquisition of Waltech, Ltd., Hong Kong, assemblers of electronic components.

During this period Control Data also established the industrial group, a business focused on industrial control systems and the company's growing expertise in the design and manufacture of small, special-purpose computers.

Thus the company's nearly insatiable appetite for the application of innovative information systems technology resulted in rapid expansion geographically and in terms of product lines. Developments were likewise dynamic in the company's primary focus on high-performance computers. In 1964–1965 work began on the 7600, the successor to the 6600, and on a supercomputer with a totally new architecture, the STAR (STring ARray processor). The demand for R&D dollars as well as money to support the development and growth of all of the new businesses was immense. Investors were enjoying returns not even imagined a mere ten years earlier. But the diversification and growth of the company also produced stress.

One day in 1966, Frank Mullaney, a strong right arm to Bill Norris since ERA days, remarked somewhat plaintively to Bob Kisch, general manager of the Computer Division and a close colleague of many years: "Whatever happened to our nice little company?" A few months later Frank left Control Data a much richer man than he had been ten years before, but in search once again of a "nice little company." Bob Kisch followed Frank soon after.

NEW FACES, NEW PLACES—1967–1970

Over the four-year period after Frank Mullaney left Control Data, the company migrated to the basic strategy and structure that would guide its existence through the 1970s. Upon Frank's departure, Bill Keye became the chief operating executive as group vice president, operations, which included computers, peripherals, and industrial products. Also in 1967 Bob Schmidt replaced his boss, George Hanson, as vice president, marketing, which included the U.S. sales organization, all the international sales subsidiaries, as well as the Data Centers Division and the computer Maintenance Services Division.

In 1968, motivated in large part by the enormous financing required in computer leasing, and enabled by its high-multiple stock, the company took on the role of "white knight" and acquired Commercial Credit Company of Baltimore, Maryland. At the time, Commercial Credit was the object of a hostile takeover attempt by Loew's, Inc. That acquisition was to provide a twenty-year enhancement to, and stabilizing element for, the company's computer business. Ironically, the lease financing motive would largely disappear within five years, thanks to the technological evolution of computing toward less expensive devices that customers could buy outright.

There was more at work in Control Data's evolution, however, than acquiring and expanding its array of new services. As the company established major new centers of operations, it developed a far more global, less U.S. Midwest–centered culture. With Commercial Credit's acquisition, Baltimore became an important center of corporate activity. European Headquarters had moved from Switzerland to Frankfurt, Germany (1963), and then to Brussels, Belgium. Both manufacturing operations and sales were growing in Asia Pacific: Japan (1964), Hong Kong, South Korea, Taiwan, as well as the growing Australian operation. Canada took on major strategic importance in 1970 when the Canadian government and Control Data forged an agreement to develop and manufacture a new line of computers at a facility near Toronto.

Discussions between company executives and government officials around the world became a part of everyday life. The topics ranged from computing standards to possible technological collaborations, to economic development policies and many discussions of how best to deal with U.S. export control laws and rules.

Change brought new faces to the company's Policy Committee, the highest-level executive group, and to its Board of Directors. In contrast to 1966, by 1970 the top two tiers of line operating executives were occupied by new people or executives who had been promoted or reassigned. These changes are reflected in the organization charts for 1957 through 1986 (at approximately five-year intervals) in Appendix 2. The makeup of the Board of Directors also changed. Compared with today's norm, there was a sizeable minority of inside directors. At Control Data, outside directors provided extremely valuable perspectives concerning technology, financial management, and policies and practices to ensure the continuation of an innovative culture. The inside directors brought both the perspectives and realities of day-to-day business to the larger questions of policy. The inside directors also gained a broader view of the company and the business environment in general, making them more ready and able to accept larger responsibilities in the future.

By the year ending December 31, 1969, Control Data's revenues had topped $1 billion, and employment grew to 45,000 people. The company was diversified both geographically and in the scope of its products and services. Control Data had long since evolved from a startup, fast-moving producer of large-scale scientific computers to a large company participating in the mainstream of the global economy. As an integral part of the economy, the company for the first time felt the impact of a national recession in 1970. This produced a downturn in the computer business that made it difficult to provide the R&D dollars necessary to support the company's proliferation of product lines. By this time, Control Data had five different product lines in development and/or production. The 6000 line consisted of the 6400, 6600, 7600, and the 8600, then under development at the Chippewa Falls, Wisconsin, laboratory. In addition, the STAR supercomputer was being designed. Other computer design efforts of the early 1960s had resulted in two additional product lines, the "lower 3000" (models 3100, 3200, 3300, 3500) and "upper 3000" (models 3400, 3600, 3800). There was also a minicomputer, the model 1700, which had been developed primarily for various process control applications. These five lines of computers were not software compatible so each of them required separate system software development and support.

The strategy envisioned in 1970 was to develop a new product line (PL) that would supercede this menagerie except for the 7600, 8600, and STAR supercomputers. Development of PL was a major effort supported in part by the government of Canada. Unfortunately, as it turned out, its overambitious design goals could not be achieved. Likewise by the end of 1970, there was developing doubt that the 8600 design could be implemented with the semiconductor technology envisioned for it. To add to the development burden, major subsystems of the STAR computer had to be redesigned. The resolution of all these computer product line problems were to be a major task for the coming decade.

More basic than product line issues, however, was the challenge of maintaining the company's innovative culture. For the first decade, the source of that culture had been most visible in its hardware design people. Would the ebullience, the excitement of developing highly innovative digital computer designs, succumb to the increasingly onerous task of rationalizing the legacy product lines? As we shall see, it did not. The many facets of innovation moved into different arenas, but ones easily as exciting as what had gone before.

A harbinger of that future came in the form of an innovation in litigation support services. In 1968 Control Data filed a private antitrust lawsuit against IBM, charging it with anticompetitive monopolistic behavior in the computer industry. At best, many viewed this action as a romantic David and Goliath confrontation; at worst, it was seen as an irrational tilting at windmills. It was neither, but rather a shrewd, bold move by Bill Norris to restructure the computer and information services industry to more effectively nurture the emerging software and information services businesses. At the very least the lawsuit's result would perhaps protect those new fields from being dominated by IBM as had happened in computer hardware. It worked. It worked for Control Data, and it worked for the industry.

The facts of the case were in Control Data's favor, and those facts were rendered all the more powerful by an information database system that the company developed specifically for litigation support in antitrust actions. Control Data's small team of lawyers was able to adroitly and effectively outmaneuver the massive legal power of its giant opponent. "David" had a slingshot that was indeed innovative!

The case was settled in January 1973. For a nominal amount of money, Control Data acquired IBM's Service Bureau Corporation (SBC). There were several other monetary and nonmonetary aspects of the settlement that amounted to a very rich frosting on the cake. The value of the settlement was deliberately played down, but internally that value was put at $700 million ($3.1 billion in 2005 dollars). Most important, Control Data acquired a large and well-known addition to its growing services business. The U.S. government followed Control Data's action with its own antitrust action, which finally ended in 1982. Meanwhile IBM walked a very fine line in the marketplace. In an attempt to ward off private and government lawsuits, IBM voluntarily implemented unbundling in 1969. With unbundling and the enormous technological change brought on by the introduction of the microprocessor-based "personal computer" in 1977, the computer industry changed fundamentally and forever.

TRANSITIONS 1971–1980

As the 1970s began, Control Data suddenly was faced with the task of rationalizing its business and product lines and at the same time transferring its innovative energy from hardware design to the domain of *services.* In 1971, total revenues from computing services were only $120 million. Nearly ten years later, in 1980, services accounted for $981 million, or about 36 percent of the computer business revenue. Moreover, this billion-dollar services business was growing at almost 20 percent per year. Although computer sales and rentals and the sale of OEM peripherals still represented the bulk of computer business revenues, services had become the focus of Control Data's future growth.[6]

From these numbers it is clear that the '70s had been marked by developments in services that worked to reshape Control Data. It was a decade of transition, or, more accurately, of multiple transitions: from hardware to services, from small company to large, but primarily a transition in innovation—from innovation in computer circuits to innovation of a far greater scope and at a much higher conceptual level.

It was not a smooth, continuous transition. There were ups and downs and discontinuities, and there was pain—pain to individuals and pain with respect to corporate financial performance. Indeed, the first year of the decade, 1971, except for the financing unit—Commercial Credit—the business had a bottom line loss, as it did again in 1974.

The company was no longer a computer designer's paradise. Except for a brief resurgence of that environment in the form of a newly established supercomputer subsidiary, ETA Systems in the '80s, the heady excitement in the design of digital electronic computers was replaced by a different but equally heady excitement: fulfilling the promise of applying computer and information technology. Innovation in "mips and flops" was replaced by innovation in *using* mips and flops to meet a broad array of human needs. Not everyone within the company, much less external to it, understood, accepted, and appreciated this transition. Nevertheless the relentless march of microelectronic technology, the pervasive expansion of the uses to which computers could be put, and the large installed base of legacy systems had brought new opportunities. We had to adapt. Exciting, important, and profitable computer developments continued to occur, but they were not the driving force they once had been.[7]

The computer systems and peripherals businesses changed significantly during this decade. It is an understatement to say that the first two years, 1971 and 1972, were traumatic for the company's business of delivering high-performance digital computing. By the end of 1971 it was painfully obvious that the new product line of mainframes (PL) could not be realized as envisioned.

Even more traumatic—or at least seemingly so—was the evident failure of Seymour Cray's Model 8600 design and the resignation in March 1972 of Seymour himself. After fifteen years, this legendary figure in computer design was no longer a part of Control Data Corporation. While the Model 7600 was a growing market success and would continue to enjoy that success throughout most of the '70s, the question of a successor machine hung over the company.

Control Data approached these problems pragmatically. The PL design was abandoned, and by redesigning the 6000/7000 computers to incorporate new semiconductor technology, a sequence of new computer product lines, the Cyber 70, Cyber 170, and, ultimately, Cyber 180 provided enhanced performance and a smooth evolutionary path for Control Data's customer base as well as expansion into new customers and markets. During this time, the company's operations outside the United States provided additional growth and increasing profitability while the 3000 and 1700 product lines continued to be phased out. None of these developments could rank as innovations to compare with the 6600. What they did do, however, was bring clarity and purpose to the product line jungle the company faced in 1971. One measure of success was the company's announcement by 1977 of the first-ever dividend on its common stock.

The other supercomputer development, STAR, was more fortunate than the 8600. Jim Thornton, its chief architect and designer, was not only an outstanding designer, he also had the executive ability to build an organization of competent design engineers and system architects who could carry on without him. Key members of the team who carried the work forward were Don Pagelkopf, engineering manager, and Neil Lincoln, architect, hardware, and software designer. They also had the support of some outstanding circuit technologists such as Tony Vacca. The first STAR computer was delivered to Lawrence Livermore Laboratory in 1974.

The subject of computers cannot be concluded without mention of microprocessors, the essential building block of personal computers, or PCs. The conventional view is that the "mainframe," or large computer, manufacturers including Control Data missed the technological boat in the '70s: that corporate shortsightedness on the part of the then major manufacturers resulted in their inability to sense and take advantage of the move to a more individual worker-centered (PC) view of information processing. This, in the case of Control Data, is an incorrect conclusion. Technologically the company was as capable as any of designing and developing such computers. From the outset, small computers were an essential ingredient of the company's repertoire. Indeed, an early (perhaps the first) "desktop" computer was Control Data's Model 160. This computer was a direct derivation of the large-scale 1604 technology. In fact, it was one of the company's early OEM products, sold under contract to NCR.

Small, powerful computers were a central part of Control Data's military and space business. The AN/AYK-14, in fact, has been the standard platform for military aircraft since 1976. Begun by Control Data, it continued to be improved and manufactured by the Computing Devices Division when Control Data was renamed Ceridian in 1992. In 1998, that division was sold to General Dynamics, where the AN/AYK-14 continued to be an extremely reliable, profitable product, a quarter century after its initial development. Moreover, the 6600 supercomputer in actuality consisted of an extremely fast central processing unit and ten "peripheral processors," small computers that acted as "servers," to the central processor. There was no blindness to either technological or marketplace evolution. Rather, there was a conscious and explicit strategic understanding of the company's core capability, which was to concentrate on complex computing applications. Control Data understood that it was not particularly skilled at commodity manufacturing. Instead, there was a conscious strategic decision to take the company in the direction of services.

Effective strategy rests on more than mere opportunism or the siren song of technological novelty. It rests squarely on a clear understanding of skills and competencies, the resources of the company, the ability to sense the rate and direction of technological evolution, and the ability to correlate the one with the other.

The 1970s transition in the company's other main hardware business, peripheral products, was no less dramatic. The driving force behind development of magnetic tape drives, magnetic disk drives, and the like had been the needs of the company's high-performance computers. The OEM business involving those products was a means to achieve economies of scale for both the amortization of product development costs and the reduction of direct manufacturing costs per unit.

By 1980 this situation was turned on its head. OEM and plug-compatibles had become the raison d'etre of the peripherals business. The requirements for Control Data's own computers, while important to additional volume, had become secondary in the peripheral products' business strategy. Extensive use of alliances was key to the strategic direction and growth of the OEM business. The first of these was established in 1972: Computer Peripherals, Inc., a joint venture with NCR Corporation. The largest and most important alliance for the development of the company's OEM business was formed four years later, in 1976. This joint venture with Honeywell was called Magnetic Peripherals, Inc. Later the French company Bull became a partner. These collaborative ventures were particularly important in the international expansion of the peripherals business.

The most notable marketplace change was the rapid evolution of so-called departmental computers, or minicomputers, and the emergence of the microprocessor-based personal computers in the latter half of the decade. The data storage requirements of these new markets dwarfed those of Control Data's large-scale computers.

By 1980 the Peripheral Products Company was a big and diverse business with revenues in excess of $1.1 billion. The products it produced included a broad range of magnetic disk drives with varying performance and storage capacity, magnetic tape transports, computer printers, plug-compatible disk systems for IBM computer users, optical character recognition equipment, a variety of terminals—"thin clients," as they would come to be called—and computer supplies ranging from paper products to magnetic disks and tapes.

The OEM peripherals business is by its very nature a commodity business, albeit a commodity business with a very large requirement for design and development expenditures. The attendant low-cost producer culture was in stark contrast to that of the rest of the company with its emphasis on supercomputer performance and value-added differentiation in services.

It is by no means impossible for a corporation to encompass businesses with disparate basic sources of competitive advantage and thus disparate cultures. It is, however, a very great management challenge, especially in times of crisis. Control Data's Peripheral Products Company devoted much effort to manufacturing efficiency and was proud of the results it achieved. However, in the waning years of the '70s it was taught painful lessons in efficiency by its Japanese competitors.

In April 1970, services was for the first time given explicit organizational recognition with the establishment of the Services Group. It included: Cybernet (data centers), Professional Services, Maintenance Services, Education Services, and two information services subsidiaries, Arbitron and Ticketron.

A defining moment for the services business came with the settlement of the antitrust suit against IBM and the acquisition of IBM's Service Bureau Corporation (SBC). In one stroke the company acquired not only a profitable $100 million business, but the best information and data networking expertise in the industry. Henry (Hank) White was the number two executive at SBC and the chief architect of its time-sharing network. Hank was an early participant in the SAGE continental air defense system that began development in the early 1950s. SBC also brought with it other outstanding management people who would play major roles in the development of Control Data's services business.[8]

The IBM settlement had other benefits as well. Part of the agreement was a significant grant of R&D funds by IBM to Control Data. In 1973 it was decided that the time had come to commercialize the PLATO (Programmed Logic for Automated Teaching Operations) computer-based education research that had been carried out at the University of Illinois under Donald Bitzer. As pleasant irony would have it, it was an ex-IBM star performer, John Dammeyer, who would initially lead this effort. The Control Data team he put together along with the Bitzer team at Illinois carried PLATO to commercial announcement in April 1976. The education services business, which began with the establishment in 1965 of the first Control Data Institute to train electronic technicians and programmers, now had an added dimension and a powerful technology to support it. In 1977, John W. Lacey was named president of the newly established Control Data Education Company.

Price unbundling, which separated the pricing of software and technical support services from the pricing of hardware, came also as a result of government antitrust pressures. This gave Control Data the opportunity to formally establish a profitable technical consulting business, the Professional Services Division, built on the capabilities of its sales support organization. Other technical consulting capabilities subsequently were added to this core.

Charging for hardware maintenance as a separate item had been standard practice from the earliest days of the industry. But the concept of unbundling, combined with third-party leasing companies that acted as leasing intermediaries and the increasing need for a different kind of technical support for terminals, microprocessor systems, and the increasing array of electronic devices associated with computing and information processing, led to the creation of so-called third-party maintenance businesses.

Each segment of Control Data's business, then, had gone through major transitions in the 1970s. The founding core, large-scale computing systems, although larger and more profitable than it once was, no longer drove the business, nor was the company the dominant competitor in large-scale scientific and engineering computing. That leadership had passed to Seymour's Cray Research Corporation. Control Data's computer development and manufacturing business was well on its way to being what we know today as a systems integration business. The peripheral equipment business had grown into a diversified, large-scale commodity manufacturing business whose primary market was no longer in-house computers. Services had diversified and grown by rapid internal growth and acquisition. It would carry forward the company's culture of innovation and entrepreneurship in the future. And finally, the company's leadership had changed from being principally those of the ERA–Sperry Rand heritage to a new set of executives.

THE SERVICES COMPANY—1980–1989

As the 1980s opened, the Services business had proved its strength. In 1980, Services revenues were $1.1 billion, double that of five years earlier. The diversity of services offerings also was growing.

Services had inauspicious, low-key beginnings in Control Data's earliest days. Richard C. (Dick) Gunderson recalled those days in a 1981 interview. Dick had responsibility for making the new computers, in his word, usable: "Seymour had the responsibility of designing and manufacturing the machine . . . but my responsibility was to build the support organization—software development, engineering services, customer engineering, training." More than twenty years later, that "support organization" was the solid center of Control Data's future.

In 1980, Services continued to provide data services including remote batch processing and time-sharing for scientific/engineering customers as well as for business data processing customers. Payroll and insurance processing, which was a major service of SBC, added much-needed critical mass. SBC also provided an entrée to data processing services for credit unions. Control Data's business, however, was predicated on businesses more far-reaching than traditional data processing: Arbitron provided TV and radio measurement; Ticketron provided automated ticketing for sports and entertainment events; and PLATO provided computer-based learning in centers located throughout the United States. The list of innovative services included Quorum Litigation Services, Staywell, Employee Advisory Services (EAR), Business and Technology Centers and Control Data (small) Business Advisors. This strong array of services was a good foundation on which to build a business for the future, but two major strategic issues still faced the company: 1) how to shape the future of the hardware businesses, and 2) how to finance emerging services businesses.

The hardware businesses were rapidly becoming commoditylike. Because this was where the company had its illustrious beginnings, attitudes toward its future were deeply emotional. Even more frustrating was the second issue— the company's innovations in services were generating many new business opportunities, but financing the startup costs for these businesses while maintaining growth in profits was an increasing problem. The Services profitability problem was further exacerbated by the fact that its two most mature businesses, time-sharing and remote batch processing, were eroding and being replaced by personal desktop computers.

Although in 1980 Services had healthy revenues, a promising future, and hefty challenges of its own, it had to struggle for resources with two hardware businesses that in total were more than one and a half times as big. It proved to be an arduous, painful, decade-long task.

The challenges of working out the final disposition of peripherals and the evolution of computer hardware, as well as the challenges to the continued growth of the services business, were not apparent from the company's financial results. Control Data reported excellent growth in all parts of its computer businesses. As the company finished 1980, it had experienced five years of remarkable growth, from $2.1 billion in 1976 to $3.8 billion. Earnings per share grew from $2.55 to $8.45. The growth in revenues from the sale of disk drives and other peripheral products was particularly robust.

Peripherals—A Changing Environment

The strength of the peripherals business until the '80s was based on the profits yielded by high-performance, high-capacity, high-gross-margin disk drives. Two important things changed by 1983. One was the market shift toward smaller computers and the need for much more physically compact storage media, including disk drives. The second was the new market presence of a host of startup disk drive companies in the United States and the aggressive entry of Japanese manufacturers into this business. Control Data responded in terms of manufacturing efficiencies and new product designs. But by now it had lost its leadership in the OEM market and was playing catch-up. The key success factors for peripherals had become different from the computer systems business or the services businesses. The Office of the Chairman had considered sale or a spin-off of the peripherals business as early as 1982. By 1983 the strategy to exit was the chosen path, and the only questions remaining were how and when.

The business still had an excellent reputation and a very large base of existing customers—more than eight thousand companies and end-users in its OEM, end-user, and magnetic and optical media products. Any exit strategy required first fixing the operational and management weaknesses in the business that were hidden by the robust growth of the late '70s. By 1983, these deficiencies were glaringly apparent. Fixing weaknesses that were baked into the company over many years proved to be harder than expected but was finally achieved by management changes, closing down the end-user business, and selling the business products division. In 1989, we sold a healthy disk drive business to Seagate Technology, Inc.

Levels of Service—A Growth Strategy

With the growth of services, it was necessary to have some unifying strategic concept that integrated services with the computer mainframe businesses or, alternatively, to separate the hardware business through spin-off or sale. Here we faced an entirely different set of circumstances from those present in peripherals. By the 1980s the company already was viewing its computers as "application delivery systems"—not as general purpose computing "platforms." As such, they were viewed strategically as being closely allied to the services business: for any given application there could be a stand-alone delivery system and/or a delivery system utilizing communications technology.

By 1985, Control Data, in addition to using internally developed computers, was also using equipment from IBM, Data General, Cray Research, Digital Equipment, and Zenith as elements of its various application delivery systems. In addition, subsystems and devices from more than fifty other vendors were being incorporated. Although the terminology did not come into common use until some years later, Control Data had become a "systems integrator" in a variety of application markets. As reported to the Board of Directors in March 1985: "Except for peripherals, Control Data could be viewed . . . entirely [as] a services company. More accurately said, we will provide . . . customers *solutions to problems* rather than *tools for problem solving* and will both build and buy the delivery devices used in those solutions." A condensed version of the report is in Appendix 3.

The ideas behind this Board of Directors presentation had been gestating for some time and had first been presented for management consideration as the "Levels of Service" concept. I began using the Levels of Service concept in the mid 1970s after I became the executive responsible for all of the computer systems and services businesses. It was a way to explain to a diverse group of profit centers how they related to one another.[9]

The idea was this: no matter what we were delivering, it was a service to help the customer solve their particular problems. At the most basic level of service were basic "tools"—computers. Customers were free to use these tools as best they could. At the next "level of service" we combined the tools with other assistance such as application software, supplying not only the computer but also software and consulting to help them actually *use* the system for their specific need. The third level was to do the job for the customer, to solve their problem for them, in other words provide a complete problem-solving service. The Levels of Service idea was the progenitor of the Technology Food Chain concept (see Chapter 5) that I later developed to help MBA students understand the evolution of technology and strategy. All that seems straightforward with hindsight from the twenty-first century. However, to those wrestling with the difficult problems at the time it was much less obvious.

A seeming anomaly to this overall service strategy was ETA Systems, a supercomputer company established by Control Data in 1983. What was this supercomputer, a truly high-performance "platform," doing in the midst of all this solutions and services thinking? By the early 1980s it was clear that the long-cherished innovative environment for leading-edge computer design, if it was to be fashioned at all, required establishment of a smaller independent company, free of the entanglements of the large company that Control Data had become. It was Lloyd Thorndyke who had the courage and initiative to discuss this issue with me, and, along with the other two members of the Office of the Chairman, we readily supported Lloyd's idea. We proposed to Control Data's board that a separate affiliate of the company be established in which Control Data retained a minority equity interest of no more than 40 percent.

Within the company there were misgivings about this idea of a separate affiliate. In addition, CMOS, the basic semiconductor technology proposed by the spin-off group, was quite at odds with the strong belief other computer developers in the company had in bipolar semiconductor technology. But the technology argument was not the issue. It was structure and environment, freedom to innovate without the constraints necessarily concomitant with the legacy systems of the larger business.

The ETA concept succeeded technologically beyond any other advanced design in the computer industry. The central processor of the ETA computer, the

ETA-10, had a rated arithmetic operations speed of 10 gigaflops (ten billion floating point operations per second) and was designed, built, and demonstrated within three years.

Unfortunately, software development dragged on. Even today that is hardly a unique circumstance in software development, and it was not the problem that ultimately forced Control Data to close down ETA. The problem was money. More particularly, it was the inability to actually put in place the original concept of an enterprise in which Control Data had a minority ownership. By the mid 1980s, the market for such computers was firmly in the hands of Cray Research. Investment bankers flatly refused to undertake an IPO of ETA. The search for corporate strategic partners was equally frustrating. Control Data continued to be the sole source of financial support for ETA, which by 1989 still amounted to a net loss of $50–$70 million a year. Cash to fund the effort was only one factor. More important was the pretax effect on the company's earnings that was in excess of a dollar a share.

Organizationally, ETA had achieved the environment we envisioned. Technologically, it had demonstrated design innovation equal to any in the company's history. The financial strategy for ETA clearly took into account a changed world and a changed Control Data, for Control Data was to have only a minority interest in ETA. It was this that failed to materialize.

It is part of an innovative culture to take risks. That's the name of the game. Sometimes the risk doesn't pay off. In ETA's case, the financial reality finally came home to roost. This was the hardest decision of my business career. Being CEO—which I was at the time—doesn't automatically eliminate predispositions toward technologies or product lines to which one is historically connected: but that cannot intrude on one's good judgment and it had to be done. Money ruled, and ETA's door was closed in April 1989.

Another consideration earlier in the '80s was Commercial Credit. As noted earlier, many things had changed it and the parent company. It was clear that almost twenty years of strategic synergy between the computer and financial businesses was ending. In November 1986 the IPO of nearly 82 percent of Control Data's ownership of the company was completed, and Commercial Credit began a new life in the world of financial services with Sandy Weill as its chief executive officer.

By the end of 1989 Control Data had completed its long, transformational journey from pioneering innovation in computing hardware devices to a broader and equally rewarding innovation in services—that is, in providing computer-based solutions to meet important market needs. After the ETA closedown trauma in the second quarter of 1989, the company returned to operating profitability in the second half of the year.

As the new decade of the '90s began, Control Data was the company with computer and information services as the core of its being, built by more than three decades of innovation from tens of thousands of dedicated employees.

OBSERVATIONS

The decade of the final transition from hardware to services was also a decade of management transition. At its beginning I became president of Control Data, at its midpoint I succeeded Bill Norris as chairman, and at its end I retired. When Bill retired at the end of 1985, we established the William C. Norris Institute, a nonprofit corporation through which his work in assisting small businesses could be continued. The Institute is now a part of the business college at the University of St. Thomas and is a unique living legacy to one of the most outstanding entrepreneurs of the computer industry.

In 1992, the name of the company was changed to Ceridian, and the rewards of more than three decades of innovation were again being realized for Control Data stockholders. But Control Data has left a far greater legacy than the institutional tribute to its founder or financial returns to its stockholders. It lives on in spin-offs of the company, in its executives who have moved on to other companies, and in the many people whose lives it touched. More importantly, Control Data has left a legacy of innovation—as guidelines and admonitions—for management of the future.

Chapter 2 On the Edge
of the Possible

I understand that in the laboratory developing this [Control Data super-computer] system there are only 34 people, including the janitor . . .
Contrasting this modest effort with our own vast development activities,
I fail to understand why we have lost our industry leadership position . . .
—T. J. Watson, chairman, IBM, in a 1963 memo

Tom Watson, the leader of the nation's largest computer company, was clearly frustrated. How could a small operation in the middle of nowhere outperform IBM? In his memo Watson referred to Control Data's Chippewa Falls, Wisconsin, laboratory where renowned super-computer designer Seymour Cray worked for ten years. As a matter of historical record, the design of the Control Data 6600 was well under way before the Chippewa Falls laboratory opened. The 6600 design group led by Seymour was previously located in a far less romantic location, an old factory called the Strutwear Building near the Company's headquarters at 501 Park Avenue in Minneapolis.

Extraordinarily innovative people in a company that thrived by knowing how to help people *be* innovative made far-reaching achievements in computer design possible. The successful development of the world's first supercomputer required an enormous amount of know-how and insight. Seymour was a key factor, but the achievement also required a management willing to take serious financial risk. While popular mythology had the 6600 built by Seymour and a team of elves in the Wisconsin forest for a few dollars a year, the truth is far different. In fiscal year 1962 Control Data's revenues were $41 million, yet the company was betting several million dollars on a facility to create a supportive environment for an individual, not to mention the tens of millions of dollars necessary to support the development of that individual's ideas.

No doubt Watson's frustration was greatly exacerbated by the fact that this was the second time in less than five years that this upstart Midwestern company had beaten IBM to the punch. Control Data's Model 1604 had left IBM's scientific computers in the dust. To counter, IBM exercised its considerable marketing muscle with special "customer support" pricing policies and other marketing tactics that only the year before had nearly put Control Data out of business—new orders for the 1604 were scarce for almost all of the 1962 fiscal year. Yet not only had the company survived, it both improved the performance of the 1604 (making it four times as powerful as anything offered by IBM or any other company) and lowered its price. Nor did the Watson memo quoted at the beginning of this chapter end the story. Instead, it marked the beginning of a decade-long struggle that culminated in a bitter antitrust lawsuit eventually settled in 1973. By then Tom Watson had retired.

From its inception, the company thrived on challenge and on taking risks and daring to be different. It did this with enormous self-confidence, perseverance, and an intuitive understanding that innovation is key to turning risk into reward and transforming "different" into conventional wisdom. The challenges the people of the company accepted fundamentally were based on a belief in the transformational power of technological innovation. Even more, the company's leadership understood that technology—know-how—resides in individuals and not in books, drawings, databases, laboratories, or interoffice memos but in individual human beings who could be given an environment that encouraged them to take reasonable chances using their *know-how.*

It is easy enough to ascribe the company's culture of creative prowess to its founder, Bill Norris. That would be unfair to the many managers and executives, individual designers, and administrative and sales people who gave shape to the business. These individuals were committed to the overall success and purpose of the company and maintained a tremendous sense of community. And there was trust.

Control Data was not a collection of clones. Technological talent ranged from awesome to mediocre. There also was no unanimity of opinion with regard to business or product strategies. For example, there was violent disagreement as to the best semiconductor technologies. For another, there was disagreement as to the relative importance of business units: those in the computer systems group looked upon themselves as the "real" Control Data. They, after all, constituted the founding core. Those in the OEM peripherals business saw themselves as the salvation of the company, because they were the cash cow that fed other businesses; and those in information services were, in their view, the wave of the future. These views were egocentric and, consequently, incomplete.

Control Data employed a mix of talent, viewpoints, energy, and personal values, from an unusually high percentage of truly dedicated individuals to a handful of free riders. Most important however, the small minority of negative influences never controlled the company's business strategy, its policies and practices, its morale, and especially not its capacity for innovation.

THE SEARCH FOR MORE POWER:
PUSHING THE LIMITS OF COMPUTERS

Innovation in the early days of Control Data centered on the design of high-performance computers. The driving force that fueled these innovations was the plethora of complex problems to be solved in science and engineering. This went back to Control Data's ancestry in Engineering Research Associates (ERA). But complex problems were not limited to military applications.

In 1859, Col. Edwin Drake struck oil in Titusville, Pennsylvania. It was not an amazing surprise. He had observed oil seeping through the soil long before he drilled his first well. Rarely is it that easy to find oil. Sinking dry wells is a time- and money-consuming operation. An early method of oil exploration involved the mapping of underground areas that showed promise of oil, but detailed maps required enormous amounts of data and complex calculations. In one method of land-based oil exploration, for example, large hydraulic pistons would pound the ground, setting off shock waves of sound that were captured by geophones. The vibrations were converted to voltage, tracked, and recorded. No matter how much data geologists collected on magnetic tape, they were limited as to the number of calculations that could be performed—and thus limited in their understanding of the true nature of underground structure.

The stakes were high. Every hole drilled cost a lot of money whether or not oil was struck. Even when a successful strike was made, geologists needed a means of mapping the field for the greatest yield possible. It is therefore easy to understand why oil companies were among the first users of supercomputers. They needed computers powerful enough to reduce their risks and increase productivity. The first of such supercomputers came from Control Data, designed by Seymour Cray.

SEYMOUR CRAY: PUTTING THE "SUPER" IN SUPERCOMPUTER

Seymour Cray's story is legendary, both inside and outside the computer world. He is recognized as one of computing history's foremost designers of high-performance computers. It was the Cray-designed Control Data computer Model 6600, announced in August 1963, that gave broad currency to the term *supercomputer*. The 6600 and its successors became the world standard for high-performance scientific and engineering calculation, and Seymour's stature grew accordingly.

The popular view of Seymour was as "the hermit of Chippewa Falls," a reclusive and eccentric genius who conjured up supercomputer designs by the light of the Wisconsin moon. But he was neither reclusive nor eccentric—well, no more eccentric than most of us—and while his conceptual skills in computer design were truly outstanding he was arguably not a genius. There is much more to genius than an extraordinary IQ.

Control Data established the Chippewa Falls laboratory not as a so-called skunk works, but rather as a creative solution to Seymour's need to employ his considerable computer design talents without what he considered the burdens of bureaucracy. The extent of Seymour's paranoia in this regard can be somewhat appreciated by his memo to Frank Mullaney regarding a newly initiated "management training program," which, he stated, would "lower morale" and "compromise performance" (see Appendix 4). In his loathing for bureaucracy, perhaps, Seymour met the quintessential prototype of an innovator.

Born September 28, 1925, in Chippewa Falls, Seymour exhibited an early fascination with electronics. He graduated with a degree in electrical engineering from the University of Minnesota. With that as a foundation, he went on to get his master's degree in mathematics. His math education proved invaluable throughout his career, giving him a genuine feeling and understanding of the mathematics involved in the complex computations customers needed to create computer-based solutions.

Following advice from one of his university professors, Seymour began work at Engineering Research Associates in St. Paul, and was thus involved in some of the earliest digital circuit and electronic digital computer designs. He found his life's work at ERA. Within eighteen months he was the project engineer leading the design of the ERA Model 1103, one of the earliest commercially successful computers designed specifically for scientific and engineering work.

Seymour demonstrated early on a highly developed sense of computing architecture that would prove most useful in solving the complex mathematics used at the leading edge of science and technology. Speed was critical in the highly iterative algorithms employed to solve such problems. For any given state of semiconductor technology Seymour understood that simplicity of the computer's "vocabulary"—in other words, its instruction set—is essential in achieving maximum speed. The more common approach of computer designers at the time was to enhance the richness of instruction set, thereby increasing circuit complexity and reducing speed. Twenty years later Seymour's idea became known as the Reduced Instruction Set Computer (RISC). Designs employing more elaborate instructions became known as Complex Instruction Set Computers (CISC).[1]

Seymour also understood that the number of binary digits (bits) used would make an important difference in the round-off errors incurred in highly iterative algorithms. The standard word length used in computers at the time was 36 bits or less. To meet the needs of scientific computation, he built a 48-bit word length into Control Data's first computer, the model 1604, and then used an even larger 60-bit word for the 6600. An even more subtle problem was the representation of negative numbers. Without going into the arcane details of the matter, Seymour's use of one's complement representation of negative numbers resulted in simple logic that generated less heat and was faster as well.

There were other architectural nuances. The numerical models used in solving fluid flow equations are particularly important in fields such as weather and high-energy physics. It was the nature of the "relaxation" method of solving these equations that resulted in including a particular instruction, the "repeat multiply add." This one instruction alone helped give Seymour's early designs a competitive advantage, and it was a basic feature of all his supercomputers. Throughout his career his particular "genius" was architecture—not just architecture in the sense of functional design, but also in the geometry necessary to realize the desired performance using a given state of semiconductor technology. Such functional designs included seemingly mundane but actually critical factors such as heat dissipation.

He continually experimented with basic semiconductor technologies to augment performance. Unfortunately, he had little interest in the nitty-gritty of the manufacturing process, and he was even less adept at managing the people he needed to assist him. In both regards, however, he had the good sense—and good fortune—to select a colleague who could do those things. In the early days that person was Jim Thornton. Later, at Control Data and, subsequently, at Cray Research it was Les Davis. Both of these individuals were highly competent design engineers in their own right. Jim was co-designer of the 6600 and the designer of the imaginative STAR computer that broke into new territory with its vector processing. Les Davis worked with Seymour through the 6600, 7600, and 8600 projects, and later conceptualized the CRAY X-MP at Cray Research. Both Jim and Les were quiet, unassuming men with excellent people skills. In effect, they were the glue that kept Seymour's team together.

A little known fact is that every supercomputer Seymour designed was a failure first and had to be reworked from scratch. This was true of the 6600, which was originally built using a semiconductor technology that in the end simply didn't work; it was true of the 7600, which began as the 6800 and failed to reach performance goals; and it was true of his last Control Data effort, the 8600, which found rebirth as the Cray 1 of his independent company, Cray Research. The development cost of each of these computers was a staggering sum for a small company like Control Data. For example, the $50 million development price tag for the 6600 in 1962 would be $320 million in 2005 dollars.

While he struggled to perfect his computer designs, Seymour struggled personally as well. Early on, even in ERA days, Seymour demonstrated an independent, contrarian personality that made it difficult for him to operate in a large corporate environment. Consequently, CEO Bill Norris and the board set up the Chippewa Falls laboratory, built on land Seymour owned. This provided Seymour a more comfortable work environment—with wonderful results.

Fifteen years after joining Control Data and ten years after opening the Chippewa Falls laboratory, Seymour left to establish his own company. Some critics have called this the typical failure of a large company to free creative people from the "stifling nature" of bureaucracy. That is far from the case. Seymour did leave because of failure—two failures, in fact—but they were much more of his own making. One failure was his latest supercomputer design, which would be called the Model 8600.

In his resignation memo Seymour wrote: "The real problem is the 8000 development work . . . there is considerable uncertainty as to the probability of success in this effort. The design work is largely complete and the hardware [semiconductor] choices have been made and are being implemented. It remains to be seen if these choices result in a really workable hardware system. . . . My guess is that there is a 50% chance of success." He went on to sketch his plans for the "Cray Research Laboratory" and his desire for a working relationship with Control Data. The potential failure of the "hardware choices" made in this design clearly weighed heavily on this proud computer designer.[2]

Perhaps more telling, however, was a different issue referred to in a memo Seymour sent three weeks earlier to Bill Norris. The subject line was "Emotional Problems." In the initial paragraph of this remarkable memorandum, he pointed to the failure of the company's development efforts concerning a new product line that would replace the existing 3000 series of computers that were the company's mainstream commercial products at the time. He wrote: "In light of the apparent failure of [N]PL to provide the major corporate technical base for future growth . . . [I foresee] a return to reliance on my work . . . for the next considerable period of time. I am not prepared to assume this responsibility."[3]

Seymour's great talent flourished at Control Data for fifteen years, producing the most advanced computer systems of the day: the Models 1604, 6600, and 7600. With far less monetary resources than its giant competitors, most notably IBM, Control Data had provided Seymour the opportunity to display his remarkable talent while freeing him from *commercial risk,* a situation he never again enjoyed.

Seymour likewise had a profound impact on Control Data. Although much has been made of his famous supercomputer designs, it was his first Control Data computer, the Model 1604, that gave the fledgling company immediate credibility in scientific and engineering circles. It was the 1604 that allowed a brash startup to outshine its established competitors. Or, as Bob Kisch, one of Control Data's earliest executives, said: "If one individual determined the kind of company Control Data would become with a reputation for outstanding technical leadership, it was Seymour Cray." And it was the 1604 that jump-started the company down that path.

Like innovators in every field, Seymour had his failures. When myths around great innovators grow, we tend to overlook the hard work and setbacks they endured. That is the reality of innovation and should be accepted as such. His failures do not detract from his successes. A leading physicist called Seymour "the Thomas Edison of supercomputing." Seymour's name is synonymous with supercomputers.

What allowed Seymour's talents to flourish and create world-renowned computing products? Something in the Control Data environment brought out the full capabilities of this cantankerous, sometimes immodest and angry individual. It clearly was something more profound than indulging him with a Wisconsin laboratory.

THE CUSTOMER FACTOR:
PUSHING THE DESIGN FRONTIER

The management consultant, professor, and writer Peter Drucker wrote that "new technologies are invariably first used simply to speed up existing processes. Only later do their truly *revolutionary possibilities become evident*" (emphasis mine). Seymour Cray's creativity rapidly expanded available computing capability. However, without the customers' creative use of those capabilities, computing breakthroughs are difficult to make. Innovative use in turn engenders new innovative technology. Creativity demands a context.

One expects to find creative technologists in high-energy physics laboratories or sophisticated geophysics laboratories in oil companies, but not in the computer department of The Church of Jesus Christ of Latter-day Saints, or the Mormon Church as it is more familiarly known. Because creativity emerges from the nuances and invention in life, it arises in unlikely places. If one had to choose a single word to describe the economic and technology philosophy of this church it would be "conservative." Yet here Control Data found in Elder Thomas S. Monson and Elder Richard G. Scott, executive director of the Church's Family History Department, kindred spirits in the innovative use of computers and information technology.

In 1844 Joseph Smith, the founder of The Church of Jesus Christ of Latter-day Saints, said at the funeral of a friend, "The greatest responsibility in this world that God has laid upon us is to seek after our dead." This grew into a central belief of the church that families can live and endure eternally if they are unified as a family in one of the church's temples. Since the church did not exist prior to the 1830s, ancestors who died earlier had no opportunity to receive the necessary temple rites or ordinances. If their names could be ascertained and family members linked together and submitted to the temple for ordinances to "seal" them together, family members would then be reunited for eternity. Thus the need and desire for genealogical research was and remains a major emphasis of the church. This need resulted in the Family History Library and FamilySearch computer systems. Church members doing research on their family lines were recording the genealogical data of many countries on microfilm for preservation and access.

By the 1980s, church filmers had gathered over a million rolls of microfilm containing the names of more than a billion deceased individuals. The original microfilm is stored in a granite vault in Utah's Wasatch Mountains. Interest in this genealogical information extended well beyond church members, and the church was anxious to share the data as widely as possible to help the millions of people around the world who were interested in discovering their roots.

Because indexes most often did not exist, searching microfilm for individual names required using the card catalog and then reading through multiple rolls of microfilm in search of an ancestor. This process was awkward and time consuming to the point of near impossibility. Indices of name information were raw and uncorrelated, which resulted in some individuals being represented multiple times in various contexts. In order to help those doing research and submitting names for temple ordinances, the church began using computer technology in the late 1960s to automate information wherever possible.

By the late 1970s, the church implemented a program to create or extract indexes of individual names from rolls of microfilm using volunteer labor from church members in their local church buildings. A decade later, only about 10 percent of the existing data had been automated, and more raw data were being added each year than could be automated by the program. Added to this indexing challenge was the church's daunting goal to create a lineage-linked record of mankind, which could be used by all people interested in pursuing their family history. This undertaking would require the use of technology that did not yet exist.

In the early 1980s the church seriously began wrestling with this problem and found in Control Data both understanding and technology under development that promised a way to create this record. Work was soon under way with a team of developers at the church and Control Data, doing what many experts in the computer field were saying was impossible. The end product was an advanced operating system, database storage, and search technology based on the largest of Control Data's mainframe computers, the Cyber 180-990E. The total cost of the project, from conception to first practical use, amounted to several million dollars.

It is interesting to note that the combined teams from Control Data and the church delivered the project on time and within budget, and they did even more than was promised. The system has since become a global network available on the Internet as FamilySearch.org. It will ultimately provide a lineage-linked file with synchronized genealogical data input and search capabilities for use by all who are interested in locating family members.

Reflecting on the more than twenty-year history of the Family History Department's computerization project, President Monson spoke of their association with Control Data with pride and even a touch of incredulity: "In case you don't know us well, I have to tell you we are not risk takers. Never before had the Church embarked on the kind of innovation and taken on the risk that was involved in the Control Data computer project." And, he added in his understated way, "We probably never will again, but there was, in [Control Data], something that gave us the courage to launch into those uncharted waters." Because they did take the risk, however, the world has gained an invaluable resource for genealogical study and discovery. Supercomputers made Control Data and Seymour Cray famous, but as The Church of Jesus Christ of Latter-day Saints vividly demonstrates, it was the unique needs of creative customers that drove us.

BOB LILLESTRAND: MEETING THE CHALLENGES OF OUTER SPACE

Bob Lillestrand was in the right line of work at the right time. The Russians launched Sputnik in 1957, and the space race began. Bob's knowledge and enthusiasm for celestial navigation fit right into U.S. interest in space travel. In 1960, Control Data hired him to work in its research division, where he analyzed computer requirements for space systems involving cislunar and interplanetary space exploration. Bob had technical abilities to be sure, but he had much more than that. He knew how to sit with government personnel in places like the Department of Defense (DoD) and the newly formed National Aeronautics and Space Administration (NASA). He listened to the challenges they were facing and presented plausible solutions to them. The result was a lot of highly confidential, sole-source contracts for Control Data and an excellent reputation throughout DoD and NASA.

Bob led an advanced technology group that developed the $469R^2$ computer, which was sufficiently small, reliable, and durable to survive years of work in outer space without maintenance. A satellite or space explorer vehicle would be equipped with duplicate systems that could "talk" to each other as well as to ground control. The systems had to be hardened enough so that they would operate wherever they were in space. The $469R^2$ was developed at a time when most computers had to be in tightly controlled environments and even then were prone to frequent downtime.

Bob didn't stop with outer space. On his own time, he demonstrated the earthbound value of a computer-based navigation system, using it to guide an expedition to the North Pole. He contributed to historical records by examining old sea logs to track the routes of explorers including Admiral Robert Peary, Sir Francis Drake, and Christopher Columbus.

Like many creative souls, Bob worked in near anonymity to the world outside of Control Data. And like many early Control Data people, Bob checked out ERA after his university graduation, but he decided to start his career at General Mills, where he worked in flour milling research. After a few years, he moved to the mechanical division, where he worked on guidance and navigation systems General Mills was building for the Jet Propulsion Laboratory. At home, he worked on another project—building an aberrascope, a telescope-like instrument that could see stars even in daylight.

In 1967, Bob helped a friend plan a snowmobile expedition to the North Pole. When Bob found out he would be left behind at the base camp while only four members of the expedition continued to the pole, he decided not to go. The Canadian government noticed his interest, though, and invited Bob to join expeditions in both 1967 and 1969. Bob's responsibility was astronavigation. Control Data supplied navigation equipment and computer-generated charts.

This experience led to creating a more precise map of Greenland by charting earlier exploration. In later years, Arctic explorer Will Steger sought Bob's help with navigation problems. These projects at long last gave Bob much-deserved recognition and put Control Data in the news, too.

A lot of innovation arises from simply being interested in wanting to know, and having the conviction to find out. Those interests manifest themselves in different ways and to different effects. Bob Lillestrand loved exploration and adventure. He found myriad ways to integrate his personal passions into his life both at work and at home.

BOB PERKINS: PLANNING AND BUILDING
THE PERIPHERALS BUSINESS

While the computers usually got the headlines in the technical world with words like faster, bigger, and better, it was the punch card readers, tape drives, and disk drives that got the data into and out of computers. Although today disk drives are considered commodities, it is sometimes hard to imagine how different they were in 1957, when IBM brought the magnetic disk drive to the computer market. That first drive, the Ramac, was the size of two refrigerators. It took a whole year's production to make hundreds of Ramacs that when *combined* held one gigabyte of storage. In 2005, the same amount of storage fits in a thumb-sized portable disk drive. An entry-level, low-cost Dell PC comes with a 20-gigabyte drive.

Back in the 1950s, the computer peripherals world was a very different place, and a man named Bob Perkins was a very different person from both Seymour Cray and Bob Lillestrand. "Perk" had an understanding and working knowledge of business realities as well as hands-on experience with design and production. Perk's name rang no bells of recognition and admiration in the larger world of the computer industry, but within the smaller world of Control Data Perk received technical homage in great measure from the engineers, designers, and executives around him.

Like Seymour and Bob, Perk was the right person in the right place at the right time. By the way, that's a part of the creative process too. In those early computing days, there were few sources for the card punches, card readers, printers, and tape and disk drives that computers needed for data input and output. The best "peripheral equipment" was available from IBM, but it was available only at retail prices. Control Data charged no markup on the devices it bought from IBM.

Control Data's executives were divided. Should the company make its own peripheral equipment? Seymour and others felt the company should stay focused on computers. But some felt that since the customer's cost for peripherals could easily be as much or more than that of the computer mainframe, there was a profit opportunity in peripherals. In an interview more than twenty years later, Perk said the decision boiled down to two fundamental issues: (1) Control Data couldn't buy at a quantity-based price structure from IBM, and (2) the company couldn't get reliability from emerging suppliers.

Perk understood the issues and the risks. At a 1959 executive management meeting, he laid out the plan for Control Data's proprietary peripheral equipment products and the need to sell those products to other computer manufacturers (OEMs). Perk understood early on that the OEM business was the only way a fledgling company could afford the development and production costs of the high-performance peripheral equipment necessary to serve its high-performance computing engines.

Perk had the technical ability to lead the equipment design, the people management skills to recruit and motivate a formidable team of experts, and the strategic business ability to understand the necessity of an OEM strategy. He had an intuitive sense of how to deal with a design culture that was deeply committed to high performance. As Perk phrased it: "Everything we do comes from a "hot-and-heavy" approach to computing design." It wasn't until years later that Perk was given the title chief engineer, but his early recruits to the company always revered him as a person with creative ideas. In fact, the design people in the peripheral products organization soon coined a descriptive term for Perk's latest product design ideas. Lloyd Thorndyke, one of his engineers and a valuable contributor both in peripheral products and later in supercomputing, explained to me in an interview years later that the then all-male engineering group referred to Perk's design ideas as PLE 1, PLE 2, and so on. "A PLE," Lloyd said, stood for "Perkins' Latest Erection."

Perk was instrumental in finding the top talent Control Data needed to implement a high-performance peripheral equipment strategy. One of his first and most significant recruits was Paul Bulver from the old gang at Univac (ERA). Paul led the design of the Control Data Model 606 magnetic tape handler. This high-performance unit served as the principal data storage device for the Model 1604 computer system, and was the first product in an OEM business that ultimately became a multi-billion-dollar business in its own right.

Perk was a straightforward, fully focused businessperson who liked to build a product and get it out the door and into customers' hands. He worked hard at business strategy, product development, and manufacturing. "There's something about research that's very comfortable if you don't have to finish it," he said. "Making products, that's a real task."

It was this pragmatic approach to business, coupled with his successful innovations, that made him a natural to head the company's Employee Entrepreneurial Advisory Office, a confidential consulting service for employees who wanted to leave to start their own business. This almost unheard of approach to fostering employee creativity will be covered more fully in chapters 4 and 5. Suffice it here to say that, of the fledgling enterprises that resulted, 80 percent of them made it past the five-year survival benchmark commonly used to judge success for start-up businesses.

JIM THORNTON: QUIET INNOVATION

Jim Thornton always received people—employees, customers, suppliers, and friends—with a smile. He was always friendly but in no way boastful or given to hyperbole. Unless pushed he had little to say about his plans and dreams, or the innovations in computer design he envisioned. He just went about the task of making reality of those dreams and innovations. He did so with determination and dedication.

There was one notable exception in Jim's experience, however: early on he got a taste of production problems when he took on the task of project engineer for Serial 1 of the ERA Model 1103 computer, which was delivered to Convair (General Dynamics) in 1954. Jim performed this task with competence, grace, and diplomacy. The grace part was not made easier by the fractious nature of the individual who was Convair's computation center manager. As a member of Convair's programming staff, I witnessed Jim in action and got some early valuable lessons in customer relations.

At Control Data Jim again worked on the 1604 and then was "co-designer" for the 6600. Just how important Jim was to the success of the 6600 is made clear in the foreword to Jim's book *Design of a Computer, The Control Data 6600,* in which Seymour wrote, "The reader can rest assured that the material presented is . . . from the best authority[,] as Mr. Thornton was personally responsible for most of the detailed design of the . . . 6600 system."

In that book Jim also pointed out the importance of the customer and the customer's need in shaping technological innovation in a section titled "Justification for Large Computers." He quotes W. J. Worlton of Los Alamos Scientific Laboratory. "If all problems of interest to science were arranged on a scale of increasing complexity and those problems marked off that have been or can be solved with present [computers], it would be obvious that the unsolved problems are largely in the domain of higher complexity." That quote is from 1968, little more than two decades after the dawn of the electronic computer age with the completion of the ENIAC computer.[4]

Much has changed in the decades since Jack Worlton's statement, but his conclusion is still valid. The advancement in scientific tools leads to the ability to pose and explore problems of ever-increasing complexity, which in turn leads to still more advancement in the tools. The creative designers of high-performance computing are one side of the Control Data equation. On the other side are the creative people who used those tools and not only formulated solutions to known problems, but also posed questions not yet even contemplated, which stimulated the innovative juices of people such as Jim Thornton.

Equally important was Jim's role as a leveling influence in the highly charged atmosphere of supercomputer design. Jim left Seymour's Chippewa group and returned to Control Data's Arden Hills operation in Minneapolis to head the Advanced Design Laboratory, a position essentially created for him by Frank Mullaney. No one was sure why Jim left Chippewa. There was certainly no clash with Seymour, who depended on Jim completely. There were rumors—which were not true—that his family was unhappy there. Frank Mullaney pleaded with Jim to stay in Chippewa. The company needed not just his talent applied to the 6600 and the soon to emerge 7600, but also his leavening influence on Seymour. But Jim was adamant. His reason was soon clear, however. He had an idea for a computer design involving an unprecedented amount of parallelism. His STAR (short for STring ARray) broke new ground in computer design.

LLOYD THORNDYKE: SEEING THE LARGER
CONTEXT OF THE COMPUTER BUSINESS

Most people tend to find their niche in a segment of a company and settle there. Lloyd Thorndyke was a notable exception. He had a scope of technical ability that few people could match. He was equally adept at solving design problems in both mechanical and electrical engineering. His first work for the company was on the Model 606 magnetic tape transport; his last was as head of ETA Systems, the company's last supercomputer development endeavor. In between he worked on an impressive array of advanced data storage and computing designs.

While demonstrating this kind of versatility is difficult for many, Lloyd had always been aware of the larger context of his work. He knew supercomputers couldn't thrive without high-performance peripherals, and he knew that the need to keep up with supercomputers drove state-of-the-art design and development of peripherals, which in turn was an enormous advantage for the company's OEM business. Looking back at the early days of the peripherals business, Lloyd said: "The [computer] systems people paid for all the development of the initial disk drives. The markup on those drives was four times manufacturing cost. We could sell them OEM at a two times markup. Our customers made money, we made money. No other OEM manufacturer had such a development advantage and the other computer companies found it easier to buy from us. We practically had guaranteed success if we were willing to take the technical risk. And we were."

More than four decades later, he recalled the 606 tape transport development with great satisfaction. "The corporation needed it so bad so the 1604 [computer] would work at capacity. It took us just 18 months from start to getting it off the production floor—and with no facilities [at the start of that process]."

In 1964, Lloyd was given a $1 million budget and told to build a disk drive business. "That put us in the disk business before anybody realized that was the thing to be in," he said.

High-performance computing is a religion. According to Lloyd, "You either believe in it or not." It was his contention that any company using standard planning could not justify going into the business of manufacturing high-performance computers and the necessary peripheral equipment. That situation left the market open to a young company. By going into the OEM business, Control Data ensured the competitiveness of its own high-performance computers, helped improve the technical superiority of its tape transports, and decreased costs because of higher volume.

Sometimes he lost patience with manufacturing engineers who changed designs on the production line, or with computer systems engineers who didn't want to listen to peripherals design engineers. "In any other company, I would have been canned," Lloyd said. When the tension got high, instead of demanding that Lloyd calm his self-described "bad attitude," Bill Norris was wise enough to create an Advanced Engineering Laboratory and put Lloyd in charge. Like Seymour's Chippewa lab, it gave an extraordinary talent room to create and produce.

In Lloyd's twenty-nine years at Control Data, "There was always a job more exciting than the one before." There were continuous challenges. In the 1960s, for example, disk drive developers didn't know why heads (the mechanisms in drives that find and read data) "flew" safely a few micrometers above the spinning disk or why they crashed into it. Lloyd installed microphones in drives to listen to the heads. "We called it a HAM kit," he said, referring to ham radio operators. Later, when his team installed the kits on customers' drives, they decided HAM would stand for Head Altitude Monitor.

Lloyd Thorndyke was another example of a talent that thrived in the Control Data environment, and he continued producing after retiring from the company. In his 70s, Lloyd took over the management of a manufacturing plant in southern Mississippi and brought his skills, drive, and Control Data experiences to bear in turning the plant around.

Lloyd Thorndyke, at 74, approaches life very much as he did at 24—with enormous enthusiasm, a great interest in seeking solutions, and an outspoken belief in his firmly held opinions and considerable contrariness. He also retains a deep understanding and appreciation of the opportunity Control Data offered him. As he says, "It's a wonder Control Data didn't fire me a dozen times." Tolerance for new ideas, even those that offend orthodoxy, is one of the hallmarks of innovative organizations.

Pragmatic Bob Perkins thrived at Control Data, and so did reclusive Seymour Cray and the gregarious and brilliant Bob Lillestrand. Quiet, good-natured Jim Thornton and contrarian Lloyd Thorndyke likewise produced product innovations at the edge of the possible. In short,

Innovators come in many different personalities.

Innovation, then, must result from other factors that can produce creativity in people of every ilk. Before exploring exactly what those factors might be, it will be useful to showcase some other innovations to which the Control Data atmosphere gave birth.

Chapter 3 Meeting Vital Needs

In the previous chapter we viewed innovation from the perspective of individuals and their particular creations. To have a more complete perspective it will help to look at things the other way around, to see how individuals will creatively respond when they are made aware of important needs. These examples also will serve to illustrate innovation beyond that which results in products—hard artifacts. They are innovations that result in soft artifacts—services to meet important needs.

PLATO: CREATING OPPORTUNITY TO LEARN

Back in 1978, when most children had never seen a computer much less touched one, five-year-old Malik Edwards loved to sit at a computer terminal in the Northside Child Development Center, a Control Data day care center in a depressed area of Minneapolis. Malik was doing second-grade math already—and loving every minute of it.

Teenager Perry Brooks hated math. That was in 1975, and he couldn't add or divide. Fortunately Perry was a student at Walbrook High School in Baltimore, Maryland. Commercial Credit, a Control Data subsidiary, had placed PLATO (Programmed Logic for Automated Teaching Operations) terminals in the school, and Perry became interested in a consumer math course. He got so interested, in fact, that he finished the course in half the allotted time. That led to an income tax course and then a job as a tax counselor.

The technology that helped in the education of Malik and Perry began in the late 1950s at the University of Illinois, when a young Ph.D. engineering student, Donald Bitzer, heard loud arguments coming from a meeting room. A lot of people had gathered there to discuss how computers could be used to teach. Bitzer hadn't been invited, but his boss told him about the meetings.

"The engineers said educators didn't know anything about technology, and educators said engineers didn't know anything about teaching," Dr. Bitzer recalled in a 1982 interview. Bitzer's response was to tell his boss, "I think I know how to build a system that will teach."

That was the beginning of PLATO, a computer-based system that came to be used by educational institutions, industry, and government to help people learn. Three full-time people including Bitzer went to work developing PLATO. However, just finding the computer time to develop a program was a huge issue. Bitzer says he was lucky to get an hour a day, and even that wasn't guaranteed: "If the computer ran 40 hours without breaking down, it was a record." This slowed down development considerably.

A Control Data sales representative, Harold Brooke, always stopped by when he was in town to see how the teaching system was going. When he saw how progress was slowed by too little computer time, he told Bitzer Control Data could supply a 1604 computer. All the university had to do was pay the insurance. For $150 a year, the university's PLATO team had a dedicated computer that also was the top computer on the market. The PLATO team was really in business then. "I don't think the 1604 ever went down. The machine performed," Bitzer said. In a half-page agreement, the university agreed to share what they learned with Control Data.

The collaboration, which began with that agreement, was, on the surface, little more than one more "education grant" by a computer vendor. But this was not one more computer vendor. It was Control Data. This modest yet auspicious beginning led to a full-fledged collaboration and the frame-breaking innovation PLATO. It was an early indicator of Control Data's remarkable ability to foster innovation beyond its walls.

Don Bitzer was not an educator per se. He did have a lifelong interest in education, and he was a teacher. But Don's love was research and using his academic discipline of electrical engineering to devise new things. He was not an employee of Control Data, but rather of the Illinois higher education system. His research and the laboratory in which he worked at Illinois was not in pedagogy, it was in military electronics. The lab was 100 percent dedicated to army, navy and air force electronics work. Some of that research work was related to the Naval Tactical Data System (NTDS) system that ERA–Sperry Univac supplied to the navy.

When asked if he always wanted to be an electrical engineer, Don responded: "Only since I was six years old." His uncle, a civil engineer, had early on showed him the fascination of solving engineering problems. He was an outstanding high school student and could choose among various prestigious colleges, including Princeton and MIT. He chose Illinois for the simple reason, as he put it, the school offered more "value-added." That is, the education process started with a far less "finished product" in its students and yet turned out outstanding scientists and business leaders. He figured he would flourish.

So in 1960 this newly minted Ph.D. was ready and eager for an academic career in engineering. He was, however, about to be touched by the innovative magic that so quintessentially characterized people associated with Control Data—even those who were its customers.

The inner city riots of the '60s lay just ahead as the decade began. But the disparities in opportunity that gave rise to them were already clear to those concerned with the social ills of large urban centers such as Chicago, Detroit, and Los Angeles. The failings of the traditional educational system were an obvious and significant factor. At the same time, proliferation of advanced technology in military and business operations greatly concerned the more thoughtful business and military leaders. How best to achieve the task of educating the necessary technicians and correct the shortcomings resulting from an inadequate public education system? Whatever the answers to these questions, it was sure to be a major economic burden.

Don Bitzer was directly involved in the use of advanced technology by the military, but he was also aware of the education problems in cities such as Chicago. This awareness intuitively led him to begin thinking of using computers and other advanced technologies to devise a new approach to training and education. So the heated discussion he overheard that day fell on a ready mind.

There was some spare time on the computer being used in the lab for military applications. Don and two associates began to use that time to work on the automated teaching problems, and the problems were formidable. Even if tutorial and other learning algorithms could be programmed for the computer—and no one had even performed that programming feat on any practical basis—there was no easy way for the learner to "communicate" with the computer. Inputs were made via punched cards, paper tape, or magnetic tape. The computer operator's input console typically consisted of toggle switches and push buttons. The results of a program were numbers and messages printed out very slowly on paper. So they began to devise keyboards and devices using TV technologies to display information for the learner. And, because more than one learner at a time could be using the system, there had to be communication links from each "learner station" to the computer, plus the system had to be capable of sharing between multiple learners. Invention, then, proceeded in multiple directions: computing algorithms for learning, display devices, and remote communications. This exciting challenge quickly caught the attention of Don's military contacts and Harold Brooke.

Harold's preparation as a salesman for the highest performance computer in the market in 1960 was somewhat outlandish to say the least. He was a railroad crane salesman for American Hoist & Derrick Co. However, if ever there was a born salesman it was Harold Brooke. At the root of his success lay an incredible curiosity and a wonderful manner of dealing with people. Harold Brooke was genuinely interested in the *success* of everyone with whom he had contact. And he was wonderfully creative in how to support them, whether it was the problems a secretary was having with her child or a Don Bitzer straining at the limits of technology to devise a new learning system. Harold Brooke decided that Control Data was going to help Don Bitzer, and he went straight to Bill Norris to tell him so. Taking advantage of Bill Norris's lifelong love for education, Harold found open-arms acceptance. The seed of a long-lasting collaboration had been sown.

The story here, however, is not only that of collaboration, but of turning the innovation, PLATO, into a business. There are many innovations that never find an audience. *The important part of creation goes beyond understanding needs, it is responding in a way that will create demand.*

In December 1973, the task of commercializing the PLATO system was assigned to John Dammeyer, who had as his principal technologist Bob Morris.

After ninety days of what Bob Morris has described as "the most intense time either he [Dammeyer] or I have ever spent," they had a plan that Bill Norris and I approved. The plan encompassed a new specially designed student workstation, new communication equipment, and networking concepts. It also envisioned a remarkably low cost of thirty-five-cents-per-student contact hour. To fund the plan we used a portion of the R&D money IBM paid Control Data as part of the lawsuit settlement in 1973. However, the plan also required collaboration with the University of Illinois and with NCR and other computer firms. The first step had to be the collaboration with the University of Illinois. Even before the plan had been completed Dammeyer and Morris contacted Don Bitzer. Bob Morris relates that experience: "Bitzer was extremely suspicious of us. He was polite and friendly, but didn't know whether to *trust* us. There is a tendency sometimes, when business and academic people get together, for the business people to look down their noses at the academics and vice versa. We spent about three days with him . . . on the first go-around. By the end of those three days, we had done two things. We had formed a very deep friendship, and we had [reached] the point where he realized that we were really competent people with a real interest in working *with* him and not *against* him. So, from that point on, that relationship improved. After awhile, it was like we were almost brothers . . .

"In the middle of all this was the U.S. government. The National Science Foundation had funded about $7 million, and they were suspicious of both the university and industry. So it took more than a year to work out all of the barriers to be able to put that agreement together."

However, Control Data and the university were determined to get started right away, as Morris related: "When it looked like it was going to be an extended period of time, Don Bitzer and I sat down and we agreed that we're gonna start now as though the agreement were intact; so we started transferring information, we started our cooperative development programs, and everything was going for that 2-plus [sic] years."

The second major piece was Control Data's own development. Not surprisingly, the initial thinking was that a viable commercial product would require developing that product from scratch using the knowledge gained from the university. However, as Bob Morris later noted: "The more we got into it, the more we found out that those people down there did a substantially better job than most research laboratories in a university. We saved a lot of money and a lot of time, in many cases, by using just what they had provided. Rather than setting up a very large software development organization to redo the software, what we did was set up a team that was made up of the software people down there as well. We used the University of Illinois as a test bed for new versions of software."

A major stumbling block for a viable commercial PLATO product was communication costs. In those pre-Internet days, communication by the PLATO workstations with the central processor had to be made via dedicated private leased lines. In 1974 the communication cost to support a workstation was exorbitant. But with the aid of Mel Doelz, a brilliant pioneer in advanced communications, we were soon able to demonstrate a 42 to 1 reduction in those costs.

PLATO was formally announced in April 1976. A massive collaborative development project based on over seven years of research and an intensive two-year development collaboration resulted in breakthrough innovation in learning systems.

The PLATO collaborative effort began, in effect, as a straightforward vendor–customer relationship. However, there evolved a truly collaborative joint project. Control Data added value to the output of this collaborative effort in the form of applications, courseware, marketing, and other complementary capabilities necessary to build a business. Don Bitzer and the university continued development of PLATO for their own educational purposes.

PLATO is but one example of how innovation resulting from technological collaboration can, with the impetus of entrepreneurship to back it up, bring gratifying results to the participants. The total effect of truly seminal innovation such as PLATO reaches out and touches many lives, inspiring people to produce their own innovation.

One of the many whose lives were changed irrevocably by this innovative system was Ray Ozzie. On March 11, 2005, the *Financial Times* reported a major move by Microsoft to enhance and underpin its efforts to upgrade its world-dominant Windows operating system. The article announced the acquisition of Ray Ozzie's latest company, Groove Networks, and his appointment to "one of its most senior technical positions." The article noted Ray Ozzie's storied background in software and the following key excerpt from his life:

Three decades ago, as Bill Gates started to lay the groundwork for Microsoft's dominance of the personal computer age, Ray Ozzie had something else on his mind. At the time a programmer at the University of Illinois, he was working on a mainframe computer system known as PLATO, a teaching system that linked to 10,000 screens. PLATO boasted rudimentary instant messaging, e-mail and "group notes" capabilities, where users could share ideas—all technologies well ahead of their time.

By his own admission, the potential suggested by PLATO later "haunted" the idealistic young programmer. While Mr. Gates was making his fortune from the standalone desktop computer, Mr. Ozzie became fixated by the potential effect on human interaction that could come from getting disconnected machines to communicate with each other.

That led eventually to Lotus Notes, the first "groupware" product designed to let workers communicate and share information. Eventually bought by IBM, Notes now has more than 100m users.

When I went to interview Don Bitzer for this book in 2003, I found Room 132 of the Daniels Hall electrical engineering and computer sciences building at North Carolina State University buzzing with activity. A small cluster of students were gesticulating and arguing at a white board. Two or three others were absorbed in their reading. Tiffany, a Ph.D. student, was engrossed in the material displayed on her flat-panel monitor. In a corner another student was questioning an older man. That was Don Bitzer, age 70, at work and now on the faculty of NC State. "It's great to see you—let's go where we can talk—Tiffany, can we use your office?" Our discussion ranged from reminiscing about the old days and PLATO development, to Don's Emmy Award for creation of the plasma display and to his current work in genetic research. His creativity, energy, and enthusiasm remind one just how much fun it can be to work with innovators. Even more rewarding is witnessing the fruits of their innovations and their lasting effects on our lives.

HOMEWORK

From its early days, Control Data looked like a hard-core engineering, product-oriented company. But it soon became obvious that the computer group's innovative culture had spread from engineering design to other departments, including employee relations, administration, marketing, and sales. Everything, every aspect of the corporation, became a lab for creative thinking because people developed an eye for creative solutions.

Before the word *telecommuting* was coined, Control Data's Human Resources department became concerned about employees who were so disabled they weren't physically able to come to work yet were still capable and even eager to work. Carol Anderson, a systems analyst at Control Data, was one such individual; an accident in 1970 left her practically immobile. For three years she was still able to get to work, but then complications from her disability kept her permanently at home. However, in 1978 Carol began working full time again—from her home. Through its new HOMEWORK program, Control Data put a computer terminal in Carol's home, where she became a courseware writer for PLATO. That experience went so well that she became a tutor to Control Data Institute students.

More than just a work opportunity, HOMEWORK opened up Carol's social world, too. Neighborhood children came over to play games and learn on the computer terminal that was connected to the nationwide CYBERNET network. Carol was able to maintain an active correspondence with other people on the network, forming lasting friendships that made her disability somewhat less restrictive. HOMEWORK is but one example of the innovations we introduced to open up new labor pools. These innovations were derived from the company's core value of concern for the whole person. All of them were made possible by computer and communication technologies.

EAR

In 1972 the State of Minnesota, like many other states, faced turmoil in its prison system. There was both prisoner unrest and employee malcontent. With vivid memories of prison riots at Attica and elsewhere, Governor Wendell Anderson established a task force to investigate and make recommendations for an ombudsman's position to serve both the prison system's employees and inmates. Governor Anderson asked Control Data for management expertise, and Norb Berg, senior vice president of administration, was appointed chair of the task force. The task force recommended an ombudsman to deal with prisoner and employee grievances. That recommendation was accepted, and implementation began. Dick Conner, a manager in the company's human resources function, was given a year's leave to participate under the company's social service leave policy.

Norb's participation sharpened his awareness of the many complex difficulties people often face in dealing with their social and work environments. Like so many at Control Data, Norb had caught Control Data's innovation bug and thrived in an environment that encouraged employees to go beyond the expected. The result was an idea for a confidential employee advisory service to serve employee needs that traditional human resource policies and practices could not meet.

There were a number of challenges in implementing such a service. The company was no longer a small start-up with employees concentrated in one location. It had grown to some forty-one thousand employees and was much more diverse in terms of occupation, place of residence, age, and family status. As with most large companies, there was a defined grievance process in place for work-related problems. The new idea would need to augment, not replace, the existing process. The envisioned intervention center needed a database of available counseling services in order to handle problems appropriately and efficiently. It needed counselors familiar with the company's organization structure, management, and employee relations resources. Another essential element was to have a true crisis management capability.

To provide that essential element, in 1974 the Employee Advisory Resource (EAR) was born. EAR was to be a twenty-four-hour, seven-day-a-week counseling and referral service with a toll-free telephone number available to all employees in the United States, and an equivalent arrangement for employees in other parts of the world. It was the first such full-time service offered by any company in the United States.[1] Its importance was vividly depicted in its first few weeks of existence. Cases ranged from child abuse to depression and threatened suicide, and all were successfully dealt with. When EAR had been in operation just a few years, it was estimated that it saved Control Data over $10 million per year in reduced absenteeism and turnover, and decreased costs for health and other benefits.

Beyond those outcomes was the important matter of improved employee relations. The following excerpt from the February 2, 1975, *Minneapolis Tribune* relates one of the hundreds of stories that lay behind that success:

> At 20, Michelle's life was coming unraveled, her perspective scrambled by a drug dependency that was swiftly eroding relationships with family, friends and co-workers at Control Data Corp. Last July she swallowed a potentially lethal overdose of barbiturates and alcohol, a suicide attempt that was aborted when she changed her mind and frantically called a friend for help. The friend phoned for an ambulance. Then she dialed a special number Michelle had given her at Control Data's Bloomington headquarters.
>
> Four days later, when Michelle was wheeled out of intensive care, Bob Jones, one of the nine full-time and part-time counselors involved in the program, was at her bedside. She was astounded. "They'd gotten me into treatment before," Michelle was saying last week, "and all I'd done was lie to them. I wasn't really buying it—just going along to get everybody off my back, and save my job. But he showed up anyway," she said. "I just couldn't believe that a company this large would really care about one individual."

The counselor got her into treatment again, arranged to place her in a halfway house for drug addicts, and convinced her that "I could reach out for help any time I needed it—that they'd always be there to listen."

She's back at work now—with no mention of her problems on her personnel record—and is assigned to a job with greater responsibility than she had before.

And she's convinced that "if it hadn't been for them, I would have succeeded [with suicide] the next time."

"Traditionally, business has had a hands-off policy," said Gene Baker, vice president of the Control Data program. "The idea has been—and still is in many companies—that if an employee keeps his personal life out of the company, the company will keep out of his personal life."

"But people don't leave their personal problems out in the parking lot," he argued, "any more than they leave their work problems on the job. And we think we've found a better way to deal with that."

"There are something like 2,000 public and private help agencies in the metropolitan area," said EAR General Manager Jim Morris, "if you include the churches, hospital and financial institutions as well as the welfare and counseling services. Our job is to make a gross evaluation—and often what starts out sounding like a marital or job-related problem might turn out to have deeper roots in, say, alcoholism—and then to find the help that's needed."

The next step was even more unorthodox. True to the company's culture and its philosophy that worked in peripheral products and data services—"if it's good for us, it must be good for others also," and "why not turn a necessary cost into a revenue-producing business?"—were put to work here, too. Control Data decided to try selling EAR services to other companies. Gene Baker, Control Data's vice president of administration for European operations, had just returned home. Gene was given the challenge of turning EAR into a revenue-producing, profit-making business. Gene selected colleague Jim Morris to help him with this task.

They succeeded. The first order was modest from a relatively small company, the Bondhus Tool Company. That sale was probably more glorious to Gene and the others in EAR than the more widely recognizable organizations that followed, such as the National Basketball Association. Companies estimated that rehabilitating or saving just ten substance abusers would more than pay for the cost of the program. By 1985 the EAR service had been sold to eighty-seven other companies and had serviced 135,000 employees in those companies. Not only did EAR become an integral part of Control Data's Employer Services business, it generated a profit margin of 21 percent.

Today Employee Assistance Programs—or EAP, as they are now known—

have an international association with thousands of companies using either in-house or external programs that serve more than twenty million people. Dr. Tom Jetzer of the Minneapolis-based Occupational Medical Consultants once said, "Norb, you deserve a Nobel prize for EAR," to which Norb responded, "Well, thanks, but it was Gene Baker and Jim Morris who made it work."

STAYWELL

The concept of serving the whole employee and the employee's family didn't stop with EAR. Poor health and physical sluggishness have been recognized as major contributors to lack of employee productivity. They likewise contribute directly to increased medical costs for employees. By the 1970s some companies were offering exercise and fitness facilities to employees. Control Data, realizing that improving and maintaining health is more than just exercising regularly, conceived of a much more holistic wellness program for its employees, which encompassed diet, lifestyle, stress reduction, safe practices in the home and while traveling, and smoking cessation assistance in addition to exercise and physical fitness. The company had acquired Life Extension Institute and, building on it, developed the comprehensive approach it was seeking. It was called Staywell. Participation in Staywell was offered to all employees on a voluntary basis. Lee Kramer, a computer systems engineer, developed the idea for Staywell, and the person who shepherded this innovative employee benefit was David Anderson. Staywell was so successful that, like EAR, it became a profit center, and in 1989 Anderson and another Staywell executive, G. L. (Bud) Anderson, teamed with a successful entrepreneur, John Tarbuck, in a management buyout to form Staywell Health Management.

OBSERVATIONS

From the stories of innovation in chapters 2 and 3 we can make five important observations:

- Innovators come in many different personalities.
- Innovators have an ability to correlate needs with technologies and resources.
- Innovation is more trial and error than inspiration.
- Innovators persevere in the face of failure.
- Innovators are willing to take risks, and they can face uncertainty with confidence and equanimity.

Throughout Control Data, diverse innovators had somehow developed a deep, instinctive understanding that technology is much more than some clever device or the mathematical expressions of physical laws, and technological innovation is much more than a moment of inspiration. *Innovation lies in the motivation and working environment of the individual beings who call themselves engineers, technologists, marketers, managers, and administrators—individuals who are more than mere mechanical participants in the organized human behavior we call a business.* How did that come to be? And how can today's enterprises replicate the imperative to innovate? The next two chapters will answer those questions.

Chapter 4 Fostering the

Courage to Innovate

The Innovation Superhighway is not only a physical infrastructure, albeit technical and electronic. It is human—a function of insight, interaction and imagination resident in the minds, hearts and hands of people around the globe.
—Debra M. Amidon, *The Innovation Superhighway: Harnessing Intellectual Capital for Prosperity*

Bob Perkins was a marvelous innovator, as evidenced in his approach to problem after problem. When the new Control Data needed a Hollerith punched card reader for its first computers, Perk put that need together with a technology resource other computer engineers might not have considered. He later recalled: "I went down to Chicago, stuck my head into what was left of an old player piano company, and learned how to do a real cheap pneumatic reader." Ideas and innovations arise from people's special connections with the world around them.

New businesses are innovative almost by definition: They come into existence as a result of an innovative idea, a new product, a new service, or a new marketing concept. If innovation is indeed the wellspring of new businesses, why do innovation capabilities so often seem to fade and become lost? Is this somehow an inevitable consequence of success, growth, and maturation, the organizational equivalent of biological aging in human beings? Do most businesses, like most people, simply lose their childlike curiosity, inquisitiveness, and sense of experimentation as they grow and mature, becoming increasingly sedate and risk-averse? Are the endless prescriptions for innovation nothing more than a futile search for an illusive fountain of youth?

Organizations are as organic in their nature as the individuals who constitute them. Business organizations can be regenerative if they have the ability to support ongoing innovation. The seeds of regeneration are sown in the earliest stages of the organization's existence and have four key attributes: acute awareness, excellent skills, inspired motivation, and a supportive infrastructure.[1] If that characterization seems obvious, all the better. Still, it is that very obviousness which misleads people. Moreover, the four attributes are interdependent and form the requisite composite for personal and organizational growth and renewal. Three attributes—awareness, competence, and inspiration—relate to personal qualities that can be nurtured, shaped, and honed through experience. I discuss these next. The fourth, a supportive infrastructure, is a purely exogenous factor supplied by the corporation—it is enabling. It allows the capacities of people to develop and find expression. I consider infrastructure in the following chapter.

AWARENESS

Awareness is the necessary underpinning of innovative creation and it is something much more profound than simply knowing about the currently available methods and technologies. Awareness involves a *correlative* ability to understand how various tools and concepts can be best brought to bear on the problem at hand. We think of people with this correlative ability as being "intuitive." Awareness is Bob Perkins, his head inside a player piano, thinking about a punch card reader. It is an ability to connect the seemingly disparate events in our lives, or as Yogi Berra might have put it, "Unless you are looking for something, you usually won't find it."

Bob Lillestrand was an innovator who was acutely aware of how to use the laws and theories of physics and mathematics to solve problems such as celestial navigation. He is no less the innovator because he didn't generate theories of his own; his gift was the power of observation and a keen ability to build on existing knowledge by combining it in unique ways.

Without question the semiconductor ranks among those inventions with the most far-reaching consequences in human history. As an innovator, Seymour Cray was aware of the possibilities the semiconductor offered, and so he was able to perceive geometric configurations of them that would result in the highest performance computers. Both Bob and Seymour are powerful examples of awareness. Both were driven by a feeling for, and a deep-seated caring about, problems that needed to be solved and, in turn, were intensely attentive to technologies they might find useful. Innovators can find solutions only when they are looking for them. In people such as Bob and Seymour, there is an innate curiosity about problem solving that heightened their awareness of the possibilities for problem resolution.

It is a considerable leap, however, from a few innovative individuals to an organization that is similarly attuned. In nearly every organization one may find a Bob Lillestrand or Seymour Cray. That does not make the company highly innovative. It is a corporate culture of awareness that is the basic building block of creative energy.

This characteristic of awareness can also be thought of as "caring curiosity." It can, like other traits or skills, be learned, and, with practice, it can be honed to rewarding sharpness. Most of us will never design a supercomputer or figure out how to navigate space vehicles. But each of us can know the satisfaction of innovation, of devising a novel solution to the oft-felt dilemma, "There's gotta be a better way." Mostly we learn this skill through experience and practice. That's not surprising. What is surprising is how few organizations know how to challenge employees and give them the opportunity to learn and practice that skill. *Of all managerial inanities none is more regrettable than to deprive people of the opportunity to learn and exercise caring curiosity—the single most important skill to corporate health and renewal.*

Control Data was one exception. The seed of the company's "awareness" culture was planted long before the company was formed, on a farm in Nebraska. In the 1930s, farmers throughout the Midwest were hit with two extraordinary problems—the Depression and the Dust Bowl, an extended period of drought. On the Norris family farm, both money and cattle feed were in short supply. Young Bill Norris, then an engineering student at the University of Nebraska, remembered that in his teens he had observed the cows picking out green thistles from the fresh hay they had been fed. There was Russian thistle tumbleweed aplenty on the farm. It was generally considered a nuisance, but Bill harvested as much of it as he could find. The neighboring farmers thought he was crazy, but it worked; the thistle nourished the cattle and kept the Norris farm going. Awareness of a pressing problem was joined with a contrarian's view of an available resource to meet an urgent need.

THE FOUR Ps

When Bill Norris became Control Data's first chief executive, he brought that cultural seed of awareness with him. The cultivation of the seed, however, involved policies and practices that evolved into four prescriptions for building awareness—the four Ps:

- *Partnering*, especially technological collaboration.
- *Possibilities* for turning necessity into opportunity.
- *Perspective*—providing opportunity for people to broaden their problem-solving experience.
- *Practicing* innovation at all levels in the company through Total Quality Management.

No one of these would have sufficed alone; they work together to inculcate alertness to possibilities so integral to a culture of innovation.

Partnering

Ever since the earliest days of the company there was always a vital energy brought through collaboration, both technological collaboration and collaboration with the public sector in finding innovative ways to address serious societal challenges such as job creation, education, and health care. Being aware of how others, including competitors, were attempting to use any given technology to meet their product or service goals is inherently eye-opening. To empathize with another person, to see the world as that individual does, requires a much deeper understanding than what simply knowing about their circumstances can offer. It requires solving a different set of problems with, more than likely, a different set of resources. In short, it stimulates innovation by stimulating an awareness that there are new and different ways to look at and solve problems.

At Control Data, collaboration began early between the company and its customers, and, even more significantly, between the company and its competitors in the computer industry. As the company grew, collaboration became far-reaching as employees became involved in the problems of a more extended community. This went far beyond permission to volunteer for causes of one's choosing. Employees were encouraged to examine societal problems as one way to explore potential opportunities for innovative information services. The example of EAR has already been mentioned. It had its roots in participation on a governor's task force.

One way this form of collaboration was accomplished was through the company's social service leave policy, which allowed employees at any level to take up to a year off with full pay and benefits to work on community, national, or international programs and projects. Social service leaves ranged in duration from a few weeks to many months. One example in particular illustrates the power of this policy in bringing out the innovative and entrepreneurial talent that is latent in people.

HILDA PRIDGEON: BUILDING THE ALZHEIMER'S ASSOCIATION
WITH COMPANY SUPPORT

Hilda Benjamin was born in Charlevoix County, Michigan, on February 20, 1926, and met her husband-to-be, Al Pridgeon, soon afterward. "We probably met in a playpen," she said more than seventy-five years later. The Benjamin family of Michigan often visited with the Pridgeon family of Indiana.

After Al's service in World War II as a B-24 gunner and aerial engineer in Europe, where he flew fifty-two missions, Al and Hilda got married and Al went to work for a drapery hardware company as a branch manager. Hilda was a secretary. At various times they lived in Dallas, Denver, Minneapolis, Chicago, and then back to Minneapolis. They had three children. The fun-loving Al enjoyed life, family, and his work to the fullest.

But when the family moved to Minneapolis the second time, Hilda sensed something was wrong. She went to work at Control Data, feeling that she needed a secure job. Soon after, Al abruptly quit his job after twenty-five years. He was only in his late forties, but something was clearly wrong. Hilda went to the family doctor and said, "I feel like I'm losing my partner." After other possibilities were ruled out, Al was diagnosed with early-onset Alzheimer's disease.

Hilda was faced with a number of dilemmas—building security by having her own career, raising her children, providing care for Al, and learning to understand and cope with a disease she was told was "rare." When Al was denied disability benefits because he had voluntarily quit his job, Hilda called EAR. EAR did more than listen. They took Hilda to the company's own law firm, which assigned a lawyer, Paul Hannah, to her case.

Paul went beyond getting Al the disability and retirement he had earned. He successfully pursued other avenues like Social Security and mortgage disability insurance. With Al's financial issues being resolved, Hilda, with the encouragement of her manager, completed her college degree while working in share-holder relations.

Having an Alzheimer's patient at home required more than financial security. She met other women dealing with the same issues. Five of them chipped in and ran a $25 advertisement in the Minneapolis newspaper, inviting families of Alzheimer's patients to a support meeting. The group got materials from the National Institute of Aging, and Control Data provided a conference room. The response was a standing-room-only crowd. "I knew then we needed to have a national organization," Hilda said. With her business background, Hilda began working nights and weekends to organize a family support group.

Then opportunity knocked in the form of an interoffice memo about Control Data's social service leave policy. Hilda wrote a proposal requesting a year off with pay and benefits to form a national organization. On August 1, 1979, her year began.

Hilda turned a room in her home into an office, but she needed furniture and supplies. A Control Data truck arrived with a typewriter, desk, filing cabinet, and office supplies. She had permission to use the company's photocopy machines at any time, and she could use company designers for her newsletter. "Anything I asked for, I got," she said. The National Institute on Aging told people what she was doing, and letters began to come in from all over the country. She did public service announcements at the local CBS affiliate. By August 28, she had registered the first nonprofit (501c3) organization for Alzheimer's in the United States. Her cofounders made public appearances; Control Data printed the newsletter and helped build a computer-based mailing list, and gave Hilda access to a WATS line for the burgeoning number of calls.

The need for a family support group was made apparent by many of the calls. Hilda recalled one desperate man in Virginia whose wife couldn't stop screaming, and he said that he wanted to kill both her and himself. Hilda called the governor's office and spoke to a legislative assistant, who got the woman admitted into a hospital. Such calls happened often.

Technically, the group was still a Minnesota organization. The National Institute on Aging invited Hilda and others to Washington, where they agreed to form a national nonprofit group. While many wanted to focus solely on research for a cure, Hilda kept reminding them that family support was equally important. The national Alzheimer's Disease and Related Disorders Association, Inc., was registered in 1980, with Hilda Pridgeon on the board of directors.

The national group began quietly, but a letter to advice columnist Dear Abby, who many years later was herself diagnosed with the disease, brought a surge of twenty-five thousand inquiries. The computer-based mailing list developed by Control Data helped answer the inquiries.

In June 2002 the Alzheimer's Association published the report *Alzheimer's Disease: The Costs to U.S. Businesses in 2002,* which concluded that "the total cost to businesses of workers who are caregivers of people with Alzheimer's disease is \$36.512 billion. The cost to businesses of healthcare for people with Alzheimer's disease is \$24.634 billion." The report went on to note that these figures combined are "equivalent to the net profits of the top ten Fortune 500 companies."

After her one-year leave, Hilda went back to work at Control Data, but her work with the Alzheimer's Association continued. She was on the board for seventeen years, during which time she traveled to chapters all over the country and met with researchers, doctors, nurses, social workers, members of Congress, and even presidents and first ladies. In a company that thrived on innovation and a culture of social responsibility, Hilda's caring activism thrived. Needs awareness—whether it is a computer designer's deeply felt understanding of the need for the best possible computing engines, or Hilda Pridgeon's firsthand experience with the needs of those dealing with Alzheimer's in a loved one—is an attribute that can be created by enlightened management.

Possibilities for Turning Necessity into Opportunity

The second prescription, turning necessity into opportunity, can easily be perceived as trite and obvious. Its execution, however, is far from trivial. The status of the computer industry when Control Data was founded forced an early recognition of the need to treat necessity as opportunity. The company's first computer was the performance leader of the industry. But the performance of the total computer system required the highest performance peripheral equipment. The question was whether to build the necessary high-performance peripherals within the company, a commitment that would be hugely expensive when comparing the costs of development and manufacturing to the relatively low volumes required.

An answer to this dilemma lay in becoming a supplier of peripherals to other competitors in the industry. The Original Equipment Manufacturer (OEM) peripherals business thus came into being. Selling to one's competitors is not a business entered into lightly. It requires a finely tuned understanding of just where one derives competitive advantage. With the OEM peripherals business, the company successfully turned necessity into opportunity.

Soon a second opportunity was identified. Computers were necessary to support internal operations: engineering, production, and administration. Why not sell the surplus computer time of these internally used computation centers to help defray some of the cost? The Data Centers Division and Cybernet were born. If there were some skeptics as to the need for the OEM peripherals business, there was a total vacuum of support for Data Centers among designers, development people, and other internal users. Management persisted.

The OEM and Data Center examples were but beginnings, although each grew to be a business with more than a billion dollars in revenues—large enough to be Fortune 500 companies. Moreover, these experiences imparted a way of thinking about turning necessity and cost into revenue and profit.

As previously mentioned, in 1969 Control Data filed a private antitrust suit against IBM. The suit was ultimately settled on terms very favorable to Control Data. The key factor in the successful prosecution of Control Data's case was a computerized database document system built to deal with antitrust issues and the enormous quantities of data involved. The database itself was destroyed as part of the settlement agreement, but the software and associated processes gave rise to another business, Quorum Litigation Services, which was ultimately sold to an ex-Control Data employee, Nasser Kazeminy, who had previously demonstrated great entrepreneurial ability. Quorum grew and prospered over the next six years. It was sold to a Fortune 500 company that mismanaged the business so badly that Nasser reacquired it, fixed it, and sold it again. Quorum changed the way lawsuits were managed in the United States by making them cost-effective and by providing more responsive and highly focused litigation support services.

Another business start-up grew out of the need to provide health assistance to employees at a time when the cost of medical insurance was rapidly escalating. It all started with a comprehensive education program to help employees understand that a healthier lifestyle could lead to both a more enjoyable life and a reduction in medical expenses for themselves as well the company. At its core this program involved improved information, training, and education. That was Control Data's kind of business. Once again internal necessity was turned into external business opportunity. The result was Staywell, which was previously described.

Often new measures or policies must be introduced into corporations, and the immediate, reflexive response is a groan: what must be done is instantly viewed as a burden. The attitude we created at Control Data was to look at everything anew and to make the best of the circumstances. Not everything in life can be controlled or avoided. However, we can control our outlook. Through case after case we demonstrated the tangible benefits of taking an unfortunate position and turning it into an advantage. Awareness must be practiced to become ingrained as a working characteristic of an organization.

Perspective

Technological collaboration and turning necessity into business opportunity are in and of themselves broadening for the participants, but there are numerous other ways to foster broadened perspective. Companies support participation in technical conferences and industry groups. These things certainly are useful to some degree, although they can all too easily become just a way of life.

Even better than exposure to new ideas at association meetings, however, is active problem solving. A relatively common sort of problem solving in industry generally is the need to establish national or international standards. Often standards are established de facto by one supplier becoming dominant in the marketplace. The classic case of the de facto is the "QWERTY" keyboard. How this occurred is described by Jay Gould in a delightful article called "*The Panda's Thumb of Technology.*"[2] Many standards, however, are established only through the arduous efforts of volunteers from companies across an industry. It is difficult to imagine a more frustrating problem-solving process: a committee of disparate members convening to agree on a single solution regarding emotionally charged issues.

Nevertheless, the experience of dealing with standards issues is an excellent example of gaining perspective through a problem-solving process external to one's company. Certainly this was one of the outcomes of the collaborative venture STAndard Computer Komponents (STACK), which was established to help a group of smaller computer and telecommunications companies gain qualification and purchasing expertise and economies of scale with regard to basic electronic components used in their products. Control Data participated in many standards-setting efforts that afforded key employees a chance to work out important industry issues.

Control Data also encouraged its rising managers to participate in boards of directors in both the for-profit and nonprofit arenas. Seeing management, employee, and technical problems in an environment outside the company is wonderfully enlightening. Companies that insulate themselves from the outside world eventually are overtaken by that world.

Practice: Total Quality Management

A vast amount of information has been produced on the Total Quality Management (TQM) movement, which, under the prodding and leadership of W. Edwards Deming, found its way into management practice globally. The thrust toward total quality resulted in such nationally accepted programs as the Baldrige National Quality Program, as well as comprehensive practices such as the "Six Sigma" program that Bob Galvin introduced at Motorola.

TQM, however, is notably absent in the literature on innovation. This is unfortunate and reflects a mistakenly limited view of TQM, as well as the general mysticism that surrounds innovation. TQM tends to suffer from the incremental perspective that "continuous improvement" imposes. It suffers even more from the idea of minimizing variations from the norm, or from the product specification. The result is that TQM is associated with operational effectiveness only and has little to do with the creation of new things—new products, new services. Actually TQM can be a training ground for innovative thinking.

At Control Data TQM was approached within a cohesive innovative culture. In introducing the practice of TQM into Control Data, I stated this as the guiding principle: "Control Data wants each employee to believe two things:

"What I think and do matters to Control Data's success."
"Always think and act on the statement, 'There's gotta be a better way!'"

Awareness is cultivated in many small ways. In some employees it will blossom into new products or new businesses, but it is a fact of life that all of us are surrounded by problems that can benefit from attention . . . if only we'd give it. Thus TQM, quite apart from its other benefits, can be a vehicle for training the mind to think in new ways and to recognize possibilities amid everyday experiences and observations.

TQM also can be reduced to just being a boring pain, the project-of-the-month from the corporate office. These are the programs to which no one commits because they are perceived to be superficial attempts at change. But it does not have to be that way. TQM can promote optimism and confidence. At the same time, TQM can instruct on the risks of innovation and the judicious acceptance of those risks, as well as on how to approach progressively complex tasks and collaborations within and between organizations. The basis for an enduring quality program is to reinforce the belief, "There's gotta be a better way!" and "I can be a part of the solution."

When executives first started pushing TQM, William (Fitz) Fitzgerald was a skeptic. Fitz came to Control Data in 1967 to work in accounting, and by the early '80s, he was head of finance for international operations.

In 1985, Fitz was put in charge of Engineering Services, the organization that kept customers' computers running. Financially, the group appeared to be doing well, but by talking to managers and visiting customers Fitz started seeing major financial and customer service problems that had been hidden from view. Largely this anomaly was due to the high profit margins associated with the sale of spare parts.

Engineering Services (ES) had the responsibility for spare parts sales. Spares were manufactured by the product division and transferred at cost to ES. ES was thus the fortunate beneficiary of the high margins associated with such sales. The result was that ES appeared to be a much more successful profit center than its actual efficiency warranted.

Business was changing, though. ES had started a so-called third-party maintenance business that served customers of other companies' IT equipment. Margins were thinner and the logistics of the spare parts system more complicated. In short, effective customer service became more difficult to achieve and much more visible.

Fitz started studying TQM. After a seminar at Conway Quality, ES worked with the consultants at Conway to develop an approach to quality customer service. As so often happens, through TQM, ES discovered that its measurement and incentives were *internally focused rather than customer focused.* A simple example is the fact that customers were concerned with uptime, not with the "parts utilization rates" that ES measured. Many companies become needlessly trapped by exclusively focusing on their own needs to the exclusion of what really matters.

Once ES changed its frame of reference, innovation soon followed. The result was new and better diagnostics software and many innovative ideas for improving the parts logistics so that field engineers had the right parts at the right time.

Bottom line: the innovations spawned by TQM paid off with happier customers, happier employees, lower costs, greater efficiency, and high profits. Bill Fitzgerald went on to apply the lessons of TQM in the Government Systems Division (GSD), where he led the group to win a Minnesota Quality Award. He is a sterling example of the fact that innovation is not limited to the Seymour Crays of the world.

SKILLS

The most immediately visible characteristic of an organization is the extent to which it is populated with highly skilled, highly intelligent people. How does this come about? It is tempting to attribute the allure of talent to compensation and factors such as lucrative stock options. It likewise is tempting to attribute an intelligent employee pool to being involved in leading-edge technologies or to the high growth prospects of an industry. While partly true, that doesn't completely explain differences between individual companies. Moreover, sustaining company attractiveness for extraordinarily gifted people over fifteen or twenty years must clearly be rooted in something more than compensation or early fascination with a new technology.

The primary reason great people join and remain with companies is the fact that people like to be associated with winners. Being a winner means financial success, but in a larger sense it also means recognition by the outside world. Within two years of Control Data's start-up, its 1604 computer set the standard for high-performance computing, and a succession of leading-edge computers continued for many years. Within the more limited circle of space and defense agencies, the company had an equally attractive reputation for superior products. As the computing and information industry grew and matured, Control Data's reputation for being at the leading edge expanded into other areas as well.

Duke University basketball coach Mike Krzyzewski is humorously but graphically clear in the matter of recruiting highly skilled basketball players for Duke: "I don't walk down the street looking for guys 5'6" and wearing glasses." He goes on to detail his search for a fit that the person must have with his culture and the values of the Duke basketball team. Recruiting highly skilled players who fit the culture has led this man's teams to eight Final Four tournament appearances in eighteen years, eight regular season Atlantic Coast Conference championships, three national championships, and international recognition for himself, including seven U.S. National Coach of the Year awards. At a "roast" of this famous coach one of his former associates put it more pungently: "C'mon! You have a team with 10 high school All-American players—you'd have to be a complete dumbass not to be a winning coach!"

Skilled players count. And talent attracts talent. No matter how individualistic innovators may think of themselves, they like to be part of a winner—an organization that has lots of talented people. Technological and innovative success is an essential and powerful recruiter of skilled people, which in turn helps ensure repeat success: a "virtuous circle" of highly skilled people, achievement, and unusual innovation is established.

However, there are always difficulties that make recruiting a tenuous matter. Just think about Minnesota's weather reputation. That was a principal reason the company established a software group in 1960 in Palo Alto, California, which, with its aerospace and other defense industries, was already a prime center for computer software talent. Dick Zemlin, who had been at Remington Rand but who had since left to go to Standard Oil of California, was asked to head this new group. Dick Zemlin had a Ph.D. in mathematics and was a talented software designer. Dick was the core magnet, drawing top people in the San Francisco Bay area (the term *Silicon Valley* was still more than a decade in the offing), as well as the West Coast, to Control Data.

A central tenet of the recruiting process was that it was the principal responsibility of line executives and not simply relegated to staff. In fact, one of the company's most effective recruiters was one of its most talented innovators, Bob Lillestrand. Companies that view recruitment as an administrative chore are missing the boat. Putting its best people out front provides an excellent opportunity for a company to showcase organizational talent.

The important thing was that the company did not just "recruit to position," it recruited the best talent. In this it reflected an affinity with another well-known Minnesotan, Bud Grant, longtime successful head coach of the Minnesota Vikings of the National Football League and member of the NFL Hall of Fame. Grant's recruiting dictum was straightforward: "Just get the best talent regardless of position."

It did not stop there, however. No matter how skilled the people of Control Data were, they had the opportunity to *improve*. This was true from the beginning but became more formalized after our PLATO system made computer-based learning available at any location. This innovation made it possible for each employee to be guaranteed forty hours of training per year—the standard that exists at many companies today. Required management training included subjects such as diversity and equal opportunity, Total Quality Management, and statistical quality control, as well as Staywell's programs. The training courses offered through PLATO included a broad spectrum, from basic math and science to writing and communication skills. There was implicit in this emphasis on training and development a strong message of the company's belief in each individual's responsibility to develop and fulfill his or her potential.

INSPIRED MOTIVATION

There are extrinsic and intrinsic factors in motivating people, in inspiring them, to go beyond merely "getting by." The *extrinsic* factors include tangibles such as incentive compensation, benefits, physical working environment, appropriate tools, and organization structures. Although Control Data's working environment encompassed some unusual policies and practices that will be noted under "Infrastructure," its use of extrinsic rewards were similar to those employed in many other companies. There were, in fact, few explicit monetary incentives to innovate. There were, of course, stock options, but nothing particularly remarkable. Of much greater importance in a highly innovative organization are *intrinsic* factors—values and beliefs. Intrinsic factors are by their nature psychological. Just as a virus mutates as it moves through a population, so does the virus of human insecurity mutate and propagate through a management hierarchy.

Factors such as trust and commitment to mission are powerful forces in helping people achieve their full potential. And they can't be as quickly and easily introduced as, say, a new pay plan. The intangible qualities within a company are harder to create and that is why there is greater variability of these factors from company to company.

Fear of Failure

Of particular importance, Control Data shaped the outpouring of innovation by alleviating the fear of failure. This characteristic of Control Data is truly distinctive. Years ago, Bill Norris and I talked about the most important factor that generated Control Data's remarkable number of product and service innovations. Our answer: the absence of fear of failure resulting from the belief that the company would back people daring to innovate in unknown territory. The innovative company engenders trust in its people.

In the vast majority of business enterprises, especially in large ones, fear of failure is pervasive. And with good reason. The consequences of failure frequently are exile to a remote part of the company, a stalled career, or termination.

It is also necessary to look at fear of failure in the context of accountability and control. Accountability is the sine qua non of performance of the corporate organization. Individual accountability is quite beyond being merely desirable. Without accountability of individual performers an organization is doomed to failure. The matter, then, begins to verge on the oxymoronic: an organization must be characterized simultaneously by strict accountability and an absence of fear of failure.

The resolution of this paradox comes from understanding project success vs. individual performance. The normative mode in project failure is that it results in each team member being labeled "a failure." This is most especially true of the project leader. In a very real sense the members of the project team are doomed to wear "yellow arm bands" and, to borrow an ice hockey term, to suffer time in "the penalty box." That is no doubt a correct and acceptable outcome if the project is a well-defined operational task. However, if one is exploring the limits of technological or human possibility, this is not acceptable at all.

One of the most compelling stories of "failure" is that of Sir Ernest Shackleton's undertaking to cross the Antarctic continent on foot in 1914. All he had to offer the twenty-seven adventurers chosen from more than five thousand volunteers was a promise of great danger, low pay, and little chance of reaching the goal. Shackleton set out on the ship *Endurance* with his crew of sailors and scientists. In an epic of legendary proportions that has become familiar in management seminars, television specials, movies, and books, the ship was frozen into the Weddell Sea ice, then crushed several months later, leaving the twenty-eight men on ice floes more than a thousand miles from any civilization. They had no communications capabilities, three lifeboats—the largest of which was twenty-two feet long—and a sextant that could be used for celestial navigation.

Their greatest resource was Shackleton himself. While the project was a failure, the journey was not. After 497 days of surviving an environment of ice and frigid water, the team found its way to Elephant Island. Land at last, but it was still an outpost where they could never expect rescue. A few crew members took the twenty-two-foot lifeboat, the *James Caird,* eight hundred miles through the Drake Passage, the most treacherous ocean passage on earth, to South Georgia Island. From there, Shackleton and two others made an extraordinary twenty-nine-mile journey across mountainous terrain to the whaling station on South Georgia.

Every one of the twenty-eight men came out of the expedition alive. They had relied on sea leopards, seals, and penguins for food and fuel. They had learned to wait patiently and to act quickly, depending on circumstances. In a project that was a "failure," Shackleton had brought out the best in himself and twenty-seven other people. They returned home as heroes. Their strengths and the lessons learned continue to inspire.

In business, we lack the clarifying starkness of a fight against frozen death— the temptation in business is to wait to see the outcome before rendering an opinion, forgetting about all of the intervening processes and the fact that the most substantive issues are the least certain. Instead, the norm is: "You screwed up; you're a goat." Seymour Cray successfully led the 1604 development but from 1958 to 1960 his efforts in designing the 6600 had failed. Many precious dollars and much time for fledgling Control Data had been lost. The same story can be told about countless innovators. Few get it right on their first try.

In his book *At Work with Thomas Edison*, Blair McCormick observes that Edison's failed experiments could be one hundred times the number of his successful ones. "Is that a 99 percent failure rate or a 1 percent success rate?"[3] Edison undertook a mining venture that failed so badly it was referred to as "Edison's Folly." He lost his fortune. "Such a venture would have crushed lesser men but he . . . put it behind him and [went] forward to earn an even greater fortune in motion pictures," McCormick wrote.

OBSERVATIONS

Seymour's first attempt in the design of the 6600 failed. Certainly he had been attempting something technologically difficult. There was nevertheless the question of whether the company would provide a second chance. This was a very visible event to the people of the company. The even more important question was how the corporation would view the individuals involved. Were they looked upon as failures? Did this mean they were incapable of productive innovation? In hindsight it may seem easy to answer those questions. In the heat of daily battle it is much more difficult. And it is not as though Control Data lacked alternatives. Other young aggressive designers who had established respectable records were at hand. Safer courses of action were available. In fact, the key follow-on product to the 1604 was the model 3600, not the 6600. The 3600 was under development and was to be delivered in 1963. But corporate support for Seymour never wavered. Not only was the 6600 project and Seymour as an individual not abandoned, he was also given visible, substantial support in the establishment of the Chippewa Laboratory. It cannot be overemphasized that this was a powerful influence on every would-be innovator, indeed on the creative ambitions of every employee, in Control Data.

The culture, the very nature of the company, was rapidly established by the success of its first major product, the 1604, and then by perseverance in the face of the initial failure of its second major product, the 6600. The extraordinary innovations and productivity exhibited over the next quarter century by literally thousands of individuals stemmed from this early refusal to stigmatize those who happen to fail while "reaching for the stars."

The efficient and effective operation of the corporate entity requires discipline: goals, milestones, and accountability. Without such discipline, products are not properly designed and manufactured, sold and delivered; and services are sloppily produced and fail to satisfy the needs they are intended to meet. Definitive processes and precise measurement underpin organizational success and continuous improvement. In the early days of the twentieth century, as mass production became a prominent feature of U.S. industry, the need for such definitiveness became more obvious with each production line. In more recent times further developments in the rigorous analysis and improvement of business processes have come about through process control, so-called process re-engineering and other quantitative techniques.

However, with the advent of the Internet there developed the belief that the basics of business success no longer obtained. This was cleverly captured in the phrase "The New Economy." The truth is that as new technology comes into the economy there are both old rules and new rules, and business success results from *synthesizing* them.

Innovation says: "Here's a way to meet a societal need in a demonstrably more cost-effective way," and entrepreneurship says: "Here's a way to create demand for that innovation." There's a definitive difference in innovation, entrepreneurship, and reaching for the stars.

There's a question of management judgment involved here. Is it a fateful Star Trek mission or just taking on a difficult task? *How one answers that question is the essence of leadership in innovation.* Those who pioneered Control Data, beginning with founder Bill Norris and technical leaders such as Jim Thornton, demonstrated such leadership. Learning and practicing this skill was passed on to those of us who succeeded them. It is a cherished legacy.

Chapter 5 Building a
Framework for Innovation

The climate in which I operated, the physical facilities, the milieu made all the difference in productivity.
—Jack Rabinow, *Inventing for Fun and Profit*

The scope and depth of innovation in Control Data was very great indeed. To a large degree, that innovation was not in the form of invention—new creations or discoveries. Rather, most innovations with known technologies worked in novel ways. There were exceptions. Jacob (Jack) Rabinow was an inventor of the first rank. A quote from his book *Inventing for Fun and Profit* appears at the head of this chapter. When Control Data acquired his company, Rabinow Engineering, in 1964, Jack was fifty-four years old and had already achieved wide acclaim for his patents. He was of Ukrainian descent, emigrating with his family from Russia in the wake of the 1917 revolution. The family first went to China, and then to the United States in 1921. He received his bachelor's and master's degrees in electrical engineering from the City College of New York.

Among his many noteworthy inventions were the first magnetic disk computer memory; a mechanism for the automatic regulation of clocks used in automobiles; the automatic letter sorting machine used by the U.S. Post Office; the so-called straight line phonograph, whose cartridge moved along a straight track rather than at the end of a swing arm; and the creation that brought Jack and Control Data together, a unique methodology for optical character reading machines. He became a vice president of Control Data and was head of its Rabinow Advanced Development Laboratory. In addition, outside of his Control Data role, he established RABCO, a company to manufacture his straight line phonographs. RABCO was subsequently sold to the Harmon-Kardon Corporation. Over his lifetime he accumulated 230 patents, a remarkable achievement!

In his quote at the head of the chapter, Jack uses the words "climate," "physical facilities," and "milieu" to describe the reasons behind a high degree of productivity at Control Data. More broadly, there are two general influences on attitudes and behavior: the person and the situation. There is a tendency to think of ourselves as autonomous actors who make our way in the world based on a constellation of character traits. We sometimes fail to see the extent to which our actions are regulated by context. Yes, we are sentient actors but always situationally placed. To ignore what the company is implicitly telling us to think and do through its overall organization is to miss a great deal of how innovation is able to surface in social settings.

There is no truly satisfactory word or phrase to describe the explicit and implicit organizational policies and practices that make up the framework within which a group of people try to carry out the task of meeting an economic need. The word "organization" is insufficient. To most people it simply means a hierarchy of lines of authority depicted in some chart. "Culture" likewise is incomplete since it involves only the values and mores of the organization. "Infrastructure," while sounding a bit like something in the province of a mechanical design engineer, is a more promising as well as more encompassing term.

INFRASTRUCTURE

The thread of innovation should be cohesively entwined in all that constitutes the corporate infrastructure in a manner that is consistent with the corporate strategy. Infrastructure to Control Data specifically meant five things: values, human resource policies, compensation and benefits, employment practices, and governance.

Values

Values find expression in the company's products and services, its dealings with customers, communities, stockholders, suppliers, and the various governments within whose purview it conducts its business.

Today, as strategy and management action have been forced to be more reactive to fast change, the need for enduring beliefs and values to guide action have assumed greater urgency. Control Data had a very strong set of values: an abiding belief in the individual; belief that innovation is the wellspring of individual, corporate and societal growth; technological collaboration as an essential component in finding solutions to complex problems; and the belief that the more complex the need, the more rewarding it is to answer its challenge.

Human Resource Policies

Employee Advisory Resource (EAR) and Staywell were developed with employee interests at the core. Building trust requires a genuine concern for someone else's well-being and respect for others' thoughts and opinions.

Control Data also was a pioneer in U.S. industry in implementing a peer review process. The peer review program was conceived and implemented to give employees with a grievance an opportunity to be heard in a relatively structured but informal setting right up to the highest echelons of the company. This process did not just ensure fairness, it also served to minimize lawsuits through informal dispute resolution.

But innovation in employee relations was not limited to problem solving as in peer review, EAR, and Staywell. One of the company's more successful employee programs was its Employee Entrepreneurial Advisory Office (EEAO). Any employee could approach EEAO on a completely confidential basis with a business idea that they wished to undertake outside the company. They could receive free technical, marketing, financial, and general business counsel with regard to their idea and the development of a business plan. If the idea involved company technology, it had to be affirmed that there was no internal interest in its development. The office consisted of one person: Bob Perkins. A network of volunteer experts did the counseling. Perk's experience and technical expertise, not to mention his reputation and coaching abilities, made him an ideal person for this unusual employee benefit.

The standard reaction to the EEAO concept was and still is: "What? You're encouraging talented, innovative employees to leave the company?!" The fact is that the most talented employees who have a burning business idea will leave anyway. As long as the company's intellectual property can be protected, it is far better to have them leave openly and with a positive relationship. In a surprising number of instances, these entrepreneurs ended up with a mutually beneficial business relationship with the company. Moreover, experience showed that nine out of ten of the would-be entrepreneurs, when faced with the reality of a start-up company, and especially the financing of it, decided to stay with Control Data and went back to work more motivated than ever.

In the first three years of its existence, some six hundred employees sought advice, and sixty-one new businesses were started, which ranged from an antique shop to a magnetic disk refurbishing shop. Fifty percent of them survived at least five years, which is an unusually high success rate for start-ups. Also, 330 new jobs were created.

Compensation and Benefit Policies

Policies regarding benefits and pay were designed to reinforce the characteristics of fairness and pay for performance. Control Data's policies from the very beginning were based on the premise that individual employees were expected to be responsible for themselves. At the same time, it was clear that as a corporation we could realize various individual benefits that were not possible for any one of us alone. So there was a sense of partnership.

This was evident in the structure of the company's pension plan. It was a defined benefit plan into which each employee paid. To the extent that employee contributions did not meet the legal future obligation funding requirements, the company made up the difference. Most important, under a clause in tax regulations, these employee contributions were made on a pretax basis. When later the IRS ruled against such pretax employee contribution plans, Control Data and one other company were grandfathered.

The policies and practices that have been mentioned—EAR, EEAO, Staywell, peer review, a pretax contributory pension plan, and the social services leave policy—all were rooted in a basic belief in the individual. This was based on a deeply held conviction that each individual has untapped potential for innovation, and each individual has a responsibility for personal growth and skill development. The role of the organization is to provide an environment that facilitates both the opportunity to practice innovation and the opportunity for personal development and well-being.

Employment Practices

Processes are the thread from which the organization fabric is woven. However, it sometimes is not clear just what the goals of those processes are. We have no difficulty understanding that the goal of operational processes is effectivity. But what precisely is the goal of people processes? In Control Data this was clear and firm: it was to be fair.

In spite of the ups and downs of its early history as a growth company, there had never been an issue of job security at Control Data. It had always been a question of the rate of hires and natural attrition. As the hardware product lines, particularly disk drives, and other peripherals became more commodity-like and more subject to economic cycles, job security became an increasing concern. To address this concern during 1979–1980, we adopted a Rings of Defense policy. This policy sought to provide a buffer to the stability of full-time jobs by the use first of outsourced contracts (this was before outsourcing entered the common business vocabulary), and secondly of part-time employees.[1] Beyond that there was established an Employee Placement Center to help ensure maximum opportunity for displaced employees to find other jobs within the company. Each displaced employee was also given the opportunity to acquire new skills if that was necessary for internal placement. While there was no guarantee to anyone of ongoing employment, it was clear from these actions that we would strive to provide as much continuity as possible.

Fair Exchange was the name we gave to cover the comprehensive set of policies that dealt with personal growth, benefits, and employment practices. The principles of Fair Exchange were the following:

From the company:
A policy which provides an increasing level of job security to the greatest number of its employees.
Management practices that ensure fair and just treatment of all employees.
Management practices that place a high value on reward for performance.
Corporate benefits and support services which recognize that personal quality of work life impacts performance.
An environment for continued self-growth and achievement, which goes beyond the training and experience, required for the present position.
From the employee:
Innovation. Generate performance improvement ideas.
Identify barriers to innovation and performance improvement.
Obtain performance improvement skills that are job related or human relations related and which increase awareness of performance.
Commitment to long term employment.

The principles of Fair Exchange served the company well through the turbulent times of the '80s. These employment ideas were put to the test within a year of being introduced as business conditions in the peripherals business deteriorated. In mid-July 1982 I reported to the board of directors that although total employment in the company had been reduced by 2 percent, it would have been 5 percent had not the Rings of Defense concept been adopted a year earlier. So, we were not perfect, but we never wavered from our intent and our principles of fairness always extended to those who were let go. Perception of fairness is critical to innovation because it engenders trust. The effective management of anxiety is one of the most important things a leader can do. People who are scared out of their wits for their jobs and their families won't be terribly inventive—except in finding ways to hunker down.

Governance and Board Policy

The board of directors is the body that sets the context within which a company operates—accountability, ethical behavior, forward-looking human resource policies, a fair and reasonable compensation policy, and, very importantly, the company's attitude toward and practice of innovation. How does the board accomplish this broad set of responsibilities?

Ideas about corporate governance have changed considerably since the '60s and '70s and particularly so in these early years of the twenty-first century. There is an increasing emphasis on the oversight, the audit, and the check and balance roles of boards of directors. This trend was galvanized in the first years of the new century with the bankruptcies of several very large companies and the disclosure of questionable accounting practices, including failures in the independent external auditing function.

Changes in laws regarding corporate governance such as Sarbanes-Oxley may be to the good, but achieving ethical behavior in business or any other human endeavor via legislation has always been and will continue to be elusive. No one would argue with the fiduciary and legal compliance responsibility of a board of directors. That, however, is nowhere close to sufficient to ensure corporate health, much less stockholder wealth.

It is no more possible to produce stockholder, customer, and employee success through scrupulous auditing than it is for individuals to ensure economic well-being by routine monitoring of blood chemistry and other physical tests. Those things are necessary and valuable but they are by no means sufficient governance mechanisms.

GOVERNANCE MECHANISMS

In simplest terms there are four mechanisms by which a board accomplishes its task. They are:

Policy
People
Money
Oversight

Each of these four mechanisms will help the board foster a climate of innovation within the company.

POLICY

A document written in 1980 and titled *Corporate Policies for Creating a New Business Culture* begins, "The inordinate amounts of attention focused on corporate governance and accountability these days are a major distraction from the grave and growing problems besetting our nation. [The] SEC chairman and a host of other spokesmen for government, academia, labor and even business itself dwell on preventing the misuse of corporate power. SEC regulations, greater public disclosure, modified laws of incorporation . . . audit committees, nomination committees . . . are at center stage. Independent outside directors are deemed necessary to keep management on the straight and narrow, and directors are being asked to function primarily as corporation cops. No one can quarrel with the need for reasonable legislation to correct deficiencies in the system or the need for surveillance. Surveillance, however, is easy. What is lacking are industrial statesmen capable of providing the leadership needed."

W. C. Norris composed that document in November 1980. It was penned in the clamor for better corporate governance. That there was a need for improved governance became very clear as, later in the decade, the unethical and sometimes illegal actions of people such as Ivan Boesky and Michael Miliken surfaced. The point was and still is that better corporate governance is much more than stringent auditing.

The document goes on to suggest several important aspects of corporate governance aimed at the essential goal of corporate growth and increasing stockholder value. Nearly a quarter of a century later there is still little evidence that we have taken this message to heart. Quite the contrary, in the wake of new and more egregious corporate accounting practices by a few large companies, the clamor is for regulation, legislation, and rigorous auditing. Here we go again.

At the very foundation of corporate and stockholder well-being is a wellspring of innovation that results in products or services that meet society's economic needs. The board's responsibility in this regard is generally expressed in such governance catechisms as to "participate in setting strategic direction." Board members can indeed provide important critique of a company's strategy. But only the people running a business can devise realistic strategic alternatives and implement the ultimate selection. What's important is the range of alternatives possible, and two things ultimately determine that range: technological innovation and money.

With regard to innovation, board members can play a much more proactive role than is presently the case. They can propose policies and practices that will help to ensure an innovative culture. So-called independent board members can be particularly valuable by working interactively with management. While there are several ways in which this can be accomplished, one of the most effective is to have insiders as well as outsiders as peers on the company's board. In the frightened search for oversight and checks and balances, this opportunity is being lost. In addition, new prohibitions against inside directors are undermining executive development. Effective directorship is a skill. Like any skill it can be learned only with practice, lots of practice. It can be learned only by doing. So, at a time when the demand for effective directors is more critical than ever, the canons of good corporate governance deny a most readily available learning opportunity—the company's own board.

The whole issue is based on the conflict of interest that is involved with inside directors. To be blunt, the current canons of effective corporate governance tell us that the company's executives can't be trusted to value the interests of the stockholders over their own: the psychological pull to feather one's own nest is just too great. Yet these very same individuals become "independent," outside directors, for companies other than their own. As such, they serve as guardians of ethical and fiscal rectitude! How's that again?

Beyond these obvious weaknesses in the insistence on board independence, it is arguable that the entire argument is flawed. There is valid research that indicates, like so many panaceas for mankind's ills, board independence is oversold if not downright invalid. In "Second Thoughts on Board Independence" (*The Corporate Board,* September/October 2002), James D. Westphal states: "After two decades of academic research in multiple disciplines . . . on the consequences of board composition there is little evidence that board independence enhances board effectiveness.

"This lack of relationship is also generally true whether board effectiveness is measured by the perceptions of corporate leaders . . . by . . . firm performance, or by . . . a variety of decisions and behaviors that are presumed to harm shareholder interest."

So there is at least room for thoughtful consideration in this matter of corporate governance beyond the function of being corporation cops. Here are a few governance innovations we introduced at Control Data.

Policies for Stimulating Innovation.   Such policies must be fashioned with a view to something more than annual performance. For example, the annual performance bugaboo can be overcome by authorizing additional expenditures for innovation beyond those needed for mere enhancement of current products and services. An important part of this is to seriously consider adjustments in annual bonus goals should innovative opportunities arise which require current expenditure for a longer-range opportunity. Not everything can be foreseen a year in advance, and the system must flexibly accommodate changing circumstances. Other examples of these policies include:

• Innovation reviews. The board should conduct semiannual reviews of the need for innovation in the company and the opportunities for such innovation. This almost always entails greater risk and short-term costs. Only the board can exercise the balance of judgment needed to authorize such undertakings. Beyond increasing board understanding and having helpful discussion of innovative initiatives, these reviews send a clear message throughout the company.
• Innovation funds. We adopted a policy to fund innovations in new fields. It was not part of the annual operating budget and was reserved for projects with a long period of development and uncertainty as to outcome. This Innovation Fund was very modest in size, $2 million a year, which represented at that time less than two tenths of one percent of the company's total innovation expenditure. The CEO administered it and only the CEO and the board were responsible for how it was spent. The funds were also set aside not just for a single year, but for three to five years.
• Fostering individual innovation. At Control Data I initiated board level reviews of our Total Quality Management process. This was a means to lend importance to individual innovation. The Employee Entrepreneurial Advisory Office (EEAO) was another means of demonstrating our belief in individual innovation and entrepreneurship.
• Small business. Providing support for small businesses is a way for the creators of most new job opportunities and of big ideas to benefit from the talent and resources of a large company, and a way for the company to invigorate entrepreneurial activities.

Schumpterian economics is a curious blend of certainty and uncertainty. The certainty is the ultimate description of the status quo. The uncertainty is how and where. Only the board can authorize the risk of exploring the unknown. The board likewise has a prime responsibility for establishing policy. Corporate policies that promote corporate health and stockholder wealth involve much more than checking for inaccuracy or malfeasance. The net effect of board policies must be to stimulate employees to think about and embrace change, that is, to ***dare to change***.

PEOPLE

The second of the four levers available to the board is people. A prime board responsibility is the selection of the CEO and evaluation of the CEO's performance. The CEO will set the tone for top management and the company as a whole. To foster innovation, it is fundamental in the selection and review of top management that they have displayed innovative capacity. Many companies that espouse creativity as a corporate trait never select managers with the criteria of creativity in mind. How serious can a company be about innovation if it is not included among the factors used to select key employees?

MONEY

The boards of most companies review and approve goals, strategies, and plans, particularly their financial quantification. However, most such quantification is little more than top-line, bottom-line and key operating ratios such as gross margins or fixed and variable ratios of expenditures. In addition, major balance sheet items and financial ratios are reviewed, approved, and monitored, as are cash flow and working capital ratios such as those dealing with receivables and inventories.

Innovation expenditure is not only absent from the standard operating statement used by most companies, it is not even defined. If there is any definition at all, companies, including their boards of directors, view the innovation effort as equivalent to R&D expenditures. This is worse than just an incomplete view of innovation, it actually limits the role of innovation to new product development. For a service business, defining R&D as innovation expenditure borders on the ridiculous. It also confines the business of innovation to a select set of people within a defined function.

In its earliest days, like most companies, Control Data only monitored and reported R&D numbers. This was clearly an inadequate view of the total expenditure of the company for technology because there was considerable technical cost incurred within customer contracts such as military and other government agreements. Accounting rules dictated that such efforts be accounted for as "cost of sales" rather than as "below the line" (gross margin line) R&D costs. In order to get a more comprehensive view of the money being spent on technology and technological innovation, the R&D cost was combined with technical expenditures accounted for as cost of sales, as well as with certain technical expenditures incurred in providing hardware and software support. This was reported as "Total Technical Effort."

Finally, as the company moved more and more into services, the board and management reviewed "innovation costs and expenses." The charts in Figures 1–4 are samples of those used in the board's review of innovation.

The board looked at innovation expenditures in each major segment of the business, including Commercial Credit, the financial services arm of the company. The charts are self-explanatory except that the "Business Development" category requires clarification: *development of a new service business is a different process than that of developing a new product for an existing business.* So for these developing business categories, quantification of innovation expense requires some definition. Here the gross expenditures—that is, *all* costs and expenses—are classified as innovation expenditure. Businesses under two years in age are designated as being "new," while businesses with a

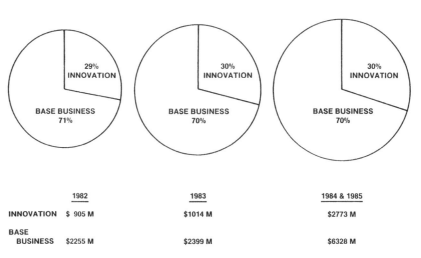

Figure 1. Information services and products—total costs and expenses

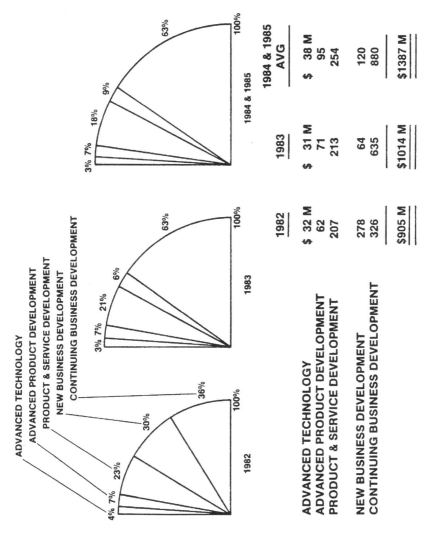

	1982	1983	1984 & 1985 AVG
ADVANCED TECHNOLOGY	$ 32 M	$ 31 M	$ 38 M
ADVANCED PRODUCT DEVELOPMENT	62	71	95
PRODUCT & SERVICE DEVELOPMENT	207	213	254
NEW BUSINESS DEVELOPMENT	278	64	120
CONTINUING BUSINESS DEVELOPMENT	326	635	880
	$905 M	$1014 M	$1387 M

Figure 2. Information services and products—gross innovation expenditures by category

93

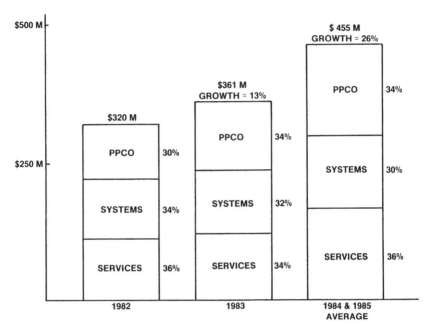

Figure 3. Information services and products—gross innovation expenditures by organization

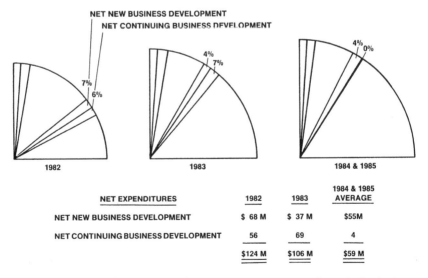

Figure 4. Information services and products—net innovation expenditures in developing businesses

longer gestation period are in the category of "continuing business development." Over time businesses must be recategorized, moving units from new business development to continuing business development. Clearly there is judgment and some degree of arbitrariness in such an analysis. However, the process not only gives the board insight as to the scope and magnitude of the innovation effort going on in the company, it establishes a board mind-set focused on innovation. Innovation becomes an integral part of the financial review process carried out by a board just as board members do when evaluating capital expenditures, marketing, and other major categories of investment and expense.

A very important aspect of the "money lever" available to the board is executive compensation, which comes under the purview of the Compensation Committee of the board. An element of executive compensation in Control Data was tied specifically to innovation. Each executive of the company, not just the product and service development executives, had to justify and explain how he/she qualified for that portion of his/her bonus. In a given year, it is quite possible for a company to be profitable but make little innovative progress. Attention to innovation ensures that the long term is attended to as well, and one of the best ways is to remind executives of that fact through the compensation plan.

OVERSIGHT

So Control Data's board was very proactive in the matter of policies for innovation, management performance, and the allocation of resources for innovation. The final function is that of board oversight. As we have seen, there were extensive board financial reviews of innovation expenditures.

Beyond numbers, however, a board needs to understand more specifically the nature of the innovative effort. While it is neither possible nor even desirable to have a detailed review of each project or new business, some key ones can be looked at in more detail in a committee of the board. In Control Data this committee was the Strategy Committee. There are other possibilities and variations, but as has been mentioned the board as a whole should have a formal innovation review as part of its standard operating procedures at least every six months.

Throughout the organization, our intent was to signal the importance of innovation and to create an environment in which it could be undertaken and duly recognized and, ultimately, in which it could thrive.

OBSERVATIONS

The stories of the many and varied innovators in Control Data give rise to four observations:

- Innovation is more trial and error than inspiration, so perseverance is essential.
- Innovators can face uncertainty with confidence and are willing to take risk.
- Innovators have the ability to correlate need with technology.
- Innovators come in many different personalities.

   In this chapter and the previous one we have seen the means by which courageous leaders and boards of directors can cultivate the characteristics essential to nurturing innovators. All this, however, is but prelude to the task of putting innovation to work, to the task of devising successful business strategy. We now turn to that task.

Part Two Technology, Innovation, and Strategy:

Strategy is a step-by-step journey of innovation in processes, products, and targeted markets.

Strategy must co-evolve with technological change and the changing nature of the world it addresses.

Technology is the strategic manager's best friend.

These three principles are at the core of strategic success. To utilize them effectively one must have mastered an understanding of the first principle that was the subject of Part 1. Unfortunately, understanding and applying all three of these principles are made more difficult because of the semantic hoarfrost that encrusts two of their key words—"technology" and "strategy"—as a result of their overuse and misuse. So the first task is to strip away that distortion and reveal the underlying and straightforward meaning of both words. Then it is possible to clearly see how to go about the commonsense tasks involved in applying the three principles.

Chapter 6 Journeys
in Strategic Space

A fine morning . . . we proceeded on a few miles to the three forks of the
Missouri . . . those three forks are nearly of a size, the north fork appears to
have the most water and must be considered as the one best calculated
for us to ascend.
—*Journals of Lewis and Clark,* July 25, 1805

The decision facing Lewis and Clark at the three forks of the Missouri
is an apt metaphor for the choices available to business strategists as
they seek the best path toward competitive success. It will be useful to
set the stage for consideration of such strategic choices by looking at
the nature of the landscape within which they are made and the nature
of the obstacles facing Control Data as it came upon the scene in the
first decade of the computer industry's existence.

First, Control Data faced a truly tough short-term obstacle: with
only $600,000 in capital the company had to have a successful first
product, and have it fast. The company accomplished that with the
Model 1604 computer. A contract for the 1604 was obtained in the
first six months of the company's existence, and when it was delivered

the company was less than three years old. Thus Control Data was born in an environment of doing "the impossible."

There were much tougher long-term obstacles to survival and growth. Looming over the whole competitive landscape was mighty IBM. That was for starters. Control Data's major competitors were divisions or subsidiaries of much larger companies: Bendix, General Electric, Honeywell, Sperry Rand, and Xerox. All these companies had proud histories and far greater resources.

Finally, the long-term issue was much more complex than just battling IBM and the other pretenders to industry leadership. Long-term survival meant successfully anticipating the rapid evolution of microelectronics and computer technology. In 1957 Control Data had to envision that a then mere laboratory curiosity, the integrated circuit and computers built using them, would in a short span of time become a commodity. At the same time just keeping up with the technology change of the moment was sufficient to try the innovative capacity of the best and brightest.

It is sadly ironic that in an industry arising from revolutionary technological change many of the companies that were pioneers generally failed to fully appreciate or understand the basic nature of technology evolution and its ultimate consequences to them and to the very structure of the industry. Of course, in the early stages of a new technology, it is common to have to do everything for oneself, in effect to be vertically integrated. But competitors in the early computer industry clung to this mode of meeting needs for such things as logic circuit components and peripheral equipment long after they were widely available and had little value as competitive differentiators. Control Data was the exception: in coping with this longer term issue Control Data demonstrated a precocious appreciation of strategy and the effect of technological evolution.

It was an exception not because of some secret storehouse of knowledge about technology and the evolution of strategy. In the beginning, there was no storehouse available to be had. It was an exception because we intuitively knew that among our strengths were creativity, an emphasis on value-added, and an inherent desire to use computing in the most complex applications possible. Control Data could never have been the low-cost competitor. Value-added would be the hallmark of its strategic differentiation. The same decisions face companies today. For example, despite mounting recommendations from industry pundits and analysts for Apple Computer to produce a low-cost computer to capture market share, it has steadfastly resisted—owing to its strategy to remain on the edge of new technologies and to be a premium value-added producer.

The preceding chapter explored the policies and practices in Control Data that allowed it to excel in the search for innovation and to achieve success in the difficult task of strategic technology management. In the next two chapters we will step back and look at strategy more abstractly—specifically to advance a conceptual framework for strategic thinking.

TECHNOLOGY AND STRATEGY

Creating and applying new knowledge—new technology—has long been the key to economic success. In today's world, however, business people feel a new urgency in this age-old task because of the increasing resources required for technological advances as well as the accelerating rate of global technology diffusion. This requires strategic thinking about technology beyond its application to new product development.

The task of managing technology is integral to, and essentially synonymous with, strategic management of the enterprise.

At this point it is probably necessary to remind the reader of the definition of technology: technology is not esoteric science and certainly not just information technology. Technology is *know-how.*

Effective technology management requires understanding the evolution, maturation, and diffusion of technologies throughout the global economy. Strategic understanding begins with appreciating the basic kinds of change that affect competitive strategies. Social, economic, and demographic change result from factors far beyond the control of any individual firm. Rather, the successful business must react to and try to use these changes to their advantage. Even in government policy making, where business has a clear responsibility to participate, the individual firm is unlikely to have a significant influence on decisions. Technology management, on the other hand, resides squarely with the company's leaders. Technology is potentially available from both society at large and from the minds and skills of the firm's employees. The managerial task is to capture this know-how more rapidly and effectively than competitors. *Thus technology is the change factor most responsive to creative management action.* Basic to this managerial task is creating an organizational culture where change is looked upon as an opportunity rather than a threat, and where the search for innovation is the focus of attention at all levels in the organization.

Such was the case at Control Data, so much so that few of us realized, much less articulated, that this mode of business management was a very different way of life. It was as natural and effortless as breathing. To be sure, there had to be intense energy applied to the usual tasks such as product development, product line strategy, managing R&D budgets, and such. These activities, even today, are ones that many companies believe encompass the entire scope of technology management. It is work enough to occupy management full-time, but it is not sufficient.

Due to the stringent financial and other resource limitations of a small but rapidly growing company, we were forced to think from day one: "Okay, to realize my goals, I need a whole set of technologies, products, subsystems, and capabilities, but there is no way we can do all of them ourselves. Somehow they've got to be sorted out." In effect, we had to ask ourselves two critical questions:

Which technologies are those that, although they are absolutely essential to our business, *in the long run* are likely to be the same ones everybody else requires and thus will offer us no competitive distinctiveness?

Which are those, on the other hand, that are so distinctive that they will provide competitive advantage and will win the game?

Therein lie the roots of the necessary and sufficient technology concept that will be discussed more fully later in this chapter.

As an unknown start-up, we also routinely had to face the question of "Control who?" No matter how superior the company's product might be, possession of great technology and ideas doesn't necessarily produce great sales.

Answering the question of "Control who?" did have its lighter moments. In 1963 the Australian Commonwealth Scientific Industrial Research Organization (CSIRO) and the Commonwealth Bureau of Census and Statistics were contemplating the purchase of Control Data computers costing some $8.5 million ($54.0 million in 2005 dollars). After considering the recommendation of their technical people, two members of the CSIRO Board were dispatched to see who this company really was. Walter Ives, board chairman of CSIRO, and fellow board member Sir Arthur Coles, founder and chairman of Coles stores in Australia, were assigned that task. Because I was director of international operations and the corporate executive responsible for the Australian subsidiary, I arranged meetings and tours for them and had the responsibility of meeting them at the Minneapolis/St. Paul airport. We had no company cars, my personal vehicle at the time was a 1957 Plymouth, Bill Norris's car was in worse shape than mine, and Control Data's Australian managing director advised that hiring a limo might be too ostentatious. So I rented a red "carry-all," as they were then known, later to become today's SUV. Back then it was basically an enclosed truck with seats. Many years later, Walter Ives, with whom I have developed a lifelong friendship, told me that although a bit taken aback, he and Sir Arthur decided that any company that would send "a kid in a red truck" to seal a multimillion-dollar sale must have incredibly great confidence in its product. We got the order.

STRATEGY

The task of devising strategy involves determining one's source of competitive advantage. The process of determination covers the spectrum from "gut feel" to exhaustive computer analysis of massive databases. Prescriptions for successful strategies range from time-honored nostrums such as "location, location, location" in retailing and real estate to erudite academic formulations addressing the competitiveness of national economies.

As Control Data embarked upon its strategic journey, business mostly followed the planning model derived from the military experience of the two world wars—especially World War II. The typical five-year strategic plan amounted to little more than a numerical extrapolation based on "more of the same." Perhaps one of the earliest derivatives of World War II experiences was the "learning curve" that simply put into a formula what had been observed in action, namely that for each doubling of production volume costs would reduce by some percentage, typically in the range of 20 percent to 30 percent. Strategy became a simplistic drive, you might even say a mindless exercise, for volume and market share. In the 1970s another strategic concept was introduced by the Boston Consulting Group. This approach to strategy is basically a portfolio analysis technique in which a company's products and services are categorized in a matrix of four quadrants. The two dimensions of the matrix are market share and rate of market growth. The resulting categories are:

- high growth and high share
- low growth and high share
- low growth and low share
- high growth and low share

The businesses belonging to these four quadrants were dubbed, respectively, "star," "cash cow," "dog," and "question mark," terminology still employed today.

Another framework for strategic analysis was the so-called SWOT analysis (Strengths, Weaknesses, Opportunities, Threats), which came into vogue in the late '70s. In essence, a SWOT analysis is a combination of the external environment (threats, opportunities) and the internal situation (strengths, weaknesses). It is helpful but not very rigorous and, furthermore, is somewhat subjective in analysis of the four factors.

Over the last twenty years of the twentieth century, academic approaches to strategic analysis began to move from these more limited ideas. One of the earliest and most widely adopted frameworks for more rigorous evaluation of the industry (external) environment affecting strategic success was Michael Porter's "Five Forces" Model.[1] The five forces are buyer power, supplier power, the threat of new entrants, the threat of substitutes, and the intensity of competition. Strategy, in this context, involved building barriers to one or more of these external forces that would allow a company to extract above-average profits or "rents" in the more general terminology of economists. This is easier in industries deemed "attractive" than in those deemed "unattractive," the latter being industries for which the external forces are all strong. A classic unattractive industry would be the airlines industry.

However, levels of profitability clearly vary more *within* industries than *across* attractive and unattractive ones. For example, note the success of Southwest Airlines in terms of profitability in the otherwise brutal airline industry. Why? The reason has to be internal to the competing companies themselves rather than just the nature of the external forces affecting them. This situation has given rise to viewing strategy in terms of internal capabilities, and the idea of some "core competence" has emerged as the source of competitive advantage. This is a step in the right direction even though in practice it can be difficult to ascertain the degree to which competencies are truly distinctive and thus provide a competitive advantage.

Alas, this strategic insight has proved inadequate in another way. As shown by Dorothy Leonard-Barton, capabilities once sufficient for competitive advantage when buffeted by change can actually become barriers to adaptation.[2] They become "core rigidities." The concept of *dynamic capabilities* was born to deal with this paradox of competencies and rigidities. By the early 1990s this concept of dynamic capabilities had progressed to the point that an overview to the approach was published by David Teece, Gary Pesaro, and Amy Shuen in their paper "Dynamic Capabilities and Strategic Management."[3] This explicitly introduced change as an important factor in the strategic thinking process and thus was another step forward. By that time, however, the early computer industry participants had mostly disappeared. Either they simply had gone out of existence, or they merged or were otherwise assimilated into some other enterprise.

In spite of these developments in academic thinking about business strategy, for the most part it is still analyzed and taught as a collection of discrete and dynamically inadequate methodologies for gaining competitive advantage: "product differentiation," "low-cost producer," "first mover," or "fast follower." While these are useful ways of looking at strategic alternatives, they do not provide a unified way of understanding the *dynamic* forces that alter the sources of competitive advantage. They are built on an academic foundation of economics, and unfortunately most economic models do not encompass technological change but rather focus on supply–demand equilibria. As a result, business education, thought, and practice have been shaped within an inadequate framework.

There have been exceptions to such thinking. The Austrian economist Joseph Schumpeter immigrated to the United States in 1932 and joined the faculty at Harvard. There he put forth the provocative argument that entrepreneurship and the process of "creative destruction" resulting from technological change are the driving forces of economic cycles. He published his most important work, *Capitalism, Socialism and Democracy,* in 1942.[4] It languished in the shadow of John Maynard Keynes.

There have been other economists who focused on technology and innovation. Edwin Mansfield was one of the earliest to undertake serious empirical studies of technological innovation.[5] In 1982 Richard Nelson and Sidney Winter published their landmark book, *An Evolutionary Theory of Economic Change.*[6] They focused directly on change. In their model, the functioning of an enterprise comprises a set of "routines." Thus know-how—technology—is embedded in every activity of the enterprise, and the search for and selection of new routines—that is, technologies—is continuous.

There were others, such as F. M. Scherer and Zvi Griliches, who studied the effects of technological change on business strategy and the resulting evolutionary nature of strategy.[7] However, until recent years such thinking was far from mainstream economic thinking, national economic policy formulation, and practicing business strategists. As far as the idea of strategic "management of technology" was concerned, the business and academic worlds were still struggling with the very definition of the term in the late '80s.

"Static Equilibria" was a concept inconceivable in Control Data. Its strategic thinking pulsated from the influence of the dynamic forces of the world around it, particularly the technological evolution of electronics and magnetics. We were immersed in Schumpterian change. I vividly remember the shock I felt, after retiring from Control Data in 1990 and starting to teach strategy to MBA students, in trying to convince myself, much less my students, that using Michael Porter's "five forces" framework would suffice for those whose task it was to devise effective strategy.

Control Data's understanding of technology and its evolution, and the implications for successful strategy, was intuitive. The company's strategy was quintessentially based on belief in our capability for innovation—a belief that had roots in the company's prehistory during the '30s, when Bill Norris solved the problem of feeding his cows by using Russian thistle weed, and was reinforced by the urgent wartime experience of innovation in enemy code breaking. At the time of its launch, the company was in harmony with the need for innovation to satisfy the scientific and engineering community's clamor for faster computation speeds and ever higher data storage bit densities. Later it was fueled by the anguished cry of the disadvantaged and economically deprived people of the inner city, as well as the more widespread need for better education and healthcare—and for jobs.

STRATEGIC SPACE

My forty-plus years as a business executive and as an educator of other executives have taught me that a more helpful view of strategy is as an ongoing journey through what I call "Strategic Space," as illustrated in Figure 5. This simple metaphor of space defines a firm's strategic position at any point in time as comprising three elements:

- Markets
- Products
- Processes

We can then view strategy as a change in position with respect to one or more of these elements. In essence, we move strategically in a space of three "dimensions." As in the real world, there is most definitely a time dimension as well. Each move will reposition the firm, and over time we thus shape a strategic journey.

Viewing strategy within such a space–time world helps us understand what each strategic move entails with regard to product, process, and market—and to anticipate the consequences accordingly. The incorporation of "process" in the model may not be immediately obvious, but new processes can be just as integral to effective strategy as a new product or movement to a new market. Note that "process" as used here is not narrowly defined as manufacturing or pro-

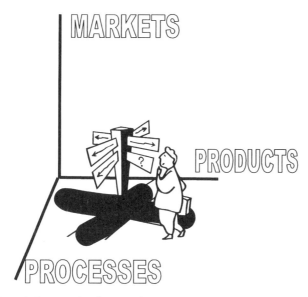

Figure 5. Strategic Space—classification of strategic options

duction processes. Competitive advantage can, in fact, come from any process, including administrative, marketing, information, and financial processes, (for example, the "routines" of Nelson and Winter).

Like the space of our familiar physical world, Strategic Space is in no way inert. There are powerful forces at work. Just as in the physical world we experience solar and radiation energy, winds ranging from gentle to tornadic, and sometimes violent movements of earth and water, so too is Strategic Space buffeted by changing social values, government policy and regulation, demographic and economic change, and *technology.* At any given point in this Strategic Space time, the relative intensity and nature of these forces will determine industry structure and the probability of a given strategy's success. It does little good to carefully analyze a situation presumed to be static that will in reality change tomorrow. Strategy, by its very nature, must deal with the future, not the present simply transported to a future time.

So management needs to look at the fundamental dynamics of change. Clearly it is important to understand, or even anticipate, economic change, demographic change, and changing societal values. Even participation in government regulation and policy formulation is somewhat limited by the very nature of that process. Once again, of the several evolutionary forces at work in the space–time world through which a business journeys, technology is management's only friend, or more precisely, technology is the only hope management has for any friend at all. Any successful friendship, of course, is built on understanding and appreciation of the nature of your friend.

Managers, as well as academics, generally fail to deal with technology, their most powerful strategic tool, as an integral factor in strategy formulation.

In everyday management this failure takes three forms:

1. an inadequate understanding of necessary and sufficient technologies;
2. a focus on product technologies rather than process technologies;
3. an inability to properly assess the time and cost of converting technology push into market pull.

NECESSARY TECHNOLOGY
VERSUS SUFFICIENT TECHNOLOGY

Bill Norris once said to me that he wished to be cremated when he died. I asked why. "Because," he said, "all the cemeteries will ultimately have to be covered over for IBM factories, and I don't want to be buried under those assholes."[8] This sardonic, if somewhat raw, bit of Bill's humor revealed a deep and profound understanding of the commoditization inevitable in the evolution of computers, and how one remains competitive in the face of that commoditization. More precisely, it underscores that competitiveness hinges on the distinctions logicians would make between "necessary" and "sufficient" know-how (technology). Devising successful strategies involves being able to discern those technologies that are required to compete but that are not of themselves sufficient to yield competitive advantage. These are the "necessary" technologies. They are the tickets to the game.

Beyond that, successful strategy involves being able to identify those technologies, either existing or potential, that secure competitive advantage by differentiating a firm from its competitors. These are the "sufficient" technologies. Say, for example, a firm that makes bicycles wishes to distinguish itself by making the lightest weight bike. It should focus its attention on the technology of lightweight materials and architectures. All the other technologies that go into a bicycle are necessary but should not be the focus of the firm's attention. Such thinking was a way of life for us at Control Data from the very beginning. We began with a single intense focus: design for high performance . . . all else being necessary but secondary.

Although this idea seems straightforward, in practice the ability of business leaders to distinguish between necessary and sufficient technologies is surprisingly rare. Even this singular ability is not enough, however. Whether a technology is sufficient or merely necessary is a function of time; those that are at one time sufficient will most assuredly become merely necessary at a later time. Prolonged fine-tuning of today's "sufficient technology," denying its natural transition from sufficient to necessary, is a recipe for strategic disaster. The importance of understanding these dynamics of change is made clear by looking at the microelectronics and computer industries and the experience of Control Data.

In the early stages of the computer industry, competitive advantage came from differentiation in any or all of the several components of a computer—logic circuits, storage devices, and systems software such as operating systems and data management systems. As the industry matured, the nature of competitive advantage changed. This began early on with data storage—the computer's "memory" devices. In the 1960s, a lively OEM business in magnetic core storage existed. Many computer manufacturers bought rather than built these memory devices for their computers. By the time semiconductor memories became standard in the 1970s, almost all manufacturers (IBM was a notable exception) met their needs by buying these standard components from merchant semiconductor companies such as Intel.

By the 1980s, the logic circuit, the component most valued in the earlier decades as competitive differentiator, was no longer the industry's focal point. Almost all the larger original computer companies resisted and failed to change. As technology advanced, they continued to spend vastly increasing sums of money on research and for production facilities for proprietary logic chips that, with the exception of certain niche markets, had become outdated technology differentiators. They failed to switch the focus of their technology to software and systems integration know-how, which by then were the sufficient technologies of competitive differentiation. New entrants, such as Apple, bought microprocessors from merchant semiconductor companies (Motorola and others) and concentrated their efforts on other technologies, such as human interface technology, that would give them differentiation. It was the continued focus on technologies no longer *sufficient* for competitive advantage, rather than technological change *per se,* that inexorably took its toll on those older, now mostly forgotten, companies that failed to adapt.

Today, while it is still *necessary* for systems companies such as Dell or Hewlett-Packard to have state-of-the-art system components, competitive advantage must come from a higher-order skill. Moreover, the mere task of maintaining "state of the art" in any given component has become increasingly

R&D intensive, and the need for economies of scale begins to dominate—thus the dominance of Intel in microprocessor technology. The need for the systems integration task, which was supplied by the vertically integrated computer companies in the 1960s, still exists.[9] The difference is that it is no longer possible for any one company to supply all the *necessary* technologies that are to be integrated. Rather, those technologies are, to one degree or another, supplied by the specialist firms, and technology *sufficient* for competitive advantage to the "systems" company must come from integration skills—though not from those skills alone. Continued maturation has meant that marketing skills have become dominant in the matter of competitive differentiation. Witness the success of Dell and the failure of Compaq with regard to direct marketing. Thus "skills" do not necessarily mean those involved in product design: Dell still has the highest margins in its class even though it uses a microprocessor equivalent to or even identical with others.

Control Data was guided by two beliefs that led it down a different path. First, "turning necessity into opportunity," and second, the usefulness of "technological collaboration." High-capacity reliable data storage devices were a *necessary* technology to the success of high-performance computers. To have those devices at an affordable price meant collaborating with competitors. The result was an OEM peripheral products business that took on a life of its own.

Control Data's strategies demonstrated profound understanding of the rapid rate of change of computer technologies from "sufficient" to "necessary," and further that just keeping the necessary technologies competitive was increasingly expensive. That example was there for all to see, but not many did. Control Data was taken to task both at the time (the 1970s) and in hindsight by some inside the company, including a board member, and others outside (primarily the wizards of the financial community) for being tied to the mainframe "dinosaur" and failing to move to the world of personal computers. But that criticism missed the point of the company's strategy, which was being built around information services. From 1970 my personal and very specific goal was to move the company to a more distinctive level of differentiation—computer-based information services. Even in the 1980s, a scant decade before the services avalanche came upon the information technology business, Control Data's "services strategy" was looked upon with derision. That is but one more illustration that pioneers are the ones with arrows in their backs. It is best to prepare yourself for that.

The period since 1985 in the microelectronics and computer industries has been aptly described as chaotic. The rapid rate of technological change in these industries was and still is obvious to all participants. Mere awareness of that rate of change, however, was of little help in the 1980s in understanding the coming structural change in the industry, nor is it now of much help in devising strategies for the future. It was not at all obvious to many that industry evolution inevitably would change "sufficient" technologies into merely "necessary" ones. It also was not obvious that this change would restructure the industry from one composed of vertically integrated systems houses to a horizontally structured industry composed of firms producing various parts of the computer system, and most particularly to one where the importance of services is strategically dominant. Services means information services and application-specific services as well as new methods of marketing.

This maturation process is not unique to the computer industry. The dynamics of change can and do vary from industry to industry, but successful strategy always must be built on clear understanding of the necessary technologies that are to be obtained as economically and efficiently as possible, and of the sufficient technologies that are to be the intense focus of proprietary effort. Even more vital is having the judgment to be able to ascertain how they will be defined in five, ten, or more years. Control Data anticipated that change in the computer industry by more than twenty years. Others did not.

As a notable example, it took a monumental upheaval and shock for IBM to get the message, including a dramatic change in going outside the company for a new CEO at the end of the '80s. Finally, by the end of the '90s, IBM understood that "services" was more meaningful as a business strategy than simply as those services used to support the users of their computer hardware.

The foregoing examples all involve change in the product dimension of Strategic Space. But technological evolution also has implications with regard to change in the market dimension—that is, new applications—and in the process dimension. One of the more dramatic examples in this last regard has to do with the *selling process.* In 1990 it would have been easy for Compaq to anticipate direct selling. Certainly embracing direct selling would have been traumatic for its established market channel of distribution. However, by 2001 the only answer for Compaq was to be acquired. The limited consideration of change and evolution in the process dimension of Strategic Space leads to the second failing common in strategic management.

NEGLECT OF PROCESS TECHNOLOGIES

Something that did not fit well in the Control Data culture was a focus on process technology. An exception to this was the company's information services business, for which competitive advantage resulted primarily from superior process. The "discovery" in 1972 of the importance of process was crucial in turning Arbitron, the radio and TV audience measurement service, from a business that lost money every year but one since its founding in 1947 into the most profitable business unit in Control Data with a return on assets in excess of 40 percent.

Control Data was founded on product differentiation, and that remained its primary cultural focus. Competitive posture was heavily weighted toward product features. The thought of finding competitive superiority through the processes of not only manufacturing but also of design, support, and administration did not come easily. In 1981, for example, faced with intense competition in its floppy disk drive business, Control Data hired a consultant to investigate possible dumping by Japanese competitors. What was discovered was that Control Data's overhead costs, particularly overhead engineering support costs, were greater than its direct manufacturing costs and were the principal noncompetitive factor. The balance sheet impact of this neglect of processes and the negative implications for cash flow were severe. The need for a focus on being a low-cost competitor ultimately resulted in the sale of the $2 billion disk drive business to Seagate.

Ironically, this relegation of process technologies to a lower priority occurred in spite of management's continuing emphasis, beginning in 1977, on the newly emerging management concept of total quality management (TQM) with its focus on continuing process improvement. But as is evident from the floppy disk drive example previously mentioned, it took a long time for TQM to move from the manufacturing floor to the key support functions. The culture of the company was a deeply ingrained one of "value-added," meaning the features, advantages, and benefits of its products and services. The processes by which they were developed, produced, and sold were important but not seen as a competitive differentiation.

This failing in strategic management of focusing on product technologies while neglecting process technologies is all too common. Thinking of process technologies as meaning production processes compounds this failure. As noted in the Arbitron example, service businesses are less prone to this shortcoming because services are inherently process oriented. People in service businesses have nowhere else to look for competitive advantage. In product businesses, the design of the product is an all too tempting trap.

The following example taken from outside the computer industry illustrates how process technologies can revolutionize an industry just as decidedly as a new or substitute product can. It also shows that "mature" industries are not immune to technological innovation and upheaval.

The story is that of Pilkington Bros., PLC. In 1958, after seven years of effort, Alastair Pilkington perfected a new process for the manufacture of plate glass. At that time, plate glass was manufactured by a cumbersome, capital- and labor-intensive process of pouring plates of glass that were then ground and polished until both surfaces were smooth and parallel. The process had remained unchanged for over a century, except for refinements and incremental improvements in the grinding and polishing steps. Pilkington's new product process—in which glass was "fire finished" by floating on a bath of molten tin—cut energy and labor requirements in half, saved the 15–25 percent of glass that was ground away by the earlier process, reduced capital investment by one third, and reduced space requirements by one half. It also propelled Pilkington from an industry leader within the U.K. glass-making industry to a global industry leader. The new process transformed the competitive economics and structure of a centuries-old industry.

By any measure this was a breakthrough technology. It yielded a competitive advantage to its originator as decidedly as any new product could have done. One only needs to look at what information technologies have done in package delivery—such as Federal Express—or retailing—such as Wal-Mart—to see that process technology is a fruitful source of competitive advantage.

Development of new and superior processes can also be a means of market entry when there are already well-established competitors. The market for dynamic random access memory (DRAM) chips is a case in point. In the late '70s, U.S. semiconductor manufacturers dominated the DRAM market. In 1975, five Japanese electronics manufacturers (Fujitsu, Hitachi, Mitsubishi Electric, NEC, Toshiba), with the urging and financial support of the Ministry of International Trade and Industry (MITI), began a technological collaboration, the "VLSI" consortium. VLSI was focused on developing superior technologies for producing very-large-scale integrated circuits by 1980. As a result of this five-year focused effort, these companies were shipping 64,000-bit chips well before their U.S. competitors, and by 1985 they had come to dominate the DRAM market. By then, most U.S. companies, including Intel, had made the painful decision to exit that segment of the semiconductor market.

Competitive advantage results from a clear understanding of the technological state of the industry. This understanding allows resources to be focused on those technologies that will lead to differentiation, whether they are process technologies or product technologies. As is clear within the computer industry, what constitutes a "sufficient" technology not only changes over time, it can change very rapidly. The advent of the Internet is but the most recent example of this.

TECHNOLOGY PUSH VERSUS MARKET PULL

A third strategic admonition is an inadequate ability to discriminate technology *push* (newly feasible technologies) from market *pull* (market demand). Not that push and pull aren't familiar terms. Most any article on technology transfer, collaborative R&D consortia, or the issue of how best to capitalize on the capabilities of the national laboratories will talk about technology push and market pull. Generally implicit in those analyses, however, is the notion that a kind of matchmaking process is needed in which needs are aligned to technologies. Market *need,* however is not the same as market *demand.*

The problem lies in the fact that most formal business education and experience is concerned with established, well-defined markets where need and demand are practically synonymous and can be studied by means of rigorous market research. Competitive advantage is seen as some sort of differentiation in satisfying a well-quantified demand. Most consumer products fall in this category. Strategy becomes mostly a matter of marketing innovation. Strategic management certainly requires understanding basic market research. But much more than that is necessary. Strategic management requires understanding how to bridge the gap between a perceived market need and actual market demand. This gap can be very large indeed, and it is a gap into which many start-ups heedlessly plunge. It requires understanding what is necessary to generate demand for innovations or technologies that have the potential to restructure entire markets or for technologies that meet inchoate needs and have the potential to create new markets.

Again, the development of the microelectronics industry provides an example. Fairchild and Texas Instruments filed patents for the integrated circuit in 1958–1959. By 1961, three years later, there was still no U.S. commercial market for integrated circuits. In 1961, however, President John F. Kennedy announced the famous "man-on-the-moon" goal, and that single stroke generated a market pull for integrated circuits. The government remained the sole market for integrated circuits until 1964, and the primary one until 1968. By 1968, much had been learned about both the integrated circuit manufacturing process and applications using that product. It still took a leap of entrepreneurship for Bob Noyce, Gordon Moore, and their colleagues to found Intel in 1968. It had taken ten years to generate sufficient market pull to begin commercialization of one of the most revolutionary technology developments in all of history. In this case, government's pursuit of a critical new mission provided the necessary initial impetus to create market demand.

At Control Data, we frequently experienced this challenge of demand creation. Perhaps in none of our endeavors was this truer than with PLATO, the computer-based learning system. The shortcomings of elementary and secondary education were not only numerous and readily obvious, they had been documented in many competent and responsible studies.[10] Bringing this innovation to market was an arduous task. It simply did not fit the "standard model," that is, it was difficult for practitioners—the teachers—to utilize PLATO within the framework of pedagogy they were trained to use. Demand could be created in a few pioneering institutions, but a mass market proved very difficult to generate because it meant, essentially, a reeducation of teachers. Properly used, PLATO not only offered an attractive and attention-holding methodology for delivering information to the learner, it offered a convenient system of exercise and feedback to check progress in comprehension. Even more than that, it had the potential to make the teacher a true coach who could provide highly individualized attention to students.

Bringing PLATO to market took many forms. In its most familiar form, the PLATO software and certain associated courseware were sold as part of a stand-alone computer system. This system was marketed to both universities and businesses. PLATO also was employed in Control Data's network of training centers, the Control Data Institutes. It was successfully delivered as a service in such difficult learning conditions as prisons, where many inmates experienced, for the first time, individualized support for learning. Some 125 PLATO learning centers were opened to bring the benefits of continuing education to the general public. The centers also were used to provide certification services.

But the public education system, potentially the most needy beneficiary of this new technology, never was a significantly penetrated market. The ingrained habits of this two-hundred-year-old and impossibly unwieldy system proved to be a truly difficult barrier to creating demand.

Not until two hundred years after the introduction of the movable type printing press in the mid-fifteenth century was the textbook commonly used in education. The difficulty lay not with the technology—movable type printing—but rather with the inability of the education system to change, to modify its pedagogical methods. Slowness to adapt still plagues education. Advanced electronic education technologies are now nearly a half-century old.

Use of flight and other simulators in training is even older. Yet computers, telecommunication, and simulators are still not the basic tools of the mainstream education process. Although the slowness of education to adopt new technologies, and thus create a market *demand* for them, may be extreme, it is by no means an exception.

Peter Drucker has said that the Internet is the most revolutionary innovation since the railroad in the nineteenth century. The Internet is so revolutionary that it gave rise to a belief that it would sweep away the past. The "new economy" with the Internet at its core would obviate the "old economy," and management was deluged with stories of the war between the two: "Bricks vs. Clicks" and recipes to survive the transition from old to new, such as, "Cannibalize Yourself." Certainly there have been instances of sweeping change. The advent of eBay became life-threatening indeed to the small retail shop for secondhand goods. And in some categories, the war between bricks and clicks brought considerable financial pain for the traditional retailer and the Internet-based newcomer, such as Barnes and Noble and Amazon.com.

For the most part, however, such sweeping generalizations ignore the fact that new technologies only *add* complexity to the management task rather than sweep away its extant challenges. The semantics implicit in the word *versus* in the popular phrase "bricks vs. clicks" are misleading. The Internet offered *one more* sales channel—essentially a direct selling channel. Not only was there the challenge to manufacturers and their retailers to understand something new to many of them—direct selling—there was the more complex task for the manufacturer of multichannel marketing.

As for the Internet-based economy itself, the irrational plunge of investors into almost any dot-com, no matter how flimsy its business fundamentals, particularly the fundamental of creating demand, led to such widespread failure that soon the byword of the financial community had changed from "the new economy" to "the technology bubble has burst."

While the computer and information services industries offer many other examples of the challenge of demand creation, taking a look at a quite different market and technology is helpful in appreciating this task of demand creation. The story of Edward Marshall Boehm, Inc., provides a beautiful (literally!) as well as a simple and powerful example of creating market demand.

Early in their marriage, Helen Boehm urged her husband, Edward, who was working as an assistant veterinarian, to get serious about his sculpture avocation. He researched ancient ways of handling clay and finally developed his own formula for hard paste porcelain that had the properties and translucence that were to be key to the beauty of Boehm objects. Hard paste porcelain technology was not unknown, but its formulation was a closely guarded secret of the fine porcelain houses of Europe and Asia. There was no equivalent technology in the United States until Boehm developed his formula.

However, art and technology, no matter how unique, do not suffice to make a successful enterprise. Their modest basement start-up in 1954 needed to attract the attention of the marketplace. To do this, Helen hit upon the idea of presenting a Boehm sculpture to President Dwight Eisenhower. She was successful, and thus established a tradition that Eisenhower and succeeding presidents commissioned Boehm to design and provide porcelain figure gifts for foreign dignitaries. The high point came when President Nixon made his historic trip to China in 1972 and commissioned Boehm, Inc., to create a new symbol of world peace as a gift to the people of China. Boehm's massive porcelain of two swans became world renowned.[11] Awareness of, and a desire to own, Boehm porcelain grew steadily from the publicity following the Eisenhower gift. Helen Boehm had created a most effective "reference sale."

As early as the late 1960s, Control Data, perceiving the long-term difficulty in achieving the economies of scale and process expertise to compete in the inevitable commoditization of computer hardware, began a strategic move into computer and information services. The company's true competence, even in developing scientific computers, was understanding and solving difficult *applications* of computers. So by concentrating on the greater added value inherent in computer-based services, it began a process of differentiation from its mainframe competitors. The potential need was clear for computer-based processing services, networking, groupware, computer-managed and mediated learning, and information databases. It certainly presented plenty of opportunity for innovation, but the process of generating viable businesses was to be a long and arduous process spanning two decades, due to the need for market education and the expensive matter of modifying patterns of human behavior. While we in Control Data, unlike Helen Boehm, could not create a presidential reference sale, we did work to create high-profile business customers and reference sales for our fledgling services. It also took, as has been pointed out with PLATO and the public education system, more than a "try it, you'll like it" approach to educate potential customers to the point where they wanted to buy.

Creating demand is nothing new, but with more advanced and complex technologies customer education requires as much innovativeness as creating the product or service in the first place. Learning this lesson can be very painful and very expensive. The advent of broadband voice and data wireless communications took the telecommunications industry down a path so treacherous that by 2001–2002 the industry virtually imploded and witnessed the bankruptcy of some of its largest companies. Commenting in the September 2002 issue of *Technology Review,* writer Michael Schrage correctly and succinctly put the matter this way: "The telecom sector remains a fabulous market for innovative uses of bandwidth. But innovation shouldn't mean getting people to use *more* bandwidth, it should be about getting people to change their bandwidth *behavior.*"

New technologies often are faced with undefined or poorly defined markets and thus with weak market pull. Educating the market, changing people's behaviors, and systemic changes take not only persistence and determination, but also time and money. If this concept seems straightforward, why is it that management so frequently underestimates the task? At the root of this is the very nature of human behavior.

One must start with the proposition that in the most rudimentary sense every need is being met in some fashion. A need may be met poorly, very slowly, or at great cost, but we attempt to meet needs and solve problems with the technologies that are available to us, whether the need involves feeding ourselves or doing engineering design. For example, the widespread use of electronic technologies in education required behavior change—in the way teachers teach and the way courses are organized. Such behavioral changes come slowly no matter how obvious the advantages. A principal example, although difficult to believe today, was the great trauma associated with the introduction of word-processing systems into the office twenty years ago. Most secretaries vigorously resisted the change, some going to the extent of hiding their old typewriters and secretly using them instead of the new machines. Worse than that, in some cases management decided the best way to use this new technology was to create a centralized "word-processing pool" to provide word processing. These reactions to technology were not Luddite-like aversions but more simply an aversion to change, to supplanting one way of satisfying a need with another.

Those concerned with technology transfer and technology commercialization need to focus on barriers that stand between the existence of a need and the creation of genuine market pull. Furthermore, it is frequently and regretfully the case that generations must change before new technologies are fully embraced.

Managers need something to help them understand the evolutionary nature of technologies and industries; something to help them understand which technologies, at any given time, are necessary and which are sufficient to secure competitive advantage; and something to help them understand industry structure, its technology underpinnings, and barriers to creating demand for new technologies. The concept of the Technology Food Chain is a practical tool that helps to meet that need. We will turn to that in the next chapter.

Chapter 7 The Care and Feeding of Strategy— The Technology Food Chain

Today, success in the global marketplace means creating and applying new knowledge—which is to say new technology—faster than one's competitors. That is the fundamental law in this competitive world.
—Erich Bloch, Distinguished Fellow, Council on Competitiveness

The Technology Food Chain (TFC) uses the food chain metaphor to explain the role of added value know-how (technology) as one moves from basic science to products, to systems, and finally to services. A simplified technology food chain for the computer and information services industry is shown in Figure 6. Also shown is an analogous chain for the simpler matter of fish, fishing, and eating fish. At each stage of the chain, beyond basic science, know-how is applied to pre-existing technology in the form of products, processes, and tools to fashion a new class of products that meet a higher order need. Thus, each step in this food chain "feeds on" the technology that has been employed to create the predecessor products, processes, and tools. Services represent the final step in the TFC.

The Technology Food Chain is not to be confused with the "value chain" concept that is common in business. The value chain concept

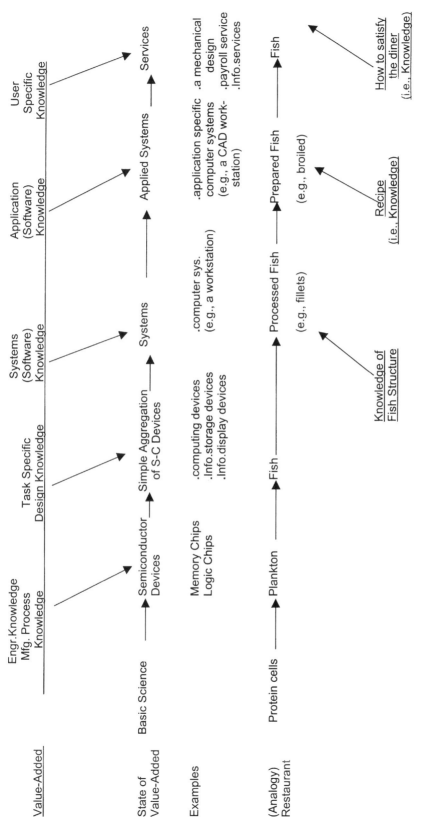

Figure 6. Technology Food Chain—computer and information services industry

is used in two different ways. One is to describe the sequential steps by which a company converts inputs into its product or service, such as the steps of design, manufacturing, marketing, and distribution. The second is the "supply chain" concept that is used to depict the sequence and types of companies that provide *inputs* to a company (referred to as "upstream" elements of the supply chain) and the sequence and types of businesses that buy the company's *outputs* and either add additional value or sell it directly to the ultimate consumer (referred to as "downstream" elements of the supply chain).

A Technology Food Chain is another matter. It depicts for an industry or subindustry the stages from basic science to the ultimate stage by which some need is met. At each stage technology (know-how) is added to the output of the previous stages. Each stage is dependent on *all* of the stages that precede it.

The TFC for the computer and information services industry shown in Figure 6 demonstrates these dependencies. In the early days of the industry, companies operated at multiple stages or, in some cases, *all* stages of the TFC, for they had no alternative to meet their dependence on them. As the industry matured this would change, but whether they operated at more than one stage, that is, were more or less vertically integrated, was a matter of economic choice.

A key difference of the Technology Food Chain, when compared with the value or supply chain, is the perspective it provides in understanding the types of know-how required at each stage. This is essential to determining what kind of know-how is merely a requisite to a product or service—in other words, *necessary* know-how (technology)—and what kind of know-how provides a distinctive advantage—in other words, *sufficient* know-how (technology). It also is helpful to anticipate how know-how may evolve over time and thus *change the source of competitive advantage* in the future.

Again in Figure 6 we can see that as more and more *applications* of computers and microelectronics are devised, the demand for components, subsystems, and systems rapidly increases, and those stages of the TFC become more and more commoditylike. The source of competitive advantage in those stages— the sufficient technology for strategic success—becomes that which yields low cost. At the same time, however, it is necessary to continue expenditures to enhance product features and performance.

The Technology Food Chain metaphor, then, is a useful heuristic in several ways. It makes clear the basic technological forces at work in an industry and how they change as an industry matures. It also clearly shows the potential sources of competitive advantage at all stages of industry development. Knowing where your business is on the food chain clarifies which technologies are the sources of competitive advantage and which are simply necessary. For emerging technologies, the Technology Food Chain helps to make clear that there is an absence of market pull. For mature industries, it offers a reminder that technological change at earlier stages in the chain can dramatically alter industry structure and economics. In addition, for mature industries, the Technology Food Chain also highlights the critical importance of process technologies and the importance of economies of scale and scope. This was the case in the Pilkington Bros. story told in the last chapter.

In the early stages of any industry, engineering design is the primary determinant of competitive advantage. The "better mousetrap" mode of thinking predominates. But while products at this stage potentially have market pull from many applications that will incorporate them, in the beginning the operative word is *potentially*. Those applications are performed in a completely different way based on completely different technologies. The example of computer-aided design illustrates this situation. While engineering design was certainly an activity being performed long before computers came on the scene, it took more than a quarter of a century after computers were developed before computer-aided engineering design developed significant market pull for computers. This delay was due, in part, to the need for the evolution of complementary technological capabilities such as graphics and software, but it was largely due to an established system of engineering design that rested on massive amounts of data in the form of old engineering drawings. The previously mentioned example of books not being adopted in education for two hundred years after the invention of the movable type printing press is another example of a need being filled by a different technology and the consequent delay in adoption of a new one. In short, if a new technology depends on market pull from needs further along the food chain, we must recognize that those needs are currently being met in some totally different way and that replacing existing ways of meeting a need will be time consuming and expensive.

The Technology Food Chain also helps clarify how sources of competitive advantage change as industries mature. As understanding increases about technologies at the beginning of the TFC, more and more uses are found, creating new applications and increasing demand for those basic technologies. However, since knowledge of them has become widely diffused, competitive differentiation is hard to achieve. Economies of scale become important both in production and in the amortization of R&D costs. Superior processes—not just in production, but in development, marketing, and administration—assume a dominant position in competitive differentiation.

Some of the original competitors will make this transition by focusing on process technology. Their basic strategy will be to optimize their existing position in the TFC. They will become efficient and effective commodity businesses. This does not mean they can ignore product technologies or the need for increasing R&D expenditure. Intel is a good example. The company must continuously strive for better and better chips, but it is process technology and scale that advances their leadership position.

Some competitors will move along the food chain to seek advantage by adding engineering know-how to build systems—and then perhaps move on to application-specific systems. The final step in the industry maturation process is services based on the predecessor products and systems. The fact that the final stage of the TFC is services has fundamental implications for the business strategist and deserves closer examination. The best way to start that examination is to repeat the assertion: *No Product Satisfies a Need: Needs Are Met by Services.*

At first blush this seems to be nonsensical. But stop and consider that products are *used* in some process and it is the process that meets the need. Let's use a very simple product as an example: the hammer. The needs for which hammers are employed are many, say to build a house. But hammers don't build houses—people do. People with the need for a house may buy the hammer (and other tools) and build the house themselves. In this instance the product is used in a *self-service*. Or the people with the need may use a hierarchy of other businesses to satisfy the need for a house; they hire a general contractor—a service—who hires one or more subcontractors—services—who in turn hire carpenters and laborers who use the hammer. And so it is with the need for transportation. An automobile may be utilized as a self-service to get from here to there, or it may be used by a service company—a taxi service—to meet the need for transportation.

As technology advances an interesting phenomenon occurs; some products are so complex they can be used *only* by a sophisticated services organization, for example, a space vehicle. On the other hand technology can simplify the use of products so that self-service becomes more possible. On the one hand hardly anyone is capable of performing engine maintenance on an automobile; on the other hand many people use self-service gasoline pumps, buy groceries, or purchase airline tickets. It is basically information and electronics that makes it possible.

The lesson here is that those responsible for product strategy always need to be thinking beyond their immediate customer and in terms of the ultimate process in which their product will be used to provide service. And those responsible for service strategies always need to be thinking of technology changes that will drastically change or even eliminate the need for their service. "Smart" products and "smart" materials are obviously becoming more widely available. The question may be raised as to whether robots soon will be "products" that are capable of providing services to meet human need.

As we proceed up the food chain, there is know-how added at each stage. It is the precedent know-how investment in the systems that makes a service possible. Service companies purchase most of this value-added knowledge in the systems on which their service platforms are based. The service firm's *proprietary* value-added knowledge tends to be application specific. Finally, then, this quest for competitive advantage through proprietary knowledge causes the service end of the food chain to become more and more market segmented. In retail services, for example, this has developed in an interesting way: on the one hand there has been the rise of "big box" retailers such as Wal-Mart, appealing to the low-cost buyer, and on the other proliferation of boutiques with narrow-market focus such as luxury goods and specialties. All of that is overlaid with direct selling via the Internet, which emphasizes convenience.

Market segmentation is inevitable as the technologies mature and diffuse. Thus the competitive appeal of a service cannot rest solely on the technological features of the products used to perform it. Suppose one is offering a remote information service based on computerized database management. In the early stages of the industry, the competitive advantage of the service might rest entirely on the speed of the computer and/or the features of the database manager. But when those product technologies mature and become widely available, a firm can distinguish its service only by appealing to a more specific customer type, that is, *market segment.* Otherwise one simply competes on price. And this is an expensive, low-margin place to be.

It is important to note, however, that as industries mature and product differentiation becomes more difficult to achieve, products do not necessarily become less R&D intensive. Nor does production of such products necessarily become less capital intensive. One only need look at the semiconductor industry, where both development cost and production line capital costs increased some tenfold over the course of the 1980s. Economies of scale and scope become increasingly necessary as industry maturation proceeds.

The classic response to the need for scale and scope has been vertical integration—handling every element of TFC internally. But that response also produced companies less flexible and less responsive to rapid technological change.

As industries mature, growing R&D and capital intensity may make vertical integration less appealing, if not downright impossible. Instead, firms seek out technological collaborations and strategic alliances. The rapid proliferation of alliances in the microelectronics and computer industries in recent years is in large part the result of such rapidly escalating resource demands.

In considering the specific case of technological collaboration, the participants usually think about what value—resources or technology—each of them brings to the collaboration. The Technology Food Chain makes clear, however, that it is equally important that participants have a very clear understanding of the added value each participant will apply to the results, *the output,* of the collaboration. Said another way, the output of technological collaboration should not be viewed in and of itself as a marketable product, for without some differentiation, the alliance partners will all end up selling the same thing. The result will clearly be a mutually destructive price war. The only other alternative is worse, at least from the consumer's view, and that is that the collaborators will collude to divide up the market. It is obviously much easier for competitors to collaborate with regard to technologies involved in areas of the food chain that *precede* their own position, since while both require such necessary technologies, they are free to add their proprietary know-how. This was exactly the case with Control Data and its competitors. Each had its own computer design, which was the competitive differentiation, but they could collaborate to design and produce *necessary* peripheral equipment such as disk drives.

Southwest Airlines gains competitive advantage through the homogeneity of its fleet and, consequently, lower parts and maintenance costs. That observation leads to an intriguing speculation: would some sort of collaboration with regard to parts and maintenance for different types of airplanes provide some much needed relief for industry participants?

The Technology Food Chain also illustrates why there will likely be problems in technological collaborations among companies that are at different points in the chain. What is competitive advantage for one may simply be a building block technology for another. Thus, the collaborators may have sharply different views on sharing technology. For example, for those designing computers a computer-aided design system is a tool, a necessary technology, but for the supplier of computer-aided design systems it is the feature of the system itself that provides competitive distinction.

The Technology Food Chain helps us to understand that in a world of increasing technological complexity, the old "make or buy" strategic crossroads has become a three-way fork: "make, buy, or collaborate." The answer as to which fork to take may not be as clear as was Clark's decision at the three forks of the Missouri, but the answer is no less key to having a successful journey. Firms can obtain necessary technologies by being vertically integrated—by making these things for themselves—or by buying those technologies through licensing or component purchase, or by sharing development and/or production risk and cost with others. The collaboration option has also been called "virtual vertical integration."

Over the last two decades of the twentieth century, collaboration took on ever more complex forms. Collaboration, with regard to computer and semi-conductor technologies, first gained widespread acceptance with the establishment in 1981–1982 of the Micro-electronics and Computer Technology Corporation (MCC), and the Semi-conductor Research Corporation (SRC). Further impetus was given through the R&D Act of 1984, which clarified and simplified antitrust regulations with respect to such collaboration.

Collaboration for manufacturing and other operational functions became widespread in the 1980s through so-called outsourcing and joint ventures. By the 1990s even product design was being accomplished through collaboration, so that a new term, "the virtual company," was coined.

However it is achieved, ***superior utilization of technology*** is the most important ingredient of economic success for nations, as well as for corporations, large and small. Concepts and issues of innovation encompass both macroeconomic policy for a nation, and business strategy for the firm. Improved performance in innovation and in managing technology is key for the future company. It is also key for the future society.

In both national economic policy formulation and business strategy formulation, there is a considerable knowledge base with regard to technology and innovation. There is even a lot of well-intended action. However, the results are all too frequently poor. Without a well-defined conceptual framework, the knowledge cannot effectively be brought to bear, and much of the action is unproductive. Even though the concepts of Strategic Space and the Technology Food Chain were never explicitly articulated in Control Data by myself or anyone else, they were part of the implicit thinking process that shaped Control Data's innovation.

Understanding strategy and achieving strategic success can be daunting. Some years ago Andy Griffith recorded a hilarious story titled "What it Was Was Football." In this vignette an unknowing, unwitting country bumpkin finds himself enveloped and herded along by a football crowd. Upon emerging into the stadium he takes the field before him to be "some kind of cow pasture" and the football to be a "pumpkin." At the end of a puzzling experience he states: "I finally figured it out: the idea was to run with that pum'kin from one end of the cow pasture to the other without either being knocked down or steppin' in something!" Business strategy can't be reduced to cow pastures and cow pies, but achieving strategic success can be made less confusing and more familiar. It begins with understanding the TFC and thinking of strategy as solving the problem of charting a profitable journey.

Each strategic move will entail choosing among the strategic trichotomy: make, buy, collaborate.

The next three chapters will explore in more detail Control Data's journey through Strategic Space and some of the more important steps it took in terms of growth through strategic alliances, acquisition, and internal growth.

Part Three Forging a Strategic Journey:
The Decision Trichotomy—

Collaborate, Buy, or Make

Business literature, not to mention everyday business conversation, about implementing strategy sooner or later raises the question: "Do we make or buy?" There is also an extensive and separate body of writing about so-called strategic alliances. However, these are actually inextricably related matters in strategic thinking. Each step of a strategic journey involves a decision to make (whether to rely on internal resources), to buy (whether to contract for or otherwise acquire), or to collaborate by means of some form of shared endeavor. Part Three highlights certain frequently overlooked aspects of each approach. It is particularly concerned with the fifth principle: **Collaboration, especially technological collaboration, is a powerful strategic tool.**

Chapter 8 Collaborate to Compete

For cooperation to prove stable the future must have a sufficiently large shadow.
—*The Evolution of Cooperation,* Robert Axelrod

For the adventurer in Strategic Space, the most keenly felt issue is that of limited resources. This is particularly true for the start-up company, and even more, it is a paramount problem for an advanced technology start-up such as Control Data. The market opportunity is tantalizing. There is talent and confidence, desire and enthusiasm. The know-how that will yield competitive advantage and market demand seems clear: in Control Data's case it was the ability through *innovative design* to extract maximum computer performance and competitive superiority. But there are all these other "must dos," such as supporting subsystems and market access through good distribution channels, things that will help turn potential into reality. Where is the money for all that? How is it possible to develop the needed capabilities in time to hit the window of opportunity? Even more daunting is the ongoing necessity of exploring more advanced technologies from which competitive advantage can be fashioned even before the technology of the current product is fully developed and deployed. The potential resolution to these issues lies in three alternative directions:

• Make
• Buy
• Collaborate

With limited resources, a new company out of necessity must seek collaboration. Such was the case at Control Data. However, there developed in the company both a mindset and a skill set that made collaboration a part of its strategic thinking long after its status as start-up had passed and it had become a multi-billion-dollar enterprise. In the later years of the twentieth century, *collaborative* undertakings, or, in the common vernacular, "strategic alliances," became a common phenomenon in the business world. In the last two decades of the twentieth century the number of strategic alliances among U.S., E.C., and Japanese firms grew fortyfold. It is estimated that in 2005 alliances will be the source of 30 percent of the revenues in the top one thousand U.S. public companies.

Such ubiquity, however, has not necessarily resulted in better understanding of the basics of collaborative arrangements in achieving their potential. The failure rate is thought to be around 40–60 percent. Because Control Data's extensive use of alliances occurred in an environment in which they were uncommon and continued to be a primary component of its strategy, I am in a position to state with the clarity of hindsight what works and what doesn't.

First, it's necessary to discuss the meaning of the term *strategic alliance:* what such a partnership is and, equally important, what it is not. This may seem unnecessary for a term in such common use, but the very casualness of its usage almost guarantees that a word or phrase becomes warped as to its meaning. Witness the bastardization of the meaning of the slang word "cool," which originally referred to something "interestingly different" or, perhaps better, "bordering on wonderfully bizarre," into simply "great," "really nice," or "attractive." So the term *strategic alliance,* and arguably there is no such thing as a *nonstrategic* alliance, has come to mean almost anything one does with another party: a contractual relationship, a simple vendor customer relationship, an acquisition, a license agreement, or whatever. By denoting all arrangements as "strategic alliances," they are given a degree of profundity that inflates the importance of the partnership—that gives them all equal standing.

An acquisition is *not* an alliance. It is simply a means of subsuming the other party's interests and capacities into one's own. A simple buy–sell arrangement or technology acquisition via licensing is not an alliance, but simply an ordinary arms-length business transaction.

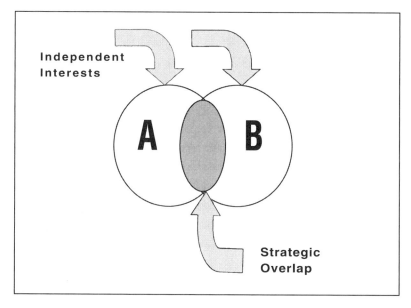

Figure 7. Strategic Alliances

A strategic alliance, first of all, involves a pooling of resources between two or more parties. Second, it should be a non-zero-sum relationship; both parties give to the other and yet *retain* what they gave and in addition gain from the relationship. Third, and most essential, true alliances have strategic overlap. Put it this way: I have my objectives and strategies for achieving them, you have yours. We determine that we can each achieve our independent objectives by collaborating in *some portions* of our strategies. Pictorially, this can be represented through a Venn diagram by the overlap of two domains, *A* and *B*, where *A* and *B* represent the domain of the respective strategies of the two parties. The overlap simply says that some portion of those strategies can best be achieved by pursuing them jointly. There remains, nevertheless, unique strategies that are each company's own.

PURPOSES OF STRATEGIC ALLIANCES

There are three, *and only three,* purposes to strategic alliances:

- Technology
- Market Access
- Complementary Capabilities

Complementary capabilities refer to the manufacturing, distribution, selling, financing, and administrative resources that are necessary to bring an innovation to market.

Technology

In today's world the time and cost associated with developing (make) or acquiring (buy) all the requisite technologies are great. The answer to this dilemma is the third alternative, collaboration. The key to *technological* collaboration is to understand which are the "necessary" technologies to be in the game—that is, those that you must have just to compete. And further, it is imperative to understand those technologies that will distinguish your service or product from its competitors. To recall the language we used earlier, these are the technologies that are "sufficient" to yield competitive advantage. Control Data's establishment of Computer Peripherals, Inc. (CPI), and Magnetic Peripherals, Inc. (MPI), are excellent examples of a collaborative effort to produce a necessary technology.

CPI was formed in 1972 as the first major strategic alliance in Control Data's peripherals business. We set up CPI with NCR to manufacture so-called unit record equipment—primarily input-output equipment for reading and outputting Hollerith cards, which were known more commonly as IBM cards because IBM so dominated the market for such devices long before electronic digital computers came into existence.[1] Unit record devices were in no way a competitive differentiator for computers, but they were nonetheless necessary to the functioning of a computer system. For a PC or a laptop computer the mouse or keyboard are similar necessary technologies.

Control Data managed the joint venture. The output was sold to the parent owners at a fully loaded manufacturing cost plus a fee to cover R&D expenditures. NCR procured the equipment for incorporation into its own computer systems. Control Data did likewise, but Control Data also was free to market the devices to other computer companies. There was no contractual constraint to prohibit NCR from engaging in this OEM marketing activity, nor for antitrust reasons could there have been, but they had little desire to do so because of the necessary investment in building the marketing and administrative structure necessary to support an OEM business. On the other hand, Control Data already had an experienced OEM organization and the benefits of the larger manufacturing volumes flowed to both partners in terms of reduced costs.

Some three years after the establishment of CPI, Control Data established with the Honeywell Corporation a joint venture of far more significant impact. In April 1975 MPI was established to design and manufacture magnetic disk storage systems. Honeywell owned 30 percent and Control Data owned 70 percent of the enterprise. Subsequently, with the alliance of Honeywell and the Bull Company in France, Bull became a small equity holder in MPI. Although NCR was not an equity owner in MPI, because of its long-standing relationship as a major OEM customer of Control Data, NCR actually held a seat on the Technology Planning Committee of MPI.

The operating arrangement of MPI was similar to that of CPI. There was a formal board of directors of the company, but there was a technology planning committee and extensive deliberation and debate over product strategy and emerging magnetic disk drive technologies. Control Data supplied the management and technical people for MPI. MPI provided the scale necessary for Control Data to become the second largest producer of disk storage equipment next to IBM, and the largest OEM producer of disk storage. The OEM business not only resulted in lower cost peripherals for Control Data computers, it became a business contributing significant revenues and profits.

NCR AND THE ADVANCED DEVELOPMENT LABORATORY (ADL)

In the course of little more than two decades from the founding of the computer industry, maturation in the Technology Food Chain had progressed to the point that the technological features of the hardware were no longer sufficient to secure competitive advantage as differentiation became ever more a function of applications software. And yet the performance of the basic computer had to continue to improve just to be in the game. In 1973 this led Control Data and NCR to establish the Advanced Development Laboratory (ADL) to study and begin preliminary development of a mainframe computer that would serve as the product line backbone of both companies. There were actually two physical facilities, one located near NCR's operations in Escondido, California, and the other near Control Data in the Twin Cities. There were reasons, both practical and psychological, for the arrangement. The practical reason was that it made it easier to tap the engineering and software talent of both companies. The psychological reason was that it helped to maintain a sense of equality between the two partners.

That this arrangement worked was a testimony to the trust that had been built between NCR and Control Data, the two companies' experience at technological collaboration, and the evolution of the industry along its Technology Food Chain. Both NCR and Control Data's strategies had evolved to the point where the focus was increasingly on application systems. Moreover, the applications of their respective market segments were considerably different: NCR dealt principally in financial and retail markets, while Control Data was more focused on scientific and engineering applications.

Control Data had been struggling with its computer product line strategy for several years. The PL-50 (aka NPL) design simply had failed to achieve the integration of its several legacy product lines. The solution at that point, the Cyber 170, was essentially a 6000-based design. The migration of the 3000L product line customers had been a brute force affair. Now the time had come to begin the design of the Cyber 170 follow-on. Not surprisingly, migration of the existing customer base was a major concern. Fortunately, a major technological benefit of the collaboration came in the form of a "dual mode" computer without the significant performance degradation that characterized previous industry attempts at emulating an older design on the new computer.

The technical problems, particularly the basic operating system software, were particularly vexing. However, the advanced development lab worked well. Both companies provided highly skilled technical people. There were inevitably differences and even acrimony, but thanks to leadership skills of people such as Derrell (Sam) Slais, Tom Elrod, and Ed Michels, these were well handled.

This collaboration was integral to the very core of both companies' business strategy. The responsibility for oversight of it had to be at the level of ultimate strategic responsibility. The Control Data executives were Tom Kamp, head of the peripheral products business; John Lacey, senior vice president of corporate plans and controls; and me, president of the Systems and Services Company. The three executives of NCR held similar high-level positions. We met monthly to review progress, address problems, and explore further potential. Unfortunately there were no direct commercial flights between NCR's headquarters in Dayton, Ohio, and Control Data in the Twin Cities, and Control Data had no corporate aircraft. But this not so trivial time–cost problem was handled with pragmatic efficiency. Since there were nonstop flights from both the Twin Cities and Dayton to Milwaukee, the monthly meetings were held at the Milwaukee airport in an unused FAA office. The facility offered spartan furnishings with government-issue desks and chairs of uncertain vintage but much more certain discomfort. Consequently, presentations and discussions were crisp and to the point.

The specification and preliminary design effort was well along by the end of 1975. Control Data had expended a lot of effort on its own with regard to customer migration and by that point had decided on certain features that we felt were mandatory in the new machine's basic design if we were to be able to effect that migration. These were presented to our NCR colleagues in that sparse FAA office, and, following the presentation, instead of the usual lively argument there was a dead silence. NCR asked for a brief adjournment. They returned to say that our presentation made them realize that by comparison they had inadequately probed migration issues. They requested time to study the matter. That was agreed to, and after some months they returned with the startling news that, for their applications, they simply didn't require the high-performance computers that Control Data did. They felt, therefore, that while the work at ADL was technologically interesting, it was very expensive and most likely would not solve their long-term product strategy needs.

ADL was closed down. The two companies continued their collaboration in disk drives and other peripherals, but the common mainframe computer was not to be. So ADL "failed," but most certainly it had not failed in a larger sense. One of the most difficult problems for the strategist is that of perspective. "Walking in the moccasins of another" is not simply a matter of understanding and tolerance. It is to gain insight—perspective—by actually working on real problems together. Each may bring different tools to the problem-solving effort, or each may be sharing a common tool to use on differing problems. Either way both gain perspective, understanding, and respect. As a result, Control Data went on to develop its highly successful Cyber 180 product line and NCR its highly successful "tower" series of minicomputers.

SRC AND MCC

By the end of the 1970s the computer industry was still, some three decades after its birth, best described as being driven by unbridled individualism and entrepreneurship. In one sense that was an excellent state of affairs because the rate of technological change continued to be explosive. There was, however, a fatal flaw in this. The applications deriving from the explosive growth of microelectronics technology were making proprietary advancement in basic technology, computers, and applications software by every participant enormously expensive and nearly impossible in terms of global competitiveness. Some industry leaders, such as Bob Noyce of Intel, were sounding alarms. Control Data had also been working diligently to bring about broad technological collaboration. Mostly, however, companies continued in their paths of proprietary technology development across the entire Technology Food Chain, from basic semiconductor technology to application systems and services.

Although there was much talk about Japanese threats to the U.S. semiconductor and computer industries, by 1981 there were no initiatives underway to actually bring about broad-based technological cooperation by U.S. companies. In order to foster and bolster support for technological collaboration, in April 1981 I spoke to the principal computer industry association, the Computer Business Equipment Manufacturers Association (CBEMA). A condensed version of that speech is in Appendix 5. A few excerpts will serve as a good introduction to two important technological collaborations in which Control Data played a major role.

"In recent months, there have been a number of comments in the press to the effect that microelectronics 'will be the crude oil of the '80s.' This is a seemingly apt reference to the opportunity microelectronic technology offers to those who would dominate world trade in the future. Perhaps unwittingly it also implies an unfortunate policy and strategic direction the U.S. computer industry is pursuing . . . one that in the long run can only lead to a declining competitive position. We are, in fact, at a vital crossroads in the evolution of microelectronic technology and its application to economic growth. The inappropriateness of the 'oil analogy' will serve as a good vehicle to describe the nature of the decisions we are about to make at this crossroads."

The speech goes on to summarize the fallacy in using the oil analogy by pointing out the differences in ownership, production, and use of a critical *physical resource,* oil, and a *knowledge resource,* microelectronics. Competition for the former is a zero-sum game, for the latter it is a non-zero-sum game. Intelligent, knowledgeable people exist in every nation, in every race, in every land on earth. Controlling knowledge is a far different matter than controlling oil. For all practical purposes, long-term it can't be done. This was the crux of the matter. The key to the success of U.S. microelectronics and computer companies was to ensure self-benefit by sharing rather than falling into the trap of adopting strategies and policies that treated knowledge as a barrel of oil.

The speech continued:

"Finally, there is a third important disparity between oil and microelectronics: the 'applications' of oil are relatively limited and relatively cheap—you refine, you burn it, you convert it. . . . There are around 750 refineries in the world. Now a refinery costs only $500 million or so and the design engineering part of that cost is only $45 million. Even a leading chemical company like DuPont spends only $450 million per year on *new* applications of petroleum derivatives. These sums of money are small when compared to research and development associated with the application of semiconductors.

"The application of semiconductor technology is still so labor-intensive that the demand for money and people to pursue them is mind-boggling. IBM, alone, spends in design engineering costs the equivalent of thirty refineries a year. And that is basically for one application of microelectronics—making calculators. According to *Business Week,* the total U.S. computer industry spends over $3 billion per year. Worldwide, all applications of semiconductors consume nearly seven billion R&D dollars. At that rate, in less than five years, we will exceed the engineering costs associated with all the refineries that exist—and the application of microelectronics is still in its infancy."

The speech concluded with a call for a broad-based cooperation in advanced microelectronics, based on four basic principles:

1. Cooperation must be limited to research, development, and production—not marketing.
2. Cooperation must be broad-based—it is not limited to just a few participants.
3. Cooperation must focus on advanced technology—those technologies that are five to ten years out in front of those in today's products.
4. Each participant must have a clear value-added strategy that can provide [its own] marketplace distinctiveness.

Based on these principles it was suggested that a cooperative program be constructed. Called Microelectronic Enterprises, Inc. (MEI), it would develop state-of-the-art microelectronic technology for its shareholders.

The "MEI" of this speech, presented as a concrete proposal, was a conscious effort to get business people and political leaders out of the hand-wringing, lamentation mode that had characterized discussion of U.S. competitiveness in microelectronics and into a mode of debating and acting on a specific proposal: embark on a new path in which strategic alliances would be a central part of corporate strategy and economic policy. The concepts presented in the MEI proposal actually came into being in the form of two broad-based collaborations, the Semi-conductor Research Corporation (SRC) and the Microelectronics and Computer Technology Corporation (MCC). Subsequently Congress passed the National Cooperative Research Act of 1984, and within the next ten years more than 250 consortia and collaborative alliances had been formed. A brief synopsis of MCC and SRC will illustrate the changed thinking regarding technological collaborations that began to pervade the industry.

SRC was formed under the leadership of Bob Noyce of Intel, then chairman of the Semi-conductor Industry Association (SIA), and Erich Bloch, then at

IBM and later a Distinguished Fellow at the Council on Competitiveness. I served on the interim board of directors that guided the actual formation of SRC. The announcement of SRC was made by the SIA in December 1981.

The initial concept for SRC was that companies would pool all or a portion of their university research grant monies and work collaboratively to prioritize and focus those research dollars. Equally important was the objective of having a greater pool of graduate students who were being trained in disciplines critical to the semiconductor industry.

Larry Sumney has effectively led SRC, located in the Research Triangle Park in North Carolina, from the time of its formation. Over time SRC has expanded the scope of its work from the core research grant programs, but perhaps most important it taught its participants their first lessons in the effectiveness of the "collaborate" path of the basic strategic trichotomy.

In August 1987, SRC had an important offspring—SEMATECH—that was more hands-on collaborative by the member companies. SEMATECH was focused on the fabrication technologies necessary to build integrated circuits well beyond the then current state-of-the-art technology. SEMATECH played an important role in restoring global competitiveness to U.S. industry in terms of semiconductor manufacturing technology.

MCC was a more difficult concept of technological collaboration and in 1982 was the most advanced yet envisioned. It was to be an umbrella organization within whose framework specific collaborative development projects could be proposed by member companies and, if approved, executed by those and any other interested MCC shareholders. Thus the number of participants for a specific project could be from two to the total number of MCC stockholder companies.

The idea for MCC was first presented to representatives of twenty companies, trade associations, universities, and government agencies in Orlando, Florida, on February 19, 1982.[2] However, the general idea of collaboration in basic microelectronics and computing had already been privately explored by Bill Norris and me over the course of the previous three years in meetings with Ed Spencer, the CEO of Honeywell, Bob Galvin, CEO of Motorola, and Bill Anderson, CEO of NCR. The results of these discussions could best be described as inconclusive, so we finally decided that getting everybody together in one room would provide the best shot at bringing about some action.

There were three notable absences from the Orlando meeting: IBM, Intel, and Sperry Univac. Sperry's abhorrence of technological collaboration was clearly stated by H. Glenn Harvey, vice president for strategic planning and development at Sperry Univac: "The very essence of our business technology is the chips and electronics. To willingly put the core of your R&D thrust outside your own control and share it with competitors is basically unattractive." There were two principal reasons that IBM did not participate: first, it felt that, in some of the key proposed areas of collaboration such as computer-aided design, it was so far ahead of the industry that the company was unclear whether it could benefit. Second, antitrust concerns were still dominant in IBM's thinking. The settlement of the Control Data and Justice Department antitrust lawsuits was still all too fresh in the corporate mind.

At the meeting in Orlando there was a surprising amount of support for doing something to meet the obvious threats to the U.S. semiconductor and computer industries. John Lacey, Control Data's executive vice president of technology and planning, presented a straw horse along the lines of the "MEI" concept of my CBEMA speech. A steering committee was established with myself and George Scalise of Advanced Micro Devices (AMD) as co-chairs. The first meeting of that committee was held in April and subsequently met monthly. Subgroups met between these monthly meetings to hammer out the initial technology projects and the various organizational, staffing, intellectual property, and administrative matters that had to be resolved.

The steering committee ultimately decided that the name of this groundbreaking collaborative effort would be the Microelectronics and Computer Technology Corporation (MCC).[3] It was envisioned as an umbrella organization to promote individual and diverse projects by and among the companies that would be its shareholders. It was further quickly realized that because of the diversity of these companies, which would include not only computer manufacturers and semiconductor companies but also the U.S. government as well as other industrial firms that used microelectronics, not every company or organization would want to participate in every project. There was even some discussion between Gordon Bell, then with Digital Equipment Corporation (DEC), and me that MCC could in effect be a "virtual organization." In this approach it would not be necessary for all MCC projects to be co-located. This proved to be too elusive an idea for most of the members of the steering committee. In the end, thanks to generous support by the City of Austin, Texas, and the University of Texas, MCC was housed in a new and most attractive facility in Austin.

There was another issue that at the time was felt to be a formidable obstacle to technological collaboration. It was the threat of antitrust action against those participating. The essential factor in determining antitrust behavior is of course

that of determining if a given behavior is anticompetitive. That's straightforward enough in concept, but arcane in the extreme when it comes to proving
guilt or innocence. Understanding that MCC would be engaging in development of broadly applicable technologies, those of us from Control Data were
confident of our ground. After all, we had had the rigorous training ground of
our antitrust lawsuit against IBM. So I began each meeting of the steering committee with a comment along the lines of: "Antitrust is not an issue. What we
are doing is forging a collaboration to increase competition, not to reduce it. So
let's move on to what matters."

The critical issue was neither location nor antitrust. The critical issue was
to decide upon and launch a set of projects of long-term technological importance to the shareholders of MCC, and to do this in a manner that would
demonstrate meaningful success along the way. It was also most important
to ensure utilization by the partner companies of the technology MCC developed. So "technology transfer" was a prime concern of the steering committee.

As far as what research areas and specific projects within those would be most
meaningful, the committee chose nineteen technologies of potential interest.
Thanks to some excellent work by the task teams chosen to investigate them
and look for projects of highest priority, within a short time four initial projects
were chosen: advanced computer architecture (ACA), software, packaging, and
computer-aided design/computer-aided manufacturing (CAD/CAM).

To address the twin challenges of research excellence and effective technology transfer from MCC projects back to the parents, it was decided that project
personnel could either be on loan from the sponsoring companies or could be
permanent employees of MCC recruited from those companies or elsewhere.
In addition the participating companies would provide technical people on
short-term assignments who would function as technical liaison between the
projects and the parents.

There was a question, however, of the caliber of the people whom the parent
companies would decide to release to these longer-term projects. Admiral
Bobby Ray Inman, who was recruited to be MCC's first CEO was certainly dis-
appointed in that regard. As he put it at the time: "I have no wish to preside
over a turkey farm."[4] That may have been a bit harsh, but there was perhaps
justification. As things turned out, the projects were heavily populated with
outsiders. That may have been good for the quality of the research, but it only
exacerbated the already challenging task of technology transfer back to the parent companies. Without extensive involvement in these projects of individuals

from the parent companies, utilization of project results became notably more difficult.

Effective utilization of the technologies developed at MCC was only one aspect of the broader issue of intellectual property. The original proposition had been for MCC to have ownership, and royalties would be charged for patents or for demonstrable packages of know-how. For project participants, royalties would become a cash charge only after they exceeded the contributions made to the project. Since project costs were to be shared equally by all participants whether large or small, this arrangement of charging in proportion to the benefit received seemed to be most equitable. If the complementary skills and assets of larger companies allowed them to benefit more, they would also, in the long run, pay more.

The proposal to charge royalties to participants not surprisingly met with a less than enthusiastic response: "Pay royalties on technology that I have paid to develop? Not on your life!" So participants received royalty-free licenses. There was to be no licensing to third parties until three years after a technology's first use by a member company. Three years seemed more than generous in terms of first mover advantage.

In almost any research and development effort there are technologies developed that are peripheral to the original objectives. Here too there was a question of how to deal with this "fallout" technology. Suppose an employee of MCC wanted to use it to start a spin out from MCC. Would this be allowed? No. At least, that was the original policy. Later this would change. MCC was plowing new ground in terms of technological collaboration.

MCC was formally incorporated as a for-profit company in December of 1982.[5] The steering committee became its first board of directors, and operations were under way early in 1983. It had not been a smooth and seamless endeavor, but it certainly was a historic one.

Did MCC succeed in the sense of the original intention to help ensure U.S. "predominance and preeminence in microelectronics and computing"? There certainly have been those who question this. In his book *Technology Fountainheads,* Raymond Long says: "In retrospect, the viability and sustainability of MCC's original mission . . . must be questioned." He goes on to point out as major failures the lack of support by the U.S. government and IBM. But this is mistaken. U.S. government representatives participated by invitation in the steering committee meetings leading up to MCC's founding. They evidenced great support. It was a conscious decision by the board at its first meeting after Inman's appointment that MCC would not *initially* seek government participation that we knew to be available. We felt that we had to prove that we as an industry would support technological collaboration and were not just seeking yet another government handout. We did that. Later, when Grant Dove became the CEO of MCC, this policy was no longer necessary and government-funded projects were both sought and obtained. As for IBM, the reason for this lack of participation has already been described. It took a far larger financial impact than the threat of competition from Japan for IBM to develop a mindset open to collaboration and strategic alliance.

Consortia, simply because they involve many collaborators, are a much more difficult form of technological collaboration than a simple partnership. Because they frequently deal with the exploration of advanced technologies that may be several years ahead of those in use in current products, and because such technologies may not ever even work out, there is greater risk. The problems of technology transfer or, more accurately stated, technology utilization, are also much more difficult. Some participants may never be able to use the technologies even if proven feasible, and in any event the ability to capitalize on them will vary from one company to another. R&D consortia, then, are much more prone to being labeled as "failures." But that simply is a wrong-headed view. Exploration is essential. The risk of failure is always there. The advantage of collaboration is to share the risk that is a concomitant aspect of any venture into new territory.

It is a strongly held opinion by many who have been involved in the microelectronics industry and computers that MCC did, indeed, realize the vision we had in forming it. Because of that pivotal endeavor, eyes previously occluded were opened to the benefits of collaboration. The R&D Act of 1984 was a direct result of MCC efforts. In short, a whole new era of technological collaboration was born. MCC, SRC, and SEMATECH did much more than produce a few advanced technologies; they educated the U.S. microelectronics and computer industries as to the problems, pitfalls, and enormous benefits of technological collaboration. The world leadership of the U.S. companies in those two industries is extant and demonstrable evidence of MCC's success.

PLATO

The technological collaboration with the University of Illinois has been described in Chapter 3. This collaboration extended well beyond the research phase and into the commercialization of the technology. This alliance between a private company and a university resulted in technology that was seminal in the field of computer-mediated learning.

Market Access

The second purpose of strategic alliance is market access. Marketing, sales, distribution, and related functions are complementary capabilities. *Access* is a different, and frequently a much more difficult, challenge.

A company's ability to market its products in certain countries may be limited because of trade barriers or political constraints. Such may be the case when a given market is dominated by a firm whose products are different yet related or complementary to one's own. Even in the absence of overt political restrictions cultural differences may inhibit a company's ability to access a market by means of its traditional methods. In such instances a joint venture or some other form of an alliance may be necessary. However, not every would-be alliance works out.

PHILIPS

Control Data had scarcely embarked on its journey in Strategic Space before it faced a major crossroads. The successful launch of the Model 1604 in 1960 quickly generated the interest among members of the global scientific community because of its superior performance. Through NSA, the British Intelligence Service procured and had installed a 1604 by the end of 1961. The Weizmann Institute in Rehovot, Israel, also exhibited early interest and ultimately procured a 1604 in 1962 with the help of World Bank funding. Beyond that, Control Data's prehistory at ERA and Remington Rand had made its principals acutely aware of the global scientific community and its potential for the company to achieve the scale needed to realize an appropriate return on the expenditures involved in the design and development of high-performance computers.

On the other hand IBM had already shown it would not let Control Data's encroachment on this scientific and engineering portion of its markets go unchallenged. Thus the window of opportunity for achieving global scale would be small. But resources, people, and especially money were very tight. This was the exact moment when IBM's U.S. marketing ploys—excessive discounts and bundled services, to name two—resulted in a drying up of Control Data orders. Moreover, Seymour Cray was being supported full tilt in his new supercomputer efforts.

In addition to internal and competitive demands, there were the political, economic, and cultural barriers to a U.S. start-up company attempting to make inroads internationally. For all these reasons the top management of Control

Data was more than open to the idea of a collaborative partnership with a non-U.S. company. Such an alliance would allow the company to more quickly grasp the opportunity inherent in the global marketplace, and most especially in Europe.

The Dutch Company Philips also was faced with a strategic dilemma. It was an established electrical and electronics enterprise that had expanded not only throughout Europe, but in North America and Asia as well. Philips North America, headquartered in the United States, had indeed almost become the "tail that wagged the dog." To avoid having Nazi Germany gain access to its U.S. assets, Philips had placed its stock in North America Philips in an independent U.S. trust. The trustees of that stock and the management of NA Philips itself possessed therefore, both technically and economically, a position of independence within the parent company. This independence had flourished because of the economic boom in the United States following World War II.

But Philips had no substantial computer expertise, either in the United States or elsewhere. What it did have, however, was an appreciation of the importance of this new technology. Philips wanted to be in the computer business. Its choice was make, buy, or form an alliance.

"Make" was impractical. Computer design expertise was scarce. "Buy," that is, acquire a company? Well sure, but which one? Not market-leader IBM. Large companies such as Sperry Rand, ICL, or Burroughs were either too big or diverse or constrained by national politics. Perhaps some small player would fill the bill.

The Dutch mentality was not much given to collaboration. Even the word "collaboration" had a negative connotation from World War II that was still acute in the 1960s. But a "partnership," one that the company could dominate, might be a good way for Philips to acquire the needed expertise and market presence it desired. Control Data's size and reputation made it a most promising "partner" candidate.

So discussions began between the two businesses, one very large and one very small, but both with important and *overlapping* needs. This was fertile ground. The first contact is lost in history, but by the beginning of 1962 talks were going forward in earnest. J. G. Miles, a corporate vice president, was in the vanguard. Frank Mullaney, corporate treasurer Ed Strickland, director Bob Leach, and of course Bill Norris were involved. By the spring, however, it was clear there was an impasse. Philips's partnership position was that the company would own 70 percent of the proposed joint venture that would operate in Europe and, in addition, would own 30 percent of Control Data Corporation. The Control Data position was a 50–50 joint venture in Europe. Period! In consequence of this impasse, by the summer of 1962 Control Data initiated its plans to go it alone in Europe, and by fall Ed Strickland was in place as head of that operation with headquarters in Lucerne, Switzerland.

What happened here? There seemed to be a strong strategic reason and pragmatic driving forces—the need for technological expertise in Philips's case, and Control Data's need for money and market access—that would have provided the basis for a meaningful collaboration. Yet it did not occur. It is a fair question to ask, "Why?"

The answer is *trust*. Philips's culture was not one of trust; it was "dominate or be dominated," a culture certainly accentuated by the experience with Nazi Germany. In the minds of Control Data's executives, while collaboration was in general readily embraced, there was a basic mistrust of large companies. The company, after all, came into being because of disillusionment with Remington Rand. The Philips proposal seemed little more than a "bear hug," an ill-disguised attempt at a takeover. Philips could easily be accused of failing the most rudimentary principal of collaboration, "Know your potential partner." That would be the wrong conclusion. Philips was thorough in its research. They knew Control Data, its principals, its history. All this knowledge, however, was filtered through a prism of corporate desire to dominate. So a true partnership was not to be on terms which we could accept.

What is important in this story is that even though there were overlapping strategic interests between the two parties and they brought complementary capabilities to the table, one essential ingredient was missing—*trust.*

CANADA

With regard to market access, it will be useful to look at an alliance that stemmed directly from, and in the end furthered, Control Data's globalization. In this alliance there were also strong elements of technology acquisition and financing. This collaboration was with the government of Canada—more specifically, with its Department of Industry, Trade and Commerce (DITC). This alliance was a clear-cut case of the overlap of two independent strategies. DITC had an announced purpose of promoting computer design and manufacturing in Canada. It needed tangible and visible results of that policy and had financial wherewithal to assist it to that end. Control Data was attempting an ambitious new product line strategy that would provide a smooth migration path for its multiple computer product lines that had evolved over the preceding dozen years. Control Data's financial resources were strained. In addition to the new product line to replace the 3000L and 3000U, there were two super-computer efforts: the 8600 follow-on to the 7600 and the ongoing STAR development.

Control Data had only a small marketing contingent in Canada but a great interest in its growth and overall development in that marketplace. In 1963, when Control Data acquired the computer division of the Bendix Corporation, it acquired the computer sales and support portion of Bendix's ComDev affiliate. In 1969 it acquired all of ComDev. So the company had a presence in Canada with both its marketing and sales operations and in military electronics.

The idea of moving some computer development "south" from Minneapolis to Toronto had some natural appeal. Bob Hall, the newly appointed group vice president for systems, was charged to make it happen. In spite of the political problems involving the U.S. government and international technology transfer, Canadian vs. U.S. export control differences, and the disruptive Quebec separatist movement, an agreement was reached.[6]

The reason this was possible at all, it must be emphasized, was that there was fundamental common ground in the strategies the two parties were pursuing to achieve their quite independent objectives. For both there was intense motivation, economic and political on the one hand, financial and technological on the other.

Further witness to the intensity of that motivation is the fact that the collaboration even survived a major failure on Control Data's part to develop the computer design that it had chosen as the basis for the collaboration. As it turned out, that product could not achieve the required cost performance. This was hardly a unique occurrence in the design and development of computers. But it is one thing for it to occur within the sheltered walls of Seymour's Chippewa Laboratory. It is quite another for it to occur in the full political glare of the administrative and legislative oversight of a national government. But a replacement design for the flawed PL-50 was soon developed, and the collaboration continued a vigorous course. The new computer design was to become the basis for Control Data's highly successful Cyber 170 product line, and Control Data was committed to produce over half of its worldwide need for the Model 173 of that line in Canada.

This was a pioneering collaboration in the information technology field. Many governments were spending large sums of money in futile attempts to bolster indigenous computer companies. The Canadian approach was to leverage the technology of a nonindigenous company, Control Data, to spawn companies that would be suppliers to Control Data. DITC, in the end, invested some $15 million in the Cyber 173 development. This modest number represented a significant investment for DITC. Moreover, Control Data was a partner that more than matched the government's funds, and was willing and able to share technology with other entities in Canada. Thus the collaboration with DITC encompassed not only market access, but also technology and financing. Obtaining financing, of course, is a most essential complementary capability.

Complementary Capabilities

STACK

In calling for the establishment of "MEI," which took form as MCC and SRC, I emphasized the billions of research dollars being spent on duplicative precompetitive technologies. Duplication of expenses in the computer industry, however, was not limited to research. Still another form of desirable cost saving through collaboration was in the matter of electronic components and in the ancillary costs of such complementary capabilities as specification, qualification, and testing and quality assurance.

An intuitive feel that there was duplication and waste in these matters gave rise to informal explorations in the late 1960s with ICL as to potential collaboration. These initiatives were not driven by top management directive, but rather by midmanagement and working-level engineers who had absorbed the lessons of collaborative enterprise. The result was that in 1974, STAndard Computer Komponenten, gmbh (STACK) was founded in Germany by Control Data, ICL, Ltd., the Plessey Company, Ltd., and Nixdorf Computer AG. The business objectives of STACK were straightforward and to the point:

1. To reduce the cost of ownership of semiconductor components required by member companies.
2. To improve members' capabilities by providing a continuing, coordinated, and disciplined interchange of information.

STACK significantly benefited Control Data as well as all its other member companies. STACK reduced our component cost ownership by 50 percent. More components were bought to STACK's very first common specification, SPEC0001, than any other in the industry at the time.

The membership in STACK grew, but it also migrated away from computer companies and ultimately became primarily a consortium of European telecom companies. STACK still exists and is headquartered in the United Kingdom, having moved from Germany in 1980.

DRIVING FORCES TO UNDERTAKE ALLIANCES

So the *purpose* of establishing alliances is straightforward: technology, market access, or some complementary capability. But the question is why? There is always the choice of taking either the *make* or the *buy* strategic alternative. Either of these two is more straightforward than the collaborate path. Alliances by their nature are more cumbersome, more difficult to manage and inevitably involve compromise, accommodation, and trade-off. So what drives a company down the alliance path? There are four basic forces that push businesses in that direction.

1. Magnitude of Required Resources. As technology becomes more and more complex and expensive, resource requirements expand geometrically.

   One solution to today's very large and growing resource requirement of technology and product development is larger and larger corporations. But huge corporations have their own set of problems, and because of this in recent years we have witnessed an extraordinary degree of *disaggregation:* spin-offs and other downsizing restructurings of various forms. The search for necessary resource and risk sharing through strategic alliance is a result of these basic forces.

   The requirement for risk and resource sharing through collaboration will not lessen. In fact, we are already at the stage where requisite resources for some endeavors—such as space exploration, high-energy physics, and environmental issues—are beyond the capacity of not only any single company, but any single country.

2. Know-How and Expertise. Even if funds are available, it is not always possible to undertake a desired strategy because the critical skills are not available in the company. In addition, it is not feasible that those skills simply can be "bought." This is particularly true if they are scarce or hard to acquire because, for example, the skills are geographically distant relative to the location of the need.

3. Time to Market. Time to market has become increasingly important in seeking competitive advantage. Collaborations and alliances may be the best way

to shorten the crucial path in commercializing an innovation—even if it is more expensive and even if some initial compromise is necessary with regard to cost.

4. Political Barriers. Political and trade barriers are historically one of the most common reasons for alliances. But cultural diversity and the need to understand local markets, even in the absence of actual legal requirements, is a powerful motivator for international business alliances.

STRUCTURE OF ALLIANCES

Alliances are most commonly conceived to take the form of equity joint ventures between the allying parties. But important alliances may also take the form of contractual agreements. The use of the word "contract" is not intended to imply of necessity a document in the narrow legal sense. The contract may be written or oral, it may express only a framework for collaboration—a memorandum of understanding (MOU), so to speak—or it may be a formal partnership agreement. As has been mentioned a technology license is nothing more than a buy–sell agreement, but such agreements may be part of a contractual or equity joint venture alliance.

Of course, equity joint ventures require a lot of formal documentation. This documentation may be implicitly accepted by the parties as evidence of due diligence and thoughtful articulation of expectations. In actual fact, all too often the equity joint venture turns out to be a mistaken substitute for meaningful articulation of goals and objectives. As a general rule of thumb, it is advisable to approach any equity joint venture as if it were a contractual type alliance. Spell out duties, responsibilities, expectations, and strategic purposes of the partners as though it were in fact a memorandum of agreement between them rather than just an investment by them in this third-party company. It was the careful understanding and articulation of interests between DITC in Canada and Control Data that ensured the survival of the collaboration in spite of the demise of the original vehicle of collaboration. In that instance, of course, there could be no equity joint venture between DITC and Control Data, but the lesson of constructing a thorough and careful contractual relationship was nonetheless clear.

There is vast literature on fashioning success in "strategic alliances." There are even templates and checklists. But there are some easy-to-remember, basic principles that can guide an executive team in constructing and managing successful alliances. The first of these, strategic overlap, has already been mentioned. It is not enough to "think" or "believe" that there is strategic overlap between the parties. It must be articulated and tested. This overlap must be viewed in its *time dimension* as well. One year? Ten years? Does it have a milestone dependency? Does it have a market maturity dependency?

Although a company's basic goals, objectives, and broad strategies may be stable over long periods of time, specific strategic initiatives can and do have relatively short time frames. Good strategy must be flexible and responsive to barriers and opportunities. So, if an alliance is to be a means of carrying out strategy, it too will be subject to such change and must be structured so that it can respond, change, grow, and, when appropriate, simply cease to be. That is the *second basic principle, flexibility.*

The necessity for strategic overlap and of flexibility gives rise to three underlying principles with regard to structure:

• **First, responsibility must be positioned at the level in the organization with the final authority for the strategy involved.**

This generally implies that this will occur at the CEO level, although in large diversified companies it may be at the group, subsidiary, or independent division level. The key is the involvement of the executive with the vision of strategic need, responsibility for strategic change, and accountability for results.

• **Second, strategic overlap is not a one-time determination.**

Changes in strategy can have significant effect on the need for and purpose of a collaboration. This was the case with NCR and Control Data in their ADL collaboration. These changes must be carefully monitored by the responsible executives in the governance of the alliance. Furthermore, two types of top-level committees should be established to support this ongoing analysis of strategic overlap as well as overall management of the alliance. One is an executive board or committee (the top executive from each partner) and the other a technology or product/service planning committee.

• **Third, flexibility starts with the basic form of the alliance.**

There is a perhaps all-too-human tendency to build "entities," separate management hierarchies with the separate physical and human resources felt necessary for the task. In this regard, separate equity joint ventures—freestanding legal entities—are used more often than they should be. In technological collaboration in particular, joint projects can be structured without even physical co-location much less embodying the project in a separate legal entity. On the other hand, collaboration and alliance is difficult and fragile. A more permanent structure—even a physical edifice—can be useful in strengthening long-term resolve of the partners. It is necessary to weigh this against the inevitable lack of flexibility in the functioning of the alliance. Control Data's alliance with NCR encompassed several different forms: a separate legal entity, CPI; a separate but unincorporated group, the Advanced Development Laboratory, which actually occupied two physical locations; a joint planning group; and contractual OEM agreements for magnetic disk drives.

OBSERVATIONS

Successful technology alliances are, in the final analysis, not so much about technology *generation* as they are about technology *utilization*. So-called technology transfer has received much attention from governments, economists and other academics, and, naturally, businesses. Whoever first coined the term *technology "transfer"* did all those interested parties an enormous disservice. The word "transfer" implies the transport of a *thing* from one place or organization to another. Once again, as with the oil analogy used in my CBEMA speech, we are semantically imprisoned by words that treat technology as a "thing" rather than as "know-how."

People learn about and make use of know-how on a very personal basis. More frequently than not this process takes place one-on-one. You do not, therefore, transfer technology from a collaboration back to the partners. Rather individuals, those in the collaboration and their colleagues in their respective parent companies, work together to utilize whatever new knowledge has been generated.

Successful alliances are non-zero-sum in nature. All too often alliances are approached with a view of gaining technology, capabilities, and expertise at the expense of one's partner(s). It is essential that each party in the alliance clearly articulate in advance what the benefit is expected to be and what each thinks the benefit to the other parties will be.

It has been shown empirically that a common characteristic of a successful alliance is *trust*. By trust is meant an abiding belief that your partner will do what is expected even under the most trying circumstances. Such a belief generally must evolve, and it evolves through observing behavior.

Collaborating to be more competitive, then, comes down to these straightforward principles:

- Thinking in terms of technology *utilization*, not technology *transfer*.
- A successful alliance is a non-zero-sum game. That doesn't mean that each party must benefit equally, but it does mean *mutual* benefit.
- Trust is built, step by step, as the people involved in the management and execution of an alliance demonstrate both competence and caring in its implementation.

Chapter 9 The Art of Acquisition

[Mergers] are, like second marriages, a triumph of hope over experience. Corporate mergers have even higher failure rates than the liaisons of Hollywood Stars.
—"How Mergers Go Wrong," *The Economist,* July 22, 2002

Acquisitions are no less the fateful temptation to the voyager in Strategic Space than the Sirens and their melodious songs were to Odysseus and his crew in their ten-year travails following the Trojan War. However, few captains of industry have the good sense to stuff the ears of their fellow adventurers with wax and lash themselves to the mast, as did Odysseus. The corporate skeletons that result are no less striking and foreboding than the mythological remains that surrounded those Sirens and their enchanting melodies.

Having experienced my full share of such tortuous adventures and the special allure of becoming a serial acquirer, I have selected a few examples to illustrate some basic understandings of the art of successful acquisition and what they can mean to a company's growth. The basic question of course is, "Why acquire?" And if there is a strategically meaningful purpose—unfettered by mere *desire for growth*—the more difficult question is, "What makes for success?" The key to success is the same as that in building an environment of innovation, and is very straightforward: *it is people,* and Control Data's very first acquisition, Cedar Engineering, is a good example of this.

The acquisition of Cedar Engineering occurred a mere two months after Control Data began operations. Cedar Engineering was a company engaged in building servomotors and gyroscopes. It was small and close at hand in a suburb of Minneapolis, and its people were known to the founders of Control Data. This was a modest transaction, but it was felt that it could bring greater credibility for the company's military and government prospects. Cedar was quickly absorbed into the company as a division on January 31, 1958. The vice president of engineering at Cedar, Tom Kamp, was later chosen to head the newly formed peripheral products division in Control Data. He provided the single-minded drive necessary to build an independent OEM peripherals business in the midst of an engulfing sea of computer designers. The peripherals business had to serve the internal demands of the likes of Seymour Cray and Jim Thornton and at the same time pursue a course of serving the very companies with whom they were in competition! No small task.

The Cedar division and, later, the Peripheral Products division were to be the source of executives who would play key roles in the company's international expansion: Gene Baker in administration and Jack Karnowski in finance. Marv Rogers, who joined Cedar about a year after the acquisition, would later serve as Control Data's senior financial executive for fourteen years, until 1986. Over the years acquisitions would continue to contribute to the development of the OEM peripherals business.[1]

Acquisitions were important to Control Data in many ways other than its OEM business, but before turning to them it will be useful to look at the basics regarding acquisitions.

BASIC PRINCIPLES IN THE ART OF ACQUISITION

Before the cart of success can be considered with any plausibility it is important first to consider the horse of rationale. The first question to which there needs to be a clear and unambiguous answer concerns why a company should embark on this route at all. If the answer to this question is, "To grow," then not only does it indicate that the acquirer lacks strategy, but that the ensuing acquisition is almost certain to be a failure. *There is no such thing as an "acquisition strategy."*

Growth

Growth and rate of growth targets are certainly legitimate objectives for a business. However, the important objective is not growth in and of itself, but having competitive products and services that will *result* in growth. Strategy and strategic thinking are about meeting that objective. The term "growth strategy" or "strategy for growth" is prima facie evidence of a company's failure to understand strategy, and more than likely its failure to fully appreciate what the sources of growth truly are.

Companies in newly emerging industries, such as was the case with Control Data in the '60s, don't have to work very hard to see the potential for new products and services. Strategy has to do with fashioning the means of taking advantage of opportunities, and frequently the means of doing so was through acquisitions.

Products and services in mature markets, on the other hand, have a basic growth rate determined by the growth of the market. Faster growth for a company means very simply either taking market share from one's competitors, or finding new markets and/or new products and services. The hard way to gain market share is to devise a competitive advantage. In mature markets that competitive advantage likely will be achieved by means of a superior *process* such as marketing, channels of distribution, financing, production, or information systems.

The easy way, the temptress tells us, is to acquire. The chorus of the temptation is: "Everyone else is doing it, so why don't we?" At this point growth has turned from being an outcome resulting from meeting needs through innovation to being the driving force of corporate action, and it evokes willy-nilly results. In essence, acquisitions become activities in search of a reason.

Strategic thinking is a search for an innovative, a competitively superior, way to meet some need. Each step toward that objective involves a move in the three dimensions of Strategic Space: products, processes, and markets. To make these moves we need technologies, market access, and complementary assets.[2]

If all these requirements can be met internally, fine. It may be, however, that they have to be acquired externally. Technologies can be obtained by means of licensing. Complementary assets can be realized by means of a contractual relationship or a collaborative alliance. Market access can be gained in various contractual forms or by means of joint ventures and other alliances. Technology, market access, and complementary assets also can be obtained by the acquisition of a company or a particular business unit of a company. Even if the financial and people resources can be marshaled internally to meet strategic aims, time to market may dictate acquisition. Naturally, buying anything within a circumscribed time period can be an expensive proposition, but if the potential gains cannot be delayed, it may be the action that must be taken.

In summary, acquisition is particularly useful as a means of gaining technologies *sufficient* to accrue competitive differentiation. Small companies and start-ups are particularly rich sources of such differentiating technologies. So acquisition is an important and even a powerful tool at the disposal of the traveler in Strategic Space. Like any powerful tool, however, the first priority is to know when *not* to use it.

Another danger signal for sure-fire failure is the fallacious reasoning of the defensive acquisition: "If we don't, somebody else will." It is difficult to conceive of a less propitious frame of mind for an organization to undertake an extremely difficult and risky task than, "Well, I surely don't want to but I guess I have to." Hello? This will increase shareholder value?

There is, of course, the more callous defensive takeover that is simply to acquire and dismantle a competitor. While this scarcely can be dubbed making a success of an acquisition, it is at least brutally honest. It is also almost inevitably very expensive. If the acquisition has little potential other than a tenuous market share, it is probably just as well to let someone else have it.

Most acquisitions fall somewhere between the blind search for growth and the defensively motivated. Here too, however, failure can result if there is not a clear understanding of which technologies are sufficient for competitive differentiation and which are only necessary to be in the game. As already noted, acquisition may be an excellent alternative to in-house development of *sufficient* technologies. For necessary technologies, it may be more attractive to pursue less intrusive forms of obtaining synergies such as a partnership or licensing or some other form of contractual relationship. It was for this reason that, after the initial start-up acquisitions for the peripheral products business, we built and grew that business via the collaboration path, principally MPI and CPI. On the other hand, CEIR and SBC brought to the company's services business distinguishing technologies and capabilities that were key to competitive advantage.

ACQUISITIONS THAT MADE A DIFFERENCE

CEIR

Even during its earliest years, Control Data was making tentative moves in the direction of computer-based information and data processing services, and one of the ways it was doing this was by means of acquisitions. Between 1962 and

1966 these included Scientific Computers, Inc., Meiscon, Computer Tech, Computech, Inc., and Samarugi & Sons. These acquisitions brought new expertise in computer consulting, computer application software, programming services, and data center operations. In 1968 the acquisition of CEIR, Inc., was pivotal with regard to the future of the services business.

During World War II there was a small but unheralded group set up under Dr. C. W. ("Robby") Robinson called the Committee for Economic and Industrial Research (CEIR). The core group in CEIR decided to apply their wartime expertise to the needs of the postwar commercial world. Data collection and information analysis on a massive scale required the use of electronic digital computers. Clients required consulting services on how to utilize these databases and thus was born one of the earliest computer-based information services companies.

CEIR not only had information expertise, it had the innovative idea that it could better serve its customers via a new technology developed at MIT. Known as "time sharing," it was a way for multiple users to be simultaneously connected to a computer via communication lines. CEIR's time-sharing system used IBM computers, not Control Data's. No matter—even "big blue" could be tolerated when it was useful to do so, and this was right in sync with Control Data's strategy of making large-scale computers available on a service basis to those who could not afford the cost of large, expensive systems.

At that time, Control Data's computation services were provided on a "batch" basis whereby users submitted a program and its associated data as a job (batch), and the data center computers ran each job in sequence with results returned to the user. By 1968 this was already being done remotely using telecommunications. However, the computer still was executing these jobs sequentially rather than working on several of them simultaneously. Large, multijob submissions to the same computer could make the queue extremely long and frustrate users.

Designers of computers had devised multitasking hardware in order to achieve much greater performance. But up to this point making use of that capability had not yet reached the software world. Much of a computer's potential lay idle when any given program was being executed. Time-sharing software would change all that by coordinating multiple programs running at the same time. So access to this promising technology in tandem with applications and professional consulting expertise made CEIR a company of great interest. For their part, the people in CEIR recognized in Control Data the innovative environment in which their technologies could reach full commercial realization.

But within the CEIR organization lay a hidden gem that would outshine the original motivation for its acquisition. There is serendipity as well as grief in the acquisition world. In this case the serendipity came in the form of the American Research Bureau. CEIR had acquired American Research Bureau (ARB), a company founded and run by a skilled research statistician who was convinced he could devise a radio and television audience measurement service superior to that of the well-established A. C. Nielsen Company. ARB struggled, and by 1968, the year Control Data acquired CEIR, it had never known a positive bottom line.

In 1970 Control Data set up Services as a formal corporate business unit, and ARB became part of my direct responsibility. Since it was a conspicuously unprofitable part of my group, it was a matter for immediate attention. I undertook a field tour of ARB's major customers and for the first time came face-to-face with the comic strip character Pogo's famous maxim: "We have met the enemy and he is us." I had never realized just how fortunate I had been in the market environment of my previous experiences. Customers may have had problems, but the company's computers and associated services were viewed with admiration, and there was a mutual desire to do well. Not so with ARB's customers. They just wanted it to go away, even though they were most desirous of a different alternative to the A. C. Nielsen Company. In successive tongue-lashings from customers covering a period of ten days, I thought over and over: "How could an organization so absolutely and completely offend its customers?" Something had to change—no, *everything* had to change, and that started at the top.

I badly needed someone steeped in the broadcast industry. I knew where to go. That contact was the result of yet another acquisition, an automatic ticketing company named Ticketron. Tom Moore had been president of ABC. In a bitter takeover attempt of ABC Tom was the insider favoring the merger. When it failed, Tom was out and, thanks to Kirk Kerkorian and the Bronfman family interests, he was given a "holding pattern" position as chairman of Ticketron. Control Data bought out the Bronfman interest in Ticketron, and Tom and I became good friends. I sought Tom's advice regarding a top executive in the broadcasting industry. Tom had the answer: Ted Shaker had been president of ABC Television under Tom. Ted and I met in New York, and I knew I had my answer. Ted took over ARB and, by concentrating on customer needs rather than just statistics methodology, within a year had transformed it into a vibrant, customer-oriented, and highly profitable enterprise. In terms of return on assets, ARB soon became Control Data's most profitable services business. More than that, it once again reminded me of a lesson I had known since my earliest days in the industry: high-performance computing is fascinating, but it is in its application to information service *needs* that true added value was to be realized. Thank you, Ted Shaker! It was a lesson not to be forgotten.

SBC

Life in the early computer industry seemed to be nothing but opportunity. Growth and evolution of basic technologies in semiconductor and magnetic media were taking place at a dizzying pace. And new opportunities for new applications of those technologies in new directions were opening at such a rate as to provide the rosiest of prospects for the future. One factor and one alone, however, overshadowed the evolving industry. Through bundling of software and support services into its equipment lease pricing policy, at every turn IBM thwarted the ambitions of would-be participants in services. In 1968 those in Control Data, coping with day-to-day sales and marketing and attempting to fashion winning strategies for the future, decided to challenge these anticompetitive practices. The facts were not only obvious to us, but also well documented in our historical files that had been accumulated over the previous decade. Relief as a result of direct action by the U.S. Justice Department or the FTC seemed a remote possibility at best. We determined that a private antitrust suit against IBM was a necessary course of action in spite of the obvious difficulties, resource demands, and daring it required. In December 1968 that antitrust suit was filed.

A larger goal of the lawsuit was a basic restructuring of the nature of competition in the industry, not by a breakup of IBM as some advocated, but by ensuring that the burgeoning markets for software and services would be available to us and other would-be participants. That was a lofty goal. At the same time the more important goal was to gain specific and immediate enhancements for Control Data's business.

The story of the lawsuit is a fascinating one, but much too long to be a part of the narrative of this book. What was of particular interest to Control Data was the augmentation of its newly emerging businesses in data processing, consulting, and education services. As the opportunity to settle the lawsuit emerged four years after its filing, the terms of the settlement became of great strategic importance. During the negotiation IBM put forth the choice between two acquisitions at a price far below their actual value. These were the

Service Bureau Corporation (SBC) and Science Research Associates (SRA). The former was a data processing company providing payroll and other commercial data processing services, as well as time-sharing services. SRA was a well-established purveyor of education materials. The choice was to broaden the scope of Control Data's existing data centers business and provide critical mass to its time-sharing services, or to provide a much needed revenue underpinning to the PLATO education services. With regard to PLATO, there was the crucial need to provide financial sustenance for the anticipated long haul process of demand creation for computer-based education. SRA was not a computer-based service, but it was an established and recognized player in education. On the other hand, SBC could perhaps provide the tipping point for Control Data's computation services that would lead to market dominance.

Bill Norris and I discussed the issue. Our counterproposal was that we would take *both* and sacrifice some of the other monetary considerations under negotiation. I will never forget the knowing smile on IBM negotiating team leader Paul Rizzo's face when he said, "No, Bob, it's one or the other, not both."[3] It was to be SBC, because of its relative importance in bringing critical mass to the data services business. SBC brought both technology in network systems and knowledgeable people to Control Data. Henry (Hank) White, who was SBC's number two executive, ultimately became an executive vice president of Control Data, and Dave White, then responsible for SBC's time-sharing business would become the executive in charge of all Control Data's data services businesses.

Acquisitions are a fragile undertaking. If trust is the essential ingredient of successful collaboration, eliciting trust in the people of an acquired company is an even more tenuous matter. SBC was run by Control Data as a totally separate business unit. It did not report to me, the executive responsible for Control Data's services business, but directly to the CEO, Bill Norris. It was a full five years—and only after the departure of SBC's president, Jack Williams, who returned to a successful career at IBM—that SBC was melded into Control Data's services business unit, and then it was Hank White who became the executive responsible for all data services. Not only did SBC provide the anticipated critical mass, it was to be the core of the "Employer Services" business unit that gave Control Data needed profitability to survive the expensive transition from hardware to services by the end of the 1980s. What gave Control Data this key boost toward becoming a services business was its deft handling of the computerized database of IBM's transgressions. Innovation in lawsuits can be fully as important as innovation in supercomputers.

Control Systems Division, Daystrom Corporation

Control Data's first prospectus clearly stated that the company would engage both in the electronic data processing market and in "automatic control for industrial, scientific and military uses."

True to this stated intent, one of the earliest acquisitions, April 1, 1960, was Minneapolis-based Control Corporation. Founded in 1935, Control Corporation supplied supervisory control systems for electric utilities and for natural gas and petroleum pipeline operators. Several other related acquisitions were added over five years to form the Industrial Group.[4]

These organizations engaged in a variety of industrial control systems, data acquisition systems, analog to digital conversion equipment, and wastewater treatment and air pollution monitoring and control systems. The Industrial Group was early evidence of Control Data's interest in being something other than one more digital computer manufacturer. These early "application systems" led the way and were important steps toward developing markets for Control Data in the utility, manufacturing, and leisure industries. Daystrom Corporation's Control Systems Division (CSD) became part of that group in August 1963. Control Data brought sales and marketing capability that CSD, as a small stand-alone business, could not afford. The operations of CSD enjoyed a high degree of autonomy due to the nature of its product and its La Jolla, California, location. Though remote from Control Data's headquarters in Minneapolis, the business itself became an integral part of the Industrial Group's strategy. Paul Miller, the general manager of CSD, was promoted to an executive position in the parent company, holding increasingly responsible positions for computer systems and corporate sales and marketing, which included all the company's international sales and marketing subsidiaries, and finally serving as chairman and CEO of Commercial Credit Company.

For a firsthand account of this acquisition we have the following excerpts from the memoirs of N. L. (Nate) Dickinson:[5]

"Selling [for] a small company is a very broadening experience. You visit the accounting department and General Manager to discuss costs and prices, you go to manufacturing to find out why the computer is late, then you go to the programming department to find out why the software is late, and then to the quality control department to find out why they are holding up the entire system. It goes on and on. Almost all of these were experiences that I had never had—I loved it.

"When CDC bought us (1963), their annual revenue was $63,000,000 and they had 3500 employees. When I retired from CDC in 1984, their revenue was $5,000,000,000 and they had 60,000 employees. CDC had a very aggressive strategy for growth by acquisition in the 1960s and at roughly the same time they bought us they bought a similar company in Los Angeles called AD-COMP. They did pretty much what we did except they didn't build their own computers; they bought 160-A's from CDC and then they built the input/output equipment and wrote the software. Both of us however, were in the on-line, real-time, monitoring and control computer business. In late 1965 CDC merged these two divisions into one with the surviving location being La Jolla but the surviving management being from ADCOMP.

"I was promoted to Assistant to the General Manager. It worked out well. I liked Joe Looney and he liked me. He was older than I and an energetic, risk-taking entrepreneur who had started ADCOMP with his and some investors' money. Consequentially he knew a great deal about a number of things that I knew almost nothing about. I had not, at 40 years of age, ever managed anything except myself—give or take some efforts to manage [my wife] Elizabeth and the kids. I knew almost nothing about budgets, salary structures, hiring and firing, profits and losses, assets—there was a long list.

"We had [several] crises that year. The Director of Manufacturing quit and I spent several months as Acting Director of Manufacturing. Then Director of Quality Assurance quit and I spent several months as Acting Director of Quality Assurance. Then the Director of Programming quit, and guess what, I acted in that position for a few months. All in all, it was a very worthwhile time for me."

The acquisition and combination of Control Systems and ADCOMP, as Nate's memoirs indicate, need not be traumatic. Through careful and caring management of the people involved the experience can provide them with the opportunity to grow and prepare them for greater responsibility. The Control Systems Division of Daystrom was an especially rich source of executive talent. In addition to Paul Miller and Nate, their colleague E. J. (Manny) Otis also became an important executive in the company and played key roles in its international expansion in Europe, Asia, the Middle East, and the USSR.

Computer Division, Bendix Corporation

Within two years of the delivery of the first Model 1604, forty-one of these million-dollar systems had been installed. This early success overshadowed another surprising story, that of the small derivative computer the 160 (later

160A). By 1962 more than two hundred had been installed. However, this computer required a different mode of installation and ongoing maintenance than did its larger and more expensive brother, the 1604. These differences included computer installations over a much wider geographic area, smaller-scale installations, and no need for on-site, resident maintenance people. At first the company had attempted to control these new challenges by limiting sales of the 160 to the geographic regions surrounding 1604 installations. This proved unfeasible because the widespread appeal of this small but very capable computer soon resulted in a much broader market. Clearly there was a need for a maintenance support service not available within Control Data.

The Bendix Computer Division had experienced great success with its small-scale computer, the G-15. It had also developed the infrastructure necessary to support several hundred G-15 installations. Here was a potential ready-made answer to the maintenance requirement of the growing number of 160 and 160A computers.

As it happened, Bendix, with upwardly mobile eyes, had launched into the mainframe market with its Model G-20. This proved to be not only technologically difficult, but financially disadvantageous. The parent company was open to a solution. Control Data's offer to buy the division for stock had great appeal as a solution to the problem. Because of a high price/earnings ratio, stock was also a cheap form of "cash" for Control Data. As a result of this acquisition, with one stroke Control Data acquired an essential complementary asset, that of a support system of top quality for its rapidly growing installed base of computers.

The Bendix product lines, the G-15 and G-20, were simply phased out. This was achieved in an orderly although, admittedly, not a perfectly smooth fashion. As an interesting sidebar, two executives who were not part of the acquired operation but who were given responsibility for managing it would later become key members of the top executive team at Control Data. John Lacey became general manager of the company's Standard Systems Division, president of the Education Company, and, subsequently, executive vice president of technology. John played a key role in the company's collaborative undertakings with NCR and the groundbreaking consortium MCC. Bob Schmidt would become the corporate vice president of marketing and sales and later, as vice chairman, would be responsible for collaborations with the Soviet Union.

As with any acquisition there are hidden assets. In this instance they included Bendix sales operations in Mexico, Japan, and Canada. Coincidentally, the international aspects of the Bendix acquisition also helped launch my own rise in the company. The Mexico connection was a manufacturers' representative who had sold a G-20 to the University of Mexico. This representative, who had come to Mexico from Chicago, achieved remarkable results. Only later did we learn that both his presence in Mexico and his success with the university were achieved because of his connections in the Mexican Communist Party. In Japan Bendix's distributor was C. Itoh & Co. This connection provided Control Data an entry into that tightly circumscribed market. The third key international asset of the Bendix acquisition was its equity stake in Computing Devices of Canada, Inc. This company would provide both an entree into the Canadian military systems market and much more substance to our early sales expansion into Canada. Computing Devices became a wholly owned subsidiary in 1969 and ultimately a major part of the company's Government Systems Group. In fact, the name of that group was later changed to Computing Devices International.

Someone had to look after these widely dispersed operations. With little logic other than expediency, that task was given to me, along with the title of director of international operations. In addition to these direct sales operations, I was supposed to organize technical support for the new European operations and provide home office administrative support for all these organizations. With this conglomerate mess of responsibilities I reported to the corporate vice president, marketing, whose authority did not include the European operations. They were headquartered in Switzerland and reported directly to Bill Norris. Suffice it to say that for me it proved to be an intriguing learning opportunity: I discovered the subtleties of pursuing global enterprise and, more important, learned to deal with the intricacies of relationships among a set of truly iconoclastic corporate executives.

In contrast with the peripheral equipment OEM strategy that encompassed many acquisitions and strategic alliances, computer systems strategy continued as a "make" strategy deriving from the core competency of the founders. The Bendix acquisition was not growth in terms of revenues, but rather acquisition of complementary capabilities necessary for an effective maintenance organization. This acquisition not only brought talented people, but it also served as a vehicle for executive growth both for the individuals in the acquired company and for those such as Bob Schmidt, John Lacey, and me who were given new and weightier responsibilities. This was not mere happenstance, but rather a guiding principle of Control Data's acquisitions. The technology, the complementary capabilities, or the market access gained via acquisition will most likely attenuate or disappear over time. But given a chance to grow, the people involved can go on to new innovations and new responsibilities.

Commercial Credit Company

The Bendix acquisition was an important step in acquiring an important complementary capability. Five years later, in 1968, the acquisition of Commercial Credit Company (CCC) provided even more crucial complementary financing capability. Moreover CCC brought substantial earnings and expanded the horizons of this quintessentially Midwestern technology enterprise run by engineers-turned-business-people.

CCC was already more than half a century old when it became part of Control Data. It started in 1912 as a commercial finance company, making loans to businesses that were secured by accounts receivables and inventories—what we know today as asset-based lending. Its rise to corporate eminence began after World War I when it became a major provider of financing for personal automobiles. This began by an association with Maxwell Motor Company and its successor, the Chrysler Corporation. CCC had a preferred, if not exclusive, position with Chrysler as a provider of both wholesale and retail financing. By 1934 Chrysler held a minority equity position in CCC, and the arrangement was broken up only when the federal government initiated antitrust action against GMAC (General Motors), CIT (Ford), and CCC (Chrysler) in 1938. The outcome was a consent decree limiting the incestuous relationships between the finance companies and their auto manufacturer associates.

CCC meanwhile had further expanded the scope of its business to include aircraft financing (Aviation Credit Corp., 1929), factoring of receivables (Textile Banking Co., 1933), bad debt insurance (American Credit Indemnity, 1936), and consumer loans (1939). The onset of World War II brought much of CCC's financing business to a standstill as production of automobiles, trucks, and general aviation aircraft was converted to war production. In response, the company acquired a number of nonfinancial service companies to augment revenues and earnings. The strategy worked well during the war and into the 1950s.

However, by the mid-1960s CCC was a company in trouble. In particular, there were severe losses in its Textile Banking Company and one of its manufacturing businesses acquired during World War II, Grabler Manufacturing Company. Coupled with the decline in its personal automobile financing, the company suffered a significant earnings decline in 1965 and no growth over the next two years. In late 1967 Laurence Tisch of Loew's Inc. contacted Berthold Muecke, the CEO at CCC. Muecke, who was on the verge of retirement, rebuffed Tisch's offer to "discuss mutual interests." In early 1968 Don Jones was elected president and CEO of CCC, with Jess Willard as chairman and CFO. Tisch renewed the pursuit, and on April 25 called to say that Loew's now held just under 10 percent of CCC's 10,614,000 shares and was ready to make a tender offer for the remainder. It was clear that what Tisch had in mind was the potential of a cheap acquisition that could be broken up and sold off with a handsome cash return.

Harold Hammer, vice president of finance at Control Data, had been looking for a year and a half for a financial services firm to acquire. Word of Commercial Credit's plight reached Hammer and following a hurried phone call to Bill Norris at his fishing retreat in northern Minnesota on June 5, 1968, he called Don Jones. Control Data's high multiple stock price allowed it to easily best the offer by Tisch. Just seventy-one days later, the merger between Control Data and Commercial Credit was complete. It was generally referred to internally as a "combination" rather than a "merger."

At a special stockholders meeting on August 15, 1968, at which stockholders voted on the merger, Bill Norris said: "This is a milestone in the affairs of two great companies—Control Data and Commercial Credit—as we unite into one organization. The marriage of the massive technological resources of Control Data with the massive financial resources of Commercial Credit will produce an environment of greatly expanded opportunities for both companies." It was to be a fortuitous and fruitful combination and could be judged to have ensured the long-term future of both businesses.

For Control Data there would be the financial wherewithal to support the leasing of its large-scale computers. Ironically, within five years of the merger the original driving force of Control Data's acquisition of CCC was fast disappearing. The advent of small computers and of third-party leasing companies changed the financial structure of competition from one based on leasing computers by the computer manufacturers to an outright sale business. Moreover, Control Data's source of income was increasingly from its services businesses and the OEM peripherals business. By 1980 financing the lease of Control Data's multi-million-dollar mainframe computers was a minor factor.

For Commercial Credit there would be the needed stability to restructure and rethink its business. Commercial Credit rapidly regained prosperity, and its profits sustained Control Data's business during the difficult years of the early '70s. By the late '70s Control Data's other businesses were flourishing again, and by 1980 profits for the corporation, which had been steadily increasing for the five years following 1975, reached a record $8.45 per share.

As Control Data's strategy continued to evolve and moved along the Technology Food Chain toward services, it continued to search for synergies between financial and information services. For example, marketing to members of professional organizations such as the National Education Association (NEA) teachers' union now included training and certification services as well as financial services. One of the largest businesses was certification of brokers, using PLATO, undertaken at the behest of the National Association of Securities Dealers, a service still in existence.

However, evolution continued along its inexorable path, and by the late '80s it was time for the two businesses to go their separate ways. Among other things, Control Data's stock price did not reflect its having become an information services company. Rather, as a mixture of financial services, computer hardware, and information services the price/earnings ratio was lower than it should otherwise have been. Finally, Control Data's 1985 financial crisis brought matters to a head.

During 1985 and 1986, Control Data and CCC restructured a significant portion of Commercial Credit's business. "Plan B," as it was labeled internally, provided a roadmap for the divestiture of CCC's international leasing business, business loans, Canadian consumer finance, ERA and Relocation Realty real estate services, unprofitable consumer finance business in selected states, factoring, and casualty insurance activities. The timely and efficient execution of this plan during 1985–1986 made the company more profitable and consequently more attractive to potential acquirers. However, the effort to sell was initially unsuccessful and was still ongoing when I was approached by Sanford (Sandy) Weill. Sandy was still seeking a vehicle upon which to build the world-class financial institution of his dream. Sandy proposed an initial public offering (IPO) of Commercial Credit with himself and his management team making a modest investment of $5 million in the company. In November 1986, an IPO of $662 million for slightly more than 80 percent of CCC was completed. Control Data thus obtained a huge cash infusion and Sandy was off on his new adventure. The rest, as they say, is history. Commercial Credit subsequently merged with Primerica and assumed the Primerica name. It then merged with Traveler's Group and assumed that name. Finally Traveler's merged with Citicorp and became today's global financial giant, Citigroup. Commercial Credit (now Citifinancial) is the flourishing consumer finance business of that company.

By any measure the acquisition of Commercial Credit by Control Data was a stellar success. This was by no means a sure thing. *The Economist* article already referenced states: "Most mergers we have looked at were defensive meaning that they were under threat . . . when a company merges to escape a threat, it often imports its problems into the marriage." Before the merger, the outstanding threat to Commercial Credit was an unwanted takeover. The threat to Control Data without CCC was an inability to adequately finance the lease of computers. To that must be added that it is difficult to conceive of two cultures so totally at odds with one another, that of a staid "Eastern Establishment" half-century-old financial business and that of an upstart Midwestern high-technology business little more than a decade old. And yet it worked. It worked because the cultural gap was clearly recognized. There was a conscious and concerted effort by Control Data not to impose its will, its personnel practices and policies, and most of all its management style on the acquired company. Rather, the need to establish *trust* was clearly understood and guided everyday management action.

Don Jones and Jess Willard became respected members of Control Data's board of directors, bringing a financial perspective the board badly needed. Marv Rogers, the CFO at Control Data who succeeded Harold Hammer, became a member of the CCC board and was an active contributor to CCC's revitalized success. Not the least of his contributions: Marv was one of the primary architects of "Plan B," which laid the foundation for the subsequent success of the IPO. Over the ensuing years management talent moved from one organization to the other with comparative ease. In all, an examination of the management rosters over the twenty years the companies were combined shows more than two dozen senior executives who moved from one company to the other.[6] All of these individuals gained experience and perspective that helped make them better executives.

Control Data and Commercial Credit both maintained their original identities and learned to profit from what could be viewed at the start only as a symbiotic relationship, using the best of what each had to offer. Perhaps the story is best surmised by Joe Minutilli, the CEO at the time of Sandy Weill's IPO of the company: "Control Data gained financial stability and Commercial Credit gained the license to *breathe* the fresh air of new ventures and the *room* to succeed (or fail) in them." Commercial Credit was an acquisition that brought very necessary capabilities to the company. Lease financing would not distinguish the company's computers competitively per se, but without it we could not even be in the game.

GUIDELINES FOR SUCCESSFUL ACQUISITIONS

Even if an acquisition passes the test as the best way to attain technology or complementary capabilities, or is the best way to gain market access, success is far from assured. My experience with Control Data's acquisitions drives home three basic principles:

1. At the root of success are people. That is common sense, but in practice it is all too easily, and frequently, overlooked.
2. Like snowflakes no two acquisitions will be the same, and it is attention to subtle variations that make the difference. It doesn't, however, imbue them with snowflakelike beauty!
3. An acquisition must also be managed at the level of the strategic decision maker responsible for the division, business unit, or product line the acquisition is intended to enhance. In the case of an alliance, executive oversight at the appropriate level of responsibility may be temporary given that critical strategic overlap may change or even disappear. In the case of an acquisition the overlap is, by definition, total. If it is not so at the beginning, it must be made so by modification of the respective strategies of acquirer and acquired. And only the person responsible for strategy can make such decisions rationally. The strategic decision maker is not defined by title or level. A division general manager may be nothing more than a "railroader," and someone else may determine where the tracks are going. In some organizations there is strategic autonomy at the level of quite small business units.

Of paramount importance is the necessity of dealing carefully and fairly with the people in the acquired company. And that begins at the top. There are many unknowns, and the level of trust is very low and the level of anxiety is very high—not only at the outset, but also sometimes for an extended period of time. Frequently only the CEO has the necessary perspective, as well as the respect required.

Commercial Credit reported to Bill Norris. His role as CEO was the strategic and operational reason for this. But because he was also chairman of the board of directors, Commercial Credit was placed in a position of particular prestige. To reinforce this, Jess Willard and Don Jones, chairman and CEO of Commercial Credit (CCC), respectively, became members of Control Data's board. CCC retained its own board of directors. This was more than cosmetic attention to CCC's external relationships such as those with its banks. It was dictated by the very different nature of the two businesses and their respective cultures.

Placing responsibility for an acquired company at a level higher than would be thought "normal" may sometimes be necessary because of special circumstances. For example, when, as a result of the settlement of the IBM antitrust suit, SBC was forced into a shotgun marriage with Control Data, it also was kept independent and reported to Bill Norris rather than to me as head of the company's services businesses. This one act demonstrated to the people of SBC just how important they were.

On the other hand, a Control Data executive was immediately put in charge of the computer division of Bendix, and its function of critical interest, the computer maintenance services, was made the responsibility of the company's existing business unit. So the degree of integration is not fixed, but rather depends both on the strategic reason of the acquisition—technology, complementary capability, or market access—*and on the circumstances.*

As has been noted, trust is the essential underpinning of a successful strategic alliance. And it certainly is crucial to a successful acquisition. In a partnership there is opportunity and time for trust to develop. This was the case between Control Data and NCR, as the relationship grew more mutually trusting over time. It is not a simple matter to create and maintain conditions in which the merged entities are able to thrive. At the outset, there is no trust. For the acquirer, there is a feeling of superiority and, all too often, egocentric and poorly disguised gloating. For those acquired there is the exact opposite of those feelings, which are frequently exacerbated by the popular press, which labels them as failures or as deserving targets for business consumption. This is hardly an atmosphere in which trust and mutual effort develop easily.

There are no panaceas for this problem. It requires careful attention to daily attitudes, interchanges, and actions in the old as well as the new organization. A fairly straightforward rule, however—and this again derives from a clear understanding of the necessary or sufficient technology that the acquisition brings—*is to quickly establish a project of clear strategic importance and use the people in the new company to carry out that project.*

Control Data's acquisition of SBC was clearly made under the worst possible psychological circumstance—the settlement of a bitter and protracted antitrust lawsuit. There was of course lots of executive communication. That is important, but it has to be backed up by substance. With regard to SBC it happened that there was an urgent need for upgrading the company's data communication network. The network was the backbone of the company's data services business and all its internal data processing. Management of this network and its improvement were made a priority project for SBC and its talented managers and specialists in network management. This was a visible and substantive move to put SBC people in an obvious position of trust and importance.

Sometimes shock value is important in dealing with acquisitions, but there is an important distinction between shock and callousness. I was a guest at SBC's first 100% Club for its salespeople after it became part of Control Data. This was in 1973, long before casual attire had penetrated the business world, much less the rigid dress code of IBM. I entered the room attired as I might have been for a Control Data 100% Club—totally casual and wearing a velour pullover of multivaried blue tones. That wasn't shock value—that was dumb. That pullover still hangs in my closet as a personal reminder of executive insensitivity. Ironically, two decades later dress code was one of the visible signals that Lou Gerstner used to signal a new culture for IBM.

If no two acquisitions are exactly the same, then it makes sense to undertake them with flexibility coupled with rigor. One of the most salient and personal dimensions of merged operations concerns employee benefits: an area that requires thoughtful attention. It is more efficient and generally fairer to have all employees working under the same regimen of compensation and benefits. Thus the benefits of acquired employees were normally made to conform to Control Data's benefit plans. Since Control Data was an innovator in regard to employee benefits, this was not a particular problem. However, for Commercial Credit and SBC, the pension plans those organizations had in place at the time of acquisition were significantly different. Control Data had managed to adopt and retain, through a long sequence of federal legislation and IRS rulings, a defined benefit plan with employee contributions to the funding of that plan on a pretax basis. This was a major benefit to the company and still resulted in an attractive employee pension benefit. SBC had a traditional and much more generous defined-benefit plan. There were pros and cons depending on individual circumstances, and so those employees were given a choice. This was not, perhaps, a major item, but a very personal indication to people that their new company cared about them as individuals. Trust is developed in large and small steps. It is possible to be thorough and demanding and at the same time adaptive to the circumstances of each acquisition.

Acquisitions are fleeting sources of competitive advantage. The acquired technology or specific product is soon superseded. A favorable marketing channel or innovative operational process is quickly imitated by competition. The new market, especially if it is visibly attractive, is like a hot spot on a walleye lake—soon surrounded by competitive fisherman. The abiding residual of any acquisition is people: people who will devise new technology and who will refine or replace the old innovative processes with new ones or simply outfish all those competing fishermen.

Retention of talent is certainly not assured no matter how wonderful the acquiring company perceives itself to be. Nor is it a simple matter of monetary incentives or administrative mechanics. In high-growth industries, in particular, the result of an acquisition is to make instant millionaires of many of those acquired. According to their personal inclination, they can either 1) leave and start a new enterprise, or 2) retire to the beach in Hawaii. The only possible remedy for staving off those outcomes is to make sure that they are visibly and personally engaged in the success of their new company, literally and not figuratively.

OBSERVATIONS

Control Data certainly did not make a success—that is, realize the potential—of every acquisition. However, because in each and every case we had an important strategic objective and because we looked at each acquisition as an opportunity for the people involved to be more successful, Control Data had a superior track record. Such was the case with the early acquisition of CEIR and later that of SBC. We succeeded because we convinced the people who were acquired that we cared about them, were sensitive to their insecurities in a new organization, and made them feel necessary and at home.

My friend and colleague John Lacey has said that we deserve a "B+" with regard to acquisitions, and John was always a tough grader. As you look around at all those who must be graded "F," that's no small achievement. The reason for that achievement was that we strove to adhere to three ideas:

In spite of the difficulties and potential sinkholes, acquisition is, for the Strategic Space adventurer, a potentially effective tool: Acquisitions can be used to quickly add vital processes and capabilities that would take too long to put in place by means of step-by-step internal development. The question of acquisition success, however, starts with financial feasibility. Superior performance is the key to having the balance sheet and/or stock price that provides financial feasibility.

Caveat: Acquisition, the "buy" branch of the strategic trichotomy, is overused: It is overused because of impatience and misplaced emphasis on growth. The result of this is all too often a sorry mess. It is overused because of failing to understand the effectiveness of other alternatives, especially the alternative of collaboration and strategic partnership. It is overused simply because it is fashionable to do so. Too often strategic wisdom boils down to "acquire or be acquired." That is sometimes true but not nearly as often as business managers think. More frequently than not, the collaborate option is a better path.

In spite of rhetoric to the contrary, acquisitions fail because companies do not concentrate top to bottom on the people of the acquired company: Even if totally appropriate strategically, acquisitions all too often fail or do not live up to expectations. In particular, they fail because there are not explicit and specific measures put in place to engender trust and engagement. This may take the form of arbitrary imposition of human resource policies, but more frequently it is failing to follow the commonsense expedient of giving people something important to do—and not just important but visibly important to all parts of the total company.

Forego the rhetoric, concentrate on the people.

Chapter 10 "Make": Relying on Internal Resources

Success in a strange country required a curious mixture of open-mindedness and skepticism, capable of adjusting accepted ideas and practices to unfamiliar conditions . . . ingenuity and resourcefulness in the field are so continuous that the casual may not notice them.
—Bernard DeVoto, Introduction to *The Journals of Lewis and Clark*

To appreciate the challenges of the third leg of the strategic trichotomy—"make," or, more prosaically, "just do it yourself"—it is most useful to look at a company's moves to develop markets outside its familiar domestic territory.

The tug of international markets for Control Data's high-performance computers was as strong and adventurous as that which led to the long search for the Northwest Passage. In 1803 Lewis and Clark undertook their defining journey in search of a river connection between the Atlantic and the Pacific. A century and a half later Control Data began its journey of exploration in markets beyond the familiar confines of the United States scientific and engineering community. Discovering and carving out new territory is seductive whether it's land or markets.

WHY ALL THIS BOTHER?

Before taking a clearer look at the global expansion of Control Data's business, it is worthwhile to pause for a moment and think about the *why* of this enormous undertaking.

Once, when asked why he robbed banks, the infamous Willie Sutton replied, "Because that's where the money is!" There was a clear and obvious money opportunity for Control Data in non-U.S. markets. In Control Data's case, however, there were a number of factors beyond mere dollars. It was perceived that competition in global markets from giant IBM would be mitigated by foreign government concerns about IBM's market dominance. Control Data had already become a favorite of the close-knit global scientific community.

Product design and development costs were huge relative to the company's size. It was desirable to amortize those costs over as extensive a market as possible. Product performance requirements were global in nature.

In short, there was a very real financial *pull–push* at work. Each incremental revenue dollar from international expansion was extremely profitable from a pure R&D perspective. There were additional costs, of course, but they were moderate relative to development costs. Later the appeal of low cost manufacturing for various computer components and for peripheral equipment products became an additional tug from the global arena.

The global expansion question for Control Data, then, was never really *if* nor *when;* the only question was *how.* The problem of market access and the clear need for resources considerably greater than those available within a start-up company with revenues less than $50 million strongly suggested collaboration as the mechanism of choice in this strategic move. The attempt for an alliance with Philips, however, did not reach fruition. So by mid-1962 the company was proceeding on its own to set up a European marketing operation. Thus the initial and major strategic step of the company was neither acquisition nor joint venture, but rather expansion by means of its internal technological, financial, and human resources. And it would require a lot of marketing and administrative resources—money and people.

The person who had been chosen to explore the possibilities for expansion into Europe was Ed Strickland, vice president and treasurer of the company. He saw this as an opportunity not only for Control Data, but also for himself. And so it was that in the fall of 1962 an "international" operation was established in Lucerne, Switzerland, with Ed as its president. He had a small team of only four U.S. expatriates and three Swiss administrative and clerical people.

In the area of marketing expenditures, things were straightforward. The company would start up and grow its global operations within the limitations set by its internally generated revenues and profits. The growth might not be as rapid as the potential permitted, but among all of us there was a deep belief in the company's internal capacity for growth. This confidence was not misplaced, for the creativity and productivity of the sales people attracted to Control Data's international operations were no less than those of the technical people attracted to its computer development operations.

Country-level marketing and sales operations were quickly set up in Switzerland, Germany, Sweden, Holland, England, and France, all of them headed by newly recruited Europeans. The first major sale of this organization was realized within a few months: a Model 1604 computer for the Danish organization Regnecentralen. Before the end of the decade this handful of expatriate Americans and the non-U.S. people they attracted to the company were producing $150 million a year in revenues.

Administration and organizational aspects of international expansion were more problematic. From a corporate management view the business units with profit responsibility were its product divisions. Their results—revenues and profits—were measured on a worldwide basis. Dealing with customs duties, taxes, and the like was left to the international subsidiaries. Naturally, each subsidiary had to maintain appropriate legal entity financial statements. In most instances this meant accounting and record-keeping in a tri-mode: one for host country financial reporting purposes, one for tax purposes, and finally the necessary accounting records to allow the product division to do worldwide consolidation. This was all reasonably straightforward and effective when the principal products involved were high-performance, large-scale computers. Relatively speaking, the transactions were small in number and very large in value.

There were complications, however. First, in the eyes of the host country government, Control Data's country manager legally was viewed as the person responsible for all the company's affairs in the country, including those related to profits and taxes. The company's product division general managers simply regarded that person as the sales manager for that territory. Moreover the compensation plan for country managers was strictly a sales compensation plan. This made for considerable tensions as to exactly who had profit and loss responsibility for the country, not to mention overall business strategy.

Second, there also was the need to coordinate the necessary technical support from the product divisions. And third, there were myriad logistical, human resources policy, and other administrative challenges that had to be managed and coordinated. In short, from a pure product point of view, international markets were appealing, and we were able to attract talented sales and marketing people in other countries with ease. Beyond that, matters became a Byzantine maze of conflicting governmental policies and a thicket of corporate administrative issues. To address this mess, a corporate "International Operations" office, of which I was named director, was established in 1963. It proved to be quite a learning experience for a thirty-two-year-old mathematician-programmer. Almost as an afterthought, it was subsequently decided that the responsibility for any international marketing operations outside of Europe should also be put under this office. This included the Canadian marketing subsidiary, a manufacturer's representative in Mexico, the Australian marketing subsidiary, and a distributor, the C. Itoh Company, in Japan. I was permitted to increase my staff of two to three. These three people, Wil French, Bob Anderson, and Phylis Bjur, were the unsung but truly heroic laborers in facilitating Control Data's international expansion.

None of this was quite as irrational as it seems in retrospect, nor certainly as it sometimes seemed to those involved at the time. The expansion into markets outside the United States was rooted in two facts: first, the company's great strength was high-performance computers. This would continue to be the driving force of the company's early success, and that innovation was firmly rooted in the U.S. organization. Second, when endeavoring to get something new started, it was frequently necessary to explore multiple approaches and seize opportunities as they arose without overly worrying about structure; that would come in due time.

Revenues from operations outside the United States grew from zero in 1963 to more than $300 million in 1973. It would be untrue to say that each and every dollar in international revenues generated in that decade had a special tale of its own, but it surely did seem that way to those of us participating in this particular substory of Control Data's journey in Strategic Space.

THE CHALLENGE OF GOVERNMENT POLICY

Of the many forces that bedevil the adventurer in Strategic Space, none is more volatile and unpredictable than that of governmental policy and action. Technology exerts a highly positive and exciting thrust, while economic and financial factors impose their demanding constraints. The sociodemographic force lies deceptively quiet, just waiting to exact its inevitable disruptive power as generations change and society absorbs the technologies of the precedent era. But the force created by government, that seemingly remote and uninterested constructor of the framework in which all business activity exists, is as fickle and unpredictable as the unknown with which Lewis and Clark had to cope. One reason the winds of government policy and action are so unpredictable is that, as a practical matter for the Strategic Space adventurer, there is no such thing as "the government." Rather, there are a multitude of executive agencies, departments, and commissions with conflicting missions and charters. The U.S. Departments of State, Defense, Energy, and Commerce, for example can be quite at odds on matters that directly affect business strategy, particularly global strategies. In addition, there's the U.S. legislative labyrinth. And that is just for starters. There are, in addition, conflicting policies and priorities of the various ministries within and between countries.

In the early stages of Control Data's expansion into international markets, the biggest hurdle was U.S. export policy administration. Later there were greater obstacles, and we will turn to those in the next chapter. The system of export controls started in 1949 in response to the Cold War with the Soviet Union. The purpose was to deter or, if possible, prevent the Soviet Union and other Communist countries from acquiring advanced weaponry and the technology to build weaponry, and Control Data was seeking to export products employing some of the most advanced technology of the time. Export policy was based on the assumption that the West needed to prevent loss of its technological lead not only from stealth (espionage) but also from its purchase by means of commercial transactions. The United States adopted legislation known as the Export Administration Act and through a coordinating committee (COCOM) of NATO attempted to rationalize the commercial export policies and transactions of the Western allies. The Export Administration Act required that export of products such as Control Data's computers and related equipment would be permitted only with a separate site license for each sale, an "Individual Validated License" (IVL). *The IVL made it necessary to completely specify the customer and the customer's intended use of the computer, as well as where it would be physically installed.* Interpretation of whether a proposed export license would be granted, and whether it was contrary to national security interests, was not determined by formula or specification but by the judgment of individuals—a bureaucratic nightmare of gargantuan proportion.

Export licenses were administered by the Department of Commerce, but the actual review and permission involved individuals within the Department of State, the Atomic Energy Commission, the Central Intelligence Agency (CIA), the National Security Agency (NSA), the Department of Defense (DOD), and, in many instances, various military and intelligence units of these departments. The State Department viewed export licenses as leverage in implementing administration foreign policy. The Commerce Department viewed the matter in an economic context, that is, export as part of corporate health and the creation of jobs. From the DOD point of view, it was simply a matter of military security and maintaining technological superiority by the denial of products to others. Consensus, let alone consistent guidelines, was a fanciful dream. Later, after years of extraordinary intraindustry effort in which Control Data played a leading role, there evolved something known as "the PDR" that provided a formula for ascertaining an acceptable level of computer performance for export purposes. Those computers with a PDR rating below a certain level could be exported under a "general license," that is, one that was not customer-, application-, and site-specific. Those with a PDR above that level still required an IVL.

Computer export policy and issuance of licenses became a poster child of U.S. foreign policy. From Control Data's perspective foreign policy as it affected export licenses fell into three eras. The first was the pre-1978 era, during which the original anti–Soviet Union sentiment guided export policy although there was a certain flexibility developing after President Nixon's 1972 visit to the USSR. During this period, however, export policy was also used as a club against nonsignatories of the Nuclear Non-Proliferation Treaty, such as France and India.

The second period, roughly 1978–1988, commenced with the coming of the Carter administration and his national security adviser, Zbigniew Brzezinski. The Russian invasion of Afghanistan simply brought trade with Eastern Europe to a standstill. Export policy under the Carter administration had the effect of almost destroying Control Data's hard work of the previous ten years in Eastern Europe. This state of affairs continued into the Reagan administration. After 1984 it again was possible to get IVLs for nonsignatory nations to the Nuclear Non-Proliferation Treaty.

The third period began in 1989 with the Soviet withdrawal from Afghanistan and Soviet president Gorbachev's dual policy of glasnost and perestroika. It was a time that was characterized by greater appreciation of technology evolution and diffusion. A far cry from the state of affairs in the early '60s.

Through this whole saga we were relentless in the push for export licensee rulings that were based on fact rather than on fear and prejudice. We were almost always pushing for sale of computers with a PDR greater than COCOM guidelines. But we did this by working with government agencies and legislators. I do not recall a single instance of a Control Data person disparaging the people in a government agency. Rather, the attitude was respect for their position and at the same time determination to meet our goals. To succeed, we needed to underscore discussion that was based on facts of the technological state of the art and the customer's access to equivalent products and technology from other sources. We needed to build a long-term relationship with the people in various government agencies that was not prejudiced by misinformation, half-truths, or irrelevancies. We pursued and pressed for these goals and made our arguments through continuing interchange at all levels. I still remember sitting down with Alexander (Sandy) Trowbridge while he was Secretary of Commerce and trying to explain the technological obsolescence of some four-year-old computers.

If Control Data was determined to make its points there were those equally determined to refute them. Among the more outspoken were Senator Henry "Scoop" Jackson of Washington, and Richard Perle, an intelligent and highly articulate man who, as assistant secretary of defense, carried great weight in matters of foreign trade, particularly trade with the Soviets.[1] Dealing with the objections of these people was a continuous and ongoing process that frequently called for compromise on the level of computers that could be shipped. That, in turn, meant going back and reselling the Soviets on computers of less capability.

The essential point here is that the *"government's view"* is elusive because, in practice, it is made up of *individuals* who have different predilections and responsibilities. Tactical success, much less strategic success, cannot be gained by hand wringing, decrying, or denigrating. It comes from honest engagement and respect.

MAKING IT ALL HAPPEN

Within a few years of the 1962–1963 start-up of international operations, prestigious customers in science and technology around the world owned Control Data computers. These included Australia, the Commonwealth Scientific and Industrial Research Organization (CSIRO); Denmark, Regnecentralen; France, Electricité de France, and two French AEC installations; Israel, The Ministry of Defense (DOD), and Weizmann Institute; Germany, the German Weather Service and several universities including the Max Planck Institute and Aachen; Canada, the Canadian Atomic Energy Commission (AECL) and Sir George

Williams University; Mexico, the University of Mexico, Taiwan, and several research-oriented government agencies; India, the Tata Institute of Fundamental Research; and even the USSR, at the Nuclear Research Institute, Dubna. A sampling of these stories will illuminate the technological force at work in Strategic Space: technology, both the superior technology of Control Data's computers, coupled with the science and the technology needs of important worldwide customers, was a most favorable force.

The German Weather Service

One of the customers just mentioned will serve to illustrate the positive pull of technological need. The German Weather Service (GWS) was a truly prestigious customer and an integral part of the worldwide network of weather-related computer installations. GWS played a major role in establishing Control Data's global reputation.

By the mid-twentieth century the need for better and more reliable weather information was an important factor in the operation of more and more businesses, from agribusiness to transportation. It also was important in anticipating and dealing with potential weather-related disasters, and it was a crucial factor in military responsiveness. To meet this economic need, governments worldwide had become increasingly proactive. In doing so they provided an ever expanding, truly global market for large-scale, high-performance computing.

The GWS first became a Control Data customer with the procurement of the 3800 and 3400 computers. These were continuously upgraded, and by 1976 GWS was using Cyber 172, 173, and 176. In an interview Dr. Reiner Lamp, then director of the GWS Computer Center, explained the importance of advanced computing to the effectiveness of their weather forecasts: "Attention to weather and environmental factors is an important function in Germany. Our central position in Europe makes us a hub for intercontinental flights. We have a strong agriculture industry and rely on rivers and harbors for transportation and shipping. Consequently, accurate, timely weather forecasts are vital to our economy."

Using Control Data computers, the GWS was able to decrease the grid point distance in its weather models by 50 percent and to increase the number of the atmospheric levels by more than one-third. By today's standards this grid point distance of some 190 kilometers and 9 atmospheric levels is modest, but at the time they were gigantic improvements. And they were so impressive that Control Data computers became a worldwide standard.

French Atomic Energy Commission

Another global need for high-performance computing relates to nuclear energy. Here matters became far more arcane. Not only are computers essential to the study of the underlying science of high-energy physics, they are essential to designing applications with both benign and catastrophic potential. In spite of fears and complex management issues, nuclear energy is a major source of electric power and therefore an integral and positive part of a country's economy. Nuclear energy can also, of course, be used in the manufacture of weapons and deployed with destructive intent. Nowhere was this clearer to us than in the international marketplace. The example of the French AEC will serve as a curious and interesting example.

The French government had an aggressive and multifaceted national program in atomic energy. First, they had a need for nuclear powered electric generating plants. In those pre-Chernobyl, pre-Three Mile Island days the appeal of low-cost, clean nuclear power was very great indeed, and France was determined to be a leader in reducing its dependence on fossil fuels. As it turned out, they have been very successful in that regard, ultimately generating some 72 percent of the country's electricity by means of nuclear power. But France also was determined to be a member of the nuclear weapons club, thereby enhancing its status as a world power, so it had an extensive nuclear weapons development program. All this was supported by extensive basic research in high-energy physics. France participated in CERN, the European Center for Nuclear Research, but it had its own research agenda as well. For these reasons the desire to have the most powerful computers available was very great. The growing dominance of Control Data computers within scientific circles was well known to the scientists and administrators within the French research establishment. It was a major opportunity for Control Data's new European operation.

The first French atomic weapon was tested in 1960, but there remained much to be done. The French government refused to sign the Nuclear Test Ban Treaty that had been fostered by the United States and to which sixty-one other nations, including Britain and the Soviet Union, had subscribed. One way the U.S. State Department could bring pressure on the French was to deny export licenses for the high-performance computers they so desired.

On the economic front, the United States and France were also in a contretemps. There was fear of U.S. hegemony—especially with regard to economic issues—an attitude that continues today. The growing dominance of U.S.-based firms and the strength of the U.S. dollar were sources of continual discussion and concern. One thing that entered into this picture was the matter of the gold standard, which the United States continued to use to back its currency. If all this seems far removed from the matter of atomic energy research and Control Data computers, it was not. It was all perilously intertwined between the various ministries of the French government and various departments of the U.S. administration, particularly State, Commerce, and Treasury.

In 1964 we delivered a CDC 3600 to AEC Vaujours, a weapons research center. The problem surfaced, or exploded, about a year later when we received an order from that customer for an add-on central memory. A request for export license was filed with Commerce in the same manner as for the original license. And all hell broke loose! It turned out that the original license application had specified not AEC *Vaujours,* but AEC *Saclay,* a civilian nuclear research center. At the time of the second request, Commerce already knew that the machine had been delivered to Vaujours instead of Saclay but, for some unknown and inexplicable reason, had kept quiet. Some time later Gerard Beaugonin, president of Control Data France, was paid a visit by two men from the U. S. Department of Commerce, who wanted to tell him that our executives in Minneapolis were irresponsible. Gerard remembers asking them to leave his office if they had only insults to deliver.

CDC France then entered into a very difficult period, as no export licenses were granted because those responsible for them in the Commerce Department no longer trusted the accuracy of Control Data's IVL license application for France. This situation became desperate after we got an order from Electricité de France (EDF), the French power bureau, for a large 6600 system. The monthly rental was $500,000. There was a cancellation clause in case an export license could not be obtained before a certain date. At this time Hugh Donohue, an executive in the company's Washington, D.C., office, was charged with solving the problem. We learned what had probably happened with the first license negotiation, as Gerard recalled: "Somebody at State or Commerce said, 'Why don't you ask for a license for Saclay?' I suspect this was not exactly what was said, but rather an interpretation of a comment from the official saying, 'If it was for Saclay you would not have had a problem.' This was interpreted as an invitation for dissembling. No one will ever know. Everyone was clearly embarrassed. So I always thought it was a mistake." After more than a year of waiting for EDF the situation was resolved after a meeting between the French Minister of Finance and the U. S. administration. There was a quid pro quo vis-à-vis the U.S. and French differences having to do with trade issues. Gerard recalled, "I remember considering leaving Control Data at that time, but the negotiation, the details of which we will never know, ended our agony in France."

The stories of GWS and the French AEC have illustrated both the positive pull of technology in assisting global expansion as well as the barriers posed by government policy. The next example will show the positive effect that the "government as customer" can have with respect to global expansion.

A time-honored way for a company with limited resources to approach the unknown problems and unquantified size of international markets is export using distributors. Using distributors is, of course, a variant of the "buy" strategy and can be a useful approach prior to making the full "do it yourself" commitment. Such was the case with Control Data and Australia.

AUSTRALIA

E. L. Heymanson & Co. Pty. Ltd. was an archetypal manufacturers' agent. The owner, Ernest Heymanson, was in his seventies at the time of Control Data's early global expansion. Heymanson had grown from an importer of commodities and textiles to be the representative of Lockheed, North American Rockwell, and Curtis-Wright. Foreseeing the inevitable consolidation in the commercial airplane business, he decided to move into computers. Lacking any computer expertise in his organization, Mr. Heymanson acquired it in the person of E. T. (Trevor) Robinson, a scientist of considerable talent but who had to learn marketing and sales from scratch. The following are a few excerpts from Trevor's story of Control Data Australia.[2]

"Not many months into his new job, Robinson told [Heymanson] that there seemed to be only one company that met the bill and that was a little group in the United States, in Minneapolis, called Control Data Corporation, who seemed to be producing the sort of equipment that the Australian Government, and particularly the scientific and defense sectors, would be looking for."

Neither Heymanson nor Control Data's management had heard of the other. Trevor was dispatched to Minneapolis. He continued:

"To say that Control Data was bemused by the proposed arrangement is an over-simplification; the senior executives concerned had never been to Australia, they doubted there was a computer market of any description, let alone for Control Data's very powerful 1604 computer, and of course they wondered whether any local support would be available. Fortunately, one of Control Data's executives was an Englishman, John W. Lacey, who had worked with

Trevor Robinson at a British Government research establishment and, hopefully with a clear conscience, was able to reassure the company.

"Toward the end of the year two senior executives of Control Data arrived in Australia. One was Frank C. Mullany, who was the number two man to William C. Norris, and the other was Raymond C. Whitney, who was responsible for Control Data's Western Region. When questioned later as to the extent of his territory, Ray Whitney said that his territory extended westward from the Rockies around the world to the Eastern seaboard of the United States. Whitney was a superb salesman with unlimited confidence and no doubt believed his answer."

In January 1962 Heymanson became a Control Data distributor. Robinson went on:

"The Corporation's advice was to stay away from trying to concentrate on selling 1604s. Robinson felt differently. . . . He felt that the market was for large computers and, after having an opportunity to see the 3600, he decided that the Australian Bureau of Census and Statistics, the Commonwealth Scientific and Industrial Research Organization (CSIRO) and the Postmaster General's Department (Telecom) were all suitable candidates. The computer sales team consisted of Robinson, analyst John Barth and secretary Claire Manual; plainly their resources to deal with prospects were limited. This strategy ran against conventional wisdom; the Bureau of Census was regarded as certain to purchase Univac equipment, it was thought that CSIRO would buy a Ferranti Atlas and that Telecom would purchase Honeywell equipment.

"The end result, however, was that both CSIRO and the Bureau of Census and Statistics purchased Control Data equipment in virtually identical configurations which consisted of one 3600 each in Canberra with '160-Z' machines in each of the capital cities. These latter machines were invented for the occasion and a source of consternation when the orders came in. 'Who dreamed these things up?' asked Bob Kisch, Vice President responsible for Engineering.

"No doubt because Control Data at that time was flexible, adventurous and wanted the two 3600 orders, as well perhaps as the 12–15 160-Z orders, they agreed to modify its incipient design to broadly meet the order specification. The machine eventually appeared as the 3200 and was the progenitor of what was called the Lower 3000 (3000L) family.

"These two multi-million dollar orders propelled Control Data into immediate prominence. One senior IBM executive probably echoed the sentiments of many in the industry—'The Government must have rocks in their heads—

Control Data doesn't have a feather to fly with, they don't have any people, how are they ever going to support them?'

"There was good cause for worry. However, the Corporation was more than equal to the occasion. Bob Price, who at that time was a senior systems analyst at the Palo Alto facility, was appointed to take care of the Australian facility as part of a strangely assorted ragbag of responsibilities that covered both Europe and Asia. Bob Price had a strong personality . . . and was a very quick learner. He was not greatly familiar with the international scene, but was more cosmopolitan in his outlook than many of his colleagues in Minneapolis.

"Bob Price saw the need for a resident guru in Australia and recruited Robert S. Barton, a well-known designer known mostly for his work on the Burroughs B5000 machine. Bob Barton brought with him a retinue of two individuals, an engineer, Al Collins, and the other a software man, John Stockman. Barton was knowledgeable, intransigent, mischievous and capable. He charmed the Bureau of Census but he alarmed the CSIRO people. Robinson tells a typical story, which Barton incidentally denies being true. Robinson had cause to complain to Barton about Al Collins interfering with the activities of customer engineers in Canberra and by way of opening up the conversation said to Barton, 'Bob, what is Al Collins' job?' Barton closed his eyes, thought for about half a minute and then said, 'Al Collins is a genius keeper; he looks after me.'"

However that may have been, first-class hardware and software support organizations were established. Trevor concludes:

"With both good engineers and capable analysts, Control Data early began providing a level of excellent support that confounded critics and laid the foundation for much business to come."

This story clearly indicates the importance of the role of government as "customer." Robinson's writings also demonstrate, however, that by judicious use of its role as customer, government can further economic development policy. Trevor Robinson, who went on to become a senior adviser to John Button, Minister for Industry, put it this way.[3]

"In the early 1960s . . . heeding developments overseas, the Commonwealth government . . . realized that the time had come to exploit a new technology where productivity and comparative advantage could be bought off the shelf— or so it was thought! The Weapons Research Establishment, the ANZ Bank, the Defense Department, the Bureau of Census and Statistics and CSIRO all acquired U.S. manufactured computers. [Thus the government stimulated and] set the pattern for other organizations."

Not that the Australian government would be consistently wise and forward looking in its policies. For example, in the early '80s it instituted a 17.5 percent sales tax on software sales, which was an obvious inhibition to the use of commercially developed software.

OBSERVATIONS

Control Data's expansion into global markets was natural. It was, however, in no way effortless. Organizing the technical support for large, multi-million-dollar systems operating far from their home base was a logistical and training task greater than any the company had faced before. Adopting the company's human resource policies and practices truly did demand "a curious mixture of open-mindedness and skepticism, capable of adjusting accepted ideas and practices to unfamiliar conditions," as was noted in the quotation from De-Voto's book at the start of this chapter. Just as with the design of its computers, and the marketing and selling of those computers, the company attracted extraordinary talent to these administrative challenges. Gene Baker, who was the company's first manager of administration in Europe, took on all these tasks associated with our decision to "just do it yourself." He made it work. Once again, the lesson for management is *people*. Strategy involves choosing one of the "three forks of the Missouri": make, buy, or collaborate. But as we have seen, for each of those strategic forks it is people who make the strategy work.

Chapter 11 Accepting Daring and Unusual Challenges

"Take your hand out of your pocket, slowly," commanded Homa in English, then in Farsi he explained to the guard, "I told him to remove his hand." Knowing that any sudden movement would result in instant death, Homa held his breath and riveted his eyes on the young, nervous guard. He could sense his companion's fear and felt an arm lightly brush his own as the man withdrew his hand. Seeing the empty hand the guard's tense shoulders eased. Homa glanced fleetingly at his companion. The man's features were rigid and his eyes were glued to the gun barrel only inches away from his face.
—From the Memoirs of Carolyn Firouztash

The quote above is a stark reminder that threat of political upheaval and chaotic turmoil in government can transform government influence in Strategic Space from one that is benign and helpful to one that is personal and life threatening. The need for government to provide a reliable framework for economic activity becomes all too obvious when governments are poorly organized, inefficient, or in turmoil.

One of the fundamental roles of government is to champion economic growth. In earlier chapters, I offered glimpses of governments acting to stimulate utilization of advanced technology, such as the U.S. space program's role in procuring integrated circuits, or the Australian government's leadership in the adoption of computers and information technologies. There also were examples of government interventions into economic activity such as the erection of export controls. Before looking at other examples at closer range as illustrations of the interactions between government policy and business strategy, it is necessary to pause to define the role of government from the corporation's perspective in a more systematic fashion.

STRATEGY AND THE ROLE OF GOVERNMENT

The usual functional and structural way to think of government—executive branch, legislative branch, and judicial branch—is not very helpful to the strategist. Rather, it is more useful to think in terms of the *four roles* it plays in business life:

1. Regulator and arbitrator
2. Provider of a framework for, and facilitator of, economic activity
3. Customer for private sector products and services
4. Provider of products and services, that is, a competitor

Regulator and Arbitrator

Free markets and free market transactions have inherent conflicts. These conflicts are resolved by competition, negotiations, and regulations.

Competition is the most straightforward and desirable. If the customer has but one choice—that is, one supplier—the conflict is clearly one-sided. If the customer has multiple choices, the playing field is leveled, innovation is encouraged, and customers benefit.

Negotiation between businesses amounts to a process of mutual self-regulation. Its weakness can lie in grossly unequal power of, or asymmetric knowledge between, the negotiators.

Regulation is dictation of the "rules of transaction" by an overarching authority such as an agency of the government. If not dictation of transaction rules, the government agency at least provides guidelines and a framework for competition and negotiation, and a locus for arbitration of disputes arising from those processes.

In its role of regulator and arbitrator, government is involved in four broad categories of conflict:

Individual interest vs. group interest. This can be protection of competitive rights
for an individual company (for example, antitrust); for individual workers
(labor laws); for individual customers (laws against price fixing).

Societal interests vs. organizational interests. Examples are laws and regulations
regarding environmental protection, health, safety, tax, and taxation.

Interpretation and enforcement of contracts. Without some rigorous enforcement
method, transactions are not only difficult; they simply will be stultified.
This problem plagues those doing business today in Russia and China.

Protection of physical and intellectual property. There are threats both internal and
external to the nation. Physical property protection ranges from laws and law
enforcement with regard to theft and physical abuse to the maintenance of
security through national and international military forces. Protecting intellectual capital is attempted through domestic patent and copyright laws, and
by means of international agreements with respect to those laws.

It is in the roles of regulator and arbitrator that business most frequently encounters government. Too often, as perplexing and onerous as these dealings
can be, they are approached with the wrong mindset. The inclination is to see
government as an obstruction to be evaded and, consequently, the reaction is to
appeal to national sentiments to "get them off our backs." This simplistic attitude lacks understanding as to how things really work, and leads to counter-
productive behavior. It blinds business to the opportunities available to it via
collaborations with government. Control Data's global expansion was greatly
facilitated because of government partnerships in Canada and in Europe. At
the very least it behooves business to actively pursue thoughtful participation in
the governmental regulation and arbitration process. Like any human endeavor, the regulatory process suffers from human frailty and shortsightedness.
But business can help bring perspective and creative thinking to the regulation
process.

The bête noire of legislation and regulation is the law of unintended consequences. All too often legislation, regulation, and executive action produce
consequences that are not only unexpected but may even be contrary to the intent of the original action. Unintended consequences may result from poorly
constructed legislation and regulations, but more frequently it is simply due to
the complexity of the issue. In the example of electric power deregulation in
California both of those factors were present. The result? Not cheaper power
and improved generation technology, but blackouts, higher prices, manipulation and multi-billion-dollar lawsuits! More recent are the still unfolding con-

sequences of the Health Insurance Portability and Protection Act of 1996 (HIPAA), which, in total contradiction to its lofty goal of more portable health insurance, has saddled the health industry and consumers with unnecessary costs and has created new exercises in bureaucratic gymnastics.

It will be interesting, although no doubt burdensome and even painful, to see what will be the unintended consequences of the Sarbanes-Oxley governance reform legislation of 2002.

Provider of a Platform and Framework for Economic Activity

This is a more visible governmental role than regulation and arbitration. The framework within which business is conducted includes monetary and fiscal policy; physical infrastructure, including transportation, energy, and telecommunications; intellectual property systems such as patents; basic research policies; and an extensive array of health and human services. In all of these arenas, the government establishes policies and guidelines; in most of them it is a source of funding, and in some, such as health and human services, electric power generation and distribution, and advanced scientific research, it is itself a provider. For the business strategist what matters is this: effective strategy must be built with an understanding of the impact of these varied governmental activities, and understanding comes from involvement.

In the Control Data story we have seen just how important it was to be a beneficiary of government research policy and to be a supplier to some of the most important research laboratories. We also were a very active participant in the formulation of science and technology policy. This was much more than a lobbying effort, it was one of active collaboration with government, academia, and companies in studying and drafting such policies. Nor was it something left to the company's specialists. Although many of them participated, so did Bill Norris and I. Talks, task forces, and committees easily occupied 25 percent of our time. Results such as the frame-breaking Cooperative Research Act of 1984 (which addressed technological collaboration), improved export guidelines for high-performance computers, and myriad state and local government initiatives in economic development all contributed to the strategic success that Control Data enjoyed.

The essential points again are, first, to recognize that regulatory policy can be an instrument of strategic assistance and, second, that governments can be allies in furthering both corporate and national interests by setting the appropriate policies.

The Government as Customer

Government needs run the gamut from paper clips to computers and consulting and telecommunication services. It was the need for space and defense computers that was so important to the launch and growth of Control Data. There is a widespread belief in business that "doing business with the government" is too hard and should be avoided if possible. Like every market, however, this is a matter of knowledge and expertise. And once more it is not "the government" to whom you are selling, it is to individuals within a particular agency or branch thereof.

In the earliest days of the company, and for many years thereafter, Henry S. (Hank) Forrest was head of our Washington office and set the tone for successful selling to the U.S. government. Of the many Control Data people who sold to government accounts, three will always stand out in my memory: Charles (Chuck) Puglisi, Chuck Weidenfeller, and Bill Sass. These three people knew their business and their customers' needs. To them "the government" was not an unknown monolith to be feared; rather it comprised people with particular needs whom they could help by means of the company's products and services.

The Government as Provider of Products
and Services—in Other Words, as Competitor

The knee jerk reaction is that the government should not compete in the provision of products and services, that such a notion is contrary to free-market economics and therefore to a healthy economy. Again, this is a bit simplistic because thinking that way shuts the door on important strategic possibilities.

No one would deny that an important role of government is to create and enhance an infrastructure for economic growth, or, in everyday terminology, for *job creation.* This task is much more complex than providing appropriate economic or fiscal policy. A healthy job-creating economy requires a skilled and well-educated labor force, it requires assistance in technology diffusion and utilization, and it requires assistance to start-up companies, which are the major source of job creation. In all of these areas, there is the possibility of leveraging private sector innovativeness and entrepreneurship with the public sector capacity for providing essential resources and for building consensus.

The profound lesson of Lewis and Clark's journey can guide us through the wilderness of business strategy. To the innovativeness and daring of these two men were added money and resources supporting their journey. The result was the discovery of economic opportunity that reverberates to this day. Economic growth needs entrepreneurs and new ventures, but they in turn require the opportunity and critical resources for success. President Thomas Jefferson provided those to Lewis and Clark, and enlightened economic leadership can do so today.

GOVERNMENT POLICY AT WORK

Two examples from Control Data's globalization will show, in bold colors, government's role in economic activity: Japan and the countries then known as the Comecon—the USSR and its Eastern European satellites.

Japan

Control Data's venture into the Japanese market is a story of serendipity, ignorance (or, at least, cultural naiveté), and frustration. In my entire business career I never experienced the same degree of strategic disappointment. It afforded an extraordinary, though expensive, learning experience.

The serendipity occurred in March 1963 with the acquisition of the computer division of the Bendix Corporation. The C. Itoh Company in Japan was the distributor for Bendix. The plan was for Control Data to sell its products through a joint venture with C. Itoh, which would operate the business. After a three-year effort that saw little success, a more direct approach was attempted.

In 1966 Control Data incorporated Control Data Far East (CDFE), and in 1967 a Control Data Far East Branch was authorized by the Japanese government to conduct computer marketing and support functions. CDFE was also to assist C. Itoh in its selling effort of other Control Data products such as OEM peripherals. With regard to data services, in 1968 Control Data and Nippon Computer Center, Limited, (NCC) agreed to establish a 50/50 joint venture for a data center in Tokyo using a CDC 6600. In 1969 the Japanese government allowed the import of the 6600, but only for NCC's *own internal use.* However, in 1970, the Japanese government diverted the import license for NCC/CDC's 6600 computer from NCC to C. Itoh. As a result the CDC/NCC joint venture data center fell through. There was not much to show for seven years of effort.

Another year-long negotiation led to a new joint venture with C. Itoh, CD Japan, Limited. A sales agency agreement was established between it and Control Data. Although the new arrangement was more effective than the original one, it still had limited success. Working with C. Itoh the company suffered from the basic problem that C. Itoh, as a general trading company, did not have a body of expertise in high-performance computers, and Control Data's people were not knowledgeable in Japanese culture nor even very skilled in the Japanese language. In January of 1976 Control Data and C. Itoh decided to dissolve this joint venture.

The failure of the early data center effort with NCC did not discourage us from attempting new services ventures. Data Services Far East, Inc., (DSFE) was established in 1977. Just to do business DSFE was obliged to sign a number of "Nenshoes"—roughly meaning "memoranda of understanding." Between September 1976 and August 1977 there were no less than six of these in favor of Ministry of International Trade and Industry (MITI), Ministry of Post and Telegraph (MPT), Machinery and Information Services Bureau, and Nippon Telephone and Telegraph (NTT). The essence of these memoranda was to give these agencies in one form or another detailed information regarding DSFE's customers and operations. But these were minor difficulties. DSFE entered into an international leased line usage agreement with KDD, the international telecommunications carrier of Japan. The agreement contained a number of rather unusual provisions, including the requirement to submit once every three months the names and addresses of customers. The most restrictive policy was that Control Data was forbidden to pass data over the leased line other than that for the service that used the computers we operated in Cleveland, Ohio. This meant that services from other U.S. data centers could not be sold in Japan. MPT's ruling was based on the fact that in order to process services other than those in Cleveland, data from the international line would have to be switched within our internal network in the United States. Japan's signature on the International Telecommunications Treaty would have permitted such "data switching." MPT, however, simply ignored that fact. Control Data enlisted the aid of the U.S. Special Trade Representative, the Department of State, and the Department of Commerce, all to no avail. It was not until KDD applied for a Federal Communications Commission certificate, essentially to bring its packet of switched services into the United States, that there was any break in the clouds. In 1981, nearly two decades after the first data services effort, that permission was granted for internal switching within the United States.

It is difficult to summarize all of the causes of the problems in Japan, but they did include interminable delays imposed by government red tape, and the fact that we were excluded from sales to the government, universities, and organizations having government funds. There also was the requirement for import licenses, which had to be obtained one at a time, high duties imposed on imports, and subsidies granted to local industry. Hope was extended and then followed by a series of delays. Then there was the egregious refusal of the Japanese telecommunications authorities to follow the rules practiced throughout the world.

By 1983, after some twenty years, Control Data finally broke through the governmental and cultural barriers. A good relationship was established with MITI, which was anxious to market Japanese computer products and services in the United States. MITI no longer feared Control Data, and we actually began to contract with some government agencies for Cybernet services.

I found that two qualities are essential when dealing with governments:

Persistence is important, but even more essential are people knowledgeable and experienced in dealing with the intricacies of government and of local culture. Additionally, they must be able to forge personal relationships that most matter within government agencies.

In dealing with government you also need *leverage.* In the example of France, that leverage was the desirability of our exceptional technology. That was true in most other countries as well. Control Data had credibility and goodwill with most government agencies. In Japan there was no leverage; indeed, the company's technology and data services strategy proved to be a threat to the policies of some agencies such as MITI, and thus a weakness with regard to market penetration.

Eastern Europe

Just as Canada was a market that naturally drew the attention of the U.S. marketing organization, the countries of Eastern Europe were of interest to Control Data's people in Germany (West German Republic based in Bonn). The first contacts were in 1963 with the companies located in the Deutsche Democratikishe Republic (DDR). The appeal of the DDR was the availability in that country of "hard currency," meaning currency convertible into U.S. dollars. By 1966 the U.S. Department of Commerce had ruled that the Model 1604 computer, by then some eight years old, was "licensable," and three orders for these computers were obtained. The first to be installed—in 1966—was at Leuna Werke, a chemical company.

By 1967, a new subsidiary, CDC Gmbh, was founded in Vienna to pursue business in the DDR, Austria, USSR, and the Eastern European countries Poland, Czechoslovakia, Hungary, Romania, Bulgaria, and Yugoslavia. There was a two-year time lapse between obtaining an order and the realization of revenues from it. Installation required the granting of a formal export license. Because of such delays the selling process was always muddled, and sometimes even after orders were received the opportunity did not result in revenues due to the failure to receive a license. License problems had more serious consequences. For example, when license was denied for CDC's 3600 computer, the French company CII licensed the manufacture of its IRIS-50 computer to the Romanian Industrial Group for Electronics and Vacuum Technology (CIETC), a unit of the Romanian Ministry of Machine Tools and Electro Techniques. This gave CII a considerable competitive advantage.

For reasons such as this there was incentive to form joint ventures. Once export license approval was given for the product to be built in a joint venture, the output of that joint venture was freed from much (but not all!) licensing red tape. In addition, joint venture production had potential for the host country to create badly needed hard currency.

The first such arrangement was with a Yugoslav company named ISKRA. This was in 1966. It was a very modest manufacturing alliance involving the assembly of electrical cable harnesses and the assembly of printed circuit cards. These components were exported to the United States for use in Control Data. Though the operation may have been on a small scale, the problems to be solved and the obstacles to overcome were not. We learned from that modest beginning, and collaborative ventures were started in Hungary (1970) and Poland (1973).

In April of 1973 we formed the first equity joint venture agreement between a western company and the Romanian government. It was called ROM CD. This arrangement was with CIETC and was made possible by the Nixon administration's new policy of détente with the Soviet Union and increased trade with Eastern Block countries in general. Such business agreements were being encouraged, and the U.S. government and the NATO Export Coordinating Committee, COCOM, ratified this one in January 1974. Its purpose was to produce Control Data peripheral products. Ownership was 45 percent Control Data, and 55 percent Romanian. Control Data's contribution was technical know-how and support, as well as certain assembly and test equipment. CIETC's contribution consisted primarily of a new 65,000-square-foot building plus other facilities and tools.

We sent six American families to Bucharest to assist in employee training and quality control, and to initially fill key management positions. Due to the success of those training efforts, within a few years the company was operating entirely by Romanians. Long-range strategy for the company was the responsibility of a joint business committee, composed of four executives from each of the two owners.

First products of the joint venture were assembled late in 1974. Over the years Romanian sources were found for some of the critical parts needed to produce the printers, terminals, card readers, and, ultimately, disk storage modules. Qualified vendors in Romania supplied forty percent of the parts. Not only were these vendors working to strict Control Data standards, they also received approval, where necessary, by the U.S. Underwriters Laboratory. This was a remarkable accomplishment, considering barriers of distance, language, infrastructure, and experience. In the first six years the factory's output averaged 60 percent for Control Data and 40 percent for CIETC, but by 1980 the output had become 41 percent Control Data and 59 percent CIETC.

It is also worth noting that new technologies from this alliance came to Control Data. For example, we received the know-how to develop a new type of lower-cost gas discharge display panel, interfaces to the Ryad family of Eastern European–built computers for our printers and disk drives, and a new way to build transformers that cut material costs by 30 percent and had seven times less current leakage. In 1978, we signed a ten-year extension of the original agreement. The new agreement provided a basis for other joint ventures, including a data services company, a software research and development center, as well as the right for Romania to manufacture, use, and sell certain CDC computers.

After the successful experience with ROM CD, there followed other alliances in Eastern Europe, including one with ISKRA to produce minicomputers, and one with the Hungarian electronics manufacturer VIDEOTON to buy some of the output from ROM CD for inclusion in their products. VIDEOTON was also engaged to supply aluminum castings to Control Data.

As might be expected, these ventures had difficulties in bridging the gap in language and culture and in operating under a Communist regime. However, by far most of the troubles came from the U.S. government as a result of ill-defined export policy. A few examples will suffice to illustrate the point. In spite of encouragement by the Nixon administration to establish the joint venture, licenses to export the required technology were delayed so long that by the time we received a go-ahead, some of the products were outdated and not saleable. Introduction of new products was delayed, and for a time the very existence of ROM CD was imperiled. We were granted the right to export medium-speed disk drive technology, only to be denied the right to export the critical parts required to build those disk drives. When this problem was cleared up, we found that we would not be allowed to use them with the Romanian-built Felix computer, although competitors from other countries could do so.

Some products manufactured by the joint venture required no specific U.S. license to be exported from Romania, while other products could not be exported outside Romania at all. An interagency committee, as I have already noted, in effect governed U.S. export controls. It was all too painfully evident in the case of ROM CD that there is no such thing as *the* U.S. government. Then, during the Carter administration, came the embargo on additional grain sales and high technology to the Soviet Union. According to administration spokesmen, the ban was not to be applied to the other countries in the trading bloc dominated by Russia—the Comecon—but in practice, trade with Eastern Europe became even more restrictive than before. We were told repeatedly that there was too much risk of diversion to the Soviet Union, and therefore Romania had become less attractive as a trading partner. Most of these objections of course came from the Department of Defense. So much for "government" policy. But thanks to Control Data's persistence and an unusual ability to work with individuals in the various U.S. agencies, ROM CD survived these travails. It even prospered. Control Data was truly blessed by the caliber of people who helped it find a path through the Byzantine labyrinth of export controls. These ventures likewise contributed to a growing mutual understanding between us and political and business leaders in Eastern Europe.

Even so, the next example of Control Data's collaboration was most improbable. Here was a company whose very existence was due in large part to U.S. response to threats from the Soviet Union, and the technology of its supercomputers was one of the most closely controlled exports from the United States. Control Data computers were at the very core of the National Security Agency's intelligence and cryptography mission. In the intervening years since the 1957 launch of Sputnik and of Control Data, fears of the Soviet Union and of the communist threat had been the major factor shaping U.S. foreign policy and its export control policies.

So what happened in 1973? Control Data and GKNT (Soviet Academy of Science and Technology) signed a major technology and trade agreement—a so-called frame agreement for collaboration. Several things had happened in the years immediately prior to 1973 that had turned an improbability into a reality.

USSR

By 1972 nearly a quarter of a century had passed since the era of McCarthyism and its frenetic obsession with Communism's supposed insidious subversion of the United States government. However, the Cold War was as stark and unrelenting as ever. But in that year President Nixon visited the USSR and signed a broad trade agreement. That was the beginning of the so-called détente between the United States and the USSR. Subsequent to this visit, the president convened a White House meeting with several leading business executives. He saw building a commercial bridge between the United States and the USSR as an important step toward putting an end to the Cold War, or at least toward making coexistence more tenable. The president's direction fell on fertile ground in the mind of Bill Norris.

The Soviet Union, for all its flawed economic and political thinking, was a tremendous reservoir of basic science and technology. Its weakness lay in innovative and entrepreneurial utilization of that science and technology. Those attributes, on the other hand, were the great strength of the United States. In no company was this truer than Control Data. Bill Norris reasoned that with ingenuity Control Data could tap the Soviet wellspring of human capital and provide itself with a long-term source of leading edge science and technology. This was especially true in math and other sciences that would be important to the company in its drive to move along the Technology Food Chain toward software applications and services. In October 1973 Control Data and GKNT signed the ten-year Cooperative Frame Agreement, which established a coordinating committee and provided the umbrella for a broad range of cooperative activities that were to be finalized under separate contracts or specific agreements. This seminal agreement is summarized by the *New York Times* (October 24, 1973), and reproduced in full in Appendix 6.

Although portions of the activities envisioned in the frame agreement were initiated, they soon were stifled by the administration of President Jimmy Carter, which took a much less sanguine attitude toward trade with the USSR. So, while the agreement did not prove as fruitful in technology development and exchange to either the Russians or to Control Data as initially envisioned, there were successes, and without a doubt it aided in Control Data's sales of computers in the USSR. Following the signing of the frame agreement in 1973, computers were sold to the Russian Ministry of Geology and the Ministry of Chemistry.

All in all, thanks to an effort in Washington, D.C., that was both assiduous and innovative, and to corresponding undertakings in Moscow, Bucharest, and the other capital cities of Eastern Europe, Control Data had achieved a market penetration that was remarkable for that time. In contrast with the experience in Japan, we found ways to combine the basic leverage of technological desirability with the foreign policy and economic goals of the governments involved.

By 1977 Control Data products and services sold in Eastern Europe had reached a level of $30 million per year. Throughout the period 1966–1980, Control Data, not IBM, was the dominant supplier of computers to these countries with performance levels greater than that of IBM's System 370-145 or the Russian RYAD 1040. This achievement was remarkable in view of the times. No business venture ever faced greater political, economic, and emotional obstacles than did this foray into the Soviet Union and the other countries of the Eastern Bloc. There were many talented, innovative, and doggedly determined individuals who worked to bring all this about. It was truly a small but mighty band of dedicated people. And at its head was an amazing individual, Bob Schmidt. It's fitting, then, to close this part of the Control Data globalization story with Bob's statement before a joint hearing of the U.S. House of Representatives Committees on Science and Technology, Interstate and Foreign Commerce, Banking, and Finance and Urban Affairs, and the House Task Force on Industrial Innovation: "It is time we faced the world as it is. The Soviet Union is a country of 280 million whose natural resources exceed our own. The one clear area in which the United States has demonstrated superiority is commercial enterprise. To deliberately close the door on trade with the Soviet Union and Eastern Europe and compete with them only in the military and political arena is to deny ourselves our greatest strength."

Bob lived to see President Gorbachev's visit to Control Data's headquarters in 1990. The company had signed a new and far-reaching agreement with the Soviet Academy of Sciences that encompassed nuclear power safety, petroleum exploration, control of electric power generation and transmission, and software development. This was more than a mere exercise in corporate statesmanship. For Control Data there followed the sale of six of its large-scale computers.

The agreement was a prime example of the approach Control Data took with the Soviets and other international governments. It had three major features:

Technological cooperation. In this instance, based on the June 1990 U.S.–Soviet Government-to-Government Agreement in Nuclear Safety Technology Cooperation.
Financing assistance. With the Soviets it was via the credit facilities made available by the Export Import Bank.

Infrastructure development. One of significant societal importance such as nuclear safety.

Iran

The Control Data story of global expansion was one marked by success and excitement. The move into markets such as the socialist bloc countries, although
frustrating at times and always tedious, was nevertheless surprisingly successful. The Iran story is one that has particular relevance in view of the dominance
of the Middle East in the economic and political thinking in today's world.
This is a story that began with high hope, creative thinking, and early success
but that ultimately resulted in great disappointment.

Then as now, market access, much less the bitter fight between Israel and its
neighbors in the Middle East, plagued market success. Access is even more dependent on coping with the volatile and unforgiving contest for power by the
different religious sects within the Muslim world, that is, between religious
conservatives who distrust and detest the West, its beliefs and technologies, and
the more progressive sects who earnestly strive to improve their countries' economic well-being through exchange with the West.

Control Data, because of its early expansion into Israel, was effectively shut
out of many countries in the Middle East. Iran was an exception. The Shah of
Iran not only had close ties with the West, he also had a great desire to utilize information technology. His government had made education and training in
advanced technology a priority. Since the early '60s the Shah had instituted a
program of land reform, universal voting rights, profit sharing, industrializa-
tion, and education. Even so, a decade later two-thirds of the population was illiterate. At this point, however, the path of education in Iran was about to cross
with that of Control Data.

The early sales efforts in the Middle East, like much of Control Data's global
expansion, consisted of ad hoc prospecting opportunities and highly individualistic sales people. John Menoudakes was certainly such a person. By 1973
Control Data had entered into a $22 million contract with the Iranian Ministry
of Education. The fact that the contract was for the establishment of vocational
schools that had nothing to do with computers was brushed aside. That outcome, it was felt, could be realized at a later stage. Control Data had no courses
and no instructors for the vocations the contract envisioned: plumbing, typewriter repair, rudimentary electrical wiring, telephone link repair, and radio
and TV repair. What the company did have was the skill of forging collaboration with public sector entities. Right in the company's backyard was an out-

standing vocational school, one of Minnesota's Area Vocational Technical Institutes (AVTI). There also was a local district school superintendent, William (Bill) Knock, who was willing to serve as a consultant to the project. With courses licensed from AVTI and a small cadre of people including Dave States (Control Data Institute) and Brian Roth (International Customer Engineering), along with consulting assistance from Bill Knock, the project was launched. It was not all smooth sailing. Dave States likes to relate as an example the course in telephone line repair, which included lessons in pole climbing with spikes. That didn't work very well for the Iranian students; the poles there, of necessity, were concrete.

Corralling John Menoudakes was a considerable challenge in its own right. Additionally, coordinating operations and sales, and managing relations with a very high-profile customer was a management task requiring great skills. That task was finally laid at the doorstep of Nate Dickinson, the Control Data executive in Vienna who was responsible for Eastern Europe and the Soviet Union. Nate commented wryly that the Middle East was attached to his territory simply because no one in the company's European headquarters in Brussels wanted to be responsible for John Menoudakes. Throughout his career, however, Nate had demonstrated the ability to deal with the unusual and the incongruous. Iran tested that competence fully, but it worked. Sales from operations other than the vocational schools grew to some $12 million per year. Computers were installed at the University of Teheran, the Ministry of Education, the Abadan refinery, and various industrial organizations.

Because of the unavailability of qualified people in Iran, Control Data's Iranian employees were mostly expatriates from other countries. An exception was Homa Firouztash, who would be thrust into a leading, but nightmarish, role in trying to chart a course through the fundamentalist revolution of 1979–1982. Homa, after graduating from high school in Iran, received his undergraduate and Ph.D. degrees in the United States. He also married in the United States and with his wife, Carolyn, returned to Iran. Once there, and full of a driving desire to improve education, Homa went to work for the Ministry of Education while Carolyn worked as an educator and research sociologist.

Because of Control Data's involvement with the Ministry of Education, its visionary program of establishing vocational institutes, and the growth prospects for large-scale computers as well as the potential of the PLATO system, Homa soon decided to join Control Data. The vision for the future was shimmering. With PLATO, the company could show the way to bringing affordable, quality education not only to illiterate Iranians, but also to the people of the whole Middle East. Control Data Iran, with headquarters in Teheran, would become a dominant force of enlightenment from India to Athens. Alas, however, it was not to be.

The event that was to bring on the end of these lofty goals and strategies was the return to Iran of the Ayatollah Khomeini and the overthrow of the Shah in 1979. Soon after the revolution engulfed Iran, prudence dictated that the managing director, an American named Stu Bernstein, remove himself to Brussels. Homa, the deputy director, was left to pick up the reins and try to chart a course through the storm of violence and revolution. Many people expected the turmoil to be transitory and that a more stable and commonsense regime for governing the country would return within a year. After all, hadn't President Jimmy Carter recently described Iran as the "island of stability" in the Middle East?

Homa strove mightily to continue Control Data's strategy and the company's position of meeting the country's need for basic education. After 1979–1980, the Iranian hostage crisis, and a steadily increasing hostility to all things Western, most U.S. companies in Iran were either nationalized or closed. Control Data, struggling against the tide, continued to try to find a way.

The stories of physical and psychological tension are too numerous to relate here. However, excerpts from Carolyn's memoir of that time provide personal insight as to the perils encountered in a voyage in Strategic Space. One excerpt was given in this chapter heading. Other excerpts are contained in Appendix 7. Homa's story reinforces the fact that there is danger to loved ones as well as to oneself in the business journeys through Strategic Space. Carolyn was one of the last expatriate Americans to leave Iran in 1981. Homa was finally forced to escape on foot through the mountains into Pakistan.

Control Data sued the government of Iran for $28 million and finally, via a World Court ruling in June 1989, was awarded a settlement of its claims. That monetary reward of the company's efforts offered some satisfaction, but it could not compensate for the abrupt and unfortunate end of a promising relationship between us and the people of Iran. The $28 million was small conciliation compared to what was lost.

OBSERVATIONS

In the three or four decades following World War II, the conventional approach to expansion outside the United States for all companies was a separate "international division," which generally comprised legal entity subsidiaries in each country. Those subsidiaries to a large degree were treated as individual profit centers. Control Data pursued a different course. Its product divisions were treated as worldwide profit centers. Professional services, software technical support, and systems consulting were likewise thought of as worldwide functions. The term *global enterprise* would not enter the common business vernacular for more than two decades, but Control Data was already functioning as a global enterprise in 1963. The imperfections in the overlay of worldwide product line profit responsibility and geographic marketing and sales subsidiaries made for intriguing times. What was true, however, was that the essential technological resources for advanced computer and peripheral equipment innovation were focused on a global market, while allowing creative sales and marketing capabilities to flourish.

I purposely have dealt with some aspects of Control Data's global expansion that were less successful. That is unfair to those who labored through that era to effect many global successes. The reason for doing so has been to make more graphic the strategic fact of life that there is no such thing as "the government" and no such thing as unequivocal success each and every time. Working with governments is good business but not for the weak-kneed or fainthearted. It requires standing firm and seeing with eyes wide open.

In this it is necessary to remember the words of Bernard DeVoto, who, reflecting on the extraordinary journey of Lewis and Clark, said that success will come to those with not only "ingenuity and resourcefulness," but "a curious mixture of open-mindedness and skepticism."[1]

Part Four Strategies for the Unexpected and the Unusual:

Crisis is inevitable, but with innovative leadership it can be used for positive change

Public-private partnerships present important, but frequently overlooked, strategic possibilities

Opportunities for innovation are frequently found in unexpected places. Sudden change in the market, political, economic, or competitive environment may result in disruption of strategy or the current way it is being implemented. But it also likely will provide new perspective and opportunity. Contrarian thinking also can result in new and fruitful strategic paths. An excellent example of contrarian thinking is that of looking at national and local governments as desirable and effective partners.

Chapter 12 When It Hits the Fan: Perilous Journeys— Innovation in Times of Crisis

There can't be a crisis next week. My schedule is already full.
—Henry Kissinger, Secretary of State (1973–1977)

Any idiot can deal with crisis. What's tough is dealing with the day-to-day grind.
—Anton Chekov

The search for stability and certainty is as integral a part of human existence as breathing. Consciously and unconsciously we strive to find those halcyon waters where gentle breezes and smooth sailing push us toward fulfillment. But for the individual and likewise for the business traveler in Strategic Space, life is rarely so kind. No matter how well we chart a course guided by the Technology Food Chain and plan for contingencies, we cannot escape unpredictable forces quite beyond our control that sweep us in unforeseen directions.

FLEABITES VERSUS ALLIGATOR BITES

Events that block our objectives and progress can be sources of great frustration. Some companies—and people—are able to cope, quickly regain their footing, and right themselves. Others are incapacitated; still others rage against the currents they have no hope of overcoming—in either case, they aimlessly drift or vainly fight until they drown.

Crisis management starts with having resilience and courage—and being able to discriminate between the ordinary frustrations of the daily grind and challenges that are inherently strategic. Such discernment is more rare than one might think. I recall one member of my management team who had an unusual propensity to get frustrated and irritable over relatively minor problems, especially if they threatened his ego. I developed a shorthand and somewhat humorous way of helping him deal with this by labeling his issues as either fleabites or alligator bites. There were not a lot of alligator bites. Some years later, after a successful career at Control Data, he was recruited into a senior level position at another company. We remained friends and had contact from time to time. One time when we met he started to describe a management problem he was having. I quietly interrupted him and said, "Good grief, John, have you forgotten how to tell a fleabite from an alligator bite?"

The ability to deal with the day-to-day irritations while conserving one's intellect and energy to focus on dealing with true crises is a mark of an excellent executive. For just as personal voyages are interrupted or endangered by unexpected and violent storms, journeys in business strategy are beset with sudden and unexpected forces in Strategic Space. Control Data's principal times of crisis over thirty plus years cover a goodly spectrum of cause, effect, and response.

The feeling expressed in Henry Kissinger's classic comment at the onset of this chapter is all too often the same as that experienced by business people subjected to sudden violence in the forces of Strategic Space. "Alligator bites" such as a frame-breaking technological change, severe economic recession, unfair practices by a giant competitor, or the self-inflicted wounds caused by lack of management diligence result in strategic and personal pain. Dealing with them requires action that must be taken quickly and decisively. That action may involve some combination of strategic redirection, legal proceedings, painful work force reductions, and financial restructuring. Dealing with true crises requires clarity of vision, a cold appraisal free from personal bias, and desire. It also requires a willingness to take risks.

Chekov, however, strikes an equally harmonic note with regard to the realities of management. Dealing with the "fleabites" of daily operations is a wearisome matter: departure of a presumably indispensable technologist or executive, frustration at lack of business acumen in one's commercial bankers, the narrow-minded avarice of an investment banker, witless carping by special in-

terest groups who are also sometimes stockholders, and the misguided interpretation of reality by the media. Reacting to every fleabite as an alligator bite is
a sure path to mental and physical exhaustion. Fleabites do need attention, but
intense scratching only tends to inflame them. These require understanding
and patience—and a sense of humor.

Alligator bites on the other hand require immediate attention and intense
focus on corrective action. There are ways to effectively manage alligator bites
but, first, I want to briefly discuss the four serious crises that Control Data confronted.

MAJOR CHALLENGES

Crisis #1: The Shark Strikes Back

In the early days of Control Data Bill Norris once likened its existence to that
of the pilot fish that swims with agility and quick response to feed off the bits of
food scattered by the attack of a large and dangerous shark. The result of mis-
calculation is swift and fatal. Control Data's first crisis resulted from the sudden
lashing out by IBM against our troublesome intrusion into its scientific and engineering feeding ground.

The initial success of the 1604 computer raised alarm in IBM, which had
already become the dominant force in the new world of computing technology. As a result, its powerful financial and marketing weapons were deployed
to eliminate the intruder before we could grow into being a more serious
threat.

With price cuts and skillful use of its bundled price structure, IBM was able
to cut off orders for Control Data's 1604 for almost the entire year of 1960. Responding to this onslaught required aplomb and doing whatever it took to survive. To preserve precious cash there were salary reductions and myriad other
cost-cutting measures. What was not curtailed was the belief in, and the fostering of, innovation. Seymour's tour de force in computer design—the 6600—was
under way and fully funded. The company also began charting a course toward
more favorable waters—the international market for scientific and engineering
computers. It worked. Not only did the company survive in those early years of
the 1960s, the new breath of life from the international marketplace gave impetus to growth. From 1960 to 1969 revenues grew from $11 million to $570 million. The stock soared to a high of $174 per share, and using that stock currency
the company gained a much needed source of stability through the acquisition
in 1968 of the Commercial Credit Company, with assets over $4 billion. By

means of assiduous trimming of the sails and skillful navigation, the crisis was met, and new visions of growth were opened. But not for long.

Crisis #2: Economic Bear

The economic recession in the United States in 1970–1971 plunged the company's computer business into the red. In the favorable climate and the world of increasing profits of the late 1960s, we had become overly optimistic, and, when optimism meets reality, reality always prevails. In the economic downturn, commercial customers deferred orders and government customers cancelled them outright. Sales for the year fell by more than $30 million from the 1969 level of $570 million. But in anticipation of continued rapid growth, inventories had increased from $172 million at the beginning of 1969 to some $300 million at year's end. Inflation was at work as well, and the additional cost of wages and salary added another $14 million to the financial burden. The *Wall Street Journal* account was: "Control Data reported yesterday an estimated net loss for 1970 of about $2.7 million on revenue of $540 million, compared with a profit of $51.7 million, or $3.51 a share, on revenue of $570 million a year earlier. The 1970 loss includes year-end adjustments in computer operations related to an inventory write-off of $23 million before taxes, and a loss of about $5.3 million after taxes representing the company's proportionate interest in the operating losses of affiliated companies in which Control Data holds about 50% ownership."

Drastic cuts had to be made. As before, what was not cut was investment in the future. Not only had Control Data continued its investment in advanced computer architecture, more important it continued its investment in Cybernet data services and in education services. Nor did the company reduce its innovations in alleviating societal problems: it was during this time that a commitment was made to create jobs in the economically deprived Selby area of St. Paul—more on that in the next chapter.

Moreover, this time of distress was used as an opportunity to institute a crucial change in the structure and management of the company. One day early in 1970 Bill Norris talked to me about his thoughts for reorganization. He was going to divide the company into five business units, four in the computer business plus Commercial Credit. The four computer business groups were to be Computer Systems, Services, Peripheral Products and Marketing—for the first time Services was to be positioned as a corporate-level business. At the time I was vice president of sales. Bill said to me, "Bob, which group would you like to run?" There was absolutely no question in my mind, and I instantly replied,

"Services." With the wry grin that we all knew so well, Bill responded, "That's good, because that's what I was going to tell you to do." It was indicative of the still dominant product orientation of the company that, when executives of the marketing group had a goodbye gathering for me, it was more like a wake than a celebration. The feeling of many in the company was that I had been sent to Siberia. Little did they know. But I did, for I knew the Technology Food Chain was on my side.

The turbulence produced executive fallout as well. Harold Hammer, the company's CFO, resigned in 1971. As reported in the press, this was due to "policy differences" with Norris, specifically, the investments in services such as Cybernet and Control Data Institutes. The root cause was deeper than that. In his five years at the company Harold had never demonstrated an understanding of either the company's culture of innovation or the basics of managing to the evolutionary nature of technology.

Once again crisis was treated successfully, and we emerged from it a better, stronger company. Rather than looking at crisis as merely something to be dealt with, we recognized crises as new opportunities to modify the future.

Crisis #3: Too Much, Too Soon

Control Data enjoyed relatively smooth sailing for nearly fifteen years following the recession-induced crisis of 1970 and the subsequent departure of early innovators such as Jim Thornton and Seymour Cray. These were years of success both in financial terms and in the growth of services into the major business we envisioned. To be sure, there were problems and setbacks in each business area, even an operating loss for the computer business in 1974. Those things demanded attention but were rather quickly remedied.

We also encountered considerable frustration in trying to communicate the essence of the company's services strategy. The inevitable commoditization of computing hardware was generally unrecognized in the industry, the media, and the investment community. The services strategy was being built on a solid foundation of serving the computing and information needs of business via network access to information databases and computing applications. Twenty years later, in the era of the Internet, such ideas are evident.

The services strategy also embraced the more iconoclastic and community sensitive view that there was a business opportunity in the *information service requirements* that are inherent in training and education, better and more affordable healthcare and wellness services, urban renewal, and bringing deprived and disadvantaged people into the mainstream workforce. Media and investment community criticism was focused on this part of the company's business, which constituted less than 10 percent of total services revenues. The investment in the PLATO computer-based learning system was particularly targeted and was exaggerated by factors of ten or even twenty times actual expenditures. So during these fifteen years there were certainly problems and disappointments along with business growth and strategic repositioning. Generally, however, it was a time of dealing with fleabites.

Perhaps that should have been a warning; as Andy Grove so succinctly put it in the title of a book, *Only the Paranoid Survive*. We, however, were far from paranoid. Because of our confidence and optimism we too easily overrode problems such as the cancellation of a major contract with the Union Bank of Switzerland (UBS) and the seemingly endless haranguing of well-intentioned but misguided groups on topics such as Control Data's presence in South Africa and its trade with socialist countries. At the same time we were somewhat blinded by more severe internal operational issues. The belief that we could do anything, no matter how tough, and that innovation and determination would overcome all obstacles was deeply ingrained in the company's management. Therein, however, lay the source of the next crisis. The financial and management resources to accomplish so much simply were not there.

One challenge was the growing commoditization of the hardware businesses. This was not something to which we were blind. In computer systems we were working at moving up the Technology Food Chain toward application systems. We had cut back on proprietary development of computers and had entered into a collaboration with Data General to supply us with mid-range computer hardware. We made a conscious decision to buy rather than build personal computers that would be used in delivering services. In short, although still intent on developing high-end computers, the company was rapidly moving toward becoming a systems integrator rather than a builder of proprietary computer systems.

More serious was the problem in the peripherals business. By 1981 it was a $1.8 billion business with both strategic and basic management problems accumulated over two decades of exciting and enthusiastic growth. It needed a sharp, clear focus on the fundamentals of a commodity business. If ever there was a business that would have benefited from an Economic Value Added (EVA) measurement, this was it. In spite of contributing significantly to corporate operating profit, an EVA analysis would have shown it to be a steady drain on the company's financial strength. We didn't have EVA measures of business at the time, but we did have such measures as cash flow and return on invested capital (ROIC). They were enough to make clear the basic capital consuming nature of the peripherals business. But the management problems needed some correction if we were to be able to realize any value from this part of Control Data. Unfortunately the 1985 liquidity problem came too soon. And in the interim, formidable competition from Japanese companies and smaller U.S. competitors cut our OEM peripherals market share nearly in half.

By early 1985 a true liquidity crisis was rapidly developing. New financing was badly needed if we were to buy the time needed to fix the problems. One possible solution was to sell Commercial Credit. The original rationale for merger of Control Data and Commercial Credit was the financing of leased computers. That had long since faded into insignificance. We had worked hard, and not without some success, to develop strategic synergy between CCC's financial services and the computer and information services. But the overall impact of these synergies in both revenues and profits was minor. Unfortunately there were no buyers for Commercial Credit at a reasonable price.

The second effort to relieve the financial crunch was a $300 million public offering of convertible preferred stock and subordinated notes. This failed when, in view of the company's deteriorating profit forecasts for 1985, we were informed by our investment bankers that they would not support the offering. In September the banks with whom we had revolving credit lines and short-term notes of some $372 million notified us that we were in default and that they would allow no more use of these credit facilities. We would have to live day-by-day on the cash flow that we could generate. Beyond that, as things unfolded, we had to pledge the stock of Arbitron and Commercial Credit as security against the repayment of all that debt by December 31, 1986. The shit had truly hit the fan. The headlines were ominous, routinely predicting Control Data's demise. In the midst of such a crisis it truly helps to maintain a sense of humor—even gallows humor. In the fall of 1985 someone gave me a bumper sticker that read: "It's been Monday all year." I propped it up on my desk, and it never left.

The board of directors was seriously alarmed and agreed that the time had come for a change. Bill, Norb Berg, and I had been functioning as a three-person Office of the Chairman for four years, with Bill as chairman and CEO, Norb as deputy chairman, and me as president and chief operating officer. The three of us had worked together formally and informally for more than twenty years. Communication between us was open and frank. There was no jockeying or manipulation—we just went about our tasks. The company, however, now had a serious liquidity problem. The board wanted action and a single point of responsibility for that action. At the December 1985 meeting, the board elected me chairman, president, and CEO as of January 1, 1986. Little else changed in my life that New Year's Day. I had already been at work on the liquidity problem for over four months. I knew the board members personally, having served on the board for more than a decade. I was well aware of their positions on various issues. Norb and I were no longer equals in position, but we were equals in dedication to Control Data and all it stood for. Norb could not have been more supportive and helpful.

The crisis did not allow much time for philosophizing. There was work to be done: first of all, to solve the liquidity problem, and, second, to reduce the number of new initiatives so that the business was more manageable. This was not an insurmountable task; it simply required careful analysis, a willingness to take action without necessarily having all the facts, and a confident knowledge that even if we didn't do everything correctly there was no better course of action than confronting the challenge head on and tending to first priorities.

In the next twelve months the following actions were taken:

Financing. The essential task of regaining liquidity and paying the bank debt was achieved by selectively selling $150 million in excess assets and nonperforming small businesses; executing an IPO of 82 percent of Commercial Credit; and launching a successful $400 million public offering of senior notes and convertible debentures. The total cash realized from these actions, including proceeds of $530 million from the sale of Commercial Credit, was $1.28 billion. Not only was the liquidity problem solved, but the company now had $300 million in cash and was essentially debt-free. In the face of great skepticism we met the challenge of gaining market recognition of the inherent value of Control Data's businesses.

Business Focus. Rather than a goal of simply changing an ingrained tendency to undertake every new services idea that came along, it was to concentrate resources where we had the greatest opportunity of competitive advantage. In total, thirteen businesses or product lines were sold or discontinued, and by the fourth quarter of 1986 the company was again recording an operating profit.

Operating Environment. The emphasis on people and innovation in human resource policy was reemphasized. The Total Quality Management Process (TQMP) that had its roots more than six years before was given corporatewide emphasis, including regular board review. The operating environment change also included an emphasis on decentralization. In spite of Control Data's culture of individual initiative and innovation, it was, in its administrative and financial control systems, a highly centralized company. If accountability was to be truly fostered at lower levels, it was necessary to change support structures such as information systems to make that a practical possibility.

The results of these actions, all based on a cold appraisal of each situation, were gratifying. The company returned to profitability in 1987, and the investment community responded with a rapidly rising stock price. There was, at the same time, the willingness to continue longer-range investments such as those in services and the new supercomputer, the ETA-10.

To back up our belief in the future, and to recognize the sacrifices that workers had made, every employee of the company was given ten shares of stock—a financially modest but psychologically very significant gesture. The future, in spite of many uncertainties and risks, looked brighter than it had for many years.

Crisis #4: Facing the Elephant

The phrase "facing the elephant" was coined during the nineteenth-century western migration of the pioneers crossing the Great American Desert, the area between the Mississippi River and the Rocky Mountains. They had left the comfort of their farms and homes to seek out the promised wealth of the West. There was terrible deprivation and danger, and they were confronted with a mammoth challenge. Facing it took incredible tenacity and courage.

For Control Data it was a matter of leaving behind the comfortable confines of its early history and relying on its innovative roots to seek new opportunity in the changed environment of the computer and information services industry. A rational, evenhanded appraisal of our strengths and weaknesses and how they would best work in the evolving information industry markets made the course clear. It was not hardware—computers, disk drives, and other peripheral equipment—that would provide the best path toward future success. The competencies of the company did not fit with the increasing commodity nature of those businesses. It was the talent for application of information technologies, that is, services, that provided the best competitive course for the future.

Still, in the '80s we believed that while making services the main strategic thrust of the company, the computer hardware business could be a viable *adjunct* to the services strategy. It had been clear for some time, however, that the pure commodity nature of disk drives and other peripherals would not fit. By 1987 the product strategy and operational inadequacies of the peripherals business had been resolved. The business had returned to profitability. It was time to dispose of that business and use the proceeds to further develop the services business.

At the end of 1986, in my self-assessment to the board I reported on the progress since the crisis of 1985 and laid out a plan for the long term. The net assessment was as follows: "Good start; 4–5 year program in all. Major change by 1990." This turned out to be a correct assessment. In 1989 the peripherals business was sold to Seagate Technologies, Inc. Also by that time, the computer systems business had become a systems integration business focused on such application areas as weather, energy, scientific research, and engineering design.

There were two exceptions to this: Government Systems, the military products business, and ETA, the supercomputer subsidiary. Government Systems was still making computers for airborne and other military applications. Such computers, contrasted with commercial computers, were not commodities. They were application specific, and their inherent engineering and software gave them value-added. Moreover, this business also had services components, such as systems integration for military and other specialized government applications.

It was with regard to ETA that we truly had to "face the elephant." In spite of the fact that ETA had demonstrated technological innovation of the highest degree and was easily equal to any creative endeavor in the company's history, we could not sustain the software and other support expenditures necessary to bring that innovation to commercial profitability. The original intent of setting up ETA as a separate subsidiary and only retaining a minority interest had not been realized. Perhaps this was a failure in financial innovation, but it had not been for lack of effort at seeking other partners or financing alternatives. In 1989 I made the toughest decision of my career: shut down ETA and take the enormous write-off of R&D and capital investment that entailed. It involved an even greater emotional cost of terminating the dreams of a lot of people, including long-time and valued colleagues. But it was done with courage and as much caring for people as was possible. The financial blow made the headlines. The emotional blow did not, but it nonetheless struck many hearts. Ironically, there was a positive side in that the tax loss carryforward resulting from the write-off provided a major boost to Control Data's earnings from its services business in the '90s. But this was a Pyrrhic victory.

OBSERVATIONS

All such examinations of corporate crises make for enticing and at times lugubrious reading. Beyond such indulgence, however, is the essential matter of learning. What can we learn? How can we best deal with the crises that result from the vicissitudes of Strategic Space, as well as our own shortcomings in charting a course of success? Dealing with crisis, unwelcome as it may be, need not be traumatic to the extent of paralysis. As I remarked in 1985: "Crisis can produce chaos, but it can also galvanize people into change." Dealing with crisis is extraordinarily difficult primarily because, no matter what the precipitant cause, external or internal, there is the problem of ego. The Japanese learned long ago many mechanisms for dealing with "loss of face," the ultimate mechanism being suicide by hara-kiri. While I won't offer moral judgment on that course of action, it would seem that a better solution might be to learn. Learning is always better than other alternatives in dealing with adversity, that is, to have the humility to admit error, the courage to correct it, and the self-acceptance to move on without being weighed down by the past.

Actions Essential to Effective Crisis Management

Dealing with a crisis situation involves four kinds of action:

1. inducing stability
2. being creatively flexible
3. making incisive strategic assessment
4. creating new momentum

STABILITY

The emotional, psychological consequences of crisis are driven by fear—fear of the unexpected and unknown. Stabilizing such a situation demands exceptional *communication* in order to restore trust and belief. Communication with all the company's stakeholders is important, but employees must be the first priority, for it is that group of people who are essential to taking corrective action. What is required is a balance of realism and hope. People aren't fools, and the essence of trust derives from frank and realistic assessment. At the same time, however, it is essential to provide hope. Winston Churchill's communication during the darkest hours of Britain's World War II battle with Nazi Germany is classic in this regard. At the very nadir of the crisis, on June 4, 1940, he spoke these words of grit and determination in the face of odds against him and his country: "We shall not flag or fall. We shall go on to the end. We shall fight in France, we shall fight on the seas and oceans, we shall fight with growing confidence and growing strength in the air, we shall defend our island, whatever the cost may be. We shall fight on the beaches, we shall fight on the landing grounds, we shall fight in the fields and in the streets, we shall fight in the hills; we shall never surrender."

In addition to communication that provides meaningful context for action and direction as to what must be done, two other actions help to stabilize an organization caught up in crises:

A focus on work. Words help, but they cannot suffice. It is important to give people something to do, to focus their energies; in short, busy people have less time to worry. Fortunately in a crisis situation there is no shortage of tasks that must be done and no problem to identify actions that will be meaningful.

No change just for the sake of change. The most common failing of business leaders in a turnaround situation is to make wholesale organization and management changes. Not everything can be fixed at once; there must be psychological and material points of departure that ground people as they begin to move to a new destination. There is little question that organization ineffectiveness and managerial inadequacies are at the root of many problems. But if the causes of that ineffectiveness and inadequacy had been obvious, then it is reasonable to believe that they would have been fixed. What is needed is fresh perspective. Crisis managers are frequently new in their responsibilities. The "knight on a white charger" syndrome in such situations is all too common.

The important thing, however, is survival: survival for a period long enough to gain perspective and assess the situation. The superior crisis manager makes only those changes that are necessary for survival and buys time for assessment. In 1962 Control Data's actions included financial steps essential to buying time to counteract IBM's anticompetitive practices. They did not include canceling the investment in Seymour's new machine nor the plans to provide him with the laboratory in Chippewa Falls.

FLEXIBILITY

Personal flexibility is essential to the crisis manager. Don't accept anyone's preconceptions, not even your own. Be prepared to adjust and change in the face of surprises. The visible causes of crises inevitably mask hidden sources of problems. When I faced Control Data's liquidity crisis in 1985, it became painfully evident that the problem was not finance or the finance function, although certainly there were weaknesses and shortcomings in that regard. The more fundamental problem underneath was simply that of "too much too soon," an inability to manage a plethora of opportunities within the limitation of the company's managerial resources.

Many years later I became chairman and CEO of International Multifoods in the midst of a crisis with seemingly terminal consequences for the company. The obvious cause of the crisis was the financial nonperformance of a major business unit that, in turn, was ostensibly the result of a monumental failure in an ambitious management information system. Those problems were very real, but at the root of all that was a misguided attempt to manage an inherently decentralized business with centralized policies, structures, and information system. Flexibility means more than anything being intensely aware of the nuances in the situation and a willingness to learn—fast.

STRATEGIC ASSESSMENT

In any true strategic crisis there are both short-term and long-term implications. The crisis may arise because the basic business model is flawed; or it may be because original assumptions about market and technology are no longer valid, or it may simply be execution. In any event short-term strategies have to be devised to deal with exigencies of the moment. That means that the first challenge is to estimate your survival time. How long will your customers, the market, the financial community, or the organization itself give you to produce substantive change? So the first actions in a crisis have the straightforward purpose of gaining time and maneuvering room.

The basic challenge is to gain perspective on the problems causing the crisis. Obviously perspective comes from whatever factual information is available. But perspective also comes from people, especially employees and customers. Advisers and consultants are useful in distilling information, but perspective comes best by being where the action—or inaction—is.

While it is true that people will be your most invaluable source of perspective, a cautionary word is in order. Each individual views the situation through his or her own prism. Learn from *everyone,* believe *no one* completely! Remember that the *personal prism,* through which each individual views reality, is always in place.

Another common obstacle to overcome in seeking perspective is that people give answers such as: "If we would just do this, that or the other, the problem would be solved." That's understandable because in a crisis, like a mother dealing with a sick child, people desperately want the problem to be solved. But you are not looking for answers, you are looking for perspective, so the question to probe is *why* this person feels his or her answer is the right one.

With perspective diligently gathered, you will be surprised just how often, like the oracles of ancient Greece, *your answer* will be the correct one.

Action must be instantaneous. There is the action already mentioned to break people out of fear and worrying into a feeling of doing. Beyond that, realize there is never enough time, knowledge, and perspective to render a complete assessment or to wrap up your strategic conclusion in a tight and tidy package.

Action must not just be instantaneous, but also continuous in order to re-build momentum. Doing what is immediately possible to yield tangible albeit moderate results gives you time to further assess and take larger, more signifi-cant action. Just keep moving.

Qualities Essential to Effective
Crisis Management

Evoking stability out of instability, strategic assessment in the midst of strategic chaos, and taking purposeful action rather than mindless reaction require four important qualities in the crisis manager. Having lived by these ideals, I can tes-tify to their validity.

A CLEAR VIEW

Certainly an unencumbered view of the causes, effects, and characteristics of the crisis would be wonderful. The question is how to rid oneself of bias and ego. Those prisms may produce self-gratifying rainbows of color but certainly not an unobstructed view. How to achieve this? The answer, as in every other principle examined in the Control Data story, is *people.* The executives I assem-bled to help me came from without and within, but no matter where they came from, they brought new perspective. It is a serious mistake to implicitly believe all voices and views, but it is imperative to listen and, one hopes, arrive at new perspective and new thinking. It is equally wrong to surround oneself with like-minded people or obsequious sycophants.

A COLD APPRAISAL

What were the roots of the 1985 crisis? A cold appraisal was that it was too much, too soon. Contrary to the conventional view at the time, it was not Con-trol Data's ventures into the seemingly obscure land of "unmet societal needs as profitable business opportunities." It was, rather, that we had, like the kid in the candy store, availed ourselves too readily of every opportunity. We had more than we could manage. Meanwhile we were not dealing aggressively with the problems inherent in the services, computer systems, and peripheral products businesses brought on by the inevitable evolution of technology. There was too much attention to what might be the next opportunity and too little to the problems of the opportunities already in hand. Taking a hard, unbiased look at this failure fell on none other than myself. Every new services opportunity was exciting—it clearly had potential, even if poorly defined, and it was a great challenge to our capacity for innovation. What could be more enticing? And now the price had to be paid, and it was: in 1986, thirteen business units were sold or shut down. There were those outside the company, joyous in the prospect, and those within, discouraged, who viewed this as an abandonment of the "Norris era." That was nonsense. It was a cold appraisal of what it *took to survive—nothing more and nothing less.*

WILLINGNESS TO TAKE RISKS

Perhaps this is mostly a matter of personal courage. But it is also very much a matter of experience. Individuals have to be given the opportunity to take risks: to experience the thrill of success and to learn from their mistakes. They must be free from the stigma of failure. This was the most essential factor in Control Data's innovative culture. Not surprisingly, it stood us in good stead in times of crisis as well. With innovation one is venturing into the unknown. In crisis, one can never have all the facts. You have to make decisions. Seymour Cray, Jim Thornton, Bob Lillestrand, and many others took technological risks and made them work. That was part of Control Data's culture, and it likewise characterized the business decisions made in times of crisis. Those decisions also worked—not always perfectly and even at times with unanticipated consequences, but they worked.

NO LOOKING BACK

Risk taking means making decisions and acting without all the facts. Sometimes these decisions have very positive consequences, not the least of which is survival. Sometimes, however, the consequences are not so positive or are not immediate. While it is always useful to look back and learn, that is not the same as indulging in "if onlys" and wasting time second-guessing oneself. The former is healthy reflection, the latter is self-absorption and an inability to forgive oneself for being human. Ad nauseam critiques of the past can best be left to the Monday morning quarterbacks who have the time to indulge themselves. For the business executive, retrospection is a matter of learning and preparing for the future. That's what will make for a successful voyage in Strategic Space.

Chapter 13 Innovating

Beyond the Walls

Fires Set, Rocks Thrown in City Mob Outbreaks; Plymouth Ave.,
Downtown Sites Hit; Woman, Fireman Struck in Head
—*Minneapolis Tribune,* July 20, 1967

Violence Grips N. Side Again; 3 Shot, 21 Held
—*Minneapolis Star,* July 21, 1967

600 Guards Mobilized to Keep Order in City
—*Minneapolis Tribune,* July 22, 1967

The red glow of the flames reported in the daily papers of the Twin
Cities in July 1967 could do little to warm the hearts or brighten life's
prospects for the residents of the Northside area of Minneapolis.

In one corner of the metropolitan area of Minneapolis–St. Paul, however, those flames fueled what had already begun: the effort to bring
greater economic opportunity to minorities. It was one thing to read of
riots in the Watts section of Los Angeles or in the streets of Detroit or
Newark. It was quite another to see the devastation in our own backyard.

As Bill Norris, Norb Berg, and I witnessed the riotous destruction of local communities, we understood without much talk that what had been set loose in these events was the nihilism that only frustration and despair can spawn. We all felt the oppressive weight pressing down on those with sparse economic opportunity and knew that something must be done.

The solution we envisioned was twofold: education and training, and a *neighborhood* source of jobs to exercise those skills. The answer to address that seemingly impossible challenge was a new Control Data plant, Northside, in the Plymouth Avenue area where the riots had occurred.

The thinking in most quarters of U.S. business and government at this time was this: Did the wave of disillusionment and unrest urgently demand response by federal, state and local government? Of course. That's what Lyndon Johnson's Great Society was all about. But thus far the results were slow in coming and marginal in effect. Meantime, too many young people had given up hope and, all too literally, the economic resources of the country were being consumed in flames.

These and related thoughts were not so concise and well ordered in 1967 as they are in retrospect, but their essence was certainly obvious to us and they soon became distilled into one of Bill Norris's more famous quotes: "Hell, you can't do business in a society that's burning."

SOFT INNOVATION

Addressing the problem of jobs and revitalizing ghetto communities requires management and innovation, and the best place to find those qualities is in the business community. Businesses have resources and decision-making processes that afford quicker action than most government agencies can offer. Our unarticulated ideas about conducting business for the good of social welfare later evolved into a formal expression of Control Data's mission as "Addressing Society's Major Unmet Needs as Profitable Business Opportunities." This specifically meant that Control Data would serve the public purpose through computer and information services where it could. In everyday terms, it meant doing well by doing good.

Such a strategy clearly involved resources and expertise considerably beyond Control Data's internal capacity. It would involve not only other businesses, but the support and knowledge of a variety of government agencies at all levels: local, state, and federal. Thus it would take the company's demonstrated skill at collaboration to a new level of complexity—and audacity. That is, we would use familiar skills in new ways.

It is helpful to look at an analogy between innovation in producing high-performance computing equipment and innovation in fashioning higher-performance socioeconomic environments. Two factors determine computer performance: basic *circuit technology* and the *architecture* of the computer design. Similarly there exist two basic determinants of sociological and economic performance. Those are *skilled people* and *jobs*. Training and education are essential to developing the skills to perform meaningful jobs. Job creation is the result of a complex interaction of private sector initiative and innovation and public sector facilitation—in other words, *societal architecture.*

Just as Seymour Cray, Jim Thornton, and other computing innovators had brilliant insight into the interaction of semiconductor technology and computing system architecture, so too did Control Data attract and develop individuals with amazing insight into the "architecture" of public–private collaborations that would result in a higher-performance society—more and better job creation.

Throughout this book I have shown that there are various forms of innovation, and not all are confined to new products or services. Some commentators have referred to nontechnical innovations as "soft innovations," and I'll retain that language with the caveat that the term does not do justice to the difficulty and messiness of innovations of this ilk. "Soft" makes them sound easy or less important, and I can assure you that they are neither.

As in the case of Northside, one variant of soft innovation involves public–private collaborations outside of the corporation—in full public view and under the bright glare of elected public officials. Thus the inevitable false starts, frustration, and rethinking that are inherent in all innovation are not shielded from the media's lack of understanding and penchant for second-guessing. Innovation, in this arena, requires more single-minded, dogged determination than in any other. It also requires a very thick skin: In pursuit of this seemingly laudable and creative approach to some of the most intransigent societal problems, Control Data would be simultaneously accused of "foggy-minded-do-good-ism" (by some conservative commentators) and of "trying to make money off the backs of the poor" (by those of a more liberal bent). The antiapartheid groups vociferously railed against the company's efforts in South Africa, including using computer-based education to raise the education opportunity for black people. Just to leave no stone of criticism unturned, antiwar protestors used the forum of the company's annual meeting to present Bill Norris with the "black sword of ignominy," in protest of Control Data–supplied computers to the defense department. Stone-faced, Bill took the sword and laid it aside without comment. These fleabites, while irritating, did not deter us from our strategic course.

INNOVATION IN THE LOCATION AND
STRUCTURE OF PRODUCTION FACILITIES

The Northside Case

The genesis venture in job creation was a manufacturing plant in the heart of the scene of the Minneapolis riots. So-called inner city plants were not unique even then, but the creativity that went into Control Data's Minneapolis Northside plant turned it into a remarkable performer. The initial instructions were to make it "an integral part of the production of our high performance computers." And not just an integral part but a *sole source* integral part. As to how to do this, the answer was, "Whatever it takes." It had to perform to the standards of any of the company's manufacturing facilities. This meant it was necessary, particularly in the beginning, to provide some unusual services for its employees.

The Northside plant, when it opened on January 15, 1968, was built to employ more than 230 people. It was expressly intended to provide jobs *in the neighborhood.* Before we began work on the plant, we sought out the neighborhood leaders, who had an interest in its betterment—and who could advise on issues related to staffing, training, and such. To build in any neighborhood it is critical to first get to know the people of that neighborhood. The company began its own learning process. As Roger Wheeler, general manager of personnel services, described it: "We developed a work rule funnel. We made the rules wider and more flexible in the beginning, then narrowed them gradually. In six months, they were the same as in other plants. We worked with black leadership. We looked at the 4-page employee application form. There was a suspicion that the selection process screened out minorities. We threw out the long form and did a one-page application that essentially required checkmarks. We eliminated questions like, 'Have you ever been arrested?' We screened people *in* rather than screening them *out.* We kept the physical [examination], but not as a screening tool."

The plant's average employment comprised 65 percent blacks and American Indians, and 35 percent whites. Half were female. The employee profile included:

- High school dropouts.
- High school graduates who still needed help in reading and math.
- People with only part-time or seasonal job experience.
- Women receiving Aid to Families with Dependent Children.
- The unemployed and those with no apparent residence.
- People with prison records.

There was a high turnover rate at first. Many in assembly jobs had no work experience. There was lots of management pressure and community attention. Gary Lohn, an Augsburg College graduate, started work part-time to gather data on the operation of inner city plants, and especially to track the causes of turnover and absenteeism. He became a full-time employee at Northside doing research that, as he put it, "sounded like a hell of a lot more fun than analyzing plans for Shell Oil in downtown Chicago." Gary's report on social services and inner city plants speaks for itself. He wrote: "It's a very clear goal in terms of operating—take the jobs to the people, but make the plant work. Maybe a half-dozen companies did the first part, but not the second."

Northside was the sole source of peripheral controllers for Control Data's computer systems. It *had* to work. The computer business was booming in 1968–1969 and quantities kept increasing. It was a fishbowl experience with community leaders and journalists watching every move. We were experimenting on the run.

Several years later, in the early '70s, Gary Lohn wrote: "The plant had stabilized. Many of the people who came in as welfare mothers with no work experience were now first-line supervisors . . . they were more familiar with some of the people and some of the problems and some of the games than the guys from the suburbs, so they could handle some of the counseling kind of stuff."

This was uncharted territory, and what was needed could not be anticipated. For example, we knew that there would be good reason to have personal and legal counseling. The Twin Cities law firm Oppenheimer, Wolff and Donnelly agreed to provide free legal help. Two lawyers came in two afternoons a week. However, it was soon evident as operations got under way that more than just legal assistance would be required; for example, a bail bondsman would be needed—especially on Monday mornings.

Like many other Control Data innovations, this one had the power to attract highly skilled people: as the proficiency level of the plant increased, more and more people wanted in. Success begets success, and skill attracts skill. Two early leaders in to the Northside project were Bill English and Fred Green. Bill went on to become a vice president in Government Systems, and Fred, after great success at Control Data, ended up running his own independent company. Norma Anderson, who came to Control Data from the government's Head Start program and who went on to become a vice president of the company, was intrigued by the idea of a developmental day care center. Early on we discovered that one of the major reasons for absenteeism and turnover was lack of child care. In response Control Data started one of the first on-site day care centers. Because of Norma, the center not only fulfilled its role in assisting employees of the plant, but it also became a magnet for other parents in the community, and over the next several years served as a model program for many such day care centers across the country.

The Selby Bindery Case

Establishing the Northside plant was a response to a perceived need for creating a more stable community in which to do business while improving conditions of the community in which it was based. It was an innovative coupling of that perceived need with the basic business need for high-quality, low-cost manufacturing that enabled the idea to take hold.

Other collaborations followed. In 1970 the St. Paul Urban Coalition expressed the need for jobs if there was to be any prospect for correcting the social ills that beset the people of the Selby Community of St. Paul. Norb Berg was a member of the Urban Coalition. As he listened to the discussion he asked a simple question: "How many jobs does it take to make a difference?" Fifty, it was said, would be a great help. On the spot Norb made his decision and committed Control Data to provide that number. He had no idea what those jobs might be or how to deal with the myriad problems that might be involved. But considering that Control Data employed some ten thousand people in the Twin Cities, fifty seemed a manageable number.

Imagine our consternation, then, when, within days of Norb's commitment, the annual budgeting process made it clear that there would have to be a *reduction* in the manufacturing employment in the Twin Cities! But a commitment was a commitment if any level of trust was to be built between the company and the community. What was needed was a way to match community need with company need. There was such a match. We needed to consolidate the technical and other publication requirements of the computer division—which at the time were dispersed and inefficient—into a single facility. The work included punching, printing, stapling, collating, and shipping. The idea was further developed and gave rise to another innovation: operating the proposed bindery on a split shift basis by attracting single mothers who would work in the mornings, and by using high school and college students for after-school hours.

There are always leaders or potential leaders who can galvanize the support needed. Selby area resident Dick Mangram was such a person. Dick became the general manager and, some years later, head of the buyout group that took over the operation. Also, two neighborhood women, Betty Barr and Lucille Archer, were attracted to the opportunity and became not just exemplary employees, but first-line supervisors in the new plant. The Selby bindery did more than just fulfill the fifty-job commitment. It ultimately employed several hundred people and attracted business from companies other than Control Data. It became a source of pride for the community. There never was any graffiti on the building. The facility planners, Pat Conway and Ron Cauldwell, insisted that there be a basketball hoop in the parking lot and that it *always* have a net. It was the only net in the neighborhood. Commitment is demonstrated in ways large and small.

The Selby Bindery received national attention. It was featured on the *Today Show* and attracted visits from figures such as Supreme Court Chief Justice Warren Burger, boxer George Foreman, Jesse Jackson, John Kenneth Galbraith, every Minnesota governor of the period, Senator Orrin Hatch, and then-Secretary of Labor Ray Marshall. Most important, many of the students who worked there were able to go on to college and escape the clutches of poverty and lack of opportunity. The three daughters of Ernie and Mary Peyton are striking examples: one earned a Ph.D. degree, one a master's degree, and one a B.A. degree. The Peytons' daughter Gwen became assistant superintendent of the Minneapolis School District.

The operation had not only the leadership of Dick Mangram, Betty Barr, and Lucille Archer, but also the support and counsel from Control Data executives. These people were unsung innovators in matching a need to available resources and technology. Whenever I think of a problem as being "too hard," I remember Selby. Leadership, collaboration, and innovation can overcome seemingly impossible obstacles. Like Northside, it demonstrates the originality and tenacity that creativity demands when responding to discernable needs.

The World Distribution Center Case

If the Selby bindery was an innovative venture into new territory of job creation and community involvement, the next major Control Data initiative in St. Paul was a demonstration of equal ingenuity and assiduity by the office of the mayor of St. Paul, George Latimer. In the late '60s Control Data was scratching, patching, and improvising to meet the need for worldwide distribution of the spare parts necessary to maintain its now far-flung computer installations and the OEM customers of its peripheral equipment. The maintenance organization had made a careful study of its needs. It developed the plan for a new, highly efficient distribution system whose central hub would be a brand new World Distribution Center (WDC) to be located in a Minneapolis suburb. The projected start of construction was December 1977, with completion one year later. George Latimer and his right-hand man, Dick Broeker, were talking to Norb and Pat Conway about Control Data, what the Selby bindery had meant, and future possibilities. Norb mentioned the WDC but felt that it would be impractical because of the short schedule for starting and completing the facility. George and Dick took that as a challenge. In fact, they later told me, "The tight time was essential. It gave our organizations a sense of urgency." Urgency can be a great motivator; it was, for example, the growing competition from Japanese electronics and computer companies that led to the development of the MCC research consortium.

One aspect of the WDC undertaking serves to illustrate its magnitude and complexity. Obtaining the site for it in St. Paul involved condemning thirty-two homes in the Selby–Dale area. Obtaining permission and agreement from the owners and residents and, at the same time, producing a positive attitude about the project was no small task. And it had to be done quickly or Control Data would go back to its original plan of building in the suburbs. Those who believe that a project bringing hundreds of jobs and infrastructure improvement receives instant acceptance simply have not experienced the skepticism that dominates blighted communities. Fortunately there was community activist Dr. Jim Shelton, who took on the project as a personal mission. His effort made it happen. The site was cleared, construction began, and the WDC leaped from vision to reality.

Three other key ingredients were at work in this project to allow Control Data and St. Paul to make the collaboration successful. First of all was *trust*. "Trust," said George, "was built one step at a time. It started with two people, Steve Maxwell, an African American judge, and Norb Berg, who were both members of the Urban Coalition." Trust grew with the successful undertaking of the Selby project. It was built up within the community. It developed in city government agencies such as planning and economic development. George said that "Control Data's actions induced a feeling of credibility and trust in some pretty hardened bureaucrats." St. Paul, he pointed out, also had something of a head start, because, in spite of many problems common to blighted urban communities, it had a much better than average availability of skilled people.

Two other factors, George told me, were, first, that those involved had no qualms about "How do we look in this matter? There was no fear of public, political, or legal fall out." Innovation is never for the fainthearted. And second, these collaborative undertakings were to be managed at the top. "Delegation," he noted, "causes good ideas to disappear like fog on a sunny day." So the essential principles of successful strategic alliances between corporations are likewise applicable in public–private collaboration: Trust cannot be wished into existence, it must be built step-by-step; responsibility for the alliance must reside at the executive level responsible for strategy; and, there must always be a surfeit of courage.

THE HARD LESSONS OF SOFT INNOVATION

Northside, Selby, and the WDC were three examples of bringing jobs to people rather than vice versa, and of being willing to resolve a knot of diverse social problems. We had many other plants that local communities depended on, and we always took our responsibilities in these areas very seriously. Campton was a plant located in rural Kentucky. There were plants in smaller towns in Minnesota such as Bemidji, Cambridge, Faribault, Redwood Falls, and Spring Grove. Certainly one of the more challenging was a facility in the heart of Washington, D.C., that brought jobs and pride to the people of a blighted section of our nation's capital.

There were disappointments as well as remarkable successes. What was most important, however, was the innovative development of new approaches in everything from real estate management by people such as Pat Conway and Ron Cauldwell to new human resource policies like Roger Wheeler's "funnel" application process. There were likewise innovative approaches to skill development in hitherto underutilized workers and employing the talents of community leaders such as Dick Mangram and Jim Shelton. Dynamic political leaders, George Latimer in St. Paul and Henry Cisneros in San Antonio, were essential to success.

Control Data's urban and rural area plants were receiving national attention within two years of the Northside initial venture. An article titled "Ghetto Jobs—It Works, But Will It?" appeared in the September 1970 issue of *Government Executive*. The article described the great success at the Selby plant and pointed out the difficulty in maintaining initiative as companies have economic downturns such as those Control Data and other computer companies were experiencing in 1970–1971. In a sidebar, it provides this summary of lessons learned (my comments are in bracketed text following some of the bulleted items):

> Quite apart from the business facts of it, Control Data has learned a great deal about involvement and communication with people as it has moved into the ghetto and rural poverty pockets of the Nation—so much so that it now offers a course in Minority Group Dynamics to others interested in tracking the same path. The mistakes made and lessons learned fill a catalog. Here is a summary of what every socially-minded corporation ought to consider:

> • Always under-promise and over-deliver to the people. [To win enduring support, it is imperative to meet people's expectations. That is more easily done by conservatively estimating what is achievable rather than hyping the prospects of programs and subsequently disappointing people.]
> • You have to be very, very careful about the person you put in charge of the plant. [It is extremely important to probe the character and sensitivities of management to find the person who is tolerant of diversity and respectful of employees in his or her employment.]
> • The employees are going to need personal counselors. [It often is assumed that everyone has the resources and networks to readily respond to life's big and little problems. Not so. For many people, professional assistance is outside their grasp. Those who are economically disadvantaged have problems very much like yours and mine but lack access to the people and resources to help resolve them. For example, many of us can find answers to our legal, family, and financial problems through professional connections, extended family, and money: for instance, we can pick up the phone, get three minutes of advice from a lawyer and be done with the darn thing. Such a trivial frustration can be a terrible burden to those less fortunate. This fact led us to supply counselors and attorneys for employees in need of assistance.]
> • From a people standpoint, every new plant is not necessarily the same as every other one. [Communities aren't identical, and neither are the needs of the people within them. It would have been inappropriate to apply one set of policies across every neighborhood in which we did business. In our Campton facility, for instance, there was no need for day care. If day care goes awry, there are sixteen dozen relatives to pick up the slack. One thing we did have to change there, however, was our standing policy against nepotism; otherwise we would have been able to hire only one person in the community.]
> • Before you put a plant in an area, send diplomatic envoys in to establish commu-

nity relations, learn the local mores, local politics. [In order to overcome the inherent suspicion and credibility gap, make it clear that if you are not wanted, you are not coming in. The cause must be mutual and voluntary—not one purely of persuasion, that is, of getting people to affirm what you were going to do anyway. The worst thing you can do is put a big announcement in the newspaper. Nothing can get shot down quicker than if the local community, which is going to benefit, first hears about it in the local paper.]

- Find out what kinds of people really are "hard core."
- Hire people as you find them. [You start with where you are and not with where you desire them to be. The only way to make positive change is to plan based on realistic assessments of the current state of affairs.]
- Be willing to train people at their own pace. [People bring different bundles of skill sets to the workplace and different capacities to learn new things at different speeds. This means that training has to be customized to the person in order to bring that person up to acceptable levels of performance.]
- Offer the same starting pay. [Don't treat new employees as if you are doing them a favor and ought to be thankful that they have a job at all—thereby justifying below-standard treatment. Relationships must be reciprocal. You have hired them to do a job and the expectation is that they will. Therefore, pay them and give them benefits according to what the job is worth.]

The full list is a good deal longer. Probably the best summary came not from Control Data management but from a local African-American resident and (once militant) employee in one ghetto plant during one of the frequent management–employee meetings. He said: "I hope you help prove once and for all the old assumption that black people don't want to work is wrong."

We did. And beyond that we demonstrated that we had the skills to forge collaboration between ourselves and the public sector to better achieve the objectives of both. In the process, thousands of jobs were produced and new opportunities opened to those previously without much hope.

If, as already noted, technological collaboration is the sine qua non of robust business growth, public—private collaboration is that and more to robust societal growth. But it must not be taken for granted that these collaborations will last forever. The strategic overlap—that is, the overlap of community and company need—may go away, and it is best if everyone involved is thinking about that eventuality. I remember that when we opened the plant in Bemidji, a small town in northern Minnesota, a celebration was planned by all our local friends and partners. That was fine, but we were already concerned about what to do when the plant would have to be closed because the technology change would make it obsolete. Bill Norris even injected into his dedication speech a comment on planning for closing the plant in five–seven years. It was not especially well received. But the point Bill made was a most important one. We could all rejoice in the circumstance: the strategic overlap that brought Control Data and the community into a mutually beneficial alliance. However, the future rests not on clinging to the benefit of the moment. It rests on the degree to which we use that benefit to develop skills and perspective to be applied in the future.

Chapter 14 Extraordinary Innovation, Extraordinary Collaboration

No problem is more eye opening and perspective enhancing than witnessing firsthand the ravenous effects of severe deprivation on other human beings.
—Robert M. Price

The examples in the preceding chapter illustrate some of the ways in which Control Data used its internal manufacturing and operational assets to enhance job creation in blighted urban and rural areas. Innovation in job creation, however, was not limited to that. Various new services were devised to foster small business formation and job creation in more direct ways. Each of these services required collaboration with the public sector.

FOSTERING JOB CREATION

Business and Technology Centers (BTCs)

The first of three new services provided a facility where small businesses could be given the support that would help ensure their survival. A Business and Technology Center is a physical location where multiple new or existing small businesses could reside and have access to training and education via the PLATO learning system, management and technical consulting services, administrative and clerical services such as payroll, and accounting and human resources. In addition, by co-locating, small businesses would have better opportunity to share operating and management problems.

The first BTC opened in 1979 and was located in downtown St. Paul in an abandoned facility. Subsequently the BTC became part of the standard repertoire for economic development employed by City Venture, about which more will soon be said. Ultimately, more than twenty BTCs were established.[1]

The BTC idea involved a lot of creative real estate procurement and management. One of the most conspicuous BTCs was in downtown Minneapolis, adjacent to the Hubert H. Humphrey Metrodome, the new home of the Minnesota Vikings National Football League team and the Minnesota Twins, a Major League Baseball team.

While the real estate procurement aspect of these endeavors was done with great creativity and imagination, the ongoing management of the properties was not a proven strength of the company, and much had to be learned in that regard. Profitably managing a myriad of small tenants proved to be a challenge.

The BTC concept, however, was so appealing that soon the "business incubator" became a standard tool of economic developers in both public and private sectors. Universities also have used similar models to facilitate utilization of technology developed by their researchers.

Small Business Advisory Services

Providing management and technical expertise to small business was integral to the BTC concept. This idea of providing such services was formalized in a new business called Control Data Business Advisors, Inc. (CDBAI). The task of establishing this business was initially given to one of the company's entrepreneurial business supplies executives, Peter Bailey. CDBAI established offices in several of the BTCs and in other locations as well. CDBAI had a small core of full-time functional experts, and in addition marshaled a wide range of consulting expertise in the local areas in which they were located. All Control Data employees who had talents that were potentially marketable to small business were listed in its data bank of consulting expertise and were made available on a part-time basis. George Troy, who later moved from an executive position in Commercial Credit to take over responsibility for CDBAI, described its origins and motivation in his chapter of the book *Corporate Creativity.*[2] I cite him at length since he appropriately expresses Control Data's extraordinary flair for entrepreneurship.

> The subject of entrepreneurship has always been close to Control Data's heart. I would like to portray some of the entrepreneurial flavor of Control Data's history, a synopsis of our continuing involvement in and commitment to entrepreneurship, and some thoughts on where we want it to take us.
>
> Peter Drucker once said, "Business has only two basic functions, marketing and innovation." In broadest terms it is innovation that the entrepreneur provides—the idea, the technology, the new process or procedure that offers, on one hand, an increase in real productivity and requires, on the other, a substantial measure of risk. I say "real productivity" because there is no shortage of "paper entrepreneurs"—people capable of tremendous creativity in accounting or finance or legal theory but whose work really involves rearranging existing assets and has no direct contribution to aggregate gain and economic productivity. Also, the extent of the risk taken by a paper entrepreneur usually extends no further than his or her own job, whereas the entrepreneurial activity we are concerned with typically carries with it the potential success or failure of an entire venture. *If it succeeds, the real gains will include perhaps the most important of all productivity considerations, job creation.*
>
> Several years ago Control Data concluded that we could realize additional income from our own past investments by making available to smaller companies our underused or dated technology, along with professional and management expertise and support services. One expression of this is the creation of business and technology centers. These are physical plants that provide various combinations of consulting services, laboratories, manufacturing, and office space as well as other services that facilitate the start-up and growth of small businesses. Economies of scale make it possible to provide business and technology center tenants . . . with needed facilities and services of higher quality at considerably lower cost than they could get elsewhere.
>
> Control Data is also assisting small business by promoting public and private cooperation across a broad front. One effort is the Minnesota Cooperation Office (MCO). The MCO's approach is simple. An entrepreneur has an idea for a new product or service and wants to start a company. He or she comes to the MCO, and MCO helps develop a business plan and obtain financing. The permanent staff of the MCO is small, but a volunteer advisory panel of engineers, scientists, and executives evaluate and assist in preparation of the business plans. Because the plans are expertly conceived, the chances of receiving financing and achieving economic viability are increased accordingly.
>
> In addition, Control Data is active in the Minnesota Seed Capital Fund and the Help Start a Company Program, both of which do what their names suggest.[3]
>
> Another major business thrust is my organization, Control Data Business Advi-

sors. Our senior management recognized that smaller companies had a need for experienced professional assistance. Major consulting firms typically have no interest in these companies, and the resources they do have access to—local accounting firms, for example—are by nature rather limited. At the same time, the expertise required by these companies did exist within Control Data. So Business Advisors was formed to identify that expertise and market it. The company was set up with key Control Data employees, and we were given access to the rest of the 50,000 Control Data people around the country as a talent pool from which to draw resources.

We were also given the ability to cannibalize Control Data's internal operations for anything it was felt could be sold externally. Right away we found a series of things like occupational analysis and employee attitude surveys that, with some very simple repackaging, amounted to more than $1 million in revenue in my organization last year. We are doing this same thing in the financial area and with [information] technology.

Control Data has a number of [information] technologies that—by the company's standards—are outdated but that still have a market and a use. Business Advisors will be in a position of identifying these and selling them to smaller firms throughout the country.

Business Advisors and these other efforts serve a number of purposes. They further Control Data's business strategy by addressing the need for job creation through a healthy small business sector. They also provide potentially lucrative markets for Control Data's goods and services.

CDBAI was but one more way in which Control Data people were stimulated to think expansively. *Many people have dormant talents in their job of the moment—waiting for expression.* Many companies believe that allowing employees to reach beyond the stated job description is a loser's game because it diverts attention and productive energy away from what needs to be expressly performed. But this construes innovation as a zero-sum game. It assumes that the time one devotes to the job is fixed, but creative minds do not spontaneously shut down at 5 p.m. Many are just getting going when the sun sets. The loser's game is depriving organizations of the best employees have to offer by artificially restricting the areas in which they may contribute. Gaining additional problem-solving experience dramatically increased the awareness that is so essential to innovation.

City Venture

The problem of urban revitalization was an urgent need as demonstrated early on by experiences in Minneapolis and St. Paul. It could only be addressed by providing local residents with the opportunity to have decent jobs and adequate training and skill development to secure those jobs. That's straightforward enough, but the task of mustering the requisite resources is truly difficult. To attack this problem, Control Data initiated a consortium called City Venture Corporation, and provided several executives for that operation, including its president, Herb Trader. The following excerpt from an essay written by Bill Norris and titled "Technology Innovation and the Prudent Man" is a succinct description of City Venture in the first years of its existence:

> Clearly, major societal needs are interrelated, so successful efforts to address them must be similarly interrelated. For example, unemployment is reduced with better education; jobs are created by developing new sources of energy . . . conversely, these kinds of opportunities are needed if a meaningful livelihood from entrepreneurial enterprise is to be made available to millions more people. Because of the diverse and extensive capabilities required in building and rebuilding urban areas, a consortium approach is required, and, for the first time, adequate resources have been brought together by City Venture in a unique and efficient pooling of the resources of individual organizations. At present, the large corporate participants in City Venture include Control Data, Reynolds Metals, Dayton-Hudson, Honeywell, St. Paul Companies, Northwest Bancorporation, First Bank System, Minneapolis Star and Tribune Company and Medtronic. Small organizations include a construction company and an architectural firm; last, but not least, are the American Lutheran Church and the United Church of Christ. That's a highly unusual group of organizations.
>
> More specifically, City Venture plans and manages the implementation of innovative and comprehensive programs for both the revitalization of existing urban areas and for creating new cities.
>
> The approach mandates that any plan for building and restoring a community must be based on meeting residents' needs for high quality, accessible and affordable education and training, and, even more important, decent jobs. Under this approach, small enterprises are a major source of jobs, as well as important means for building, rebuilding and maintaining housing and commercial centers. Small businesses also participate in providing health care, education and other social services, as well as food production, processing and distribution, and waste recycling.
>
> City Venture is two years old, but in that time contracts have been obtained for projects in Minneapolis, Toledo, Philadelphia, Baltimore, St. Paul and Miami.
>
> To give you some indication of the impact of a typical City Venture project, let me quote from a recent speech by Mr. George Haigh, CEO of Toledo Trust Inc., and one of the leaders responsible for the effort to revitalize the Warren-Sherman area in Toledo:
>
> "The project began with a neighborhood that suffered unemployment in excess of 32 percent; inadequate, run-down housing; low household incomes; inadequate

shopping; lack of small business; and lack of recreational facilities. Crime, arson, and pride-sapping neighborhood decay were all too evident. Using City Venture, a Minneapolis-based corporation, as a catalyst and gaining the trust and active decision-making involvement of neighborhood people, neighborhood organizations, the City of Toledo, and several private businesses, a unique program began to rapidly take shape. Not a program featuring handouts, but, rather, one that would provide improved neighborhood housing, training and education for hundreds, over a thousand additional neighborhood jobs, a new business and technology center to help minority business, a new shopping center, new parks for recreational use—and the list goes on. Most importantly, however, is that these programs are all investments that are aimed at producing profit for the private sector, pride for the neighborhood and real opportunities for people."

Right or wrong, this was the vision we had to help those in the inner city restore their communities. Yes, it took creativity and persistence to fuse a multitude of interests into a unified plan of action. The fact that we succeeded at all in this may be sufficient cause for satisfaction. But even more rewarding is the understanding that conceiving of and developing new social architectures is a creative endeavor and no less awe-inspiring than creativity in science and technology. There was a need and an attendant vision was shaped through community efforts. The goal was to replace despair with hope and vibrancy. With the assistance of many fine organizations and community leaders, we worked to make that possible.

Rural Ventures

Following the pattern established by City Venture, a new consortium called Rural Ventures, Inc., was put in place in 1980 to address the fact that small family farms generally were economically depressed and would soon disappear— uprooted as swiftly and thoroughly as Dorothy's farm in Kansas. Quite apart from the cultural desirability of the small family farm, increasingly questions were being raised about the overspecialization, the energy dependence, and the transportation demands of megafarms. On its own, Control Data had initiated the purchase of 1,200 acres of land in Princeton, Minnesota, with the intent of making that land available to ten–fifteen small farmers. Control Data initially would rent the land to the tenant farmer and subsequently allow them to purchase it on favorable terms.

The Rural Ventures consortium consisted of the five dioceses of the Minnesota Catholic Church, the SuperValu Company and the large cooperative Land O' Lakes. Brian Roth, general manager of Agriculture Technology Products and Services, explained the idea underpinning the initiative in this way: "Large scale farms and small scale farms historically have been equated with successful and unsuccessful. That's an erroneous rating. It really is well-managed farms vs. poorly managed ones. And poor management isn't always the [farmer's] fault. It can mean the manager doesn't have the tools that are available to the larger scale producer."

Computer technology was, of course, the underpinning of the plan to achieve this better management by the small-scale farmer. Not only would there be some ten management systems ranging from planning crops, livestock choice, and herd management to accounting and marketing. There would also be a data bank of agricultural technology and computer-based training with the courseware written through the cooperative efforts of some fifteen universities and other organizations.

By means of these information and management systems the recipients could achieve higher production per acre with lower capital investment and fossil fuel consumption.

The obstacle of capital was—and still is—a major hurdle for the would-be small farmer. The Rural Ventures endeavor sought to overcome this obstacle by the expedience of sharing that cost. The equipment necessary for operations: tractors, plows, planting and tilling equipment, and combines and other harvesting machines would be shared. The total cost could easily amount to half a million dollars or more but when divided among the dozen or so farms would become much more manageable.

The target net income for these small farmers was $25,000–$30,000 on a gross income of $300,000. These figures in 2005 dollars would be $70,000 and $700,000 respectively. It was an ambitious undertaking and was viewed with even more skepticism than had greeted many of Control Data's ventures. One somewhat benign criticism ran along these lines: "I certainly look upon Control Data as well-meaning . . . on the face of things," said Ed Grady, manager of Minnesota Farm Bureau Federation Information Division. "But I'm not at all assured that theirs is the right route to go if you want to enhance or improve viable agriculture either immediately or long range."

Others were considerably more caustic. In the face of the skeptics, Rural Ventures achieved some notable successes and won contracts with a Native American Alaska development corporation for an agricultural plan for a native village in an area above the Arctic Circle. Because of the extended daylight that far north, the cabbages were unbelievably huge! Rural Ventures also had a contract with the State of Virginia to prepare a development plan for a region of ten low-income counties in that state. Rural Ventures never achieved the widespread success originally envisioned, but it reaffirmed that information technology can improve farm management skills and that, in yet another sector of the economy, public–private collaboration is a powerful tool.

Control Data's innovative architectures for job creation such as City Venture, CDBAI, Rural Ventures, MCO, Minnesota Seed Capital Fund, BTCs, and manufacturing plants in inner city and rural areas, created thousands of jobs. And not just jobs, but ones highly leveraged for positive economic and social impact. The lesson they have for business and government leaders, however, is much more profound than job creation statistics: complex, deeply rooted economic and social problems are highly resistant to solutions by legislation, and market forces are sadly weak in such circumstances; but by collaboration that draws on the strengths of business and government, seemingly intransigent problems give way. *Poverty and despair give way to productivity and hope.*

EDUCATION AND SKILL DEVELOPMENT

The two basic determinants of sociological and economic performance are jobs and skilled people to fill those jobs. Having invested heavily in innovative ways to promote job creation, we needed to dedicate more time to the matter of locating skilled people to fill jobs. As described in relation to the Northside plant, this is more than posting notices on the Internet or, in those days, running help wanted ads. A more proactive approach is recognizing and tapping labor pools that have been unused because of inadequate skills.

The PLATO system proved to be the ideal means of efficiently reaching prospective workers to provide enhanced training in a variety of nonacademic settings. In this instance, without the obstacles thrown up by an entrenched, close-minded education system, there was remarkable success.

Fair Break

Fair Break was a program developed and designed to attack the causes of chronic unemployment. The program was for those who lacked:

• A functional level of literacy
• Occupational skill training
• A high school diploma or its equivalent
• Adequate job search skills
• Appropriate work attitudes and behaviors
• Confidence and self-esteem

Fair Break began as an internal Control Data program. It made good business sense to train people to work in the company's inner-city plants. The people trained through this internal program proved its efficacy, and, once again, we believed an internal program could be successfully deployed to meet extant social needs.

Fair Break was composed of several segments, all or any of which could fit into an existing program designed to help the disadvantaged, undereducated and unemployed. Those segments included:

Remediation Services. These included Basic Skills Learning and General Educational Development (GED) instruction. Basic Skills comprised reading, mathematics, and language from the third- to the eighth-grade level.

Personal Development Services. This segment's purpose was to increase each person's self-confidence and independence. It included group support counseling and instruction in life management skills: money management, credit, insurance, and investment. The skills and knowledge gained helped participants manage their financial resources and function as informed consumers.

Job Search Training. Instruction and practice were combined with emotional support and encouragement in a systematic approach to self-guided job placement.

Staff Development. The Fair Break program included a training course for staff development and was called "The Helping Relationship." The emphasis was on developing coaching and communication skills that were essential for the effective implementation of the program.

Fair Break utilized a number of instructional methods to present information to participants. Audiovisual materials, texts, individual and group counseling, role-play, and simulation were all part of the training package. PLATO computer-based education was integral. Computer-based education proved itself particularly effective with people who had a history of difficulty with more traditional educational methods, and it proved to be a highly effective alternative delivery system. One of the chief advantages of Fair Break was its flexibility. Its products and services could be integrated with existing employment preparation programs to meet specific client needs.

The first Fair Break program began in May 1978 in St. Paul, Minnesota, under Title IV of the Comprehensive Employment and Training Act. Goals for the initial program period included an 80 percent completion of basic skills, 50 percent GED certification, and 50 percent placement in full-time, unsubsidized employment. All of these program goals were met. Ultimately Fair Break was used by more than fifty agencies nationwide, helping to meet the needs of the disadvantaged. Those served included: young people, welfare recipients, prison inmates, Native Americans, displaced homemakers, and disadvantaged adults. A subsequent evaluation of three Fair Break programs showed a GED completion total of 92.6 percent, and a program outcome of 76.3 percent employment placement.

REQUISITES FOR SUCCESS

The personalities and background of the people who were the progenitors of the foregoing innovations in public–private collaboration are as varied as those of Control Data's original innovators in high-performance computing. These people were not professionals at economic development, nor were they social scientists, nor specialists in agronomy. Indeed many of them came from the mainstream of the computer business or the Commercial Credit finance business. Yet they demonstrated wonderful creativity and innovation in addressing a variety of very difficult problems. It was, once again, the environment for innovation created by Control Data's values, policies, and practices that allowed these people to exercise their remarkable diversity of talent.

There was another ingredient in these success stories: the nature and quality of corporate governance provided by the company's board of directors, and the active support and involvement of top management. Otherwise, they would have remained simply hobbies to be tinkered with in someone's spare time, which is to say, never. These experiences with public–private relationships have led me to the following observations and conclusions.

Policies for Fostering Cooperation

Most company executives do not think of cooperation with other companies, and certainly not with government. A board can encourage, even insist upon, participation in at least one consortium. The possibilities are numerous: environmental protection and enhancement; water resources; improved energy sources; urban revitalization; more affordable healthcare; and education. The cost of such participation is relatively small; the benefits to the corporation can be very great. Participation in such consortia will generate sales for existing products and services. More important, because such efforts frequently involve the use of emerging technologies, the company will be among the first to discover opportunities for new products and services. Aside from these direct benefits, the company also benefits from the exposure of its executives to the problems that come from a rainbow of causes.

Strategy is a problem-solving process that, with practice in a variety of settings, can be learned and fine-tuned. A person's problem-solving ability develops with knowledge, perspective, and practice. Perspective comes from engagement; from witnessing firsthand how others must grapple with challenging, and often life-threatening, problems. As noted at the head of this chapter: No problem is more eye-opening and perspective enhancing than witnessing firsthand the ravenous effects of severe deprivation on other human beings.

Fostering cooperation with government is a challenge. But the potential benefits to everyone make that a challenge worth the effort. One of the most important skills of a true business leader is an ability to marshal resources. The government has money. It also has within its various agencies the knowledge and skills to carry out their missions. By coordinating and aggregating resources and skills, business can at one and the same time enhance its business and make government agencies' very large expenditures more effective.

Engendering Trust

Inherent in these enterprises is the board's responsibility to ensure that the corporation is viewed with trust by all its stakeholders. As we have seen, trust is the basic underpinning of successful technological collaboration. And so it is with public–private collaborations—perhaps even more so. In business, many transactions are short-term and succeed because both parties are enriched when they abide by the rules of exchange. The net benefits of compliance surpass the costs. There often is a much longer time horizon when working with public institutions, and there are also interruptions in continuity.

There are many reasons for these discontinuities. The most common is that time frames often are not synchronous. Generally, business is thought of as having a very short-term orientation, with all the emphasis on quarterly earnings—and that is true. But in terms of strategy, whether product development strategies or those that entail the creation of new technologies to improve value-creating processes, business horizons are much longer. Strategic goals in these cases frequently span multiple years, not just multiple quarters. These time horizons are even longer when the exploration and development of new markets is involved.

All too often public policy and legislative actions are dictated by the next election. Anyone who has been involved in the most basic need of all—that for excellence in public education—knows the frustration of trying to execute strategies for reform over multiple administrations—each of which, ironically, has normally proclaimed education to be a top priority. Continuity and longevity of the individuals who conceive of and implement private sector alliances are problems. With the electoral process this is even a greater difficulty, and while many administrators of the executive branch survive multiple electoral changes, this isn't the case at the all-important policy level, where alliances are forged.

To withstand these periodic project discontinuities, there must be respect for one another's interests and a willingness to persevere—not head for the hills—when there are signs of trouble. In a word, there must be "trust." Not all public-private ventures are able to survive significant changes, but the only way they have a chance of enduring at all is by knowing that each party will stick to its word and have the flexibility to find ways around unforeseen obstacles. Trust comes from demonstrated action, not talk.

Business and government, particularly in the United States, are cast in adversarial roles. Government all too often behaves as though business is a necessary evil to be circumscribed as tightly as possible, while the business attitude is simply to "get the government off my back." This is not a psychology upon which mutual trust and collaboration for greater societal good can be built. It is not even a simple matter of competition between two segments of society; it is the sort of antagonism inherent in religious or ethnic conflicts. We have also learned from the experience of Control Data that such a situation *does not* have to exist and that the trust necessary to meaningful public–private alliances can be made to exist. *It takes leadership.*

Innovation that results in "hard" artifacts, such as high-performance computers, is easily grasped, and consequently it achieves public recognition much more rapidly by becoming part of the common vernacular—for example, "super computer," "PC," or, moving back in time a bit, "fridge." Innovations that result in "soft" technology are less likely to have that same level of public visibility that makes them a part of everyday talk. All too often they take on the aspects of passing fads, if they get noticed at all. This problem has particularly plagued improvements in education and training processes. Economic development suffers even more. These social innovations not only lie outside the limelight, they are frequently and needlessly reinvented.

Yet while Control Data's stunning computing innovations such as the 1604 or the 6600 are now only curiosities to be looked at in computer museums, the company is fortunate in that many of its innovations in economic development and education exist today. Perhaps the single greatest legacy of Control Data is that its innovations in public–private partnerships for the betterment of society not only linger, but they have become part of the common vernacular—for example, terms such as "wellness" in the health care profession, "place and space" or "computer mediated learning" in training and education, terms such as "EAR" or "EAP" in human resource employee counseling, and the "business incubator" in economic development. It may be overly generous to take exclusive credit for these terms, but there is no doubt that Control Data was present during their formation and shaped their meanings.

SUCCESS AND FAILURE

The cornerstone of all these public–private collaborative ventures was the need for computer technology to deliver information and education services to a broader base of recipients at less cost and in less time. For Control Data, these undertakings were not philanthropy or altruism. By no means, however, were the company's intentions ever predatory. Public–private collaboration was rooted in genuine service interests that were able to take advantage of Control Data's basic technological capabilities.

Each business was undertaken with the full expectation of profitability and an acceptable return on investment. The critical difference was that the time necessary to achieve those returns was extended beyond the normal ones for computer hardware and more traditional computational data services. On a discounted cash flow basis, then, the company was willing to accept a somewhat lower return, but in terms of current rates of return at any point after profitability was achieved, the results would be equal to any other business.

The implications of this are twofold:

It is necessary to have the cash to support the more extended time frame of product and market development involved in such business.

In order to manage the operating statement (P&L) at a level acceptable to the stockholders the number of such businesses under development at any given time must be carefully controlled.

OBSERVATIONS

In this latter regard, Control Data lacked the ability to just say "no" to a good idea. Too many companies have the reverse problem. By continually saying "no" to innovative ideas or, worse yet, by labeling as "failures" those who fail in the attempt at risky innovation, they end up having nothing to which to say "no!" But embracing too many good ideas simultaneously runs the very real risk of being unable to respond to unexpected financial difficulties. The financial crisis of 1985 had the sobering and beneficial effect of giving us more balanced judgment in that regard.

The essential underpinning of any strategic alliance is a common overlap of the independent strategic interest of the parties to the alliance. This is difficult enough in alliances between companies. Strategies are too often weak in their articulation of the necessary and sufficient technologies that constitute the search for competitive advantage. Rather than seeking necessary technologies via collaboration and focusing internal efforts on the value-added technologies that will be sufficient to yield competitive advantage, companies more frequently proceed toward alliances with a vague search for scale, market access, or just "growth."

In public–private alliances, the problem reaches a whole new level of difficulty. Who is trying to achieve what? The reasons for this level of difficulty are several. First, for the most part government agencies do not even have *strategies*. They have objectives and they operate under legislated policies. At some level of abstraction a "policy" may be considered a strategy, but in the practical world of public–private collaboration mere policy won't suffice. To find the strategic overlap necessary for successful collaboration, the parties must consider *policy objectives* and determine if there is a means by which mutual action will simultaneously assist in reaching those objectives and at the same time benefit the company.

Second, the measures of success for public and private organizations are totally different. Measurement and effective management of costs are inherent in the success of both. However, without a straightforward definition of, and accounting for, the "top line" (revenues in the private sector organization), the discipline of the "bottom line" as a measure of success disappears in public sector accountability.

In spite of these difficulties, with perspective and creative thinking the necessary strategic overlap between public and private sector entities can be forged. It is a matter of carefully focusing on needs. If you can't find common ground in that area, there is little sense in going any further. As Control Data's examples have demonstrated, the optimal way to understand one another's needs is through involvement in community and national affairs. That is precisely what we encouraged executives and other employees to do.

Trust essential to these alliances does not come from wishful thinking or corporate proclamation; it is built up by working on mutual problems with candor and commitment. As with private sector collaboration, public–private endeavors must be managed from the top. Only then can the necessary sense of urgency be developed and maintained to overcome the inevitable obstacles and strategy changes. For Control Data, this level of oversight and commitment meant board support as well as top management involvement. Within the public sector, the active participation of the executive responsible for policy is requisite.

Finally, public–private partnerships are great training ground for organizational flexibility. Organizations that find uncertainty distasteful, and that have difficulty adapting to unforeseen events, will never succeed at working with public institutions. The problems that will be encountered in these relationships can never be fully anticipated—they require ongoing assessment, adjustment, and commitment. As Control Data's example so classically illustrates, these basic guidelines, if faithfully followed, can result in mutual benefit to the community and to the corporation.

Epilogue

I am inclined to believe that my beloved [King] Arthur of the Future is sitting this very moment among his learned friends in the Combination Room of the College of Life. . . . When [the world] is ready to listen to reason, if it ever is, they will issue from their rath in joy and power: and then, perhaps, they will give us happiness in the world once more and chivalry, and the old medieval blessing of certain simple people who tried at any rate in their own small way to still the ancient brutal dream of Attila the Hun.

—T. H. White, *The Book of Merlyn,* the unpublished conclusion to *The Once and Future King*

In the legend of King Arthur, T. H. White found the inspiration to tell a story that distills the dreams and flaws of mankind. *The Once and Future King* not only became a best seller, but later spawned the enormously successful musical "Camelot." The word *Camelot* has become part of everyday vernacular, meaning a time or place in which the better part of human nature succeeds in setting higher values in spite of all mankind's shortcomings.

This book began with two questions: why do businesses exist, and why, assuming there is a reason for their existence, are they relatively short lived? Control Data's journey through Strategic Space over some thirty-three years provides profound perspective on those questions. The company focused on meeting human need through innovation in computer and information technology. At the outset, that need was an urgent demand for vastly improved computation and communication. As the company grew in its power to innovate it developed a broader understanding of information as a vehicle to reclaim society's castoffs for productive contributions to societal and economic health.

Control Data not only survived the pioneering perils of Strategic Space, it charted a rewarding course because of a deep-rooted and intuitive understanding of the source of innovation—people. Because of that understanding it succeeded, in spite of shortcomings, in setting higher values and creating an extraordinary level of innovation. As a result it evolved with, adapted to, and effectively used technological change.

As we have seen from Control Data's strategic journey, seven simple and powerful principles of effective strategic management emerge.

THE SEVEN PRINCIPLES OF SUCCESSFUL STRATEGY

Innovators are made, not born.

Strategy is a step-by-step journey of innovation in processes, products, and targeted markets.

Strategy must co-evolve with the technological change and the changing nature of the world it addresses.

Technology is the strategic manager's best friend.

Collaboration, especially technological collaboration, is a powerful strategic tool.

Crisis is inevitable, but with innovative leadership it can be used for positive change.

Public–private partnerships present important but frequently overlooked strategic possibilities.

These principles have the common thread that strategy and strategic management are all about *people*. They also involve coping with uncertainty.

There is a particular emotional undertone to the word "uncertainty," more than any other term in the strategic lexicon. Other words used in strategic analysis such as "capabilities," "competitive threat," "opportunity," "strength," and "weakness" represent factors that may be positive or negative, pleasant or unpleasant in their implication, but the words in and of themselves do not evoke fear. "Uncertainty," on the other hand, is something most of us fear. It directly implies not knowing exactly what's going on, and thus not knowing exactly what to do.

The natural reaction is to invent prescriptions for coping with uncertainty—to fend it off, to box it in, to react in some way. Basically, however, defensive reactions are only temporarily effective. The underlying uneasiness is still present and most people remain hesitant and fearful. Those with courage, however, know that, contrary to conventional wisdom, uncertainty is a positive force. Uncertainty gives rise to opportunities, opportunities for innovation and regeneration. In the face of uncertainty, *the courage to dare is the courage to innovate.*

The fear of uncertainty and the anxiety it generates permeate our lives. The drive to dispel it is so great that we grasp at forecasts as *predictions* of things to come. So desperate are we to have somebody foretell the future that we place heavy measures of faith in our forecasts, forgetting the whims of the marketplace and the changing nature of reality.

The need for certainty is as old as man. In ancient Greece, oracles were held in awe because, seemingly, they had the ability to foretell the future. And many times—but not always—they did, for they were strategic thinkers, not forecasters. There was nothing mysterious about it. *The oracles were simply human databases.* People flocked to them. Rich men, poor men, kings, and slaves came, leaving behind their bits of knowledge. Using this vast resource of information, more often than not the oracles were truly able to advise people that certain things would happen unless steps were taken to change them. The oracles also knew very well how to put the appropriate spin and caveats on their predictions by means of ritual and clever wording.

Uncertainty was essential to the oracles. For quite different reasons, it is essential to us. Without it, strategic planning and its component forecasts will invariably become a purely mechanistic substitute for *thinking.* Uncertainty is different than *risk.* Risk is calculable based on known facts and probabilities. Uncertainty results from facing the *unknown.* It evokes not calculation but fear. Yet people do face and deal with the mysteries of the unknown. They overcome fear, they innovate, strategize, and improvise to find a path to the future. Thus it was with Lewis and Clark, with Benjamin Franklin, with Henry Ford, with Michael Dell, and thus it was with Control Data.

Essential to being able to deal with uncertainty is *trust.* Trust stems from demonstrated performance and *demonstrated understanding* at each step of the way. Trust enables employee innovation, trust enables successful alliances, trust enables the ability to perform well in unknown territory, and, paramount, trust engenders belief in ourselves and permits us to cope by fostering the hope so essential to dealing with crisis.

In its early days, the computer industry was characterized as "IBM and the BUNCH," reflecting IBM's dominance and the secondary status of Burroughs, Univac, NCR, Control Data, and Honeywell. Of the BUNCH only Control Data evolved on its own. Burroughs and Univac ultimately became UNISYS, Honeywell exited the computer business entirely, and NCR was subject to the trauma of being both acquired and divested by AT&T, as that communications giant struggled with changing technology and industry structure.

Control Data was a start-up company and the only member of the BUNCH to survive the early years of the computer industry intact. There was no a priori reason that dictated the failure of the others to adapt and grow. They all had far greater resources than did Control Data. Their shortcomings were the failure to perceive that *mere technological change is not the same as evolution along the Technology Food Chain* and the failure to understand and employ collaboration as a principal means of achieving strategic objectives.

In view of the foregoing, it is all the more ironic that Control Data, which did understand and which followed a strategic evolution based on that understanding, is generally believed not to exist. This somewhat curious outcome is worthy of consideration.

With the stock market collapse of 2000–2002, much has been written to the effect that *rampant greed* was at its root and characterized the essence of the financial and business community in the 1990s. There is certainly justification for such an analysis of the excesses and outright inanities evident in the behavior of many financial and business executives in those years, but it fails to fully explain the business story that unfolded. Behavior rooted in greed is not new and has often led to manipulation and fraud in business and finance. For that matter, excess and extra-legal business practices are a constant threat to the functioning of free markets.

The 1990s were different. No previous period of modern business more visibly reflected such rampant solipsism, the self-based assumption of reality, as did these years in which a new generation of business people reached positions of financial and executive power. Greed can be destructive, but it can have positive as well as negative consequences. It does not compare in its deleterious effects with the results of power being exercised by executives operating under the belief that there is no reality other than *self.*

Control Data did not escape this affectation of changed management values in the 1990s. The *creation* of value through innovation was transformed into *realization* of value by means of portfolio management; manipulation replaced management; creation of new product and service businesses was replaced by buying and selling businesses. This transformation was capped by changing the name of the company in 1992 to a contrived and meaningless word: *Ceridian.* That too was indicative of yet one more business fad of the '90s—to adopt bizarrely contrived names for businesses that are not, in any rational sense, helpful to their customers.

Although renamed and culturally transformed, Control Data survived and even prospered if the measure is limited to increase in stockholder value. The inherent value of the innovations, nurtured over the preceding thirty years, was the wherewithal that provided the ability to realize stockholder value. Its transformation over the preceding two decades into a services company made it all possible. Over those years we had understood that its competency lay in innovation, in creatively adding value as it evolved along the Technology Food Chain. The company survived and returned value as a result of following this path to the future.

While the value created remained, the soul of the company was lost. Its capacity for innovation, for devising new ways to meet societal need, for promulgating public–private partnerships as a means to that end, for building the awareness, motivation, infrastructure, and skills in its employees, was gone. So it is hardly surprising that Control Data is believed not to exist anymore. But that is not true. It has simply been moved from front-page news to the stock listings.

The lessons learned, the values inculcated in Control Data's people, its innovations in services, its understanding of the power of technological and public–private collaboration, all appeared lost. But were they? Not at all. The heart of Control Data—its people, and, in particular, management people—carried these seeds with them and planted them in organizations of every ilk all over the world. Control Data's management people moved into positions of leadership in over one hundred companies, nonprofit organizations, and public agencies. A partial list of spin-offs and start-ups by former Control Data employees is in Appendix 8.

Two of them will serve to illustrate the wellspring Control Data has been for enlightened entrepreneurship. As the strategic evolution of Control Data from hardware to services neared completion, not only was it necessary to resolve the future of major hardware units such as peripheral products, but smaller hardware business units were also affected. One was VTC, a unit set up originally to explore certain leading-edge semiconductor technologies, and also to provide at least limited semiconductor production capability.

Larry Jodsaas had a successful executive career in the company, including stints in Peripheral Products and Computer Systems, and as the corporate staff executive responsible for quality. With a portion of VTC, Larry saw an opportunity to have his own business, and with that business demonstrate the superior skills he knew he had developed. It certainly wasn't easy in the beginning, but slowly the business became successful. Larry not only engendered trust and loyalty in the hard times, he rewarded all his people by sharing the profits with them when those years came around. Success finally attracted attention from larger players in the semiconductor industry. A portion of the business was sold to Lucent Technologies for more than $100 million. Larry further rewarded the trust and diligence of his employees by sharing with them 20 percent of the profits from that sale.

The second example is that of Nasser Kazeminy. Nasser joined Control Data in 1969 as a computer programmer. He headed the Logistics System Design Group that was responsible for creating a worldwide logistics system. During his Control Data career, Nasser also held important positions in the Education Group and the Peripherals Group. It was while working for the Peripherals Group that he saw an opportunity for a service that Control Data was not already providing for its customers—that of low-cost, tax-leveraged leases for peripheral products. With Control Data's blessing, Nasser left to found a leasing company focused initially on the peripheral market. Control Data's customers benefited by lower monthly fees, and the company improved its cash flow. Working with a number of other computer companies and major corporations, Nasser went on to build the largest privately held leasing company in the United States. Later, when Control Data began divesting some of its businesses, Nasser recognized that some of these innovative companies were conceptually and technologically ahead of their time, but built on solid foundations. Nasser was prepared to invest, work hard, and wait for the world to catch up. He consistently treated the Control Data employees he acquired fairly and maintained Control Data's philosophy centered on *individual innovation*. One of the first of the businesses he acquired from Control Data was Quorum Litigation Services, which grew out of the IBM antitrust suit. Nasser also acquired the PLATO Industrial Technical Systems Education Services Division. The engine created by PLATO was used to develop an entirely new industry of information technology certification, now employing more than two hundred thousand people worldwide, with technology used by 95 percent of the computerized testing and certification market. This company eventually merged with Sylvan Learning Systems and later sold for over $775 million.

Control Data's Credit Union Division was also acquired by Nasser. The company, renamed XP Systems, provided complete turnkey banking services for over three hundred major credit unions nationally and was later sold to a Fortune 500 company. A spin-off company, Digital Insight, leveraged on the competencies of XP Systems and developed broad Internet-based home banking services for middle market financial institutions. Today, over five million users avail themselves of these services on a daily basis. The company is now publicly traded with a market value that has approached $800 million. Nasser also acquired other companies from Control Data, all of which were very successful. As he put it, "There was not a loser in the bunch. The technology and vision behind them was sound."

Nasser believes that the success of these companies was not so much a result of what he did, but rather the contributions made by the bright, loyal, and innovative executives surrounding him. He used Control Data's philosophies to motivate his exceptional management teams to achievements beyond everyone's expectations. Over the course of fourteen years, over forty-six multimillionaires were created by Nasser's companies.

THE CONTROL DATA LEGACY

The legacy of Control Data is more far reaching than mere statistics or anecdotes, no matter how intriguing. It was instrumental in changing the very structure of the computer industry through unbundling of software and services from hardware products.

The company was a pioneer and trendsetter in forming strategic alliances in the computer and information technology industry. These ranged from the early alliance with NCR to the multicompany disk drive joint-venture Magnetic Peripherals, Inc., and to the Microelectronics and Computer Technology Corporation (MCC) for advanced research and development in computer technology.

Control Data firmly established the information services businesses that have become a key strategic thrust of the industry. Perhaps most notable in that regard is that today the company's old nemesis, IBM, now embraces services as its key future strategy.

By turning internal necessity into business opportunity, Control Data was a pioneer in outsourcing as a way of freeing resources to concentrate on proprietary value-added. More than that, by establishing and working with small business, Control Data pioneered the networked corporation, which has taken the form of the so-called virtual company.

It vividly demonstrated, as a remarkable private sector enterprise, that public–private collaboration can work to the advantage of business and the communities that they serve.

In addressing "unmet societal needs as profitable business opportunities" Control Data demonstrated that such needs can be turned, in Peter Drucker's words, from being "capital *consuming* to capital *generating.*" This concept also lives on in the National Center for Social Entrepreneurs (NCSE), which was founded by fellow Control Data board member Judson (Sandy) Bemis and me. NCSE continues to help nonprofit organizations become more self-sustaining and more effective in delivering their services to more people by using core capabilities in innovative and profitable, revenue generating ways.

Even its specific major innovations such as supercomputers, network services, optical character recognition devices, computer-based mediated learning, business incubators, and space and military guidance systems have proliferated and live on under a variety of names. The financial services of Commercial Credit were the launching pad for today's largest financial services company, Citigroup, currently headed by a former Commercial Credit (Control Data) lawyer, Charles Prince.

Innovation in job creation and economic development services included the Business and Technology Centers (BTCs) and small business advisory services (CDBAI). There were urban and rural based enterprises: Northside, Selby, City Venture, Rural Ventures, Prison Ventures.

Innovation in human resources policy may be the greatest legacy of all. Such innovation was rooted in the recognition that every employee is a whole person: the Employee Advisory Resource (EAR), the Wellness Program (Staywell), pioneering use of flexible hours and personal days off, the Employee Entrepreneurial Advisory Office (EEAO). All these innovative policies are a lasting legacy of human resource practice.

The people in Control Data were a wellspring of advanced technology. This wellspring gave forth a remarkable array of innovation because:

• They believed in the mission of the company.
• They were committed to that mission.
• They were free from the stigma of failure.
• There was trust.

Once upon a time Control Data forged this legacy, which lives on today as a compass for the company of the future.

Appendix 1: Control Data Timeline

Date	Events	Acquisition	Collaboration
July 1957	Founding: Norris, Mullaney, Ryder, Drake, Forrest, Miles, Cray, Keye, Kisch, Perkins, Shekels, Zimmer		
December 1957	Initial acquisition	Cedar Engineering	
1959	Plan presented for OEM Peripherals		
1960	Start of data centers and software development Delivery of first 1604 Start of Industrial Group	Control Corporation (1960)	
1962	Revenues: $41 Million		

(*continued*)

Date	Events	Acquisition	Collaboration
	Model 606 Magnet Tape Transport		
	Delivery of Polaris navy submarine fire control computer		
	Start of international operations in Europe, Australia		
1963	Initial expansion into Asia, Mexico	Bendix	
	Expansion, Industrial Group	Computer Systems Division Daystrom	
1964	Delivery of first 6600		
	Initial expansion into Eastern Europe		
	Start of PLATO		University of Illinois/D. L. Bitzer
1965	Expansion in Canada	Computer Systems Division Computing Devices	
	Control Data Institute established		
1967	Revenues: $245 million		
	Key executives depart: F. C. Mullaney, R. N. Kisch		
	Reorganization: W. R. Keye, Operations; R. D. Schmidt, Marketing		
	Expansion in Services	CEIR	
1968	Financial Services	Commercial Credit Corp.	
	Cybernet established		
	Northside Plant opens		
	Antitrust suit vs. IBM filed		
1969	Revenues: $1.02 billion		

Date	Events	Acquisition	Collaboration
	Expansion in Canada	Computing Devices of Canada	
1970	Unbundling in computer industry Reorganization—formation of Services Group (RMP), Systems Group (RCH), Marketing Group (PGM), EDP Products Group (TGK), Commercial Credit (DSJ, CEO and JSW, Chairman) Expansion in Asia Collaboration with Canada to design and manufacture computers (PL)		Canada (DITC)
1972	Revenues: $1.15 billion NCR collaboration Committee for Social Responsibility established Seymour Cray leaves		CPI
1973	Settlement of IBM lawsuit Collaboration with NCR to design new computer line Soviet, Frame Agreement Peripherals manufacture in Eastern Europe	Service Bureau Corporation	Advanced Development Lab (ADL) USSR (GKNT) ROMCD
1974	STAR delivered to Livermore Employee Advisory Resources (EAR) established		
1975	Honeywell Collaboration		MPI
1976	PLATO introduction		

(*continued*)

Date	Events	Acquisition	Collaboration
1977	Revenues $2.3 billion First stock dividend Iran partnership to manu- facture terminals		Computer Terminals of Iran
1978	Formation of City Venture		City Venture, Inc.
1979	Staywell initiated First Business and Technology Center (BTC) Formation of Control Data Business Advisors, Inc. (CDBAI), sometimes referred to simply as BAI		
1980	Formation of Rural Ventures Corporate Executive Office formed (WCN, RMP, NRB)		Rural Ventures, Inc.
1981	Services revenues reach $1.1 billion		
1982	Revenues: $3.2 billion Collaborative technology consortium established		MCC
1983	Formation of ETA		
1985	Liquidity crisis WCN retirement (January 1, 1986) RMP Chairman and CEO		
1986	IPO of CCC		
1987	Revenues: $3.37 billion		
1989	Closedown of ETA Sale of Peripherals		
1990	RMP retirement		

Appendix 2: Organization Charts (1957–1986)

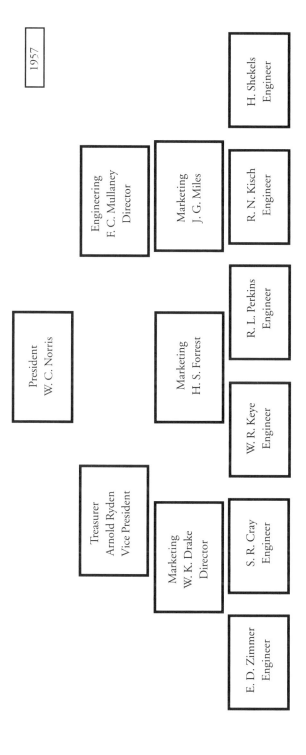

1957

President
W. C. Norris

Treasurer
Arnold Ryden
Vice President

Engineering
F. C. Mullaney
Director

Marketing
H. S. Forrest

Marketing
J. G. Miles

Marketing
W. K. Drake
Director

R. L. Perkins
Engineer

R. N. Kisch
Engineer

H. Shekels
Engineer

W. R. Keye
Engineer

S. R. Cray
Engineer

E. D. Zimmer
Engineer

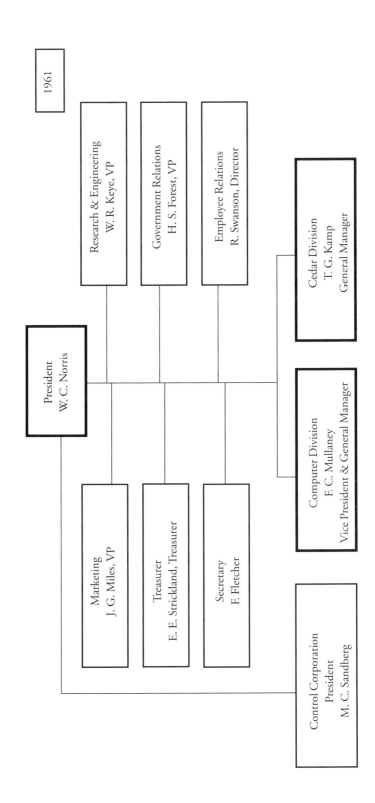

1961

President
W. C. Norris

Research & Engineering
W. R. Keye, VP

Government Relations
H. S. Forest, VP

Employee Relations
R. Swanson, Director

Marketing
J. G. Miles, VP

Treasurer
E. E. Strickland, Treasurer

Secretary
F. Fletcher

Cedar Division
T. G. Kamp
General Manager

Computer Division
F. C. Mullaney
Vice President & General Manager

Control Corporation
President
M. C. Sandberg

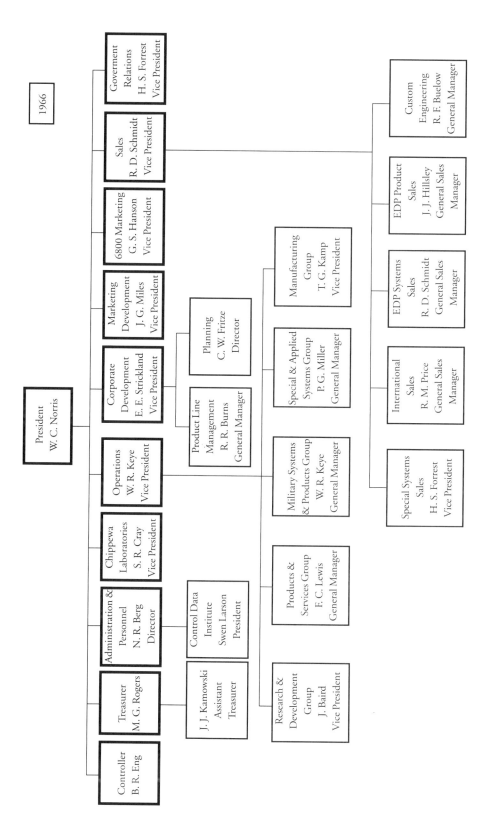

1966

President
W. C. Norris

Controller
B. R. Eng

Treasurer
M. G. Rogers

Administration &
Personnel
N. R. Berg
Director

Chippewa
Laboratories
S. R. Cray
Vice President

Operations
W. R. Keye
Vice President

Corporate
Development
E. E. Strickland
Vice President

Marketing
Development
J. G. Miles
Vice President

6800 Marketing
G. S. Hanson
Vice President

Sales
R. D. Schmidt
Vice President

Goverment
Relations
H. S. Forrest
Vice President

J. J. Kamowski
Assistant
Treasurer

Control Data
Institute
Swen Larson
President

Product Line
Management
R. R. Burns
General Manager

Planning
C. W. Fritze
Director

Research &
Development
Group
J. Baird
Vice President

Products &
Services Group
F. C. Lewis
General Manager

Military Systems
& Products Group
W. R. Keye
General Manager

Special & Applied
Systems Group
P. G. Miller
General Manager

Manufacturing
Group
T. G. Kamp
Vice President

Special Systems
Sales
H. S. Forrest
Vice President

International
Sales
R. M. Price
General Sales
Manager

EDP Systems
Sales
R. D. Schmidt
General Sales
Manager

EDP Product
Sales
J. J. Hillsley
General Sales
Manager

Custom
Engineering
R. F. Buelow
General Manager

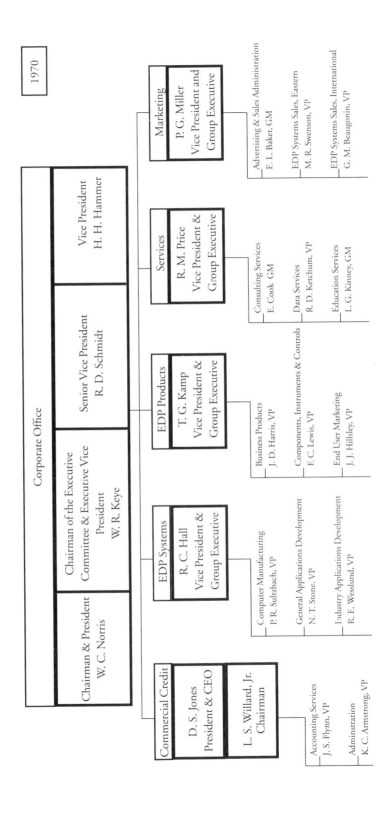

1970

Corporate Office

| Chairman & President W. C. Norris | Chairman of the Executive Committee & Executive Vice President W. R. Keye | Senior Vice President R. D. Schmidt | Vice President H. H. Hammer |

Commercial Credit
D. S. Jones
President & CEO

L. S. Willard, Jr.
Chairman

- Accounting Services
  J. S. Flynn, VP
- Administration
  K. C. Armstrong, VP

EDP Systems
R. C. Hall
Vice President &
Group Executive

- Computer Manufacturing
  P. R. Sultzbach, VP
- General Applications Development
  N. T. Stone, VP
- Industry Applications Development
  R. E. Wesslund, VP

EDP Products
T. G. Kamp
Vice President &
Group Executive

- Business Products
  J. D. Harris, VP
- Components, Instruments & Controls
  F. C. Lewis, VP
- End User Marketing
  J. J. Hillsley, VP

Services
R. M. Price
Vice President &
Group Executive

- Consulting Services
  E. Cook GM
- Data Services
  R. D. Ketchum, VP
- Education Services
  L. G. Kinney, GM

Marketing
P. G. Miller
Vice President and
Group Executive

- Advertising & Sales Administration
  E. L. Baker, GM
- EDP Systems Sales, Eastern
  M. R. Swenson, VP
- EDP Systems Sales, International
  G. M. Beaugonin, VP

EDP Sytems Sales, Western
V. E. Seiling, GM

European & Resale Systems
G. S. Weller, VP

Product & Applications Market
D. H. Wentworth, GM

Systems & Industry Marketing
L. D. Findley, VP

Maintenance Services
J. D. Kee, GM

Specialized Data Services
R. M. Price

OEM Marketing
G. R. Brown, VP

Peripheral Products Operations
C. G. Smith, VP

Terminals & OCR Operations
P. J. Bulver, VP

Corporate Staff

B. R. Eng, VP Accounting Services
N. R. Berg, VP Administration & Personnel
H. P. Donaghue, Assistant to the President
S. R. Cray, VP Chippewa Labs
J. W. Lacey, VP Corporate Development
W. P. Moyles, VP Corporate Growth
M. G. Rogers, VP Financial Planning
H. S. Forrest, VP Government Relations
R. C. Chinn, VP Manufacturing
J. G. Miles, VP Marketing Development
J. Baird, VP Research
R. A. Worsing, VP Software & Engineering

Space & Defense
R. H. Scherer, VP

Systems Development
E. J. Otis, VP

Consumer Services
J. M. Sheehan

Corporate Development
D. H. Brill, Sr. VP

Debt Management
N. W. Cameron, VP

Investment
Management
L. C. Dilatush, VP

Legal
C. H. Brown, VP

Risk Administration
F. W. Meier, VP

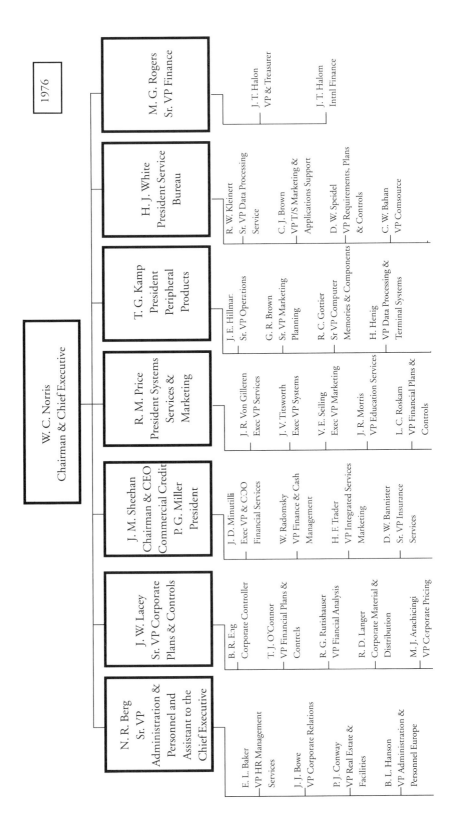

1976

W. C. Norris
Chairman & Chief Executive

N. R. Berg
Sr. VP
Administration &
Personnel and
Assistant to the
Chief Executive

- E. L. Baker
  VP HR Management
  Services
- J. J. Bowe
  VP Corporate Relations
- P. J. Conway
  VP Real Estate &
  Facilities
- B. L. Hanson
  VP Administration &
  Personnel Europe

J. W. Lacey
Sr. VP Corporate
Plans & Controls

- B. R. Erg
  Corporate Controller
- T. J. O'Connor
  VP Financial Plans &
  Controls
- R. G. Rutishauser
  VP Fiancial Analysis
- R. D. Langer
  Corporate Material &
  Distribution
- M. J. Arachicingi
  VP Corporate Pricing

J. M. Sheehan
Chairman & CEO
Commercial Credit
P. G. Miller
President

- J. D. Minutilli
  Exec VP & COO
  Financial Services
- W. Radomsky
  VP Finance & Cash
  Management
- H. F. Trader
  VP Integrated Services
  Marketing
- D. W. Bannister
  Sr. VP Insurance
  Services

R. M. Price
President Systems
Services &
Marketing

- J. R. Von Gilleren
  Exec VP Services
- J. V. Titsworth
  Exec VP Systems
- V. E. Seiling
  Exec VP Marketing
- J. R. Morris
  VP Education Services
- L. C. Roskam
  VP Financial Plans &
  Controls

T. G. Kamp
President
Peripheral
Products

- J. E. Hillmar
  Sr. VP Operations
- G. R. Brown
  Sr. VP Marketing
  Planning
- R. C. Gortier
  Sr. VP Computer
  Memories & Components
- H. Henig
  VP Data Processing &
  Terminal Systems

H. J. White
President Service
Bureau

- R. W. Kleinert
  Sr. VP Data Processing
  Service
- C. J. Brown
  VP T/S Marketing &
  Applications Support
- D. W. Speidel
  VP Requirements, Plans
  & Controls
- C. W. Bahan
  VP Comsource

M. G. Rogers
Sr. VP Finance

- J. T. Halon
  VP & Treasurer
- J. T. Halom
  Intnl Finance

R. B. Hawkins
VP & Sr. Staff Officer
Legal Affairs & Corporate
Secretary

G. H. Lohn
HR Development & Public
Affairs

E. G. Vargon
VP Labor Relations

R. G. Wheeler
VP Corporate Personnel

3

J. J. Karnowski
VP & Assistant Treasurer

B. C. Imbert
VP Corporate Business
Strategy

R. H. Smith
VP & Exec Assistant

G. G. Smith
Sr. VP Education
Services

D. H. Brill
Exec VP Economic &
Technical Services

R. E. Dunn
VP Financial Planning
& Control

D. M. Noer
VP Personnel

C. H. Brown
VP & General Counsel

G. F. Troy
VP Corporate
Development

F. R. Dawe
VP Personnel &
Administration

R. E. Wesslund
VP & Assistant to the
President

P. G. Bailey
VP Business Products

W. T. Brayer
President Magnetic
Peripherals Incorporated

G. R. Brown
OEM Marketing and
Eastern European Ops

B. E. Johnson
VP Personnel &
Administration

G. H. Ashbridge
VP New Business
Planning

R.C. Pflager
GM Contracts

T. S. White
VP T/S Development

S. H. Beach
VP & General Counsel

J. J Shaffery
Controller

W. J. Goldstrohm
Dir Personnel &
Administration

J. F. Lowrie
Mgr Special Business
Programs

J. E. Matzinger
Mgr System Operation

C. R. McEwen
Dir Communications

271

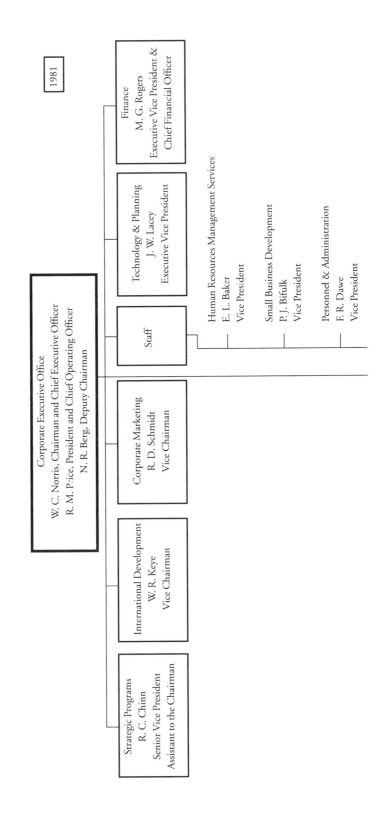

1981

Corporate Executive Office
W. C. Norris, Chairman and Chief Executive Officer
R. M. Price, President and Chief Operating Officer
N. R. Berg, Deputy Chairman

Strategic Programs
R. C. Chinn
Senior Vice President
Assistant to the Chairman

International Development
W. R. Keye
Vice Chairman

Corporate Marketing
R. D. Schmidt
Vice Chairman

Staff

Technology & Planning
J. W. Lacey
Executive Vice President

Finance
M. G. Rogers
Executive Vice President &
Chief Financial Officer

Human Resources Management Services
E. L. Baker
Vice President

Small Business Development
P. J. Bifulk
Vice President

Personnel & Administration
F. R. Dawe
Vice President

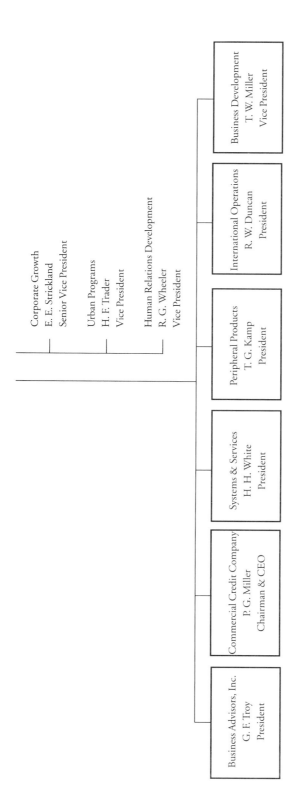

Corporate Growth
E. E. Strickland
Senior Vice President

Urban Programs
H. F. Trader
Vice President

Human Relations Development
R. G. Wheeler
Vice President

Business Advisors, Inc.
G. F. Troy
President

Commercial Credit Company
P. G. Miller
Chairman & CEO

Systems & Services
H. H. White
President

Peripheral Products
T. G. Kamp
President

International Operations
R. W. Duncan
President

Business Development
T. W. Miller
Vice President

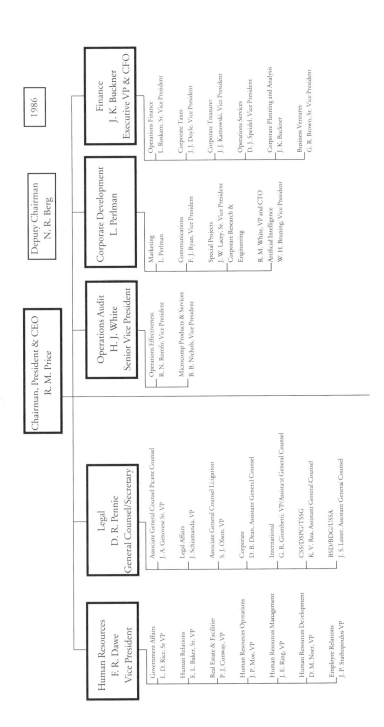

1986

Chairman, President & CEO
R. M. Price

Deputy Chairman
N. R. Berg

Human Resources
F. R. Dawe
Vice President

- Government Affairs
  L. D. Rice, Sr VP
- Human Relations
  E. L. Baker, Sr. VP
- Real Estate & Facilities
  P. J. Conway, VP
- Human Resources Operations
  J. P. Moe, VP
- Human Resources Management
  J. E. Ring, VP
- Human Resources Development
  D. M. Noer, VP
- Employee Relations
  J. P. Stathopoulos VP

Legal
D. R. Pennie
General Counsel/Secretary

- Associate General Counsel Patent Counsel
  J. A. Genovese Sr. VP
- Legal Affairs
  J. Schiamanda, VP
- Associate General Counsel Litigation
  S. J. Olson, VP
- Corporate
  D. B. Dean, Assistant General Counsel
- International
  G. R. Giombetti, VP/Assistant General Counsel
- CSS/DSPG/TSSG
  K. V. Rea, Assistant General Counsel
- BSD/BDG/USSA
  J. S. Lester, Assistant General Counsel

Operations Audit
H. J. White
Senior Vice President

- Operations Effectiveness
  R. N. Romfo, Vice President
- Microcomp Products & Services
  B. B. Nichols, Vice President

Corporate Development
L. Perlman

- Marketing
  L. Perlman
- Communications
  F. J. Ryan, Vice President
- Special Projects
  J. W. Lacey, Sr. Vice President
- Corporate Research &
  Engineering
  R. M. White, VP and CTO
- Artificial Intelligence
  W. H. Bruning, Vice President

Finance
J. K. Buckner
Executive VP & CFO

- Operations Finance
  L. Roskam, Sr. Vice President
- Corporate Taxes
  J. J. Doyle, Vice President
- Corporate Treasurer
  J. J. Karnowski, Vice President
- Operations Services
  D. J. Speidel, Vice President
- Corporate Planning and Analysis
  J. K. Buckner
- Business Ventures
  G. R. Brown, Sr. Vice President

Business Services
D. P. White, President

- Business Development
  G. F. Troy, Vice President
- F. I. S./Micrognosis
  A. J. Martin, Vice President
- Arbitron Ratings
  T. R. Shaker, Chairman & CEO
- Control Data Business Centers
  P. M. Delaney, President
- Marketing Services
  D. E. Vacheron, Vice President
- Network Information Services
  C. J. Brown, Sr. Vice President
- NIS Operations and Network Operations
  J. E. Matzinger, Vice President
- Financial Plans & Controls
  J. M. Hudgens, Vice President
- Human Resources
  R. A. Rich, Vice President

Data Storage Products
L. Perlman, President

- Components
  J. E. Ousley, Vice President
- Large Disk
  A. E. Netten, Vice President
- Small Disk
  W. J. Miller, Vice President
- Sales & Marketing
  P. K. Nagle, Vice President
- Research & Advanced Technology
  L. Perlman
- Strategic Operations Planning
  J. B. Keffeler, Vice President
- MPI Operations
  A. H. Abola, Vice President
- Communications
  L. J. Jadwin, Director
- Financial Plans & Controls
  K. J. Muehleck, Vice President
- Human Resources
  J. P. Gougouris, Vice President

Government Systems
B. T. Jones, President

- U.S. Operations
  R. E. Handberg, Vice President
- Computing Devices
  J. W. Fawcett, Vice President
- Technology Center
  R. L. Lillestrand, Vice President
- Electronic CAD
  W. C. Jacqes, General Manager
- Government Systems Marketing
  H. E. Julsen, Vice President
- Planning/Development
  T. L. Petrzelka, Vice President
- Strategic & Business Development
  N. J. Contardi, Director
- Government Systems Security
  P. E. Myers, General Manager
- Contracts
  R. E. Jensen, Sr. Consultant
- Information Resources
  J. N. Benson, General Manager
- Investment & Cash Management
  G. J. Hubbs, Vice President
- TQMP
  C. M. Miller, Consultant
- Financial Plans & Controls
  D. J. Dolan, Vice President
- Human Resources
  D.G. Rogosheska, Vice President

Systems and Services
T. C. Roberts, President

- Scientific Engineering & Systems Services
  L. E. Jodsaas, President
- Technology Support Services Group
  T. W. Miller, President
- International
  T. C. Roberts
- Financial Plans & Controls
  J. R. Eickhoff, Vice President
- Human Resources
  A. P. Stathopoulos, Vice President
- ETA Systems
  L. M. Thorndyke, Chairman & CEP

Commercial Credit Company
J. D. Minutilli, Chairman, President & CEO

- Consulting & Bank Services
  W. B. Turley, President
- American Health & Life
  M.A. Griver, President
- Investment Recovery
  G. P. Shaw, Sr. Vice President
- McCullagl Leasing
  J. A. Blessing, President
- International Financial Services
  J. B. Morrell, President
- Gulf Insurance
  J. D. Nolan, President
- American Credit Indemnity
  H. A. Leggs, President
- Corporate Services
  W. D. Rowe, Sr. Vice President
- Legal Affairs
  C. O. Prince, Sr. Vice President
- Finance
  R. M. Sheridan, Sr. VP and CFO
- Human Resources
  B. L. Mannes, Vice President

Appendix 3: Robert Price Presentation to the Control Data Corporation Board of Directors (March 14, 1985)

INTRODUCTION

When describing the supercomputer market to you in January I emphasized that to understand that part of the business the central fact to remember was unusually high risk—both technical risk and market risk. The computer mainframe business is of course also high risk—as GE, RCA, and many smaller competitors have discovered. But that is not the major point to be emphasized for those of us who are the minor players in the mainframe segment of the industry. The word to remember is "discipline." If that puzzles you somewhat, let me explain. A journey through time in this part of the computer business is best thought of as "a search for survival." That journey takes place in an environment which is harsh and unforgiving. Small mistakes can lead to great tragedy and even extinction. And the results of those mistakes may only surface five or ten years out. Now a wilderness explorer cannot simply sit and wait—he must move—quickly yet decisively and deliberately. Panic, chasing rainbows, dashing in many directions is fatal. It is well known that skill, desire, good peripheral vision, and above all *discipline* are the essentials of survival in such an environment.

THE TIME OF HOPE—1958–1964

In the early years Control Data's evolution was rapid, even though it was small and had already suffered badly from IBM's predatory practices. A broad range of

277

products from desk-size computers—160, 160-A (a sort of prehistoric version of the micro-computer) through what today would be called minicomputers (924, 3100), to large computers (1604, 3600), and of course the about to be 6600 supercomputer. In other words there was a full line of hardware applicable to any type of problem. Control Data's actual sales were still largely to the scientific and engineering area except in international where a small research and engineer market and less entrenched IBM competition made the commercial market more appealing and more available (we became the major suppliers to the insurance industry in Mexico, for example).

REALITY—1965-1971

By the mid-sixties it was evident—at least to Bill if not to most in the industry—that the reality of the situation was that general purpose computers—the so-called mainframe business—would not be sufficient to provide long-term stability and growth for a company in the computer industry. Control Data's moves into services and peripherals were by then under way.

Understanding reality, however, does not necessarily mean that one can adapt to it either quickly or easily and so actually Control Data looked at from an overall perspective moved ahead aggressively in computer mainframes—seeking new, more commercially oriented markets such as automotive and airlines as well as geographic expansion. From 1965 through 1970 development of extensive hardware and software continued.

ADJUSTMENT—1972-1974

So the adjustment began. A careful evaluation of where we were—strengths, weaknesses, and best opportunities for growth. And the answer was to build on the 6600/7600 architecture and *its* strongest markets. In case that seems obvious from the vantage point of 1985 let me remind you that that chosen foundation—scientific supercomputers—was definitely an item of noninterest in our industry at that time—IBM's and the industry's thrust was toward a one vendor, general purpose computer to satisfy all needs for a company; in the Vietnam backlash, space program moon landing completion, general "greening of America" psychology, and scientific and engineering computing were way below the recognition threshold of most market researchers; the 6600 was eight years old; with the failure of the 8600 Seymour's mystique was severely tarnished; our largest customer base was for the (totally incompatible) lower 3000 systems; our international business, much more commercially oriented, was vital to our financial health; and we had devoted several years to the development of the PL design and architecture. It was then that some of us learned the true definition of a strategic decision: one that involves *pain*. Anything else is just humdrum choosing between noncatastrophic alternatives. We also learned that *discipline* as well as dedication and creativity make strategic decisions become reality.

THE PLAN

The plan called for phaseout of the lower 3000 product line and the upper 3000 product line, and the migration of those customers to 6000 computers—primarily by sheer brute strength—i.e., the sales force ability to sway customers. It also called for the slow and painful consolidation of the three product lines as embodied in the various operating systems of Cyber 70 to one, and then and only then migration of those customers to the new system. The final problem was cost and time to do that. Many of the features such as initial memory we wanted for our new line were already coming into the marketplace in a significant way. That was in 1973—the plan to be executed covered a period of ten years.

SUCCESS—AT LEAST TO SOME DEGREE

At the start of that ten year trek the conventional wisdom was that Control Data would soon exit the computer mainframe business (and thus exit business entirely). *Forbes* and *Fortune,* among others, confidently predicted our demise. Today, however, with the wonderful warp of hindsight we find quotes such as "Norris realized early that a computer company committed to a mainframe product line was an architect of its own doom." And "Control Data is a survivor. It is not caught in the vise that the rest of the bunch find themselves in." On the other hand, it hardly seems necessary to add that criticism has not evaporated—only shifted to other aspects of the business—and there are even murmurs now and then that services should be abandoned or severely curtailed.

In any event what should be said is, the performance of Control Data's product development and sales people from 1973 to 1984 was one of the most determined, disciplined, as well as creative episodes in the history of the computer industry. Less than that would have meant the end of that part of our business.

Yet did that effort yield superior financial performance? Or did it even secure the future of the business? No. More than that the pretax return on invested capital for the past three years, while higher than ever, has averaged less than 15 percent, while the corporate goal/performance norm is 20 percent or greater. There is no great probability that this relationship will ever change.

TRENDS AND IMPLICATIONS

The basic reason for the financial pressure is of course the competitive structure of the industry. On the other hand, that statement itself, while true, doesn't help much to provide much in the way of clues for survival. There are some more detailed trends which can help however. So next I'll review those trends. Obviously they do not tell the whole story of something so complex, but they provide a basic understanding of the challenges. And they also help to truly appreciate that "discipline" is the basic characteristic necessary for survival.

To earn the same number of dollars you have to sell three hundred times as many units—in constant dollars that becomes more than one thousand times as many units. Or, put another way, in constant dollars we have to sell forty-two S-Os to equal $1.8 million (1960) and the S-O is thirty times more computer than the 1604. Such statistics are not merely characteristics of twenty, or ten, or five years' time lapse. In 1984 we installed 23 percent more computers than in 1983 in order to maintain essentially flat revenue. In 1985 we plan to install more than 50 percent more computers to achieve a 7 percent revenue growth. If ever anything was more illustrative of running harder to stand still, I don't know it. For the user price/performance reduction is good. From an overall economic viewpoint it is good. For a would-be participant in the industry—it is a challenge. More than creativity is required. Volume production is required. Many have tried vertical integration—and paid dearly. Through cooperation and leveraging off the volume of others Control Data has done better. For example we have always relied on the viability of the U.S. merchant semiconductor industry, and it was the threatened extinction of the semiconductor industry that was one major impetus behind MCC. That threat is, by the way, not entirely gone, and further cooperation with enterprises such as VTC may well be required.

STRATEGIC RESPONSE—RECAPITULATION

Let me pause now and recapitulate.

Strategic Diversification. Our basic response to strategic threat of IBM to the computer mainframe business was diversification into peripheral products and services. That diversification has provided both the financial and strategic freedom necessary for survival of the mainframe business.

Narrower product and market focus. A necessary secondary response has been to maintain a narrow market and product focus. And we have been fortunate. The world has evolved so that our chosen areas of focus, i.e., science and engineering, is more important today than ever. The concomitant result of that evolution, however, is that more and more competition is developing. Not only has IBM made clear its intention to reenter and extract its "normal" market share, but also in the past two–three years at least three new small companies have entered the scientific general purpose computer arena.

Technical expense and creativity. Even with basic business diversification and narrower product focus for our computers, increased technical expenditure as a percentage of revenue has been necessary, and increased technical effort leveraging through cooperation has likewise been required.

Moreover only great creativity by our people has allowed Control Data to respond to the escalating competitive demands for price performance and features—and, by the way, not only respond but achieve superior performance and features. The same degree of creativity and success I will repeat has not been achieved with regard to *product cost or reliability.* That is now the major focus of attention for computers systems.

The availability of commercial credit. The availability allowed us to cope with the enormous financing requirements imposed by IBM with its lease oriented pricing structure. That has been rapidly changing since 1979 to a purchase as opposed to lease profile. IBM's rental revenues in five years have gone from roughly half their total income to less than one quarter. This change is both a response by IBM to Japan and an industry result of the exponential growth of specialized workstations based on microcomputers. These devices are for the most part sold rather than leased. In any event, while a purchase dominant business has its own set of potential pitfalls for large capital procurements such as general purpose mainframes, it does reduce the asset intensity and associated financing burden of that business. So this problem will diminish rather than increase.

THE FUTURE

So where do we go from here? This is a segment of the industry with enormous competitive constraints: expensive technology, rapid change, large capital requirements, and historically lower than desired financial returns. But the future is not entirely bleak.

Why? First of all because Control Data's computer systems business is the result of an enormous wellspring of market and product innovation that is very much in line with basic trends. I have mentioned market trends. Architecturally the industry is moving more and more from the general purpose computer to the specifically designed *application* system. Currently this is more a function of software than underlying hardware. Advances in micro-electronic technology, however, are accelerating the possibilities for the hardware as well. Within ten years the general purpose computer as we have known it could well be mostly a thing of the past. We will look to application specific "work stations" linked together by local and remote networks as appropriate. So the trend is simultaneously specialization and integration. If that seems an oxymoron it is nevertheless true. Our computer systems business can have an increasingly viable role as "specialization" becomes more prevalent. Not surprisingly, in services where the focus is on solutions we have twenty years' experience in integrating diverse elements to produce those solutions. In short there is a rapid merging—already evident in many applications such as education and computer-aided design—of our systems and services businesses.

That is a brief look at *why* the future holds promise. The second question is *how* do we fulfill the promise? How do we evolve from this point on?

For applications delivery we use equipment from IBM, Data General, Cray, DEC, Zenith, and over fifty other vendors. That gives us better insight into what our own hardware is best used for, and it has provided both a broad perspective of the industry and the ability to discipline the amount and type of internal hardware development.

The key, then, is applications and, beyond that, new and improved marketing approaches. That, as it happens, is exactly the same statement made about what we have historically called computer services. And so, in that sense, except for peripherals Control Data could be viewed as becoming entirely a services company. More *accurately* said, we will provide our customers *solutions to problems* rather than *tools* for *problem solving,* and we will both build and buy the delivery devices used in those solutions. But what about these applications to which I keep referring? They don't come for free, and their development costs could put us right back in financial margin quandary with which we have struggled. Any major application system will take five to ten years (or longer) to bring to a reasonable state of market acceptance and cost at least $50–$100 million. The example of PLATO is widely publicized. In CAD for mechanical engineering applications we are spending nearly $20 million a year. CAD for electronic engineering applications is equally costly. For one application in the health care area—the Pathlab system now entering its third model—we have spent $2 million a year for ten years. In the utilities industry today we have the Cadillac energy management system offering. Today we even obtain some orders without going through competitive bids. This is not an accident, nor is it cheap—we have been in the energy management systems business for fifteen years and since 1982 alone have spent some $45 million on this application area.

I could go on, but even these few examples indicate we have built up over the years a considerable base of applications on which to build. Investment must continue—between systems and services over the next three years some $300 million of our total innovation expense will be for applications.

CLOSE

We have survived because we have been able to sense emerging trends before others and have had the strategic discipline to follow a highly focused strategy. Technical effort requirements in order to pursue the applications strategy necessary to future survival could easily double technical costs as a percent of revenue. All this will require creativity, innovation, and disciplined selection of application markets.

Appendix 4: Seymour Cray Letters

March 7, 1960

To: F. C. Mullaney
From: S. R. Cray
Subj.: End of An Era

I believe the initiation last week of a full blown management training program heralds the end of an era of purely technical supervision. This past two years has been a most interesting experiment for me and one from which I have derived considerable satisfaction. The loosely managed system with strictly technical supervision, which has come to be known as the "family plan", has performed with fewer people than I had thought possible. The dangers advertised as basic to this approach have been greatly exaggerated. The key is sustained technical competence at all levels. This can only be accomplished by supervising personnel working a reasonable portion of their time at technical work. Conventional management philosophy is not a requirement to achieve the end result.

I was somewhat surprised at the scope of the management training program and the emphasis given it. Your directive making attendance mandatory for all key engineering personnel makes it difficult to ignore. Attendance would of course have been very spotty without this emphasis. Several of the engineering personnel have unsuccessfully opposed such in-plant training at RRU and feel rather strongly about it. I imagine our maverick system is embarrassing to the corporate staff who, by definition, should establish such general policies. It is inevitable therefore that an effort should be made to educate the technical people in conventional management philosophy. The present course is obviously not one of discussing philosophy but of teaching a doctrine. The instructor cannot help this. The decision was made in hiring this type of man.

Immediate reaction to education is going to lower morale on the part of some key employees. Long term reaction will probably be a compromising organization. With this will go compromised performance. I guess we are a big enough company now to support this. As you know, I am a poor compromiser and will probably give you trouble in this thing. I hope you will understand my inflexible position and seek a replacement for me if this is anything but an academic exercise. I am not planning on attending further training sessions.

S. R. Cray

2/14/72

TO: W C Norris
FROM: S R Cray
SUBJ: Emotional Problems

This memo is on a different subject than my normal correspondence with you, but because of the recent developments in Control Data technical direction I believe it is important and urgent that I present as clearly as possible my emotional attitude toward the company and the implications it has on our continuing relationship. I have not experienced any recent traumatic emotional event that alters my attitude toward Control Data. Rather, the gradual erosion of emotional involvement in the Corporation's activities has brought me to a point of possible action. This is a matter of special concern in light of the apparent failure of PL to provide the major corporate technical base for future growth and a resulting return to reliance on my work as an alternate for the next considerable period of time. I am not prepared to assume this responsibility.

Let me review briefly the fifteen years of Control Data history from the standpoint of my emotional involvement. When the company was initially formed I was eager to get away from the large corporation environment and work in a small group with simple straightforward relationships. This turned out to be everything I expected of it in early Control Data history. I need not dwell on this point, because I am sure you understand my feelings at this point in time. The picture became an unsatisfactory one for me during the period of rapid growth and increasing depth of management in the early 1960s. The solution for me was to move to Chippewa and establish a small relatively isolated group which I could emotionally handle. Again you understood the situation and supported this rather unusual move, for which I am most grateful. This solution has worked for a decade, which is remarkable when one thinks about it.

Traumatic events in the later 1960s caused me to resign from the Board of Directors and further withdraw from overall corporate affairs. This period was traumatic for me because several of my personal friends found their own limits of tolerance, and I was emotionally involved with them. Clearly I would not have been with Control Data at this period had it not been for the Chippewa arrangement. The games grown men play in corporate life I find revolting, and I cannot personally participate. At this point in time I would have liked to leave and form (or join) a small company, but I felt a real obligation to continue working for Control Data as a result of your support in establishing the Chippewa Laboratory; and I rejected such thoughts categorically.

Ten years have now passed since moving to Chippewa, and two major products were developed and delivered to customers and to larger corporate development. The obligation which I felt in the 1960s has slowly been amortized, and I now feel a residual of zero. My remaining with Control Data in recent years has been the result of technical interest in continuing the evolution of my own ideas, which I nevertheless consider to be Control Data property. This evolution may be nearing an end. The 8000 development work is aimed at substantial improvement in speed of computation for very large number crunching problems. Many radical departures are being made in module construction techniques, and there are serious problems not yet solved. In the past few months some unexpected basic problems have appeared in the metallurgy of the low temperature solders which we were relying on for module assembly. The significance of these problems has been realized only recently, and the solution may require prolonged work. There is little question that an 8600 of the type I have described can be built. The question is one of range of application if more exotic techniques are required, resulting in less competitive performance. I think these matters will reach a decision point before the end of 1972. If further work in this direction seems to me to be slow and difficult, I do not think that I want to personally pursue it. In this case I am emotionally at the point where completely new work, quite possibly not directly involving computers, is of considerable appeal to me. I think I part ways with Control Data in this case.

What then do I suggest for Control Data? Whether the 8000 work continues or not, I think some other course for the major technical base of the Corporation is desirable. It should be supervised by an individual who has a good technical background but not the personality tolerance problems that I have. The obvious choice for this job is Jim Thornton. STAR performance has been disappointing to date. It also has been educational for Jim. He should be in an excellent position to evaluate the integrated circuit technology vs discrete components and plot an evolutionary course from CYBER hardware to newer technology for future years. I think this should be done.

S.R.C.

March 6, 1972

TO: W. C. Norris
FROM: S. R. Cray
SUBJECT: Thoughts on Separation

Since my last memo to you, my thinking has crystalized to the point of knowing generally what I want to do. This consists of establishing my own company to pursue research into large computer technology.

The timing of this activity and the general arrangements for initiating it remain to be worked out. In thinking about my relationship with Control Data, several factors appear important. The most urgent of these is minimizing the impact of my action on Control Data employees and on external opinion regarding Control Data's future. Another is the impact on the work current at Chippewa Laboratory. Also important to me is the future relationship with Control Data and with you personally. Finally, I am concerned about my own conflicts of interest and possible solutions to these problems.

Let me review briefly the current status of the work I am doing for Control Data. There are three parts to this. One is the corporate planning for future technical programs within the company. A second is the 8000 development work in Chippewa. The last is the 7600 production in Chippewa. The last is not really a problem since Serial No. 11 is due to be delivered in November and I am not personally involved in the final steps of this production. The first can be handled on a consulting basis. The real problem is the 8000 development work. The 8000 prototype is approaching the initial hardware checkout phase. There is considerable uncertainty as to the probability of success in this effort. The design work is largely complete and the hardware choices have been made and are being implemented. It remains to be seen if these choices result in a really workable hardware system. If the prototype can be made to work in the near future, the 8000 program can proceed to commitment of deliverable products for 1974 or 1975. If not, the approach should be abandoned or a major change of direction initiated. There is no way of determining the degree of success before late fall of this year and it may still be uncertain then. My guess is that there is a 50% chance of success.

Let me propose a scenario for my future activities. This makes assumptions which are sheer speculation on my part but may be helpful for planning purposes in our discussions later this week. First let me assume that I continue to work one-half time for Control Data until the 8000 work feasibility is established. This will likely take six months to a year to determine. My presence at Chippewa Lab and real interest in the outcome of the work should improve its probability of success.

Now let me speculate on what I will do with the other one-half of my time and possible conflicts it presents. Assume I form a corporation in Wisconsin with an initial capitalization of $2 million. Assume this corporation is called Cray Research Laboratory. Of the original money required, $1 million comes out of my pocket and the other million from the pockets of a dozen personal friends {I include you in this category and unique opportunity}. There is no public offering and no need for publicity.

During this coming summer a 10,000 square foot building is built on my property about 1/4 mile from Chippewa Laboratory. A two year program of basic research into large computer design problems is initiated. This is done by me and a small group of people {6–8}.

The intent of this two year program is to find some really basic new method of building computers using lasers, mirrors, semiconductors, or who knows what. Assume that this effort is successful. In 1974 a public stock offering raises capitalization to $10 million and a development program is initiated to build and deliver a small number of very large equipments to meet specialized computing requirements. The general idea would be to sell equipments and/or designs to large corporations or to very daring end users.

There surely are potential conflicts of interest in the above division of my time. There are also problems with Control Data employees who may want to work in my new company. Fortunately the latter problem is limited by the size and character of the new company. All of the problems are minimized if there is an on-going and developing relationship between Control Data and Cray Research Laboratory. I can see no reason why this is not possible. Control Data may well profit from buying completed designs with a minimal risk at a higher than cost price. There may be mutually desirable short-term R&D-type projects as well. In the extreme view there would be little difference from the current relation with Chippewa Lab except that the accounting of money would be lumpy rather than continuous. I obviously need your help in proceeding any further along these lines.

Seymour R. Cray

Appendix 5: Robert Price Speech to CBEMA Panel—"Microelectronics: 'The Crude Oil of the '80s'" (April 7, 1981)

In recent months, there have been a number of comments in the press to the effect that Microelectronics "will be the crude oil of the '80s." This is a seemingly apt reference to the opportunity Microelectronic Technology offers to those who would dominate world trade in the future. Perhaps unwittingly it also implies an unfortunate policy and strategic direction the U.S. computer industry is pursuing . . . one which in the long run can only lead to a declining competitive position. My remarks today will center on this dilemma. For we are, in fact, at a vital crossroads in the evolution of microelectronic technology and its application to economic growth. The "oil" analogy, or rather its inappropriateness will serve as a good vehicle to describe the nature and importance of the decisions we are about to make at this crossroads.

How we in the computer industry treat this issue of microelectronic development—more than any other single factor—will determine the economic future of this country. And since our political future is inextricably tied to our economic future, there is a whole lot more at stake here than mere prosperity.

In the next eighteen months or so, either explicitly or implicitly, our industry is going to decide which path it will take. There are only two paths, and as you have correctly guessed they fall into the biblical mold—one right, one wrong.

I'll come back to that in a moment but, first, let's return to our oil analogy . . . and its misleading implications.

Oil is a physical resource and it is relatively widespread compared to some other important minerals. But even it is limited to certain geographic areas. A very small minority—less than seven percent—of the world's nations control the major deposits. And the major industrialized nations are for the most part dependent rather than self-sufficient. As a physical resource oil must be pumped, put into pipes or containers, and physically moved before it can be of use to anybody. So it is easily controlled. In recent years, we have learned the hard way what that means. If you have it, you have it—and the other guy doesn't. He's got to buy, and even beg, to get it from you—or he may possibly kill you to get it. But when he does get it from you—by whatever means—he has it and you don't. It's a zero-sum game.

Microelectronics, on the other hand, is knowledge. Well, there is a little sand and some other physical matter involved, but microelectronics for strategic considerations is knowledge. And here is the first crucial distinction which makes the oil analogy misleading. Intelligent, knowledgeable people exist in every nation, in every race, on every land on earth. Controlling knowledge is obviously a different ballgame than controlling a physical quantity such as oil. For all practical purposes it can't be done.

Now certainly the development and use of high technology requires more than the presence of intelligent, knowledgeable people. A whole economic, educational, and political infrastructure is also required. But such an infrastructure also exists to the degree necessary in every country with whom we compete. Thus, one can argue only within a relatively limited range about who has the potential to do what in the area of microelectronics. The point is that, as opposed to oil or any physical resource, knowledge, and specifically the knowledge of microelectronics, is more widely diffused, more easily transported, and more readily accessible than any other resource which has ever been essential to human development. All of our international competitors have enough of this vital resource to create economic mischief.

There is a second important difference: knowledge transactions as opposed to oil transactions are not zero-sum events. If I have know-how and I sell it to you, I've still got it. The trick is to turn this non-zero-sum attribute to our advantage.

And right here we have come to the crux of the matter—the essence of the crossroads decision we face. We can treat knowledge transactions according to their true nature—non-zero-sum events—or we can fall into the trap of setting corporate strategy and government policy as though they were zero-sum. The first will allow us to retain a position of leadership. The second, in the long run, will reduce us to second-rate status. The way to take advantage of the true nature of knowledge is to work cooperatively. Which means: I share with you in such a way as to *add* to my know-how. We *both* gain. And if the transaction is well conceived we both gain to the same relative degree.

Finally, there is a third important disparity between oil and microelectronics: the "Applications" of oil are relatively limited and relatively cheap—you refine, you burn it, you convert it. There are around 750 refineries in the world. Now a refinery costs only 500 million dollars or so and the design engineering part of that cost is only $45 million. The most familiar application of oil is the internal combustion engine—a relatively inexpensive device in engineering terms. Even a leading chemical company like DuPont spends only $450 million per year on *new* applications of petroleum derivatives. These sums of money are small when compared to research and development associated with the application of semiconductors.

And application of semiconductor technology is still so labor-intensive that the demand for money and people to pursue them is mind-boggling. IBM, alone, spends in design engineering costs the equivalent of 30 refineries a year. And that is basically for one application of microelectronics—making electronic calculators. According to *Business Week,* the total U.S. computer industry spends over $3 billion per year. Worldwide, all applications of semiconductors consume nearly 7 billion R&D dollars. At that rate, in less than five years, we will exceed the engineering costs associated with all the refineries that exist, and the application of microelectronics is still in its infancy. That is one thing on which *everybody* agrees. From this perspective—that of the great difference in the number and cost of applications—acting on the belief that microelectronics is analogous to oil can clearly be seen as a road to disaster. The key strategic issue in oil is who uses the *least* amount relative to the amount available to them, whereas for microelectronics it is precisely those who can use the *most* who will win the game.

Speaking to the Sixth Solid State Circuits Conference recently, Robert Noyce said: "Since it is the growth of applications that is the source of semiconductor industry growth, it follows that the best assurance of a viable semiconductor industry in any country is the existence of viable industries using semiconductor products, and not the other way around."

And every technical or capital dollar spent on unnecessary and dissipated microelectronics research effort is a double whammy: it gains no basic knowledge *not* already available and it is money not available to achieve gains in the applications area—which is where the economic benefit truly lies.

So what is in fact happening? Everyone is out there scrambling for themselves. We are acting exactly as though we believe the oil analogy. Listen to *Business Week:* "Computer makers are having to invest a lot more money—to automate and streamline their manufacturing operations. Capital requirements have risen so rapidly that even the healthiest of the companies are scraping the bottom of their coffers." The article goes on to point out how everybody is integrating forward and backward and spending money to the limit. A couple numbers from the article will illustrate my point—in 1980 IBM spent two and one quarter billion dollars on plant automation. Datapoint is spending $50 million. That's a ratio of 45 to one. You can pick out any other numbers from the article and find similar discontinuities of scale. But my point is not to pick on Datapoint or any of the other companies mentioned. It simply points out the diffusion and duplication in our industry. If you add up the unnecessary, overlapping expenditures to advance the technology, it would undoubtedly amount to more than a billion dollars per year. In particular, everyone is out there duplicating their equally inadequate expenditures in the area of semiconductors—when they need every dollar possible to achieve value-added distinctiveness for their products and services which are based on those devices. This is even more amazing when you consider that in the area of semiconductors we are entering a totally new era. There are changes taking place in every phase of microcircuits including research, hardware, software, manufacturing and applications:

As already noted, the industry is becoming more capital intensive.

Software technology is more pervasive and more critical to advances in semiconductor technology and certainly in applying it.

There is a great shortage of technically trained personnel, especially software types. In the same address I referenced a moment ago, Bob Noyce also noted that "we must conserve design talent in the semiconductor industry . . . we must cope with the too rapid consumption of our industry's human resources."

Essentially there are only two or possibly three efforts in microcircuits that have sufficient scale and coordination to effectively cope with the changing environment: Japan, Inc.; IBM; and possibly Bell Labs. The other efforts, which include Control Data's, are fractionated and uncoordinated, and over time will not be productive enough.

And what of our government? Not surprisingly, without leadership from us there is no help there. Although the debacle in Detroit is bringing some people to their senses, we still need important policy changes and perhaps legal changes as well.

The National Science Foundation, the Department of Defense and other government agencies could do a lot to foster cooperation in microelectronic research—but rather the prevailing mood seems to mirror that of industry.

INTERNATIONAL ATTITUDES TOWARD COOPERATION

If U.S. industry does not yet understand what is going on, what is the situation in other countries?

Unfortunately for us, there is a considerably greater degree of understanding—especially in Japan.

Perspective

Everyone in our industry senses that microelectronics is the essential fuel they must have to succeed. And what they sense is right. But rather than carefully reflect on the nature of that "fuel," the knee-jerk reaction is for each company to go grab some for itself. It is hard to avoid an image of each CEO dashing out into his back yard to start drilling for oil—with a shovel. It's no accident that the "oil" analogy has come into our lexicon. It's a direct reflection of the underlying psychology of what is going on. And what is going on is *wrong.*

Sensing in some vague way the need for help, the second knee-jerk reaction sets in: the government! The government should sponsor more R&D and, of course, give better tax breaks. This appeal for government salvation was spelled out in elaborate detail by the SIA in testimony before Congress in January. We don't stop to think that to use that money effectively requires more than everybody just grabbing a piece for themselves. By contrast, the Japanese government can spend a mere $300 million over four or five years and bring Japanese industry from far behind to a state-of-the-art situation. It would take many times that amount to achieve the same degree of progress in the U.S. and that is not only wrong, it's inflationary.

But the government awakened by the alarm of industry *does* react. How? By placing embargoes on international technology transfer. Which is *not* all that wrong . . . if you believe this essential fuel that everyone seems so alarmed about can—like oil—be owned.

Meanwhile, other countries—especially Japan—are using industry cooperation and industry-government cooperation to gain leverage and are rapidly overtaking us because of our diffused, redundant and inadequate approach. And their approach is not only right—it will win the game.

We urgently need a different approach. Our dilemma is the absolute and expensive need for continually advancing the state-of-the-art in microelectronics while at the same time giving highest priority to the even more expensive task of *applying* microelectronics.

THE ANSWER—COOPERATION

And there is only one answer: broad-based technological cooperation in advanced microcircuits. Unfortunately, that is easier said than achieved. Experience teaches that the top management in most large corporations is incapable of coping with major changes before they occur. But in the case of microelectronics, it would be far too costly to wait for the impact of the changes coming to take their toll in order to establish the right climate for cooperation. We must act on the experience we have gained. That experience shows that cooperation and competition can exist simultaneously and effectively if we adhere to four basic principles:

Cooperation must be limited to research, development, and production—no marketing.
Cooperation must be broad-based—that it is not limited to just a few participants.
Cooperation must focus on advanced technology—those technologies that are five to ten years out in front of those in today's products.
Each participant must have a clear value-added strategy which can provide marketplace distinctiveness.

A Proposal

Using these basic principles, a cooperative program can be constructed. We believe an entity should be formed to perform research development and production in semiconductor technologies and products. Let me call it Microelectronic Enterprises, Inc. (MEI). MEI would develop state-of-the-art microelectronic technology and provide circuits incorporating this technology to its shareholders—but not to the merchant market.

CONCLUSION

This is our crossroads. Either the U.S. computer industry will adopt a strategy of technological cooperation on a broad basis—or it will not. If it does, there will be vitality and growth. If it does not, then there will be isolation and sickness—IBM will be the General Motors of the '90s—the rest of us won't even have to worry about it.

And so it is, where we wind up is ours to decide—and we must make that choice—now.

Appendix 6: *New York Times* article:

"Computer Accord Signed by Soviets"

COMPUTER ACCORD SIGNED BY SOVIETS

*Control Data in 10-Year Deal
for Joint Development of
Advanced Technology*

DETAILS NOT SETTLED

*Venture's Ultimate Value Put
as High as $500-Million—
National Network Sought*

By THEODORE SHABAD

The Control Data Corporation and the Soviet Government announced yesterday that they had signed a 10-year agreement to cooperate in the joint development of advanced computer technology and related services.

The cooperation accord, the first with a major computer manufacturer as well as the first such long-term pact with a United States company, was concluded at a time when the Soviet Union has ambitious plans for a national computer and data-processing network that would inject new vigor and effciency into a sluggish economy.

The research-and-development pact, which was concluded in Moscow after months of negotiations, may ultimately lead to joint manufacturing arrangements with the Russians and appears to give the Minneapolis-based concern potential primacy in the Soviet computer market.

A company spokesman said by telephone from Minnesota that the agreement represented a "major stride forward." However, he stressed that detailed projects remained to be worked out. American sources in Moscow put the ultimate worth of the agreement at perhaps $500-million.

ULTIMATE PROJECTS

One of the ultimate projects, according to unconfirmed industry reports, may be the production of computer components in Soviet plants built with Control Data assistance. These components would then be mated with United States-made components, the finished products being marketed in third countries.

Control Data is also expected to help the Soviet Union in developing the national computer network, to be used both for process control and economic planning.

According to industry sources, installation of a Soviet time-sharing network might benefit from experience gained in Control Data's own Cybernet system in the United States.

The Soviet Union has lagged far behind the United States and other industrial countries in the use of computer technology. By the beginning of 1973 it had installed more than 800 automated control systems in industrial plants as well as 1,585 computer centers.

About 480 more control systems and 510 computer centers were to be added during the year.

The computer agreement was signed yesterday for Control Data by William R. Keye, vice chairman of the board, and Robert D. Schmidt, executive vice president, and for the Soviet Union by Dzherman M. Gvishiani, a deputy chairman of the Government's State Committee for Science and Technology.

The committee, and particularly Mr. Gvishiani, who is Premier Aleskei N. Kosygin's son-in-law, have been in the forefront of Moscow's quest for advanced technology in the West.

Under the accord, joint study teams will work out cooperative projects in the design of computer mainframes and peripheral equipment as well as data-processing and communications systems and the software for such systems. Specific applications are to be explored in the general areas of medicine, education and transportation.

At the signing ceremony in Moscow, Mr. Gvishiani expressed the hope that a more specific agreement of intention to carry out particular projects would be concluded by the end of the year.

According to Tass, the Soviet press agency, he said that talks were already under way with Control Data on the construction of computer-manufacturing plants on a "compensation basis." Such compensation deals, which are being sought increasingly by the Soviet Union, would then pay back the investment with production from such plants.

The Soviet Union in the past has concluded a number of deals for the purchase of American computers, including some from the International Business Machines Corporation and Control Data.

Lately, however, Moscow has expressed interest in more permanent cooperative arrangements rather than isolated cash deals. I.B.M. has been cool to such arrangements, according to Soviet sources.

It remains to be seen how the Control Data agreement fits in with the Soviet bloc's own development of third-generation computers, the Ryad series, and to what extent United States-Soviet cooperation in computer technology will be constrained by American strategic controls on the export of very large-scale computers.

Although Control Data computers account for only about 4.5 per cent of the machines in use in the United States, the company has long been the world leader in the manufacture of very large computers, such as its 6000 series.

In recent years Control Data has become a broad-based company, including the manufacture of peripheral equipment, software and time-sharing services.

Last April the company signed a joint manufacturing agreement with Rumania to build peripheral equipment in Bucharest. Control Data was to have a 45 per cent interest in the joint venture, whose initial investment was planned at $4-million.

Appendix 7: Memoirs of Carolyn Firouztash

(Control Data Iran's Deputy Director Homa Firouztash, an Iranian national educated in the United States, struggled to maintain Control Data's presence during the Iranian revolution. His wife, Carolyn, an American-born educator working in the country, kept memoirs of that time. Here, with Carolyn's permission, are summarized excerpts from those memoirs.)

October 1978: The Shah of Iran was still in charge, but demonstrations against the government grew more violent; strikes became more frequent. The turmoil was considered temporary, but difficult to deal with. Control Data Iran began evacuating families of employees.

Getting Control Data expatriates out of Iran was no easy feat. Every day the airport was swamped with both foreigners and Iranians. People arrived seven or eight hours before their departure time and spent hours just trying to get inside the airport building.

Because of the language difficulties, Homa, who was Iranian-born and spoke Farsi, went to the airport to assist Control Data families. He always came home exhausted, often with his shirt torn. There was a great deal of pushing, shoving, yelling, fighting, and grabbing as people fought to get tickets and go through check-in. Because of the continual horrendous crush of the crowds, Homa often carried suitcases above his head for hours as he pushed through the mass of people to the airline gates. Families were separated, and children screamed with fright. Homa compared the panic and terror of being left behind to a herd of uncontrollable stampeding elephants. The Control Data spouses and children were, however, safely evacuated.

In January 1979, oil production fell to 1952 levels. Heating oil was rationed. Strikes hit both public and private sectors. The central bank was closed, schools closed, and garbage collection stopped. Power shortages were common. There was no bus service. The U.S. ambassador recommended that dependents of American business people leave the country "temporarily." Control Data stepped up its evacuation efforts, and Homa spent considerable time at airline offices and at the airport.

This evacuation proved even more difficult. There were no tickets available. Control Data's Minneapolis office talked with Pan American Airways office in New York and got a promise of 19 tickets to be secured on the first available flight out of Tehran.

Homa went to Pan Am's Tehran office to pick up the tickets. The building had been set on fire the day before. Windows were smashed and the building reeked of smoke. And there were no tickets, according to the agent. Homa pressed his case, insisting on seeing the manager. At last he got the 19 tickets and again fought his way through an even more chaotic airport to get Control Data people out of the country.

The Shah left Iran on January 16, 1979. On February 1, the Ayatollah Khomeini returned to Iran from exile.

In April, Homa had a scheduled trip to Brussels. A few days in advance, he went to the airport to check on his passport and to make sure an exit visa had been granted. There was no passport, according to the agent, and Homa was directed to an office where young revolutionaries told him that, as the manager of a business, he could not leave because no one would then be responsible for the business. His passport had been confiscated.

After some days and several encounters, the revolutionaries were convinced by Control Data's office manager, Ali Gafari, that the company would be in good hands during Homa's absence.

In October 1979, American hostages were seized at the American Embassy, beginning a 444-day ordeal. Homa arranged a way to get supplies into the embassy through Canada's embassy, but that effort ended in April 1980 after a failed hostage rescue attempt by the U.S. government. Homa and Carolyn began to make their own plans in case they needed to leave the country.

In April 1980, Homa's request to renew his passport was denied with a note saying: "Banned from leaving; refer individual to Prime Minister's section." This office was at Evin Prison, a place infamous for executions—sometimes thirty to forty a day. Most people banned from leaving the country would not voluntarily set foot in Evin.

Homa went to Evin twenty-seven times over the course of the next few months. Each time there were the same questions asked and impossible demands made. The central issue was Control Data's invoice to the university charging for a computer and services. Homa produced one document after another, but nothing seemed to satisfy the prosecutor general. Homa was told to reach an agreement with the university, but no one at the university would talk to him.

Homa became such a familiar visitor that the guards came to recognize him on sight. On one occasion, a man who was obviously visiting Evin for the first time asked the guard how long it would take to get his problem solved.

Homa, standing behind the man in line, laughed and said, "Do you see Abdul's [the guard's] long, bushy beard? Well, the first day I was here, he didn't have a hair on his face!"

The guard chuckled and said, "Yes, that's right."

There was little humor, though, in Homa's continued quests to get his passport renewed. Even when ordered to talk to Homa, the university president refused. When a letter did finally arrive, it accused Homa and Control Data of cheating "the oppressed people of Iran," and claimed that the university did not owe anything to "the bloodsucking American company."

The prosecutor general told Homa that his cousin, a computer expert, would look into the matter. As it turned out, the cousin really was a computer expert and decided that Control Data was owed money—but that the $3 million should be discounted by $1 million. Homa did not like the idea of his passport costing, in effect, $1 million. He held out for full payment. Meanwhile, in Minneapolis, Control Data sued the government of Iran, placing Homa in an even more delicate situation. In late December, a new university president sided with Homa and said the university would pay $834,000, far short of what was owed. But at least there was an acknowledgment of debt.

Homa's situation still remained precarious. As time went on, the situation for foreigners and for Iranian nationals (like Homa) who worked for American companies grew even more desperate. Carolyn, with great reluctance, flew out of Iran on the last plane allowed to leave. Homa finally escaped on foot. He hiked out of Iran through Pakistan.

Appendix 8: Spin-offs and Start-ups by Former Control Data Employees (partial list)

Aetrium
Apertus Technologies
Arbitron
Astrocom
Authorware
BlueLine Software
Capital Dimensions Venture Fund
Compton Electronics
Computer Communications
Computer Systems
Control Data Systems
Cray Computer
Cray Research
Cypress Semiconductor Minnesota
Cybernetics
Cytrol
Data 100
Date Action
DataCard
Datagraph
Data Pathing

Digital Biometrics
Drake Training
Digital Systems
Edge Computer
Educational Alternatives
Flame Industries
Fourth Shift
Ganz-Wiley
Gateway Communication
Hutchinson Technology
Institute for Advanced Technology
Intech
(Itasca Systems) IBEX
Joanne Henry & Associates
Johnson-Matthey Electronics
Materials Processing
Midwest Data System
Multi-Access
National Computer Systems
Network Systems
OnTrack Computer Systems
Premier Computer Corp.
Process Management International-Bluefire Partners
Quorum Litigation Services
Rorke Data
Star Technologies
StayWell
Sytec-Artesyn Technology
Technalysis
Technology 80
The Analyst
TRO Learning (Plato Learning)
VTC
Western Temporary Services
XP Systems
Xylogics
Zycad
Zytec

Notes

CHAPTER 1. THE ONCE AND FUTURE COMPANY

1. Erwin Tomash and Arnold A. Cowen, "The Birth of ERA: Engineering Research Associates, Inc., 1946–1955," in *A History of Computing in the Twentieth Century,* Annals of the History of Computing, Vol. 1, no. 2 (AFIPS, Inc., Oct. 1979). A nonclassified version of the Atlas computer was made and marketed as the ERA Model 1101. The number 1101 is the binary representation of the number 13, which was the navy's task number for the Atlas project. In 1956, a Model 1101 computer ultimately found its way from the air force's Arnold Engineering Center to the Rich Electronic Computing Center at the Georgia Institute of Technology. There it provided the computing power to prove out a numerical integration solution for a mixed system of partial and ordinary differential equations. The proposed methodology was the subject of my master's thesis at Georgia Tech.

2. In June 1955 Remington Rand merged with Sperry Corporation to become Sperry Rand. Later it became Univac, and still later merged with Burroughs Corporation to become Unisys. Charles T. Murray, *The Supermen, the Story of Seymour Cray and the Technical Wizards Behind the Supercomputer* (New York: Wiley and Sons, 1997).

3. In fact, Control Data revenues were $63 million within 5 years and $160 million within seven years. In terms of 2005 dollars, that represented an increase from $380 million to $943 million in just that two-year time period.

4. The actual relationship was even stronger than that. Ralph Meader, formerly of NCML, was one of the founders of ERA, and two engineers formerly of CSAW became principals in research and development at ERA.

5. C-E-I-R began life as the Council for Economic and Industrial Research, a government think tank, during World War II. It was incorporated as a nonprofit in 1952 and branched out to offer data services.

6. Commercial Credit, which had become part of Control Data in 1968, added another $1 billion to total revenues in 1980.

7. mips: millions of instructions per second; flops: floating point operations per second.

8. SAGE led to many later networking technologies and developments. Its story is related in several publications, but interesting ties to network computing, including the Internet, are contained in David L. Boslaugh, *When Computers Went to Sea: The Digitization of the United States Navy* (New York: Wiley-IEEE Computer Society Press, 2003), and M. Mitchell Waldrop, *The Dream Machine: J.C.R. Licklider and the Revolution That Made Computing Personal* (New York: Viking, 2001).

9. R. M. Price, "A Search for Survival, 1957–1985," Address to Board of Directors, March 14, 1985.

CHAPTER 2. ON THE EDGE OF THE POSSIBLE

1. The RISC/CISC architectural alternative has continued to be a source of competitive advantage debate in the industry. Intel came under considerable competitive pressure to adopt RISC in the 1980s but pragmatically chose, because of the by then near universal use of its X86 processors, to stick with the CISC design of those microprocessors.

2. Author's personal files.

3. Author's personal files.

4. The story of ENIAC, generally accepted as the first stored program electronic digital computer, is told in Scott McCartney's book *ENIAC* (New York: Walker Publishing Company, 1999).

CHAPTER 3. MEETING VITAL NEEDS

1. Kennecott Copper Corporation Mining Company had previously initiated a similar but more limited service, "Insight," for its employees in Salt Lake City.

CHAPTER 4. FOSTERING THE COURAGE TO INNOVATE

1. These four attributes, but particularly skills and awareness, are essential to the concept of "absorptive capacity," which is defined as "an ability to recognize the value of new information, assimilate it, and apply it to commercial ends." This is the definition used by W. M. Cohen and D. A. Levinthal in their 1990 article "Absorptive Capacity: A New Perspective on Learning and Innovation," *Administrative Science Quarterly,* 36 (1990): 128–152.

2. Jay Gould, "The Panda's Thumb of Technology," *Natural History,* Vol. 96, no. 1 (American Museum of Natural History, 1986).

3. Blaine McCormick, *At Work with Thomas Edison* (Canada, 2001).

CHAPTER 5. BUILDING A FRAMEWORK FOR INNOVATION

1. Outsourcing is yet one more term that has been bastardized. Originally it meant simply buying a needed product or service from an independent company, rather than handling it internally. Thanks to political expedience, it now means shifting jobs to countries with lower labor costs.

CHAPTER 6. JOURNEYS IN STRATEGIC SPACE

Epigraph: Bernard DeVoto, ed., *Journals of Lewis and Clark* (Boston: Houghton Mifflin Company, 1953).

1. Michael Porter, "Note on the Structural Analysis of Industries," Howard Business School Publishing, 1983 (9-276-054).

2. *Strategic Management Journal* (Summer 1992): 111–125.

3. David Teece, Gary Pesaro, and Amy Shuen, "Dynamic Capabilities and Strategic Management," *Strategic Management Journal* (8/7): 509–533.

4. Joseph Schumpeter, *Capitalism, Socialism and Democracy* (London: George Allen & Unwin, 1943).

5. Edwin Mansfield, *Innovation, Technology and the Economy: The Selected Essays of Edwin Mansfield* (Brookfield, Vt.: Elgar, 1995).

6. Richard Nelson and Sidney Winter, *An Evolutionary Theory of Economic Change* (Cambridge: Harvard University Press, 1982).

7. See, for example, F. M. Scherer, *New Perspectives on Economic Growth and Technological Innovation* (Washington, D.C.: Brookings Institution, 1999); Zvi Griliches, *R&D, Education, and Productivity: A Retrospective* (Cambridge: Harvard University Press, 2000); Zvi Griliches, *Productivity Issues in Services at the Micro Level: A Special Issue of the Journal of Productivity Analysis* (Boston: Kluwer, 1993).

8. Bill Norris's intuitive understanding of the commoditization of technology may have been correct, but the company he chose was a bit off the mark. Intel would have been more accurate.

9. In fact, even the systems integration task has become more specialized. With the advent of networked computers, the Internet, and massive databases it is very unusual for an organization with large communication requirements to rely on a single systems integrator. Thus the customer is apt to have separate systems integrators for computing systems and data storage systems, and most likely for different wireless and wired, internal and external communication requirements.

10. For example, the report of the National Commission on Excellence in Education (David P. Gardner, chair) titled "A Nation at Risk: The Imperative for Education Reform" (April 1983).

11. Material excerpted from Sally Friedema, "New Jersey Q&A, Helen Frangolin Boehm, 'Aggressive Salesperson or Shy Artist,'" *New York Times,* August 8, 1993; and Diane G. Lasseter, "The Boehm Empire Started in the Basement with a $1000 Loan," *Business for Central New Jersey,* September 4, 1991, 3.

CHAPTER 8. COLLABORATE TO COMPETE

1. A prior joint venture had been formed in 1962 with Holley Carburetor Company to design and produce printers, but by 1964 it had become a wholly owned operation of Control Data. It was made a part of CPI.

2. The organizations were: Advanced Micro Devices, Inc., Burroughs Corporation, Computer and Business Equipment Manufacturers Association, Control Data Corporation, Department of Defense, Digital Equipment Corporation, Electronic Industries Association, Gellman Research Associates, Harris Corporation, Honeywell, Inc., Massachusetts Institute of Technology, Motorola Corporation, National Cash Register Corporation, National Semi-conductor Corporation, Rockwell International, Signetics Corporation, Sperry Corporation, Texas Instruments, Mostek, and Xerox Corporation.

3. An extensive history and analysis of MCC is contained in David V. Gibson and Everett M. Rogers, *R&D Collaboration on Trial* (Boston: Harvard Business School Press, 1994).

4. Cited in E. Raymond Corey, *Technology Fountainheads: The Management Challenge of R&D Consortia* (Boston: Harvard Business School Press, 1997).

5. The ten founding shareholders of MCC were AMD, Control Data Corporation, DEC, Harris, Honeywell, Motorola, National Semi-conductor, NCR, RCA, and Sperry Corporation. In early 1983 they were joined by Mostek, Allied Signal, Buckbee Mears Company (BMC), and Martin-Marietta.

6. These issues as well as many other aspects of this imaginative collaborative undertaking are covered in considerable detail by John N. Vardalas in Chapter 7 of his book *The Computer Revolution in Canada* (Cambridge, MA: MIT Press, 2001).

CHAPTER 9. THE ART OF ACQUISITION

1. Among these were Holley Computer Products, originally a 1962 joint venture with the Holley Carburetor Company, Digigraphic Systems (1963 from ITEK Corporation), Electrofact NV (1963), Bridge, Inc. (1964), Rabinow Engineering (1964), the transactor business of General Time Corporation (1964), Data Display (1965), and Electronic Accounting Card Corporation (1968).

2. As pointed out in Chapter 4, the terminology "complementary assets" is that of David Teece and refers to capabilities required to actually realize the potential profits of a new technology or innovation. They include such things as sales and marketing capability, production, distribution, information systems, and support services.

3. Paul Rizzo was at that time the CFO of IBM and a candidate for the CEO position. Paul had been an outstanding football player at the University of North Carolina, a point of some ironic rivalry with my Duke University background. Interestingly, our paths would, if not quite intersect, come close together when Paul became dean of the Kenan

Flagler School of Business at UNC while, as an Executive in Residence, I was teaching a course on strategy at Duke's Fuqua School of Business. One of my illustrations was Control Data's lawsuit against IBM twenty years earlier.

4. They included Electrofact NV, the Stromberg Division of General Time Corporation, ADCOMP, Automation Control Company, and the Control Systems Division of Daystrom. The company had also set up an internal business unit, the Industrial Data Processing Division.

5. N. L. Dickinson, "The Life & Times of Nathan Look Dickinson," vol. 1 (unpublished).

6. For example, Bruce Quackenbush, the chief financial officer of Commercial Credit, became the treasurer of Control Data. Dan Brill, a former member of the Federal Reserve Board and Commercial Credit's director of international operations, helped set up its Commercial Trading International subsidiary, which played a pivotal role in the barter business—an essential element of Control Data's push into doing business in the Soviet bloc of Eastern European countries. Paul G. Miller, one of the computer business's top executives, became CEO of Commercial Credit. Bill Rowe, a top human resources and administrative executive, went from the parent company to Commercial Credit, where he assumed the top administrative job, and later was senior vice president in charge of consumer finance operations. Herb Trader went from the computer business to run John Sheehan's Integrated Services Marketing. George Troy moved from Commercial Credit to Control Data's services business, where he held a variety of positions, including running the fledgling Business Advisory Services unit. Dave Noer moved from the parent company's human resources department to become Commercial Credit's vice president of human resources.

CHAPTER 10. "MAKE": RELYING ON INTERNAL RESOURCES

1. Richard Perle was about the biggest single pain we had to endure in export license matters. It was nevertheless with considerable regret and dismay that I read in the September 6, 2004, *Chicago Tribune* that this intelligent and assiduous public servant was under investigation for failing to exercise appropriate oversight as a company director. Perle has remained a highly visible public figure and, as of this writing, is still a Defense Department adviser.

2. It is interesting to note that Trevor consistently refers to himself as "Robinson" rather than "I." This is no false humility. It is characteristic of a man who while accomplishing prodigious feats still refers to himself in the disinterested third person.

3. From E. T. Robinson, "Government Participation in the Australian Computer Industry," in *Computing in Australia: The Development of a Profession,* ed. J. M. Bennett et al. (Sydney, NSW: Hale & Iremonger, in association with the Australian Computer Society, 1994).

CHAPTER 11. ACCEPTING DARING AND UNUSUAL CHALLENGES

1. Bernard DeVoto, ed., *Journals of Lewis and Clark* (Boston: Houghton Mifflin Company, 1953).

CHAPTER 14. EXTRAORDINARY INNOVATION, EXTRAORDINARY COLLABORATION

1. Baltimore, MD; Bemidji, MN; Champaign, IL; Charleston, SC; Duluth, MN; Grand Rapids, MN; Minneapolis, MN; Monmouth, IL; Nashville, TN; Omaha, NE; Philadelphia, PA; Providence, RI; Pueblo, CO; Saginaw, MI; St. Paul, MN. In addition to the first BTC in downtown St. Paul there was an "Energy Technology Center" in that city's Energy Park Development as well as in San Antonio, TX; South Bend, IN; Stevanage, Hertfordshire, England; and Toledo, OH.

2. Raymond W. Smilor and Robert L. Kuhn, eds., *Corporate Creativity, Robust Companies and the Entrepreneurial Spirit* (Praeger Publishers, 1984).

3. MCO and MSCF along with the Microelectronics and Information Science Center—a collaboration with the University of Minnesota—ultimately made up what was called the Minnesota Network for Small Business Innovation and Job Creation.

EPILOGUE

Epigraph: *The Book of Merlyn* was not originally published with *The Once and Future King.* The manuscript for the entire book was presented to White's London publisher in 1941, but due to dislocation caused by World War II was not published for twelve years. In 1975 the Texas Press discovered the manuscript in the archives of the Humanities Research Center at the University of Texas, Austin, and the decision was made to publish it in collaboration with White's biographer, Sylvia Townsend Warner.

Index

A. C. Neilsen Company, 160

ABC Corporation, 160

"absorptive capacity" concept, innovation and, 306n.1

accountability, fear of failure and, 78–80

Acheson, Dean, xi

acquisitions strategy: basic properties of, 155–75; case studies of, 158–70; growth as rationale for, 157–58; guidelines for, 170–74; rationale for, 156; strategic alliances and, 132–33

Adams, John, 8–9

Adams, John Quincy, 9

Adamson, Norma, 229

ADCOMP, 164, 309n.4

"Addressing Society's Major Unmet Needs as Profitable Business Opportunities," 225

advanced computer architecture (ACA), in microelectronics industry, 142–44

Advanced Design Laboratory, 49–50

Advanced Development Laboratory (ADL), NCR and, 135–37, 152–53

Advanced Micro Devices (AMD), 141, 308n.1, 308n.5

AEC Saclay weapons research center, 185

AEC Vaujours weapons research center, 185

Agriculture Technology Products and Services, 241–42

Allied Signal Corporation, 308n.5

Alnes, Judy, 10

Alzheimer's Disease, 69–71

Alzheimer's Disease: The Costs to U.S. Businesses in 2003, 71

American Credit Indemnity, 167

American Hoist & Derrick Co., 56

American Research Bureau (ARB), 19, 160–61

Amidon, Debra M., 65

AN/AYK-14 platform, 27
Anderson, Bill, 140, 179
Anderson, Carol, 59–60
Anderson, David, 63
Anderson, G. L. (Bud), 63
Anderson, Wendell (Governor), 60
antitrust regulations, collaboration and, 141–44
ANZ Bank, 188
Apple Computer, 100, 109
applications of technology, Technology Food Chain and, 122
application systems, evolution of, 163–64
appraisal, crisis management and role of, 222–23
ARB Corporation, 19
arbitration, 191–93
Arbitron Corporation, 19, 29–30, 112, 215
Archer, Lucille, 230
Area Vocational Technical Institutes (AVTI), 204–5
Arnold Engineering Center, 305n.1
astronauts, backup navigational process for, 2
AT&T Corporation, 254
Atlas computer, development of, 14, 305n.1
Atomic Energy Commission, 180
At Work with Thomas Edison, 80
Australia, CDC partnerships with, 182–83, 186–89
Australian Commonwealth Scientific Industrial Research Organization (CSIRO), 102–3, 182–83, 186–89
Automation Control Company, 309n.4
Aviation Credit Corp., 167
awareness, culture of innovation and, 66–68
Axelrod, Robert, 131
Ayatollah Khomeini, 205

backup navigational process for astronauts, development of, 2

Baker, Gene, 62–63, 156
Baldridge National Quality Program, 74–75
Barr, Betty, 230
Barth, John, 187
Barton, Robert S., 188
batch-based computing, 159–61
Beaugonin, Gerard, 185–86
Bell, Gordon, 141
Bemis, Judson (Sandy), 258–59
Bendix Corporation, 20–21, 100; C. Itoh Company and, 195; ComDev affiliate, 148; Computer Division of, 164–67, 172
benefit policies, 85
Berg, Norb, 60–63, 215, 224, 229–31
Bernstein, Stu, 205
"better mousetrap" paradigm, 123
Bitzer, Donald (Dr.), 7, 29, 53–59
Bjur, Phylis, 179
Bloch, Erich, 120, 139
Board of Directors at Control Data: changes in during 1980s, 215–17; policies set by, 87–95; speech to, 277–82
Boehm, Helen, 116–17
Boesky, Ivan, 88
Bondhus Tool Company, 62
Book of Merlyn, The, 251, 310
Boslaugh, David L., 14
Boston Consulting Group, 103
"bricks vs. clicks" paradigm, 116–19
Bridge, Inc., 21, 308n.1
Brill, Dan, 309n.6
British intelligence service: Control Data sales to, 20, 145; origins of Control Data and, 8
broadband technology, demand creation and, 118–19
Broeker, Dick, 231
Bronfman family, 160
Brooke, Harold, 54, 56–59
Brooks, Perry, 54
Brown, Harold, viii, xii

Brzezinski, Zbigniew, 181
Buckbee Mears Company (BMC), 308n.5
Bull Corporation, 28
Bulver, Paul, 18, 48
Burger, Warren (Justice), 230
Burroughs Corporation, 254, 305n.2, 308n.2
Burton, John, 188
Business Advisory Services unit, 309n.6
Business and Technology Centers (BTC), 30, 236–37, 243, 258, 310n.1
business entities: economic needs met by, 5; evolution of, 1–2
business focus, crisis management and, 216
business growth, make, buy, and collaborate trichotomy, 7–8
business incubator concept, 237
business strategies, for innovation, 127–28
Business Week, 139
buyer power, in "Five Forces" model, 104

C. Itoh and Co., 21, 166, 179, 195
Canada, Control Data partnerships with, 21–22, 46, 147–49, 151–53, 179, 182–83
Canadian Atomic Energy Commission (AECL), 182–83
capital intensity, growth of, 125–28
Capitalism, Socialism and Democracy, 105
"caring curiosity" paradigm, 67
Carter, Jimmy, viii, 181, 200–201, 205
cash flow measurements, 214–15
Cauldwell, Ron, 230, 232
CDC Gmbh, 196–97
CD Japan, Limited, 195–96
Cedar Engineering, 17–18, 156
CEIR. *See* Committee for Economic and Industrial Research
Central Intelligence Agency (CIA), 180
Ceridian Corporation, 27, 35, 255
CERN. *See* European Center for Nuclear Research (CERN)

change: crisis management and role of, 220; innovation and perception of, 9; strategic space concept and, 106–8
Chekov, Anton, 209–11
Chrysler Corporation, 167
Churchill, Winston, 219–20
Church of Jesus Christ of Latter-Day Saints, The, 43–45
CIETC. *See* Romanian Industrial Group for Electronics and Vacuum Technology
CII company, 198
Cisco systems, 8
Cisneros, Henry, 232
CIT Credit Company, 167
Citifinancial, 169
Citigroup Corporation, 169, 258
City Venture, 237, 239–41, 243, 258
CMOS technology, 33
code-breaking, origins of Control Data in, 4, 8, 14–15
Coles, Arthur (Sir), 102–3
collaboration: competition and, 131–54; innovation and, 236–50; partnering strategies and, 68–71; perspective as tool for, 73; PLATO system development as example of, 56–59; policies for fostering of, 245–46; soft innovation and need for, 234–35; as strategic tool, 6, 252; Technology Food Chain and, 126–28; trust-building and, 246–48. *See also* public-private partnerships
Collins, Al, 188
Commercial Credit Company (CCC), 22, 34–35, 163, 306n.6; acquisition of, by CDC, 167–70, 211–12; innovation environment at, 245; IPO made for, 215–16; legacy of, 258–59; PLATO system and, 54; research and development initiatives in, 92–95
Commercial Trading International, 309n.6

commodification of technology, 106–8, 307n.8

commodity business, Control Data's involvement in, 27–29, 31–35

communication: importance of, in crisis management, 219–20; societal innovation and importance of, 233–34

Communications Supplementary Activity-Washington (CSAW), 14, 16, 306n.4

communication technology, PLATO system evolution and, 58

community characteristics, societal innovation and recognition of, 233

Compaq Corporation, 110–11

compensation policies, 85; societal innovation and need for, 234

competition: collaboration and, 131–54; in "Five Forces" model, 104; from government-provided services and products, 194–95; necessary vs. sufficient technology and, 108–10; process technology and, 113–14; regulation and arbitration and, 191–93; technology push vs. market pull in, 114–19

competitive advantage, Technology Food Chain and, 122–28

complementary assets, growth and, 157–58, 308n.2

complementary capabilities, strategic alliances and, 133, 149–51

Complex Instruction Set Computer (CISC), 40, 306n.1

Comprehensive Employment and Training Act (CETA), 244–45

Computech, Inc., 159

computer-aided design: evolution of, 123; in microelectronics industry, 142–44

computer architectures, development of, 40–43

Computer Business Equipment Manufacturers Association (CBEMA), 138–44, 153, 308n.2; Price speech to, 289–93

Computer Peripherals, Inc. (CPI), 28, 134–35, 153, 308n.1

Computer Services Division, 27, 212–13

Computer Systems division, 212–13, 256

Computer Tech, 159

Computing Devices of Canada, Inc., 21, 166

conflict, regulation and arbitration and, 191–93

Conner, Dick, 60

consortia, as collaboration tool, 144

contracts, interpretation and enforcement of, 192

control: fear of failure and, 78–80; of public-private partnerships, 248

Control Corporation, 163–64

Control Data Business Advisors, Inc. (CDBAI), 30–31, 237–39

Control Data Corporation (CDC): acquisitions by, 158–61; Advanced Development Laboratory partnership and, 135–37, 152–53; Business and Technology Centers project and, 236–37; Cedar Engineering acquired by, 17–18, 156; City Venture project and, 240–41; Control Systems acquisition by, 163–64; Cray's impact on, 40–43; DITC partnership with, 151–53; economic recession and, 212–13; European Headquarters for, 22; FamilySearch computer system and, 44–45; formative years of, 15–22, 254; history of, vii–ix, 1–2; Industrial Group formed by, 21, 163–64; international operations of, 176–79; launching of, 13–15; lawsuit against IBM by, 24–25, 29, 57, 72, 141, 161–62; legacy of, xi–xiii, 247–48, 257–59; life span of, 252; national distribution of small plants by, 233–35; organizational structure of, 23, 265–75; personnel changes at, 22–25; Policy Committee formed, 23; prehistory of, 4; revenue statistics for, 16, 20–21, 23,

25, 31, 37, 179, 305n.3; role of problem-solving in, 4; Rural Venture project, 241–43; Selby Bindery project, 229–30; small business advisory centers project, 237–39; spin-offs from, 255–56; stock valuations for, 17, 215; strategic planning at, 99–119; supercomputer research and, 39–43; timeline for, 261–64; transitions from 1971–1980 at, 25–30; "white knight" role of, 22

Control Data Education Company, 29

Control Data Far East (CDFE), 195–97

Control Data Institutes (CDI), 213

Control Systems Division (CSD), Daystrom Corporation, 163–64

Convair Corporation, 49

Conway, Pat, 230–32

Conway Quality, 75

Cooperative Research Act of 1984, 193

"co-opetition" concept, at Control Data, 18

core competence model, strategic planning and, 104

Corporate Creativity, 237–39

Corporate Policies for Creating a New Business Culture, 88

corporations: evolution of, 1–2; life span of, 4, 252; overlapping principles of, 5–6

cost analysis, in public-private partnerships, 249–50

Council for Economic and Industrial Research (CEIR), Control Data's acquisition of, 19, 158–61, 306n.5

counseling services, societal innovation and need for, 233

Cray, Seymour, xii; Canadian collaborations with, 148–49; CDC support for, 220; disk drive technology and, 47; formative years of Control Data and, 15–17, 52, 145; letters of, 283–87; Model 6600 and, 36–37, 80, 211–12; peripherals development and, 156; resignation

of, 26, 213, 283–87; as risk taker, 223; semiconductor technology and, 67, 226; supercomputer technology and, 39–43

Cray 1 computer model, 41

Cray Research Corporation, 30, 32, 34, 41–42

CRAY X-MP, 41

creativity, computer design and, 43–46

Credit Union Division, 257

credit union services, SBC involvement in, 30

crisis management: basic principles of, 209–11; economic recession of 1970–71 and, 212–13; Employee Advisory Resource system and, 61–63; essential actions for, 219–23; facing the elephant strategy, 217–18; flexibility and, 220–21; inducing stability and, 219–20; innovation and, 6, 8–9; momentum creation and, 222; positive change through, 252; services strategy at CDC and, 213–17; strategic assessment and, 221–22

cryptanalysis, origins of Control Data in, 14

customer relationships: emphasis on, at Control Data, 16–17, 43–45; needs assessment as part of, 53–64

Cyber 70 product line, 26

Cyber 170 product line, 26, 148–49, 183

Cyber 180–990E product line, 26, 44–45, 137

Cybernet Division, 28, 72, 197, 212–13

Dammeyer, John, 29, 56–57

database information services: Control Data's acquisition of, 19; IBM/Control Data rivalry over, 72; necessary *vs.* sufficient technology and, 108–10

Data Centers Division, 18–19, 22, 72

Data Display, 308n.1

Data General, 32, 214

Data Services Far East (DSFE), 196

Davis, Les, 41

Daystrom Corporation, Control Systems Division of, 163–64

defensive acquisition, risks of, 158

defensive takeovers, 158

Dell, Michael, 253

Dell Computers: direct-sale process of, 3; necessary *vs.* sufficient technology and, 109–10

demand creation, technology push *vs.* market pull and, 114–19

Deming, W. Edwards, 74–75

Denmark, CDC operations in, 182

departmental computers, evolution of, 28

Design of a Computer, The Control Data 6600, 49

desktop computers, Control Data's involvement with, 27

Deutsche Demokratishe Republic (DDR). *See* Germany

DeVoto, Bernard, 176

Dickinson, N. L. (Nate), 163–64, 204

Digigraphic Systems, 21, 308n.1

Digital Equipment Corporation (DEC), 32, 141, 308n.2; 308n.5

Digital Insight, 257

directorship skills, policy mechanisms and role of, 89–90

disabled employees, PLATO system and, 60

disaggregation, strategic alliances and, 150

Doelz, Mel, 58

Donohue, Hugh, 185

Dove, Grant, 144

Drake, Edwin (Col.), 38

Drake, Willis K. (Bill), 15

Drucker, Peter, 43, 116, 258

dynamic capabilities, strategic planning and concept of, 104–5

"Dynamic Capabilities and Strategic Management," 104

dynamic random access memory (DRAM) chips, 113–14

E. L. Heymanson Company, 20, 186–89

Eastern Europe, Control Data operations in, 181–82, 197–200, 202, 309n.6

Eckert-Mauchly Computer Corporation, 14–15

economic activity, platform and framework for, 193–95

economic needs, meeting of, as corporate goal, 5–6

economic recession: impact at CDC on, 212–13; job creation during, 232–34

Economic Value Added (EVA), measurement, 214–15

economies of scale, Technology Food Chain and, 123

Economist, The, 170

educational technology: CDC initiatives for, 243–45; market pull *vs.,* 115–19; PLATO system and, 53–59

Education Company, 165, 256

Education Services Division, 29

Edward Marshall Boehm, Inc., 116–19

Edwards, Malik, 53–54

Eisenhower, Dwight D., 117

Electricité de France (EDF), 21, 182, 185–86

Electrofact, N. V., 21, 308n.1, 309n.4

Electronic Accounting Card Corporation, 308n.1

Electronic Industries Association, 308n.2

Elrod, Tom, 136

Employee Advisory Resource (EAR), 30, 60–63, 69, 258; infrastructure as framework for, 84–85

Employee assistance programs (EAP), evolution of, 62–63

Employee Entrepreneurial Advisory Office (EEAO), 48, 84–85, 90, 258

Employee Placement Center, 86

Employer Services unit, 162

employment practices, at Control Data, 85–87

Energy Technology Center, 310n.1

Engineering Research Associates (ERA), 14–17, 38, 305n.1, 306n.4; Control Data's evolution and, 145; Cray's involvement with, 40; naval contracts for, 55

Engineering Services Division, 75

English, Bill, 228–29

Engstrom, Howard, 14

ENIAC computer, 49, 306n.4

entity-building, equity joint ventures and, 152–53

entrepreneurship, CDC projects for encouragement of, 237–39

equity joint ventures, structure of, 151–53

ERA 1101, development of, viii, 40

ERA 1103, development of, viii, 40, 49

ETA-10 supercomputer, 217–18

ETA Systems, 25, 33–35, 50

European Center for Nuclear Research (CERN), 20–21, 184–86

An Evolutionary Theory of Economic Change, 105

executive compensation, innovation and role of, 954

expectations, societal innovation and, 233

Export Administration Act, 180

export control laws: Control Data's policies and, 22–23; international expansion of CDC and, 180–82

export licenses, CDC international operations and, 197–200

failure: innovation and role of, 78–80; project failure, characteristics of, 79; technology transfer and, 144

Fair Break program, 243–45

Fairchild Corporation, 114

Fair Exchange program, 86

"fallout" technology, microelectronics and, 143–44

family farms, CDC support for, 241–43

Family History Library, 43–45

FamilySearch computer systems, 43–45

Federal Communications Commission, 196

Federal Express, 113

Federal Trade Commission (FTC), 161

Fernandez, Mario, xiii

financial limitations: reliance on internal resources and, 177–79; strategy and technology development and, 102–3

Financial Times, 58

financing strategies: crisis management and, 216–17; in Soviet Union-CDC partnership, 202

Firouztash, Carolyn, 190, 204–5; memoirs of, 299–301

Firouztash, Homa, 204–5, 299–301

Fitzgerald, William (Fitz), 75

"Five Forces" Model, 104, 106

Fletcher, Fremont, 14

flexibility: crisis management and, 220–21; in public-private partnerships, 250; strategic planning and, 152–53

focusing strategies: business focus, 216; crisis management and, 220

Ford, Henry, 253

foreign policy, CDC operations and, 181–82

Foreman, George, 230

Forrest, Henry S. (Hank), 194

Fortune 500 companies, life expectancy of, 4

469R² computer, 44–45

France, CDC operations in, 182, 184–86

Franklin, Benjamin, 253

French, Wil, 179

French AEC company, 21, 182

Fujitsu, 113

Galbraith, John Kenneth, 230

Galvin, Bob, 74, 140

Gellman Research Associates, 308n.2

General Dynamics, 27

General Education Development (GED) instruction, CDC program for, 244–45

General Electric, 100

General Mills, 46

General Time Corporation, 308n.1, 309n.4

Georgia Institute of Technology, 305n.1

German Weather Service (GWS), 21, 182–83

Germany, CDC operations in, 21, 182–83, 197–98

"Ghetto Jobs—It Works, But Will It?", 232–34

GKNT (Soviet Agency), 200–203

global markets: Control Data's expansion into, 8, 20–21, 27, 176–79, 182–89; export control laws and, 180–82; government partnerships and, 192

GMAC Corporation, 167

Gorbachev, Mikhail, 181, 202

Gould, Jay, 73

governance mechanisms at Control Data, 87–88

governmental partnerships: Control Data's involvement in, 9, 194; government-provided services and products, 194–95; role of trust-building, 247–48

governmental policy: economic activity platform and framework for, 193; economic growth and, 190–91; global economic activity and, 195–205; impact on Control Data of, 179–82; lack of strategy in, 249–50; strategic planning and role of, 191–95

Government Executive, 232–34

Government Services Division (GSD), 75

Grabler Manufacturing Company, 167–68

Grady, Ed, 242–43

Grant, Bud, 77

greed, as threat to free markets, 254–55

Green, Fred, 228–29

Griffith, Andy, 127–28

Griliches, Zvi, 105

Groove Networks, 58

group interest, individual interest *vs.*, 192

groupware, PLATO system as, 7

Grove, Andy, 214

growth, as motive for acquisitions, 157–58

Gunderson, Richard C. (Dick), 30

Hall, Bob, 148

Hammer, Harold, 168, 170, 213

Hannah, Paul, 69

Hanson, George, 22

hardware business, Control Data involvement in, 25–27, 31

Harris, Jim, 17–19

Harris Corporation, 308n.2; 308n.5

Harvey, H. Glenn, 140–41

Hatch, Orrin, 230

Head Start program, 229

health assistance plans, evolution of, 63, 72

Health Insurance Portability and Protection Act of 1996 (HIPPA), 193

Hewlett-Packard Corp., necessary *vs.* sufficient technology and, 109–10

Heymanson, Ernest, 186–89

hiring process, societal innovation and, 234

Hitachi Corp, 113

Holley Carburetor Company, 21, 308n.1

Holley Computer Products, 21, 308n.1

HOMEWORK program, 59–60

Honeywell, Inc., 28, 100, 254, 308n.2; 308n.5; strategic alliances with, 135

Hubert H. Humphrey Metrodome, 237

Human Resources Department, 59–60

human resources management: company infrastructure as framework for, 84–85; Employee Advisory Resource system and, 60–63

Hungary, CDC partnerships in, 198–200

IBM: competition with Control Data, 16, 19–20, 36–37, 100–101, 109, 145, 211; Control Data lawsuit against, 24–25, 29, 57, 72, 141, 161–62; dominance of, 220, 254; early years of, 14–15; equipment from, at Control Data, 32; global markets for, 177; magnetic disk drive technology of, 46–47; magnetic tape transports, 17–18; microelectronics industry and, 140–44; peripheral products for computers from, 28; System 370–145, 202; time-sharing technology and, 159

import licenses, international operations and role of, 196–97

independent directors, policy mechanisms and role of, 89–90

individual innovation, development of, 256–57

individual interest, group interest *vs.*, 192

individual performance, fear of failure and, 79

Individual Validated License (IVL), 180–82, 185

Industrial Group, formation of, 163–64

industry maturation, Technology Food Chain and, 123–28

information services and products: CDC's legacy in, 257–59; crisis management and, 213–17; development costs of, 91–95; package delivery services, 113–14; in Rural Venture project, 242–43; self-service products, 124; Technology Food Chain and, 122

information technology certification, 257

infrastructure development: innovation framework and, 83–88; in Soviet Union-CDC partnership, 203

Inman, Bobby Ray, 142

innovation: in acquisitions strategies, 155–75; awareness and, 66–68; collaboration and, 236–50; creating culture for, 65–81; crisis management and, 209–

21; definitions and terminology for, 3; in design, collaboration and, 131–33; development and fostering of, 6–7, 252; diversity of personalities and, 52; fear of failure and, 78–80; framework constructed for, 82–96; habitats for, examples of, 53–64; individual innovation, 256–57; infrastructure as framework for, 83–88; inspired motivation and, 78; international expansion and, 176–89; leadership for, 247–48; maintaining culture of, 24; management of, 248–50; Norris's comments on, vii–ix; policy mechanisms for, 87–89; principles of, 5–6; problem-solving and, 3–4; risk-taking and, 223, 253; skills and, 76–77; soft innovation, 225–35; stimulation mechanisms for, 90; strategic alliances and, 135–44; strategic planning and, 120–28; technology and, 103–6; Technology Food Chain and, 122–28; Total Quality Management and, 74–75

innovation funds, 90

innovation reviews, 90

"Insight" employee service, 306n.1

inspired motivation, innovation and, 78

insurance processing, SBC involvement in, 30

integrated circuits, technology push *vs.* market pull and, 114–19

Integrated Services Marketing, 309n.6

Intel Corporation, 114–15, 137, 139–40, 307n.8

intellectual property: microelectronics technology and, 143–44; protection of, 192

internal resources, reliance on, 176–89

international markets: CDC entry into, 176–79, 182–89; export control laws and, 180–82; Iran-CDC partnership and, 203–5

International Multifoods, 221

International Telecommunications Treaty, 196

Internet: Technology Food Chain and, 125; technology push *vs.* market pull and, 116–19

Inventing for Fun and Profit, 82

Iran, CDC operations in, 203–5

IRIS-50 computer, 198

ISKRA company, 198–200

Israel, CDC operations in, 182, 202–3

Itek Corporation, 21

Ives, Walter, 102–3

Jackson, Henry "Scoop," 182

Jackson, Jesse, 230

Japan: CDC ventures in, 195–97; competition with CDC from, 215; electronics technologies in, 113–14

Jefferson, Thomas, 195

Jet Propulsion Laboratory, 46

Jetzer, Tom (Dr.), 63

job creation: Business and Technology Centers program for, 236–37; CDC legacy in, 258–59; at CDC Northside facility, 227–29; education and skills development for, 243–45; government-provided services and products as source of, 194–95; soft innovation and, 226–27; strengths and limits of, 232–34

job search training, CDC program for, 244

job security, at Control Data, 86

Jodsaas, Larry, 256

John Adams, 8–9

Johnson, Lyndon Baines, 225

joint ventures, 127; in Eastern Europe, 198–200; Holley Carburetor Company, 21, 308n.1; structure of alliances for, 151–53; in technology, 134–35

Jones, Don, 168, 170–71

Kamp, Tom, 18, 136, 156

Karnowski, Jack, 156

Kazeminy, Nasser, 72, 256–57

KDD communications carrier (Japan), 196

Kennecott Copper Corporation Mining Company, 306n.1

Kennedy, John F., 114

Kerkorian, Kirk, 160

keyboard technology, 73; PLATO system and, 56–59

Keye, Bill, 17, 22

Keynes, John Maynard, 105

Kisch, Bob, xii, 17, 21–22, 42, 187

Kissinger, Henry, 209–10

Knock, William (Bill), 204

know-how: strategic alliances and, 150–51; technology defined as, 3, 101–3, 105, 153–54; Technology Food Chain and, 120–28

knowledge resource, strategic alliances and, 138–44

Kramer, Lee, 63

Krzyzewski, Mike, 76

Lacey, John W., 29, 136, 141, 165–67

Lamp, Reiner, Dr., 183

Land O'Lakes, 241–42

Latimer, George, 231–32

Lawrence Livermore Laboratory, viii, xii; Model 6600 at, 19–20

Leach, Bob, 17, 146

leadership: at Control Data, xii; trust-building and role of, 247–48

learning algorithms, PLATO system and, 56 59

Leonard-Barton, Dorothy, 104

Leuna Werke, 196

Levels of Service concept, 32–33

leverage, international expansion and role of, 197

Lewis and Clark expedition, 99, 127, 176–77, 180, 194–95, 253

Life Extension Institute, 63

Lillestrand, Bob, 2, 45–46, 50; disk drive

technology and, 47; innovative attributes of, 66–68; recruiting skills of, 77; as risk taker, 223

limited resources, Strategic Space and, 131–33

Lincoln, Neil, 26

liquidity problems: crisis management and, 214–16; flexibility and, 220–21

Loew's Inc., 22, 168

logic circuit, necessary *vs.* sufficient technology, example of, 109–10

Logistics System Design group, 256

Lohn, Gary, 228–29

Long, Raymond, 143

long-term planning, strategies for, 99–119

Looney, Joe, 164

Lotus Notes, evolution of, 59

Lucent Technologies, 256

macroeconomics, innovation and, 127–28

magnetic disk drive technology, Control Data and, 46–48, 50–52

Magnetic Peripherals, Inc., 28, 134–35, 257

magnetic tape transports, Control Data innovations involving, 17–18

magnitude of resources, strategic alliances and, 150

mainframe technology: decline of, 25–27; necessary *vs.* sufficient technology and, 110–11

Maintenance Services Division, 22, 29

"make, buy, or collaborate" strategy, 126–28; Philips case study, 145–47; reliance on internal resources and, 176–89

"make or buy" strategy, 126

management theory: business strategies and, 5–6; technology and, 105–6

Mangram, Dick, 230, 232

Mansfield, Edwin, 105

Manual, Claire, 187

market access: growth strategies and, 157–58; international expansion and, 177–79; strategic alliances and, 133, 145–49

market pull: Technology Food Chain and absence of, 123–28; technology push *vs.,* 114–19

market segmentation, Technology Food Chain and, 125

market strength, corporate philosophy of, 4–5

Marshall, Ray, 230

Martin-Marietta, 308n.5

Massachusetts Institute of Technology (MIT), 159, 308n.2

maturation process, necessary *vs.* sufficient technology, 111

Max Planck Institute, 182

Maxwell Motor Company, 167

McCormick, Blair, 80

McCullough, David, 8–9

Meader, Ralph, 14, 306n.4

Meiscon, 159

memorandum of understanding (MOU): Japan and CDC partnerships and, 196; strategic alliances and, 151–53

Menoudakes, John, 203

mergers, basic properties of, 155

Mexico, CDC operations in, 165–66, 183

Michels, Ed, 136

Michigan State University, 19

Microelectronic Enterprises, Inc. (MEI), 139–44

Microelectronics and Computer Technology Corporation (MCC), xiii, 127, 137–44, 165, 257, 308n.3; 308n.5

Microelectronics and Information Science Center, 243, 310n.3

microelectronic technology: expansion of, 25–26, 110–11; strategic alliances in, 137–44; technology push *vs.* market pull in, 114–19

microprocessors, Control Data's involvement with, 26–27

Microsoft Corporation, 58

Miles, J. G., 146

military contracts, Control Data's involvement in, 27

Milken, Michael, 88

Miller, Clair, xii

Miller, Paul, 163–64, 309n.6

Ministry of International Trade and Industry (MITI) (Japan), 113, 196–97

Ministry of Post and Telegraph (MPT) (Japan), 196–97

Minneapolis Tribune, 61–62

Minnesota, entrepreneurship in, 15

Minnesota Catholic Church, 241–42

Minnesota Network for Small Business Innovation and Job Creation, 310n.3

Minnesota Quality Award, 75

Minnesota Seed Capital Fund, 243

Minutilli, Joe, 170

Mitsubishi Electric, 113

Model 160/160A, development of, 19, 27, 164–65

Model 160-Z, 187

Model 606 magnetic tape, 18, 48, 50

Model 1604, 76; development of, 4, 19–20, 37, 42; Eastern European expansion and, 197–98; global impact of, 145; historical importance of, 247–48; IBM's competitiveness and, 211–12; PLATO system evolution and, 54; strategic planning and, 99–100; success of, 164–65; word length in, 40

Model 1700 minicomputer, 23

Model 3000 product lines, 23, 148

Model 3600, 185, 187, 198; development of, 19

Model 6000 line, 23

Model 6600, 19–20, 27, 80–81; crisis management concerning, 211–12; historical importance of, 247–48; history of, 36–37, 41–42, 48–49; Japan market for, 195–96; word length in, 40

Model 7600, 21, 26, 41–42

Model 8600 line, 23–24, 26, 41–42, 148

Model G-15 (Bendix), 165

Model G-20 (Bendix), 165–66

Model RYAD 1040, 202

momentum, crisis management and creation of, 222

money, innovation and role of, 91–95

Monson, Thomas S., 43, 45

Moore, Gordon, 114–15

Moore, Tom, 160–61

Morris, Bob, 56–59

Morris, Jim, 62–63

Mostek, Inc., 308n.2; 308n.5

Motorola Corporation, 109, 140, 308n.2; 308n.5

Muecke, Berthold, 166

Mullaney, Frank, viii; Australian partnership and, 187; as Control Data founder, xii, 15, 17, 21–22, 49–50; Cray and, 287; Philips project and, 146

multitasking hardware, development of, 159–61

National Aeronautics and Space Administration (NASA), Control Data and, 44–45

National Alzheimer's Disease and Related Disorders Association, Inc., 70–71

National Basketball Association, 62

National Cash Register Corporation (NCR), 27–28, 254, 308n.2; 308n.5; Advanced Development Laboratory and, 135–37, 152–53, 172; CDC alliances with, 134, 165, 257; microelectronics industry and, 140–41; PLATO system development and, 57

National Center for Social Entrepreneurs (NCSE), 258–59

National Cooperative Research Act of 1984, 139

National Education Association (NEA), Commercial Credit Corporation and, 169–70

National Institute of Aging, 70

National Science Foundation, 57

National Security Agency (NSA), 145, 181, 200

National Semi-conductor Corporation, 308n.2; 308n.5

National Tactical Data System (NTDS), 55

NATO Export Coordinating Committee (COCOM), 180–82, 198

Naval Computing Machine Laboratory (NCML), 16, 306n.4

NEC Corporation, 113

necessary technology, 108–11, 123

necessity, as opportunity, 68, 71–73, 110–11

needs awareness: case studies in, 53–64; services *vs.* products as tool for meeting, 124; soft innovation and, 225–27; technology push *vs.* market pull and, 116–19

negotiation, regulation and arbitration and, 191–93

Nelson, Richard, 105, 107

new entrants, threat of, in "Five Forces" model, 104

New York Stock Exchange (NYSE), 17

New York Times, 201, 295–97

Nielsen Company, 19

Nietzsche, Friedrich, 1

Nippon Computer Center (NCC), 195–97

Nixdorf Computer AG, 149

Nixon, Richard M., 117, 181, 201

Noer, Dave, 237–39, 309n.6

Norris, William C., vii–ix; Advanced Design Laboratory and, 51–52; Bendix Computer Division and, 166; as CEO of CDC, 71–72; CISRO project and, 102–3; City Venture project and, 240–41; codebreaking activities of, 8, 14; Commercial Credit Corporation and, 168–70; Cray and, 41, 283–87; on crisis management, 211–13; criticism of,

226–27; Data Center development and, 18–19; early life of, 67–68, 106; fear of failure discussed by, 78; founding of Control Data and, xii, 14–17, 37; humor of, 108; industry restructuring and, 24; magnetic tape transport development and, 18; microelectronics development and, 140; Northside plant and, 224–29; Philips project and, 146; PLATO system development and, 56–59; policy mechanisms designed by, 88; research and development operations and, 193; retirement of, 35, 213; SBC acquisition and, 162; on soft innovation strategy, 234–35; Soviet Union technology operations and, 201–3

North Pole expeditions, Control Data and, 46

Northside Child Development Center, 54, 229

Northside Control Data facility, 225–29, 258

Noyce, Bob, 114–15, 137, 139–40

Nuclear Non-Proliferation Treaty, 181

nuclear power, in France, 183

Nuclear Research Institute (Soviet Union), 183

Nuclear Test Ban Treaty, 184

numerical models, Cray's involvement in, 40

nurturing culture for innovation, 6–7

Occupational Medical Consultants, 63

oil exploration technology, Control Data involvement in, 38–39

Once and Future King, The, 251

100% Club, 173

Only the Paranoid Survive, 214

operating environment, crisis management and changes in, 216–17

Oppenheimer, Brown, Wolff and Leach, 17, 228

opportunity, necessity as, 68, 71–73

organizational interests, societal interests
vs., 192

organizational structure: culture of innovation and, 65–66; fear of failure culture in, 78–80; infrastructure, 83–88

original equipment manufacturing
(OEM) peripherals: Control Data's development of, 17–18, 27–28, 156; global
market for, 21; history of, 46–48, 50–
52; necessary vs. sufficient technology
and, 108–10; necessity as opportunity
in case study of, 71–73; sale of, by Control Data, 31–32; strategic alliances for,
134–44

Otis, E. J. (Manny), 164

output of collaboration, identification of,
126

outsourcing, 86, 127, 307n.1

overlapping needs, collaboration and role
of, 146–47

oversight mechanisms, innovation and
role of, 95–96

Ozzie, Ray, 58–59

Pagelkopf, Don, 26

Panda's Thumb of Technology, The, 73

Parker, John E., 14

partnering, innovation and, 68–71

payroll processing, SBC involvement in, 30

PDR formula, 181–82

pension plan, infrastructure at Control
Data for, 85

people, innovation and role of, 91

Peripheral Products Company, 28, 156,
212–14, 256

Perkins, Bob, 18, 46–48, 52, 65–66

Perle, Richard, 182, 309n.1

persistence, international expansion and
role of, 197

personal development services, CDC program for, 244

personal prism, crisis management and,
221–22

perspective: as collaboration tool, 73; in
crisis management, 222

Pesaro, Gary, 104

Peyton, Ernie and Mary, 230

Peyton, Gwen, 230

Philips company, 20; collaboration with,
144–47, 177

physical resources, strategic alliances and,
138–44

Pilkington, Alastair, 113

Pilkington Bros., PLC, 113–14, 123

plate glass, case study using, 113–14

PLATO system (Programmed Logic for
Automatic Teaching Operations), xiii–
ix; acquisition of, 257; at Business and
Technology Centers, 237; collaborative
development of, 7, 144; Commercial
Credit Corporation and, 169–70; commercialization of, 29–30; demand creation for, 115–19; education and skills
development using, 243–45; employee
training using, 77; evolution of, 53–59;
HOMEWORK program, 59–60; Iranian sales of, 204–5; media criticism of,
214; SBC acquisition and, 162

Plessey Company, Ltd., 149

PL-50 design: Canadian collaborations
with, 148–49; NCR/ADL collaboration on, 136–37

Poland, CDC partnerships in, 198

policy mechanisms at Control Data, 88–
91

policy objectives, public-private partnerships and, 249–50

political barriers: strategic alliances and,
151; to trust-building, 246–48

Porter, Michael, 104, 106

portfolio analysis, strategic planning using, 103

Present at the Creation, xi

Price, Robert M.: Australian partnership
and, 188; as CEO of CDC, 215–16; on
collaboration, 236; on innovation, 236;

Norris's comments on, viii–ix; speech
to Board of Directors by, 277–82;
speech to CBEMA panel by, 289–93
price unbundling, at Control Data, 29
Pridgeon, Al, 69
Pridgeon, Hilda, 2, 69–71
Primerica Corporation, 169–70
Prince, Charles, 258
principles for corporations, 5–6
prison systems, Employee Advisory Resource and, 60–63
Prison Ventures, 258
problem-solving: collaboration as tool for,
246; innovation and, 3–4; perspective
as tool for, 73
process technologies: neglect of, 111–14;
Technology Food Chain and, 123
product design and development: costs
of, 177–79; strategies for, 23–24
product differentiation: in Control Data,
112–14; Technology Food Chain and, 125
product technology, vs. process technology, 112–14
Professional Services Division, 29
profitability: corporate philosophy of, 4–
5; variability in, in "Five Forces" model,
104
project failure, characteristics of, 79
property, physical and intellectual, protection of, 192
proprietary value-added knowledge,
Technology Food Chain and, 125
publicly held companies, life span of, 4
public-private partnerships: CDC's legacy
in, 258–59; implications of, 248; at
Northside Control Data facility, 226–
27; as strategic tool, 6, 9, 252
Puglisi, Charles (Chuck), 194

Quackenbush, Bruce, 309n.6
Quorum Litigation Services, 30, 72, 256–
57
"QWERTY" keyboard, 73

RABCO, 83
Rabinow, Jack, 82–83
Rabinow Advanced Development Labo-
ratory, 83
Rabinow Engineering, 21, 82, 308n.1
Ramac disk drive, 47
RCA Corporation, 308n.5
Reagan, Ronald, 181
real estate management: for Business and
Technology Centers, 237; innovation
in, 232–34
recruiting of talent, barriers to, 77
Reduced Instruction Set Computer
(RISC), 40, 306n.1
Regnecentralen company, 20–21, 178,
182–83
regulation, government role in, 191–93
relaxation method of problem solving, 40
remediation services, CDC program for,
244–45
Remington Rand, 14–15, 305n.2; Control
Data's evolution and, 145
research and development (R&D): amortization of costs, 123–24; growth of,
125–28; innovation and role of, 91–95;
international expansion and, 177;
strategic alliances in, 134–44
Research and Development Act of 1984, 127
responsibility, in strategic planning, 152
return on invested capital (ROIC), crisis
management and, 214–15
Rich Electronic Computer Center, 305n.1
Rings of Defense policy, 86–87
risk-taking: crisis management and, 223;
innovation and, 253
Rizzo, Paul, 162, 308n.3
Robinson, C. W. ("Robby"), Dr., 159–61
Robinson, Trevor, xii, 186–89, 309n.2
Rockwell International, 308n.2
Rogers, Marv, 156, 170
Romanian Industrial Group for Electron-
ics and Vacuum Technology (CIETC),
198–200

ROMCD, 198–200

Roth, Brian, 204, 241–42

Rowe, Bill, 309n.6

royalties, microelectronics technology and, 143–44

rules of transaction, regulation as, 191

Rural Ventures, 241–43, 258, 264

Ryden, A. J., 14

SAGE continental air defense system, 29, 306n.8

Saint Paul Urban Coalition, 229

Samarugi & Sons, 159

Sarbones-Oxley Act, 87, 193

Sass, Bill, 194

Scalise, George, 141

Scherer, F. M., 105

Schmidt, Bob, 165–67, 202

Schrage, Michael, 118

Schumpeter, Joseph, 91, 105

Science Research Associates (SRA), 162

Scientific Computers, Inc., 159

Scott, Richard G., 43

screening tools: innovation and job creation with, 227–29; societal innovation and, 234

Seagate Technologies, Inc., 32, 112, 218

"Second Thoughts on Board Independence," 89

Selby Bindery, 258; CDC collaboration with, 229–30

self-service products, 124

selling process, strategic space concept and, 111

SEMATECH Company, 140, 144

Semi-conductor Industry Association (SIA), 139–40

Semi-conductor Research Corporation (SRC), 127, 137–44

semiconductor technology: ETA Systems, 33–34; evolution of, 67–68; strategic alliances in, 139–44

service-based product line, 25–30; growth strategies for, 32–35

Service Bureau Corporation (SBC), 24, 29–35, 162, 172–74

Services Corporation, 28, 30–35, 212–13

services strategy: crisis management and, 213–17; necessary vs. sufficient technology and, 110–11

Shackleton, Ernest (Sir), 79

Shaker, Theodore F., 19, 160–61

Sheehan, John, 309n.6

Shelton, Jim (Dr.), 231–32

Shuen, Amy, 104

Signetics Corporation, 308n.2

"Six Sigma" program, 74

skills development: CDC initiatives for, 243–45; innovation and, 76–77; soft innovation and, 226–27

Slais, Derrell (Sam), 136

small businesses: advisory services for, 237–39, 258; innovation at, 90

"smart" products and materials, development of, 125

Smith, Joseph, 43

societal architecture, 226–27

societal interests: organizational interests vs., 192; soft innovation and, 226–27

Société d'Economie et de Mathématique Appliqués, 20

soft innovation, 225–35

South Africa, CDC efforts in, 226–27

Southwest Airlines, 126

Soviet Academy of Sciences, 202

Soviet Union: CDC technology sales to, 183, 200–203, 295–97; global markets and impact of, 180–82; Sputnik launched by, 13, 45–46

space exploration, Control Data's involvement in, 27, 45–46

space program, Control Data and, 13–14

SPEC0001 design, 149–50

Spencer, Ed, 140

Sperry Corporation, 305n.2, 308n.2; 308n.5

Sperry Rand, 100; formation of, 15, 305n.2

Sperry Univac, 305n.2; microelectronics

industry and, 140–41; naval contracts for, 55

Sputnik, launching of, 13, 45–46

stability, crisis management and importance of, 219–20

staff development, CDC program for, 244

STAndard Computer Komponents (STACK), 73, 149–50

standards development, case studies in, 73

Standard Systems Division (CDC), 165

STAR (STring ARray processor), 21, 23–24, 27, 41, 50, 148

States, Dave, 204

"Static Equilibria" concept, 105–6

Staywell Health Management, 30, 63, 72, 77, 84–85, 258

Steger, Will, 46

stockholder value: of CDC, 255; corporate philosophy of, 4–5; policy mechanisms for innovation and, 88–89

Stockman, John, 188

stock market collapse (2000–2003), 254

strategic alliances: competition and, 132–33; driving forces for, 150–51; purposes of, 133–44; stakeholders' interest in, 249–50; structure of, 151–53; trust as ingredient of, 153–54

strategic overlap, in joint ventures, 151–53

Strategic Space concept: corporate longevity and, 251–52; crisis management and, 209–11; growth and, 157–58; limited resources in, 131; principles of, 106–8; Technology Food Chain and, 127–28; technology push vs. market pull in, 114–19

strategy: case studies in, 99–119; for collaboration, 245–46; development of, 103–6; evolutionary nature of, 105–6; for growth, 157–58; innovation and, 7–8; necessary vs. sufficient technology and, 108–10; principles of, 6, 252–57; technological change and, 6–8, 97, 101–3, 252; technology food chain and, 120–28

Strategy Committee, evolution of, 95–96

Strickland, Ed, xii, 20, 146–47, 177–78

substitutes, threat of, in "Five Forces" model, 104

success, requisites for, 245

sufficient technology, 108–11, 123, 157–58

Sumney, Larry, 140

supercomputers: Control Data's involvement with, 19–21; Cray's involvement in, 39–43

SuperValu Company, 241–42

supplier power, in "Five Forces" model, 104

supply chain concept, 122

SWOT analysis, strategic planning using, 103–4

Sylvan Learning Systems, 257

Systems and Services Company, 136

systems integration, 307n.9

Taiwan, CDC operations in, 183

talent recruitment: acquisitions and problems of, 174; human relations policies and, 84–85; innovation and role of, 76–77

Tarbuck, John, 63

Tata Institute of Fundamental Research, 183

teaching operations: computer-assisted technology for, 54–59. See also PLATO system

technological collaboration: in Soviet Union–CDC partnership, 202–3; strategic power of, 7–8; value identification in, 126–28

technology: acquisition as tool for, 157–58; change and, 9–10; collaboration and, xiii–ix; commodification of, 106–8; definitions and terminology concerning, 2–3; evolution of corporation and role of, 2; generation of vs. utilization of, 153–54; market pull vs., 114–19; necessary vs. sufficient technology concept, 108–11; process technology, ne-

technology (*continued*)
  glect of, 111–14; strategic alliances and,
    133–44; strategic planning and, 6–8,
    101–3, 252; strategic space concept and,
    106–8; utilization of, 127–28
Technology Food Chain (TFC): Com-
    mercial Credit Corporation and, 169–
    70; concept of, 33; crisis management
    and, 213–17; failure to perceive impor-
    tance of, 254–55; Soviet Union tech-
    nology operations and, 201–3; strategic
    alliances and, 135–44; strategic plan-
    ning and, 120–28
Technology Fountainheads, 143
"Technology Innovation and the Prudent
    Man," 240–41
Technology Review, 118
technology transfer: barriers to, 118–19;
    definition of, 153–54; in microelectron-
    ics industry, 142–44
Teece, David, 104, 308n.2
telecommuting, 59
television technology, PLATO system
    and, 56–59
Teller, Edward, viii, xii
Tercentenarians Club (Great Britain), 4
Texas Instruments, 114, 308n.2
Textile Banking Co., 167
Thorndyke, Lloyd, 18, 33, 48, 50–52
Thornton, Jim, 15–16, 41, 48–50, 52, 81;
    peripherals development and, 156; res-
    ignation of, 26, 213; as risk taker, 223;
    semiconductor technology and, 226
Ticketron Corporation, 29–30, 160
time sharing, 159–61
time to market forces, strategic alliances
    and, 150–51
Tisch, Laurence, 168
Today Show, 230
Toshiba Corporation, 113
Total Quality Management (TQM), 74–
    75, 77; crisis management and, 216–17;
    innovation and, 90; process technology
    and, 112–14

Total Technical Effort initiative, 92–95
Trader, Herb, 240, 309n.6
training programs, societal innovation
    and need for, 234
Traveler's Group, 169–70
Trowbridge, Alexander (Sandy), 182
Troy, George, 237, 309n.6
trust: collaboration, 147; in public-private
    partnerships, 249–50; soft innovation
    and role of, 231–32; strategies for en-
    gendering, 246–48; uncertainty and,
    253–54
TV advertising, audience measurement
    techniques and, 19

ultimate use, consideration of, 124–25
uncertainty, strategic planning in face of,
    253–54
unemployment, Fair Break program in re-
    sponse to, 243–45
unintended consequences, law of, 192–93
Union Bank of Switzerland (UBS), 214
UNISYS, 254, 305n.2
United States Department of Commerce,
    180–82, 196–97
United States Department of Defense
    (DoD), 180–81, 200; Control Data
    and, 44–45, 308n.2
United States Department of Energy, 180
United States Department of Industry,
    Trade and Commerce (DITC), 147–
    49, 151–53
United States Department of State, 180–
    81, 184–86, 196
United States Justice Department, 161
United States National Security Agency
    (NSA), 20
United States Navy: as Control Data's
    client, 14–16; Postgraduate School, 16
United States Special Trade Representa-
    tive, 196
Univac Corporation, 254, 305n.2
UNIVAC I, development of, viii
University of Illinois, 53–59

Vacca, Tony, 26

value chain concept, 120, 122

value creation, role of, at CDC, 255

values, infrastructure as framework for, 83–84

Venn diagram, strategic alliances and, 133

very-large-scale integrated circuits (VLSI) technology, 113

VIDEOTON, 199–200

"virtual company," evolution of, 127

virtual vertical integration, 127

Vladimi K. Zworykin Award, 53

VLSI Consortium, 113–14

von Neumann, John, viii, xii

VTC spin-off, 256

W. C. Norris Institute, 35

Walbrook High School, 54

Wall Street Journal, 212

Wal-Mart, 113, 125

Waltech, Ltd., 21

Watson, Thomas J., 36–37

Weapons Research Establishment, 188

Wedgewood, C. V., xi

Weidenfeller, Chuck, 194

Weill, Sanford, 34, 169–70

Weizmann Institute, 20, 145

Wellness Program. *See* Staywell Health Management

Westphal, James D., 89–90

"What It Was Was Football," 127–28

Wheeler, Roger, 227–29, 232

When Computers Went to Sea, 14

White, Henry (Hank), 29, 162

White, T. H., 251

Whitney, Raymond C., 187

Willard, Jess, 168, 170–71

William C. Norris Institute, ix

Williams, Jack, 162

William the Silent, xi

Windows operating system, 58

Winter, Sidney, 105, 107

word-processing systems, 118–19

World Bank, 145

World Distribution Center (WDC), 230–32

World War II, origins of Control Data and, 4

Worlton, W. J., 49

Xerox, 100

Xerox Corporation, 308n.2

XP Systems, 257

Yugoslavia, CDC partnerships in, 198–200

Zemlin, Dick, xii, 77

Zenith Corporation, 32